CONFESSIONS OF AN UNSUCCESSFUL ACTOR

BOOK ONE:

BANISHED FROM GANAIDEN

by

SIDNEY EDEN

CONFESSIONS OF AN UNSUCCESSFUL ACTOR
*Book One: Banished From Ganaiden**, by Sidney Eden

Library of Congress TXu 1-904-014 TXu 2-052-637
ISBN 978-0-9968086-1-3

Also published as a Kindlebook.

1. Memoir - History. 2. Theatre. 3. Jazz. 4. 60's Sexual Revolution.
5. African American culture.

Cover: *"Chased from the Garden of Eden by an Angel with a Fiery Sword Accompanied by Death,"* by Hans Holbein, the Younger. By permission of the Mary Evans Picture Collection London, England

Frontispiece Illustration: Lester Young playing after hours at *"The Palace of Audible Dreams,"* in 1955.

The BIRDLAND featured in this book has no connection whatsoever to the BIRDLAND currently operating in New York City.

Design, Layout: Doug Barron

Published September 2020

Printed in the United States of America

SidEden.com

sideeden7@gmail.com

* Yiddish for the Garden of Eden

To
anyone who ever hired me
or bought a ticket to see my shows
and

*a klep tzu meineh sonim!**

*a curse on my enemies.

"Every man is more than just himself;
he represents the unique… That is why every
man's story is important, eternal, sacred."
- HERMAN HESSE

"Life consists of propositions about life."
- WALLACE STEVENS

"If you tell the truth
you don't need a good memory."
– JUDGE JUDY
(HON. JUDITH SHEINDLIN)

AUTHOR'S NOTE

Upon the inauguration of Donal J. Trump

If you're looking for a "literary arc," I myself am the through-line and cannot change but only choose the events that fit my theme. The years I write about led to the devolution on which we are embarked, a nightmare where insipid cowboy music and vomitious vulgarity abound, a bad dream in which a purblind media savagely exploits us and a *Walpurgisnacht* of reactionaries, led by a megalomaniacal four-flusher steeped in the wiles of Roy Cohn, rules D.C. - a situation undreamed of months ago, yet unsurprising to this "Red Baby" whose youth was defined by Nazism, Jim Crow, anti-Semitism, and the brutal differences between Right and Left, differences that propelled me toward the Theatre, the shows in which I participated, and the people with whom I collaborated.

So, as I (or, in the early stages, my alter ego) guide you through these untold stories of Immortals, if you cannot see the through-line, fix your glasses or get a political education, though, by now, it's probably too late and you're in for it, like everyone else.

- Sidney Eden - New York City

P.S. Footnotes and appendices being impediments to pithiness, my story is designed so that the reader may skip them altogether or read them as they occur, momentarily pausing the narrative flow, but picking up a bit of extra information along the way.

Table of Contents

PRELUDE

At the Pinnacle:
Jimmy Or the "Shuberts"

I hate squares and love alliteration, though I list it as the least of my vices. I'd like to say that from the start.

1945- Hitler's racial war was over and everyone wanted to celebrate; the house lights dimmed and intermission ended. Amongst a buoyant full house in the Chicago Theatre, Paramount Studios' flagship venue, celebratory because National Socialism had run its ugly course and Hitler had surrendered only days before, my sister (who turned out to be my half-sister, a brutal fact of which I was not disabused till decades later) and I, sat in a mezzanine loge that reflected the combined tastes of Louis the Fifteenth, Barney Balaban, Sam Katz, and the aged Poobah of Paramount Pictures, the firm's fabled founder, Adolph Zukor, who smoked one cigarette a day, flaks said, and lived to be one hundred and one.

We had just seen Jack Benny, as a third rate trumpet player turned angel, hang from a skyscraper in an interminable denouement, but that was only half the reason for the packed house. Now, the boisterous celebrants shushed each other and the crowd grew still.

Abruptly, the screen flew upward, the stage lights bumped up to full, and a wall of glorious music, carefully proportioned, tightly harmonized just short of dissonance, poured forth from a bandstand which mysteriously glided downstage propelled by hidden pneumatics. And while Duke Ellington, seated at a gaudy white piano stage right, finessed the audience with his strictly *entre nous* sophistication, somewhat exaggeratedly raising his arms, as he played, exhibiting his elegant hands and fingers and cueing the orchestra simultaneously with his bobbing head, there, center stage, stood

Billy Eckstine, in the forefront of the oncoming ensemble, crooning his latest hit in his patented concupiscent baritone.

It was a rehash of "Caravan," now a significant seller for the singer, whose name was Eckstein until a nightclub owner decided it looked too Jewish. "B-Fine," because of the Petrillo recording ban and the changing nature of the music business, forced to dump his band composed of, not only mighty satellites, but monster planets, Charlie "Yardbird" Parker, Leo Parker (the baritone saxophonist and no relation to Bird), Dizzy Gillespie, Miles Davis, Fats Navarro, Sarah Vaughn, Dexter Gordon, Gene Ammons and Art Blakey, teamed up, now, with Duke for a road tour of major movies houses, playing stage shows, like this important Chicago Theatre engagement.

And enthroned like an omniscient god, at the rear of the ambulant wagon filled with black men in white tie and tails (the lone exception being a light-skinned man, with slicked back hair and rimless spectacles, the Puerto Rican-born trombonist, Juan Tizol, who, with his boss, shared the copyright to the song they were playing), surrounded not only by a full-size jazz kit but by kettle drums, strange cymbals, cowbells, woodblocks, a large triangle, hanging chimes and an enormous Chinese gong, there sat Sonny Greer, wearing an enigmatic smile and rap-tapping an obsessive Latin tattoo on his magniloquent tom-toms. It was enough to make a nine year-old want to become a drummer.

No doubt engendered by my widowed mother whose childhood was spent in the Deep South and who cursed segregation, and by my sister, a radical student, a follower of Paul Robeson, and soon to be enrolled at the new college named for our sainted President Roosevelt who had died suddenly in April of a cerebral hemorrhage, I resolved, then, something I had contemplated for some time: that I preferred people of color to their white oppressors and that their power to produce such potent Art would forever be an indispensible component of my life. Seeing Duke Ellington for the first time joyously haunts my conscious mind as vividly as the horrific pictures of the liberation of Dachau, published only days before.

Deceived as to the true identity of my antecedents, euchred of my patrimony at the age of four – an awful kind of bankruptcy – I was banished, along with my sister, a hater of Shirley Temple, and my mother, a descendent of the original settlers of the Ohio Valley and Kentucky who was disowned upon her elopement with an itinerant immigrant, Jewish salesman, my father, a mysterious man (to me) who escaped an Odessa literally aflame with anti-Semitic atrocities, at the age of six, and soon learned to speak impeccable English, banished, I say, from a large house in the suburbs and shoe-horned into a cramped apartment in the unfashionable section of Rogers Park.

Skipping what Mencken calls the "larval stage," my introduction to venery (at a distant time when pitchers pitched nine innings and most girls abstained from copulation till proper nuptials were performed) occurred on a filthy cot in an abandoned hotel, on the South Side of Chicago, with a wretched black drab of indecipherable age, while my schoolmates formed a line and waited their turns in the hallway. Not only was I, like Pozdnishef, in Tolstoy's story (Ed. note *Kreutzer Sonata)*, forever stained by my initiation, I was doubly punished for my transgression by the soon appearance of *pediculous pubis*, better known as "the crabs."

Only months before, at a time when shower stalls were a luxury reserved for the well-to-do and the ones in most apartments were slapdash affairs with overhead track-lines from which plastic curtains were suspended, and many people, young and old, preferred baths to showers of necessity, I, like many of my contemporaries, discovered my sexuality in the bathtub, in my case, while studying a picture of Rita Hayworth's cleavage oozing from a gown, by Jean Louis, as she sat in El Morocco, cuddling up with Aly Khan. I had been advised by schoolmates of this phenomenon of self-discovery, but, as a fatherless boy with only an older sister and a mother to explain the facts of life, I was disadvantaged and without proper counsel to know the true mechanics of fornication, or, for that matter, to realize that this semi-protuberance, which swaggered under a celebratory banner of superiority (*"inside leg," "jelly roll," "ding-dong,"* as in, *"I'm A Ding Dong Daddy From Duma [And You Oughta' See Me Strut My Stuff]"*), or which labored under a pejorative flag of surrender and inferiority (*"potz," "putz," "schmuck"*) a roll call Henry Louis Mencken declined to devise, that it, not the brain, is at the center of mans' gravity, and that, just as in the case of my dead father, it would be both my downfall and my salvation.

However, now, after the first ugly incident, at least according to a society on which I already frowned, I was a man.

My second amative proceeding took place in a disreputable hotel on Van Buren, nestled beneath the southeast loop in "the Loop," around the corner from Minsky's, on State Street, the object of my affection being a mature lady of joy, who wore a black bodice like Fellini's La Saraghina, in *8 1/2*, and said she was Charlie Ventura's "old lady," and I don't mean his mother or his wife. It was she who informed me of the pubic lice I had inherited from my initial dalliance and, upon my departure, with all the sincerity she could muster from her harlot's hard heart, she purred, "Come back and see me sometime," a wish to which I wish I could have acceded with a baseball bat in hand, for her temporarily docile and inviting manner concealed her true identity as an agent of the gonorrhea bug, for which she designated me a beneficiary, a swell reward for my second venture in the realm of carnal pleasure.

It is not my aim to shock, or seek the reader's sympathy, though a cynical laugh at the preposterousness of it all would be appropriate, but, since around the time of the death of my father, and even a little bit before, nurtured and informed by a series of fateful events, such as the one which follows, I learned this is predominately a world of sorrows. Despite the cynicism and sense of irony growing within me and, oppositely, because I had developed a keen interest in observing the dog-eat-dog environment in which I was a willing co-conspirator, I resolved there was no impediment to my overcoming whatever obstacles I faced in my drive to succeed.

They call it "Bughouse Square" because bugged-out people stand on boxes there and give speeches. I mean Washington Square Park, not New York, but across the street from the Newberry Library, in Chicago.

It's way past dinnertime; I'm sixteen. It's a steamy night in mid-July and the GOP's in town at the International Amphitheatre to nominate Dwight D, Eisenhower. A hungry-looking black man in his thirties is giving an angry speech to fewer than a dozen listeners, myself included, when, on a street otherwise free of traffic and parked cars, a Chrysler Crown Imperial limousine heads slowly down Walton in our direction. The stately automobile comes to a stop fifteen feet from where I'm standing and a famous and beloved comedian, wearing expensive blue suit, white shirt, blue tie uniform of the era, erupts from the passenger compartment of the presidential limo, comically scampers up to the black orator, points his finger at him, throws his head back and, after quickly salivating, spits at the black man and yells:

"Nigger, nigger, nigger!"

Then, like a thief in a pantomime, he pivots about and, in his patented comical way, scampers back on tip-toes to the luxurious car and piles in, planting himself between two fat cats, also in blue tailored suits and white linen fine as his own. They look as if they've come from a board meeting of an oil company, or from a sumptuous meal at the Stock Yard Inn. Helpless with laughter, they clutch their bellies and kick out their heels, as another fat cat, sitting in a jump seat, slams the door shut from within and the long, black car speeds away into the night.

It happened in a flash; you might not have noticed his face. But I did; I was a *shaigetz* with *saichel*, streetwise and cynical and I didn't miss a thing. The great funny man would never have gotten away with it today, nor would he have acted today as he did then, for if he had it would have been front-page news. Perhaps he was egged-on by his backseat companions. Maybe they were driving around telling dirty stories after dinner, having a ball, and someone said to the driver, "Drive by 'Bughouse Square.' Let's see what the Commies are up to tonight, yak, yak, yak." And when they arrived, someone might've said to the comedian, "I dare you to jump out and call that nigger on the soapbox 'Nigger' and spit at him."

Though it was strictly a gag to them, and they all laughed in a spirit of good fellowship while making it into a bet, it was an ugly sight to see. But just as, during the predictable campaign of 1944, my mother and I, by chance, saw FDR hustled up a ramp in a wheelchair and into Soldier Field for a campaign speech, thereby adding to my growing store of skepticism (for who would have thought he was unable to walk of his own volition?), the comedian's shocking behavior became merely another scene in a scenario in which I was pitted against a world about which I had already developed so keen a sense of the injustice of things, that I took the spitting and the use of the "n" word almost in stride. Nothing surprised me anymore.

It began with them cajoling me to sing – an enticement to be loved, for the more I performed, the more they loved me. Soon telling a story and pretending to be someone else became palliative, addictive, my solace. My pimply-faced, eighteen year-old cousin, J.D. (who turned out to be my half-brother) would grab me by the armpits and swing me atop the dining room table. My mother and father and sister, Betty, would clap their hands and boisterously request "Jeepers Creepers," or "Playmates," or another standard of the day. I learned to be loved by performing.

And that same year they dropped the A- Bombs and I saw Duke Ellington, escorted by one of my mother's beaux, for she was refined and attractive to men, I attended my first Broadway show, the touring company of *Winged Victory*, at the Civic Opera House, an extravaganza written and directed by Moss Hart, presented by the U.S. Army Air Force, and featuring a cast of one hundred soldiers, most all of whom were actors in civilian life, many of them stars of the theatre and cinema. I had seen children's theatre at the Goodman, in its beautiful wood paneled auditorium, and the puppet shows at the Seneca Hotel, but they were puerile in comparison to the slick professionalism of the presentations that emanated from New York.

Then, in quick succession, I saw Mike Todd's opulent *Up In Central Park*, at the Shubert, with memorable settings (such as the enormous merry-go-round) by Howard Bay; Olsen and Johnson's *Laffin' Room Only*, the successor to *Helzapoppin'*, in which both stars ran up and down the aisles *sprtitzing* soda from seltzer bottles, enough to make me detest "immersive" theatre forever; *State Of The Union*, the political Pulitzer Prize-winner, at the Blackstone, with crackling dialogue and taught direction; and *St. Lazare's Pharmacy*, starring Miriam Hopkins, produced by Eddie Dowling, who had just closed in *Glass Menagerie*, on Broadway, a play that opened next door to *Winged Victory*, at the smaller Civic Theatre a year before.

And, all in that same year I first saw Duke and we incinerated two hundred thousand Japanese in a couple of days and the Cubs won the pennant because all the good players were fighting the War, I saw two shows, both of which featured an "All-Black Cast," and seeing them made my future in the theatre predictable: *Anna*

Lucasta (the people seated in the vicinity of my mother, her escort and myself were appalled that grownups had taken a nine year-old to see a play about a black prostitute), and *Carmen Jones*, with its wizardly stagecraft, its swift movement from scene to scene, punctuated by pulsating drums, a stunning effect on one so uninitiated and easily impressed, and guaranteed to transport an audience from place to place. I mark it as the moment I decided to pursue a career in the Theatre, though, sometimes, I wish I had never heard those drums at all.

Exposed to hideous pictures of the lynching of black men, in the South, their lifeless bodies suspended from trees, fully-educated as to the atrocious nature of Jim Crow, initiated as a Red Baby, during the momentous election of '48, and dragged to joyful rallies on behalf of Henry Wallace and the Progressive Party (bigots called it the "Negro Party," or worse), in a darkened Chicago Stadium, I thrilled with optimism to the songs and speeches of the great activist-singer-actor-lawyer-All-American fullback, Paul Robeson, the righteous authority of diminutive W.E.B. Du Bois, bathed in a solitary spotlight, and the plaintive militancy of Woody Guthrie. But that idealism was defeated in a phenomenon erroneously labeled "a triumph of liberalism" in the form of Give 'Em Hell Harry, who would soon participate in the destruction of the Left.

Inured to disappointment, beaten up by gentiles because my name was Edelstein and shunned by some Jews because my mother was a *shikseh* (even though she immersed herself in ritual baths and sent me to *cheder* for my Bar Mitzvah), again, do not feel sorry for me; I had begun to forge the path that led to the top.

Now, more than a score of years later, I WAS there, standing in Shubert Alley, by the entrance to the flagship theatre of the same name, about to fulfill the dream of every wanna-be Broadway producer who ever lived, about to walk up the stairs and meet "the Shuberts" themselves. I was simultaneously at the pinnacle of the commercial theatre and facing total bankruptcy. I was in the toilet for one hundred thousand 1973, scumbag dollars and my back was to the *farkuckt* wall, no joke. You don't pay your debts in the theatre you're banished.

But I had a hit! An international hit I called it. I had achieved the impossible by creating a new theatre, in the bowels of a bank, out of what was really a corporate meeting room, with five hundred plush seats, in the middle of Chicago's Loop. Murals by Chagall adorned the outer lobbies and the plaza above, and, though the backstage area was inadequate, I now had a sellout production of a hitherto neglected, one hundred-ten minute, one-act play by America's greatest playwright, Eugene O'Neill, entitled *Hughie*. Even though the reviews from the tough Chicago critics were not uniformly sensational, I bought a page in *Variety* saying they were.

And by writing a well-worded letter, I motivated Clive Barnes, the influential critic for *The New York Times* and also, *The London Times*, to get on a plane, see my production, and write a review - a pre-Broadway review! In my letter I emphasized the importance of this short play and its place in the oeuvre of its creator. Barnes came through with a glowing review that appeared in both *Times* and was followed-up by raves in *Time* and *Newsweek* magazines. This made my show a certain future hit on Broadway, for how could Barnes (or those magazines) reverse his (or their) opinion(s)? Everyone who mattered on Broadway agreed.

And here's the kicker: I had no investors. I owned the entire show and no one could tell me what to do.

Now nearly every theatre owner in America (and some abroad) wanted my show, and I was about to meet the biggest of them all, "The Shuberts," though they weren't Shuberts, at all. They were "Bernie and Jerry" (Bernard B. Jacobs and Gerald L. Schoenfeld), tough lawyers who, along with General Manager, Phil Smith, controlled the Shubert Organization.

I was about to be checked in at the box-office and directed to their glittering private suite on the second floor, the brightly lit, rococo rooms from which Lee Shubert banished Brother Jake. Lee repaired to the Sardi's Building, across the street and gave Jake the Winter Garden, relegating him to mounting musicals, and, according to uncertain legend, the two barely spoke again. Now I was about to be seated across the desk of gilded ormolu upon which (I had read in books) Jake "auditioned" chorines; about to make a deal which could save my ass and prolong my ascent, at the very scene of Jake Shubert's allegedly prodigious sexual conquests.

"Don't be intimidated by the surroundings," Bernie Jacobs would soon tell me, referring to the omnipresent 18th Century furnishings, not the B and K, movie palace, *papier mache* of my youth, but the real thing, *emes.*

That I was nervous was understandable, but remember, reader, I had been putting on shows since I was a child.

"Sing, little one; go into your dance."

And along the way I'd gotten it in my head to control the whole *shmeer*, like the people I admired: Paul Robeson, Orson Welles, José Ferrer, actors who did more than just act. By 1973, I'd directed dozens of plays, many with famous actors, in stock and resident theatres, though not Broadway, that's true, but I was making a living in Chicago as an actor before *Hughie*, making commercials and acting in plays, sometimes with stars.

But I hear someone saying:

"Eugene O'Neill's *Hughie*? Hey, that's a well-known play; everyone's done that: Al Pacino, Brian Dennehy, Forrest Whitaker, For god's sake," you say, " that's a no-brainer!"

But you'd be wrong. In 1973, *Hughie* was considered artistically insignificant and commercially poisonous. It premiered, in 1958, at the Royal Dramatic Theatre, in Stockholm, to critical praise, with Bengt Ecklund in the leading role of "Erie" Smith. Five years later, it received a lukewarm reception and achieved only a brief run, with Burgess Meredith, in its first English language production, at the Theatre Royal, in Bath, England. On Broadway, the following year, starring Jason Robards, Jr., produced by Ted Mann and Joseph E. Levine (really, backed by the latter) directed by Jose Quintero, it lasted but fifty-one performances. The critics were divided on the play's worth. Mostly high-minded sissies, they were myopic and disinclined to be intellectually associated with the world of the seedy horseplayer, "Erie" Smith, O'Neill's metaphor for mankind's ongoing struggle.

In some cases it had taken years for critics to accept the master-playwright's mature works, of which *Hughie*, having been written during the same period, is a prime example. *Iceman Cometh* was a flop when first presented. Originally, *Moon For The Misbegotten* closed out of town in 1947 and failed on Broadway in 1957. Later, Actors Studio's revival of *Strange Interlude*, despite Jose Quintero's direction and Ben Gazzara's excellent performance in the leading role, also failed.

Conversely, Quintero and Ted Mann's contract with Carlotta O'Neill, effected with payment of a dollar bill, led them to revive *Desire Under The Elms*, starring George C. Scott, and *Iceman Cometh*, starring Jason, with Peter Falk, both at Circle in the Square, at its original Sheridan Square location.[1] The monumental *Long Day's Journey Into Night*, starring Fredric March and Florence Eldridge, followed in 1956.

Moon For The Misbegotten was successfully revived in the summer of 1973, in a Chicago suburb, with Jason, Ed Flanders and Colleen Dewhurst. Then, Marshall Migatz, the producer of the show, was killed while changing a tire on the Dan Ryan Expressway, on his way back from New York where, one supposes, he secured the now-razed Morosco Theatre for his show, and met with the O'Neill Estate, or both.

At this time, having signed a lease on the theatre in the bank, and seeking an opening production, I had hoped Jason would reprise his portrayal of "Erie" for me, that we could bring *Hughie* back to life. But his agent nixed it, said a new producer had stepped into the picture, and that *Moon For The Misbegotten* was coming to Broadway, after all. It won four Tonys: Dewhurst, Flanders, Quintero and for the new producers, a Special Tony Award. There was no "Best Revival" category at the time and there was no mention whatever of the late Marshall Migatz. "The Theatre is a ruthless hussy," said the noted Boston critic, Elliot Norton, referring to the no longer influential critic George Jean Nathan, O'Neill's first champion.

I considered myself to be an artist (if only a performing one); the words of the great writers meant everything to me. And strangely, like Erie Smith, I was a gambler, a horseplayer at that. But I was also a good handicapper, too; I knew the time was right for *Hughie*. And, after premiering the theatre and receiving nice reviews for the first show, but losing money for my investors, for my second show I secured the rights to *Hughie* and made a lengthy and ambitious list of those who could play the leading role of Erie Smith, a copy of which may be found in APPENDIX #1.

---

1 I studied with Quintero at his Directors' Studio, in 1954-55 and, arm around my shoulder, he introduced me to many cast members on *Iceman's* opening night, including Peter Falk, but not Jason Robards, Jr.

Like George Bernard Shaw, the physical descriptions O'Neill provides for his characters are restrictive and impractical. "Erie" he describes as in his "early forties…around medium height but appears shorter because his fat legs are too short for his body. So are his fat arms."

After Jason was eliminated I went to my next choice Ben Gazzara, the "best voice in the American Theatre."[2]

Readers might, also, question my involvement in the commercial theatre at a time when regional theatre was proliferating. Just before, and even during, *Hughie*, I was committed to a well-publicized campaign to establish a not-for-profit theatre in Evanston and, later, at Navy Pier, where the Chicago Shakespeare Company now resides. (SEE APPENDIX #2) I turned down scholarships to the Boston Conservatory of Music and, later, Goodman Theatre, for apprenticeship at the Cleveland Playhouse, the country's first professional regional theatre.

But in a day when multiple names, to the point of absurdity, are pasted above the title, and modern critics view old-time producers ("lone wolves" they call them) as just one step removed from Max Bialystok, I thought them, ideally, to be near-artists, like Diaghilev, artistic adventurers with knowledge and taste, spinners of dreams who loosen up money and make reality out of supposition, in other words, heroes worthy of the respect of a George Jean Nathan.[3] It had been on my mind to revive *Hughie* at the first opportunity. The theatre in the bowels of the bank was my chance.

The trouble was Gazzara, in addition to being brilliant in the role of "Erie" Smith, was a barracuda, a veritable wagging tail, and I the dog caught between "the Shuberts" and the other powerful entity in the commercial theatre, James M. Nederlander, Sr. (1922-2016), owner of the vaunted Palace Theatre, and many others throughout New York and other cities. A half-hour before, in his eagle's nest office overlooking Times Square from atop the Palace, I met with Jimmy (as everyone from ushers on up called him with affection and respect) for the second time. He invited me to go to Yankee Stadium with him, "The limo's right downstairs."

---

2   According to actress, Gena Rowlands, in a PBS Special about the Broadway theatre.
3   "Morning After The First Night," Alfred A. Knopf (New York) 1938, and elsewhere.

He wanted me to meet George Steinbrenner, smoke Dunhill cigars and critique scripts of London hits that wanted Broadway bookings. He came to meet me in my dinky Chicago office when *Hughie* opened. He had seen and enjoyed the production and wanted it for his theatres in Washington, Detroit and, then, Broadway. The "Shuberts" could be amiable, but they were lawyers and Jimmy was a showman; a sportsman, too. He had *cohones* (expanding his father's operations nationwide) and *rachmones*. He understood "Erie," the metaphor, and agreed the play must be presented without an accompanying piece, an idea some had, selfishly, suggested. The evening was about O'Neill and Gazzara, not the other way around.

When I initially hesitated in giving Jimmy an okay, he sent emissaries from New York - Liz McCann (Elizabeth Ireland McCann) who was a company manager, then Jimmy's consultant and who would later become the most prolific producer on Broadway, and Nelle Nugent, with whom Liz co-produced, for a time.

Liz, dressed casually in black slacks and a wide-collared, loose-fitting, white blouse, reminded me of a Dickensian character woman. In her direct, unaffected way, she pointed her finger at me, and angrily prophesized, "You're going to be sorry, Sidney! Jimmy likes you."

Liz and I had much in common. We both saved all through high school to buy Broadway show tickets. Maybe Jimmy Nederlander, who swept up backstage at his father's theatre in Detroit, and had been seeing shows since he was five,[4] had seen more shows than I, but he was fourteen years my senior, old enough to be the brother I lost as a child. Meeting him again in his office in New York, how could I say I was about to face his competitors, "the Shuberts," in a few minutes, across Jake's desk, and probably accept their offer? Was I inherently duplicitous like my bigamous father?

I had to think quickly. If we took the limo to the Stadium to see the Yankees and meet Steinbrenner, should I reveal my financial predicament? What should we discuss? It couldn't be politics. We were violently engaged in Watergate and Vietnam, and the opinions

---

4 *Razzle Dazzle*, by Michael Riedel (Simon & Shuster) 2015, page 161. Riedel's epic book includes the fact that Jimmy, in uniform, was in the box office for the first legit show I ever saw: *Winged Victory*.

of these scions of wealthy families would be unlikely to mirror my own. So, politics were verboten should we motor to the Bronx to meet George.

I would endeavor instead to direct the conversation to more favorable topics. I knew how to get a laugh. Thirty-eight years old, still an Anglo-looking, trim, leading man, I'd been playing *shtik* opposite people like Martha Raye, Dom DeLuise, Bob Crane; directed Edgar Bergen, Alan Alda, Betty Garrett, Larry Parks, and countless other farceurs and comedians, for god's sake! I could execute the punch line to obtain a "house" laugh in a five hundred-seat theatre or a thirty-five hundred seat Amphitheatre, much less in the limo or in a box at Yankee Stadium. Yes, I would charm my hosts, and should the subject arise, astound them with my knowledge of the Sport of Kings. I couldn't read a box office statement yet, but I could figure parlays in my head and Steinbrenner was important in racing and Jimmy had horses with a trainer I knew. I had been addicted to the game since Swaps beat Nashua.

But I must be careful not to reveal too much, for I was operating on uncertain terrain. At Hebrew school, where I was awarded the leading role in *Joseph And His Brothers* and Bar Mitzvahed to the huzzahs of the *shul's alter kuckers* and *shikkers* who hung out for the schnapps that followed such events, all of them agreeing my well-intoned delivery of the liturgical portions and rendition of my oration succeeded beyond any given in the collective memory of the *shul*, it became clear to me that the combination of my *goyishe* good looks and Jewish education eventuated in a serendipity that allowed me to navigate both worlds, at any level, with ease. I was a spy, a not dishonorable profession according to wartime espionage movies and the Eric Ambler novels of my youth.

Was my hesitation in accepting Jimmy's invitation because I was afraid of revealing my past, a past in which I cheated death on nine vivid occasions, the first of which occurring the day after my birth?

I could brag to them that, as a fatherless poor boy, I had raised millions of dollars and had established a theatre in San Francisco, but I was, in truth, like many actors, a shy person who could be obnoxiously outgoing when necessary, especially when selling a product in a commercial, an activity in which I was often engaged, on and off camera. But I had many secrets.

I would not be able to tell them about the times I was dead broke and, though properly dressed, walked the canyons of Park Avenue until the break of day because I hadn't a penny to my name nor a place to sleep. I couldn't tell them I'd been imprisoned twice on serious charges, though exonerated soon after.

Sybaritic, egotistical, a self-centered voluptuary, divorced twice and recently awarded custody of my infant son, I had never been in love despite the number of women, whore and non-whore alike, with whom I copulated, because I was too enchanted with myself, an old story, perhaps, but devastatingly true in my case. Idealistic, a survivor (Capricorn, The Goat), quixotic, please remember, I repeated to myself once more, "Be careful what you say. Make a mistake, you're banished - until you have another hit, if you ever do, which, most likely, you won't." Norton was right; "the Theatre is a ruthless hussy."

I wanted to go to the Stadium, not add the two powerful men to the list of those whom I had, at one time or another, through errors of judgment, stood up, or turned down a humiliating register of luminaries which included Joseph E. Levine, Duke Ellington, Bette Davis and Joe Glaser, Louis Armstrong's Outfit-connected manager who told me, years before, as his twin Dalmatians dozed on the carpet of his Park Avenue office: "Yer goin' t'the top, kid. I got confidence in ya."

Joe, beneath the tough exterior, was a very nice man, and he, too, was taken with me. Another of his clients, Dizzy Gillespie, was to portray himself in a musical I was producing about the relationship between Miles Davis and Charlie "Bird" Parker, called *Lookin' For The Man.* Joe liked my handmade shirts from Charles Dillon, who provided linen for JFK, my handcrafted shoes from Egon Dumler, who shod the Duke of Windsor, and my tailor made suits from Steven Salen, who would fashion and fit Henry Kissinger, and other ritzy *machers.* Brought up by two fashionable women, everything I wore (except my underwear), even my ties, were designed by and made for me, but I wasn't dressing for myself I was dressing to influence other people.

Joe liked the fact I was from his hometown, Chicago, liked the stories I told him of the Outfit joints I frequented as an uncontrollable (by my mother) teenager who worked in the Loop, at the big record store on State and Randolph, then, hung out in jazz clubs at night. I knew all the locations – the Hi Note, the Blue Note, the Argyle Lounge, McKee's, the Brass Rail, Jazz, Ltd. - and Joe knew I knew and he liked me for it.

"I got confidence in ya', kid." I was only twenty-six then and guess where he wanted to take me? Yankee Stadium. "I got the limo waitin' downstairs," he said.

Nine years had elapsed between invitations. I did not go to the Stadium with Jimmy because I had to honor the appointment with "the Shuberts," and I couldn't keep them waiting. Gazzara did not want to play the old National Theatre in Washington (which Jimmy, now, controlled) in the heat of August. He wasn't looking forward to the Nederlander base in Detroit either. The intimate, Shubert-controlled Booth Theatre, at the uptown corner of Shubert Alley, was the best venue for *Hughie*, and one always does what is best for the play if one is truly an artist.

And Hollywood beckoned, too. The management of the Huntington Hartford wanted the show and Gazzara wanted badly to accede to the request. My back, as I said, was to the *farkuckt* wall, but Joe Glaser was right. Regretful for my many flaws and missteps, I was nevertheless at the top now and, initially travelling in the guise of my alter ego, I want to tell you how I got there in order to rediscover, dear reader, how and why I fell from grace.

BANDITS AND BOPPERS
ON BROADWAY
THE LAST DAYS OF BIRD
AND PREZ

1

The Palace Of Audible Dreams

The Palace of *Audible Dreams* was a place where nobody would tell anybody where somebody was. It was a point of honor among those who worked there, most of whom were gamblers or just-this-side-of-the-law. They were dream purveyors operating on a rundown stretch of Broadway, a few blocks from Times Square, a tatty strip that no longer represented the Great White Way to which Mr. Cohan so enthusiastically gave his regards. It was in the middle of a concrete byway running from the Ed Sullivan Theatre to the Capitol and Lindy's, where a cup of coffee had risen to the outrageous sum of twenty-five cents, a section of the once grand boulevard now laden with wicked traps, such as the penny arcade and the camera and appliance shops that hawked "FIRE SALE!" bargains, at marked up premiums, for unwashed knuckleheads who descended upon it from the outer boroughs, New Jersey and all nations of planet earth.

And the denizens, each of whom possessed their own personal audible dream, these arrogant "record men" of the Palace of Audible Dreams, considered themselves way above "squares" and infinitely too hip to be placed in the ignominious category of guys who talked too much. It was axiomatic they keep a tight lip at all times.

So when eighteen year-old Aiden Gandy, fresh from Chicago, (by way of the famous Cleveland Playhouse) was hired as their co-worker, and Aiden's comrades from back home came looking for him, they would get the dead hand from the record salesmen with a response like: "Gandy? Never heard of no Gandy working here," they would lie, thinking they were protecting Aiden, when, in fact, they were the very ones from whom the not yet fully formed naïf required protection.

Located on 52nd and Broadway, "The Jazz Corner Of The World," across the street from Birdland (a club opened in 1949 and named after Charlie "Yardbird" Parker, the innovative alto sax player and central figure in the musical movement known as bebop), the Palace of Audible Dreams was the most famous record store in Manhattan, or maybe the whole world, and, bathed in innocence while bitten by the muse, imbued with a euphoria born of youth and self-deception, awash in the exuberant anticipation of all good things to come, Aiden Gandy, seeking fame and fortune on Broadway, rolled into Gotham driving a battered Nash Ambassador, his lone passenger an amputee in khakis, from Korea, and soon arrived upon this scene of shabby glamour.

Giving a soldier a ride was obligatory. It was a time of great conformity; there were, as yet, no beatniks, no HOWL, no Jack Kerouac. Paul Robeson had been denied a passport, and Charlie Chaplin was banned from re-entering the U.S. Most people were desperately afraid to be different and the attorney general had his list of so-called Communist organizations and their members, the Party, itself, having been outlawed in the summer.

And though Joe McCarthy had finally been rebuked by Ike, and was up for censure in the Senate, and had been discredited in the Army Hearings because he met his match in Joseph N. Welch ("Have you no decency!") and garnered a wealth of bad publicity stemming from the hi-jinx of his counselor, Roy Cohn, and Cohn's boyfriend, Private David Schine, this alcoholic Senator from Wisconsin, who cordially greeted the unfriendly witnesses (his victims) in the Senate Office Building's elevator as they rode together to the hearing room[5], where they would be forever ruined, this evil, smiling man continued to have a multitude of vociferous compatriots who insisted Pinkos and Reds were ubiquitous and possessed a subtlety which allowed them to insinuate themselves into every sphere of ordinary life, so that one had to be very careful, careful to conform.

---

5   Richard Rovere's "Senator Joe McCarthy" (1965) University of California Press

But Aiden had no intention of conforming for convention's sake, though obliging the hitchhiking soldier, in the middle of Ohio, on a bright Sunday morning in October, for Aiden was unprecedented, if only because he had been driving an automobile for merely a week. True, there were other reasons. His father, a wily Jew from Odessa (whose real name, Ganaiden, was mangled at Ellis Island by an overworked customs officer) who had been an executive, con-man, jeweler, author of detective stories and no stranger to the road, was killed in a car crash the day the Nazis raped the Netherlands. The painful morbidity of that event, and the fact that Aiden had had such an active life through high school, contributed to his reluctance, until a week ago, to learn to drive an automobile.

Accompanied by his widowed mother, a distinctive woman, a distant cousin of Woodrow Wilson, a woman whose ancient Presbyterian antecedents fought in all the American wars thus far, and twice on both sides, Aiden bought the bulbous, blue rattletrap, in which he sat, for fifty dollars, from a used car dealer in nearby Evanston. Oddly shaped and faded by the sun and Midwestern winters, it resembled an empurpled bathtub.

Aiden's sister, eight years older than he, was almost as much a mother as his real one. A radical graduate of the new college named for FDR, authoritative, patient, a born teacher, a young woman who, though attractive, resembled Aiden not at all and nurtured a healthy tan each summer while Aiden (who resembled his mother) turned red with blisters and shunned the sun, taught Aiden to drive the ugly Nash in a parking lot on Howard Street, and, in the days before a picture was required for identification on a driver's license, an older friend took the test for Aiden, and Aiden was off to the Apple (a term put in use by the jazzmen he so admired, some of whom he already knew from working in Chicago's biggest record stores). He was a quick learner but a highly inexperienced driver. He didn't even know how to change a tire.

Rebellious and independent, he was, otherwise, a model of self-sufficiency, but it would be lonely driving another six hundred miles alone, he thought to himself. Accommodating the soldier, who stood waving two hundred feet in the distance, would be prudent in case of a highway emergency. On the other hand Aiden was opposed to another war, this time with Russia, and a soldier thumbing a ride in the middle of Ohio was unlikely to share his views.

When younger, Aiden had been a close observer of the Hollywood House Un-American Activities Committee's witch hunt hearings. Each day after school, he rushed home for the afternoon newspapers in order to see what movie star's life had been ruined in testimony before the right-wing warmongers. He questioned the "police action" in Korea, headed by a compromising hero and a vice-president who, Aiden was emphatically taught to believe, had framed Alger Hiss. And he detested an administration that fried the Rosenbergs and squashed dissent by outlawing the Communist Party.

All this was against the soldier waving before him. What tipped the scales in the soldier's favor was Aiden's sense of fair play and his unwillingness to defy fate.

Only months before, while they were between productions at the Great Playhouse in Ohio, he and another young actor hitch-hiked to New York just to see some Broadway shows (among which were, *Golden Apple* at the Phoenix, the legendary production Gore Vidal selected as a device to end his *Golden Age,* and *Caine Mutiny Court Martial,* with a cast of nineteen, headed by Henry Fonda, Lloyd Nolan and John Hodiak, directed by Charles Laughton), and on that journey drivers had been kind to the teenagers. That was Aiden's first short exposure to New York; the second was with a beautiful married actress from the Great Playhouse, a devotee of Theodor Reik, engaged in an "open" marriage, who told Aiden that "man is not monogamous," and suggested they walk out at the intermission of *Teahouse Of The August Moon* (starring Burgess Meredith, Tony-winning David Wayne's replacement). It was on that trip that Aiden obtained his job at the Palace of Audible Dreams.

With the present question resolved, Aiden screeched the car with the honeycomb grille to a halt. But, when the soldier flung himself, with some effort, into the passenger seat, Aiden saw the man was missing an arm and would be useless in the event of a flat tire. He was a decade older than the teenager, wore a corporal's stripes, and was glad to know Aiden's destination was New York City.

"Whatcha' do there?" he asked.

"I'm an actor."

The military man pondered momentarily, then, pointed over his shoulder. "Well, you goin' the wrong way; Hollywood's thataway," he drawled mockingly, pointing back over his shoulder. His smiled a grim half-smile that made him slightly ominous and he had whiskey on his breath.

" I'm going to live there. I'm in the Theatre."

"What theatre is that?" the soldier, shot back. He pronounced the "a" to rhyme with "hay" as all hicks do, and peered at Aiden, with a dull look on his face.

"The Broadway stage; plays, musicals, *South Pacific, Oklaholma, Peter Pan.*"

The latter was about to open, starring Mary Martin. The year before, in Chicago, at the "House That Insull Built,"[6] Gandy had seen Jean Arthur and Boris Karloff in Leonard Bernstein's flop version of the Barrie play. He was pissed at the tone of the soldier's voice for Aiden Gandy (who skipped grades twice in grammar school and hammed it up as Sheridan Whiteside, the leading role in his senior class play, *Man Who Came to Dinner*) was a know-it-all. Not only was he one of the few to see that doomed event, he auditioned, then sang in the chorus of the Chicago Symphony Orchestra (Mahler's "Resurrection" Symphony #2) conducted by Lenny.

Oh, what magnificence! One hundred and ten instruments and a chorus of one hundred. He sat in the front row during rehearsals to hear the young maestro's witticisms and occasional references to Billie Holiday. Oh, how Lenny roused the spirits of all 214 participants, four soloists included! And Aiden resolved, "this is the music I want to hear as I'm dying," a morbid thought for one so young, but Lenny really made you think.

And serving as an usher, or purchasing tickets with money earned from his job at the flagship record store on State and Randolph, Aiden had seen nearly everything presented in Insull's auditorium, during the last two years of high school, and most everything presented by Sol Hurok at Orchestra Hall.

Steeped in Gordon Craig, enervated by the idealism of Stark Young, he had read every volume in George Jean Nathan's "Theatre

---

6   Magnate Samuel Insull, who, along with William Randolph Hearst, informed and inspired Herman J. Mankiewicz's writing of *Citizen Kane*, built the Chicago Civic Opera House.

Book Of The Year" series and had even seen the Lunts in the play Buford Caulfield so detested in the new novel by J.D. Salinger.

"Peter Pan?" The corporal ejaculated. "That's for fairies!"

" I've been in lots of plays," Aiden said, assuring his passenger, "maybe, a couple dozen. I'm going to be a director."

"A director" the soldier said, his voice dripping with even greater incredulity, "well, you still goin' in the wrong direction, boy." Later, he asked, "Say, how you long been drivin' this buggy?"

"A week," Aiden said, with a smile, swerving the tub slightly.

"A week, huh? How long you been drivin' period?"

"A week," the young man replied with his best comedic timing.

"I hope you don't gotta change no tires." Some time went by before the soldier resumed saying, "You don't say nothin' 'bout my arm."

'Were you in Korea?" Aiden asked, innocently.

"Commies done this to me," the soldier asserted and soon fell asleep.

"What a jerk!" Aiden thought to himself, and drove on into the night as the corporal snored. "What a Philistine, but I could have won him over," mused the eighteen year-old, who could sell anyone anything, ladies' shoes, phonograph records, you name it, a gift, he speculated, he must have inherited from his sometime travelling salesman father.

At dusk, when they finally turned the bend on Miller Highway and the glittering island appeared before them, Aiden's eyes ignited with Pilgrim wonder. Only then did the grim-visaged warrior awaken from a fitful sleep to say," Welcome to the wicked city." Aiden made no reply, but thought to himself, once more: "What a jerk!"

Directing Gandy where to turn along the way, the G.I. requested he be let off at Forty-Second and Seventh. And at that tawdry location he debouched awkwardly from the car by Kelvinator, waved dismissively at the handsome boy behind the wheel, and entered the lobby of the seedy hotel that stood, then, upon that legendary corner. The soldier was gone. Aiden thought little of the journey or of the corporal at the time, yet the experience remained imbedded in his memory, as seen, quoth Proust, through "the translucent alabaster of remembrance."

His joy in becoming a New Yorker was undiminished by the wounded man's insouciance for, now, after years of hearing the train draw into Grand Central Terminal every Saturday morning on the radio show, *Grand Central Station*, the famous landmark stood only two or three blocks away; he had arrived in his chosen city!

He was still sitting outside the aluminum and wired-glass doors of the old Times Square Hotel when a city bus tapped the rear bumper of his oafish car. The bus driver immediately shouted raw obscenities at our hero, rough jibes with which Aiden, as a Chicagoan, was unfamiliar.

But he did not hesitate to respond with obscenities of his own, for, due to a particular childhood incident that haunted and influenced him still, he had learned to stick up for himself, and his usual instinct when antagonized was to greet an attack with another of superior proportion.

Nevertheless, he was also, to a very limited extent, prudently aware of his self-cowardice, and, in recognition of the fact he was only good with his mouth not his fists, he soon complied with the agitated civil servant and vacated the man's territory, putting the Nash in gear and driving past the Metropolitan Opera House, on Fortieth and Seventh. The Empire Theatre, which should have been on his right, had been torn down the previous year, prompting many to opine that "the theatre is dying" and would never survive the decade.

Broadway was still a two-way street, but Seventh Avenue had been converted to a one lane southbound, so Aiden, compelled to travel up to Sixth, made a couple of wrong turns, at one point driving past the giant Roxy Theatre, at 50th and Seventh, next door to the Taft Hotel and across the street from the stage door of the Winter Garden Theatre, but he eventually found his bearings and maneuvered to his destination, the Palace of Audible Dreams. He had promised he would check-in as soon as he arrived in Manhattan. He parked directly outside the store, on Broadway, near the northwest corner of the two-way street. There was a parking meter, but it was Sunday and the Broadway theatres were closed.

A newsstand, on the corner, stood in front of Rudley's, a small diner with seating for under two dozen people, among whom, at any given time, might be some of the greatest jazz musicians of all time.

And Meyer, the chestnut man, a dead ringer for a demented Buddy Hackett, had parked his wagon to the far perimeter of the entrance to the Palace of Audible Dreams. Aiden hated the smell of burning chestnuts and came to hate Meyer as well.

This was the neighborhood one reads about in Runyon, the seat of big time gambling in Manhattan. Lindy's (or Mindy's, as Damon called it), where Arnold Rothstein once held court, was one block downtown of the store. And because of its convenient location and the fact that many who worked in the store gambled, the Palace of Audible Dreams was a hangout for bookmakers, big time and small, most of who doubled as loan sharks. Pay-offs and collections were conducted there by Runyonesque mugs with tags devised in fanciful flights of antonomasia, names such as Irving "One-Eye" Glass (whose one good eye was badly cocked and the other made of glass, which probably accounts for the oft-quoted admonishment "never bet with a cross-eyed bookmaker"), Willie "The Clutch," Morris "Mosie" Horowitz, the "runner" for the "Clutch," who, a couple of years later, on a hunch, would hold on to a $10,000 bet on Nashua to win the upcoming Derby and go into business for himself, and "Shulem" Lipshutz, all of whom took bets on any sport, and on horses, from stars and bit players appearing in shows at the nearby theatres. This included the Broadway Theatre, at the head of the block, a few steps away, on the corner of 53rd.

A Shubert theatre now, it once was B.B. Moss's Colony; the long-running *South Pacific* had closed there in January. Under refurbishment when Aiden arrived, it would reopen in December, with Gian Carlo Menotti's *Saint Of Bleecker Street*. Aiden had seen everything of Menotti's, even heard his inconsequential piano concerto in Grant Park, with the Chicago Symphony and Eddie Gordon. As a know-it-all, Aiden was a pain in the ass.

The backstage to the Broadway Theatre was adjacent to the rear delivery entrance of the Palace of Audible Dreams, and if you stood out there at actors' half-hour, before show time, you'd see, at one time or another, through the years, Ethel Merman, José Ferrer, David Wayne, Mae West, Noel Coward, Phil Silvers, Leslie Caron, Alfred Drake, Ray Bolger, alone, in mufti, or accompanied by an convoy of camp-followers, arriving at near-performance time, walking down the alley and entering the backstage of the theatre.

But the bookies took bets from anyone: restaurant owners, waiters, pimps, cops, anyone who wanted to gamble, and many did, even the owners of the store, Ziggy and Bunky, whose collective philosophy in the domain of retail selling was "Buy it, Bag it, Beat it." But they were smart and the bag that carried a purchase of record or sheet music – whatever the dream may be – classical, semi-classical, popular, jazz, folk, rock and roll, spoken, soundtrack, original cast, or unclassifiable and miscellaneous, bore the inscription: "I Found It at the Palace of Audible Dreams!"

In order to feed their souls, everybody, celebrity and commoner alike, came there to find their past or present audible dream - everybody. Aiden was not a star-fucker. He had already been around celebrities at the big-time record store in Chicago, but he made a partial list of some regulars at the Palace of Audible Dreams, and also some more occasional shoppers, to whom he sold the shop's wares. He included celebrities whom he had only observed, but his training was that of an actor and observation was endemic to his craft. The customers included:

Elizabeth Taylor & Eddie Fisher; Johnny Mercer, the co-founder and owner of Capitol Records, "Thanks for the use of the hall," he'd say in his Savannah drawl; Ezzard Charles, a great jazz fan; Jack Dempsey, always smiling and gracious; Dick Tiger, an underdog, just off the boat from Africa, he said he would win the title and did, at big odds; Milton Berle, who declined discussing the flop musical, *Seventeen*, which he had produced a couple of years earlier; Tennessee Williams, a curious, silent spectator, Aiden was the only one who knew who the playwright was when he came in to look around the commodious store, in mufti, getting lost in the show crowd which erupted from the nearby theatres, then sauntered through the store in streams, meandering from the 45's section to the 78's, from the vastly profitable sheet music racks to the lucrative LP department, where, a paltry, few years in the future, Brendan Behan would recite, for clerks and customers alike, the poems of Dylan Thomas; Julie Andrews, from her first days on Broadway, appearing in the *Boy Friend*; Willie "The Lion" Smith, loud, boastful and belligerent, and justifiably so, because he was one of the originators of jazz, a fact for which he received insufficient credit and *bubkes* in receipts; Coleman Hawkins, "The Father Of

The Saxophone," who took a relatively recent invention, rejected by most classical composers, and, through the back door provided by what churchgoing people still referred to as the "Devil's Music," turned the tenor sax into a mainstay of all music; Count Basie, unabashedly confessing the folly of his youth, warning in fatherly fashion a newly-hired young trumpeter, and decrying the addictiveness and cost of the devil drug, pointing, alternately to the right and left sides of his nose, "I got one Cadillac up this nostril and another Cadillac up this nostril!"; Marian and Jimmy Mc Partland; Charlie "Yarbird" Parker, who, speaking of tenor saxophonist, Lester "Prez" Young (so named by Billie Holiday "The President Of All Saxophone Players" and a primary forerunner of bebop) said: "I was crazy about Lester…but I wasn't influenced by Lester;" Irving Caesar, who said, "I write fast," was also Al Jolson's turn-to guy and horseracing expert, but his own royalties from "Tea For Two" (so simple even a child could write it in fifteen minutes) brought in sufficient dough to feed ten stables and he was at the racetrack every day of every meet; Jack Yellen, smallish, sweet, unassuming and prodigiously productive, who not only co-wrote the song Stephen Sondheim would say he, Sondheim, wished he had written ("Hard Hearted Hannah"), but who, much more importantly, co-authored FDR's campaign song, "Happy Days Are Here Again," which helped elect the Governor of the Empire State to the White House; Arthur Schwartz; Frankie Frisch; Charles Mingus; Lester "Prez Young, who coined much of the current jazz vocabulary, using the word "bread" for money, "eyes" (as in "I Only Have Eyes For You") meaning having a predilection for something, so that it came out, "I have eyes for the gig, but how does the bread smell?"; Stan Getz, who, so the legend goes, on meeting, for the very first time, Prez, the man he so assiduously emulated (in the bathroom of Birdland) and, saying "Hey, it's a pleasure; I love you," and Prez, eyeing "Stanley Steamer" in the bathroom mirror, saying merely "Nice eyes, carry on;" Marilyn Maxwell, Eddie Arcaro (the embodiment of "class"); Steve Allen, a former Chicagoan whose new NBC *Tonight Show* began shooting from the Hudson Theatre, on West 44th Street, the month before Aiden's job began, and Jayne Meadows (they frequently parked their red and white 1955 Buick Roadmaster convertible in front of the store, after the show, and bought a bunch of LP's, before heading home); Blossom Seeley and Bennie Fields, she, a top pop singer of the 20's, he, the other part of a world-famous vaudeville act, they were, though they had a new release on LP, fast becoming unknowns; Jackie and Roy; Eydie and Steve; Nica de Koenigswarter, née Rothschild and Thelonious Sphere Monk, the pianist who was a prime inventor of bebop, but was not, yet, at the height of his popularity, known to many as the "Mad Monk," while Nica, his new patron, was not, yet, known as the "Jazz Baroness;" William Saroyan, an avid, losing horseplayer who invited Aiden to his meager digs at the old Great Northern Hotel, on 57th Street, where he had stacks of unpublished, unproduced plays sitting on his dresser (Aiden told him he wanted to be a producer one day); Ernie Kovacks and Edie Adams; Bob Fosse & Joan McCracken, who flirted with Aiden and made goo-goo eyes in order to irritate Bobby; Henry Fonda and the Princess di Frasso; Sarah Vaughn (frequently); Everett Dirksen; Hubert H. Humphrey; Harry S. Truman, who, on his way to the premiere of a major movie, waved at Aiden, with his Stetson; Sammy Davis, Jr., a regular and a great personal friend of Ziggy and Bunky, he starred in *Mr. Wonderful*, at the Broadway, on the corner, and within months would suffer a serious car accident in which he lost one eye; Morris "Moishe" Levy, mobbed-up owner of Birdland and Roulette Records, who, despite a brawl, which cost a policeman an eye, and the mob murder of two of his business pals, escaped prosecution until 1988, when he was convicted of extortion and died of cancer at sixty-one; Horace Silver, who, originally, was a co-leader, with the great drummer, Art Blakey, of the group which became known as the "Jazz Messengers," so-named because all the band's members were of the Muslim faith; Quincy Jones (young and friendly); Clark Terry; Paul Desmond; Joe Morello, Dave Brubeck's drummer, who was blind and was escorted everywhere; Lennie Tristano, the blind teacher-pianist (ditto); Lee Konitz, a graduate of Senn High School and Lennie's most famous pupil, who, speaking of modern jazz, said of Lester Young: "He is definitely the basis of everything;" Roy "Little Jazz" Eldridge, the diminutive trumpeter who, like his idol Louis Armstrong, was, some said, sent by the Angel Gabriel; Charlie Shavers, who played as well as Roy (or anyone else, except Harry James) but not as funky; all the comics in town (when they weren't at nearby Lindy's, or at Max Asnas' Stage Deli, around the corner on Seventh Avenue, or the more distant Carnegie Deli) from Henny Youngman to Myron Cohen, from "Fat" Jack Leonard to Jackie Mason; Willie Pep, the flyweight champ who had a bar on 57th, near 9th Avenue; Walter Matthau, who bet with "Mosie," and anyone else who would take his action, playing mostly "baskets;" Teresa Brewer; Jack Klugman; Buck Henry; Sidney Poitier (intense, self-concerned, it was 1954, before *A Raisin In The Sun*, he wanted some Jamaican music); Pearl Bailey and Louis Bellson (frequently, when *House Of Flowers* was at the Alvin Theatre); Thad Jones; Art Taylor, probably the best-dressed of all the musicians, with the exception of fellow-percussionist Roy Haynes, who made George Frazier's "Ten Best Dressed Men" list in *Esquire Magazine*, but A.T. was Brooks Brothers, Roy was Chipp & Co., both off-the-rack; "Pee Wee" Marquette, the dwarf doorman cum master of ceremonies at Birdland, who carried a switchblade knife and used it to cut someone, severely, outside the club, one summer night; Earl "Bud" Powell, hospitalized frequently for schizophrenic episodes resulting from brutalization by railroad policemen, and a fight in which he was hit on the head with a bottle, mentored by Thelonious Monk, idolatrous of Art Tatum, he was the pre-eminent bebop pianist and, at his best, the standard for brilliance; Elmo Hope, Bud's boyhood friend, whose style was nearly identical to that of his chum, and who, as one of Bud's chaperones, shadowed Bud to keep him safe, but received slight recognition as a pianist; Clifford Brown and Richie Powell, Bud's brother, just before they died in a car crash on the Philadelphia Turnpike; Mitch Miller, already head honcho at Columbia Records and, at the time, the most powerful man in the business (but before the advent of his "Sing-along" TV show); George Jessel, very haughty, with Walter Winchell, a real S.O.B.; Mel Brooks and Carl Reiner; Dorothy Kilgallen, "Just one of the boys," her father was a newspaper reporter and she a committed egalitarian and "fag hag"; the girls from the Latin Quarter, with beautiful bodies and hair dyed purple; Don Budge, tennis champ, who went into the laundry business and loved jazz; Red Rodney, who replaced Miles Davis in Bird's Quintet and who, dressed in a dirty t-shirt and a filthy overcoat, hazy-eyed and looking off into the distance, incoherently begged Aiden for a copy of the cover of his new album, on Fantasy, "not the record, man, just the cover," and Aiden let him steal it before Red was busted and went to federal prison, on drug charges, for six wasted years; "Babs" Gonzalez, jazz singer, outspoken forerunner of rappers, who tried to coax Charlie Parker off of heroin and was informed by the genius, "Wait until everyone's getting rich off your style and you don't have any bread, then lecture me about drugs;" Arlene Francis & Martin Gabel, with Jim Backus (Mr. Magoo) and wife, usually in formal dress; most members of Count Basie's Band, because they played, regularly, across the street; some members of Duke Ellington's Band, including Jimmy Hamilton, when they played Basin Street West, on 51st Street; "Sugar" Ray Robinson, who parked his pink Cadillac convertible outside the store for hours as he visited Birdland and/or ate at the rib joint across the street; Ralph Meeker, a congenial man and a great jazz fan, who was chosen by director Robert Aldrich for the choice role of Mike Hammer in Mickey Spillane's *Kiss Me Deadly* (1955); and John Cassavettes, who shot much of his first film, *Shadows*, in the neighborhood, guerilla-style, usually, without a permit, a film which, along with Alexander MacKendrick's classic, *Sweet Smell Of Success* (1957), with Burt Lancaster as a thinly-disguised Winchell, gives the best portrait of the area in which the store operated in those Eisenhower years. (SEE APPENDIX #3. - GEOGRAPHY OF TIMES SQUARE AREA IN 1954.)

It was the era when people, irrespective of their sex, began addressing each other as "man," saying things were or weren't "cool," a time when it was no longer hip to be hep. It was the Golden Age of Bebop.

Co-owner of the Palace of Audible Dreams, Ziggy Zweig, a reserved man in his forties, whose cynical manner concealed his generosity of heart, kept his word. When Aiden walked into the store that Sunday evening, Ziggy introduced Aiden to the men who were working the night shift, which lasted until 4 A.M. Among them was the man on the cash register that evening, Dean Romanoff, a thin, fellow with eyeglasses, a decade older than Aiden, of whom Ziggy said, "Dean knows more about jazz than any record man alive."

Not only did the statement prove accurate, Dean, dark and aristocratic, with White Russian antecedents, became Aiden's best friend at the store and Aiden became Dean's "Kid Brudder," a nick-name given him by Mitch Miller, so that Aiden was forever known within the confines of the Palace of Audible Dreams as "Brudder," the "Kid" becoming superfluous anon.

"You know Bird's playing in the Village tonight, wish I could go but we gotta work," Dean said.

It was an opportunity Aiden refused to miss. He had never seen Charlie Parker; Bird had not played at the JATP concerts Aiden attended in Chicago. So, he obtained his work schedule from a gracious Ziggy, wrote down the address of the club where Bird was playing and said "goodbye" to Dean and the others. Then he drove his ageing vehicle downtown and parked on 33rd, between Ninth and Tenth Avenues.

He had been advised immediate sleeping accommodations were available at the Y.M.C.A., on Thirty-Fourth Street, but he was cautioned, too, that it was a well known homosexual haven, with its Spartan, single rooms, sans bathroom, and large, communal shower. But it was only five dollars a night and he planned to check out after a day or so. He ate at the diner on Thirty-Third and Ninth, then registered at the Christian facility, taking a change of clothing and leaving the bulk of his luggage and wardrobe in the car.

He had driven cross-country and was in "jake" with his new employer. Comfortably nestled in the grip of charming Cholly Knickerbocker, that disarming seducer of ambitious dreamers, Aiden, for the first time in his life, hailed a New York cab, and, with the evening in its infancy, as fervent as a zealot on the trail to Palestine, was off to see Charles Christopher Parker, Jr., "The Bird," "Yardbird," or just plain "Bird" (though often known sim-ply as "Yard"), the man viewed by many as the primary figure in American music.

And while he takes his first New York taxi ride, let the reader note that, even though he was but eighteen, Aiden's musical educa-tion was unique, for music and theatre are inextricably connected.

When Aiden's father was killed, his mother and sister minis-tered to the child's sense of loss by taking him to the Ravinia Fes-tival, in Lake Forest, where they lay on a blanket, under the stars, listening to the Chicago Symphony Orchestra, with Fritz Reiner, or Eugene Ormandy, playing chestnuts by Tchaikovsky and masterpieces by Beethoven and Brahms. Aiden wandered to the bandstand on occasion; the music spoke to him with powerful eloquence. Though he knew all the songs on the "Hit Parade," he developed a voracious appetite for classical music.

He delivered groceries, then, worked at the corner drugstore jerking sodas in order to purchase 78 RPM's in colorful albums, records that broke into pieces when dropped on the floor. He devoured the three B's and the Romantics, then all of Tchaikovsky and Chopin, and underwent a Baroque period that lasted a couple of months. He immersed himself in the orchestral poems of Scriabin, all the opuses of all the students of Rimsky-Korsakov, as well as the works of the master himself, then savoured the symphonies of Sibelius, apeing Saroyan, who had written about them glowingly.

He readily embraced Rachmaninoff, Debussy, Ravel, Richard Strauss and Mahler, then, gravitated to the cacophonies of Stravinsky, and, after studiously digesting the works of those who matriculated under Nadia Boulanger, he feasted on Hindemith, Berg, Schoenberg, Bartok, Varese, Prokofiev, Shostakovich, Khachaturian, Messiaen, and "Les Six," then backtracked for days, listening, to nothing but *"The Goldberg Variations,"* with Wanda Landowska, when re-issued on L.P. But when his sister introduced him to the sound of Duke Ellington, and he, subsequently discovered bebop, he became a jazz devotee.

A couple of years later, he obtained a most wonderful job at the largest record store in the Loop. Near the famous corner of Randolph and State, it was sandwiched in between the old bus station and Walgreen's flagship store, but, more to Aiden's liking, it was also just across the alley from the Chicago Theatre, where he had first seen Duke. The rear door of the store was only feet from the stage door of the famous movie emporium that always featured stage shows.

Fifteen year-old Aiden loved his job. Designated head of the jazz department because none of the older people liked that music, he ingratiated himself with Jazz at the Philharmonic impresario, Norman Granz, who was usually accompanied by a sassy Buddy Rich, who listened to Kenny Clarke records, Aiden played for him, and then critiqued them tersely, saying, "No technique."

Wearing polo coats, Tyrolean hats and Brooks Brothers button-down collar shirts, they stopped in the store when in town and Norman introduced Aiden to a, young unknown, pianist from Montreal named Oscar Peterson. Aiden dined at Walgreen's immense cafeteria, below the State Street level, with Ella Fitzgerald and members of Ellington's band who frequented the store and chatted with star clarinetist, Jimmy Hamilton, whom he idolized.

The job was thrilling, but he soon learned the store's aim was to sell appliances not records. Music was a lure to entrap the largely African-American clientele into buying TV's, phonographs and refrigerators at inflated prices, on usurious installment plans; that was the real moneymaker.

Aiden formed a band with himself on drums and an African-American, eight years his senior, named Tunis Aligherei, who did the heavy lifting, while Aiden did the soda-jerking, when both worked at Oris's drugstore, on Clark Street, a block from Aiden's small apartment. Tunis, who played guitar, escorted Aiden all over the South Side, even to rough places where Aiden was the only white person present. Yet, no prejudice was exhibited in his direction. At the record store, he met a tenor player, a saurian looking, twenty-one year old, named Tino, a customer who, one day, introduced himself to Aiden inquiring: "Smoke pot?"

Aiden had no idea what he meant. How could you smoke a pot? With a friend of Tino's on trumpet, the band played a couple of dives on the Northwest Side and Aiden obtained a gig for the group at a poor man's *bar mitzvah*. But after the affair, Tino and the trumpet player, both of whom were really shooting dope not puffing weed, successfully conspired to steal Aiden's set of drums in another negative, but highly educative, learning experience. Meeting Louis Armstrong, around that time, was a positive.

At Hebrew school, a couple of years back, Aiden enraged the headmaster, Rabbi Cohen by saying Louis Armstrong was Jewish, "He wears the star of David around his neck."

"There are no black Jews!" Cohen insisted, his eyes staring sternly from behind rimless glasses.

Now, Nat Hale, the head of sales for Columbia Records in Chicago, rewarded Aiden for pushing his product line by inviting him to meet Satchmo, who topped the stage show bill at the Chicago Theatre, across the alley.

"Come on, kid, I'll take you backstage to say 'hello.' It's something for your memory book," said Hale, a lovely man.

Aiden and Nat went through the back door of the store and crossed the narrow alley, which ran from State to Wabash. They entered the backstage door of the theatre and ascended the spiral, cast-iron staircase to a second floor dressing room. It was really a cubicle the size of a large closet.

And sitting against the wall in his underwear, sweating massively, wearing a fully extended white handkerchief on his head and a Star of David around his neck, was Louis Armstrong.

"Hi, Pops," he said to Aiden smiling broadly.

A "performing fool," he was exhausted and resting from his last show, straining to regain his wind for the next appearance two hours hence. Weakly, he made his toothy grin and waved at Aiden.

Satchmo called everyone "Pops" and the Star of David he wore was in honor of a Jewish family that sheltered him in his youth, something Aiden did not know at the time.

At the store, Aiden gained an important new friend in a fellow record clerk twenty years older than he whose name was Emil. Emil's nails were manicured and his steel-gray hair and cleft-chin imparted a resemblance to the Hungarian-born film star, Charles Corvin. Sporting tailor made suits and custom made shirts, with rounded stick-pin collars graced by elegant ties, Emil performed a major *mitzvah* and introduced Aiden to Eddie Gold, the head usher at the Civic Opera House, a man fondly known to the gay community as "The Phantom Of The Opera." He allowed Aiden to usher there, which explains why Aiden saw everything presented on that stage during the years 1951 to 1953. (SEE APPENDIX #4.)

He not only studied *Der Ring Des Nibelungen* in high school music class with his diligent teacher, Ms. Ford, he saw the whole damn thing and *Die Meistersinger*, too. He saw all the reproductions of the great Diaghilev in the 1951-52 tour of Ballet Russes De Monte Carlo[7], with settings by Bakst, Matisse and Picasso. He saw Ballet Theatre, all touring productions of the New York City Ballet

---

7   This was around the time of the great Pressburger-Powell film *Red Shoes*, (1948), which Aiden saw over and again.

and the New York City Opera, Sadler's Wells and the Metropolitan Opera (which produced *The Ring* that year). He had seen Lotte Lehmann in one of her numerous farewell tours, and even experienced a folk song phase, listening to Josh White, Big Bill Broonzy, Pete Seeger, Big John Hooker, Sonny Terry and Brownie McGhee. Earnestly Aiden abhorred the bastardization of blues by whites, thought R&B banal, and barely tolerated country and bluegrass, except for Hank Williams, Robert Foster and Chet Atkins, of course.

Working at the record store, one day Aiden opened a box shipment of ten-inch records. It was Bill Haley's dreadful "cover" of Chuck Berry's "Rock Around The Clock," one of the most important records ever made. Elvis Presley made his first record that July. For years, blues records made by and for African-Americans were called "race records" by those who manufactured and sold them. People began referring to the genre as "rhythm & blues." Then, only months before Aiden started work at the record emporium, the term "rock and roll" was coined and popularized by Cleveland disk jockey Alan Freed. Aiden saw it all happen; this thing called rock and roll developed during the period he worked at the store and it was a music our hero, with a few exceptions, detested his whole life long.[8]

As far as Aiden was concerned, nothing compared to bebop[9] because it amalgamated all great music and created something even more sophisticated.

Lester Young was a radical who showed jazz could be "cool;" it need not be "hot" to be good. The great bop pianist, Barry Harris, said, "Bebop began with Lester Young...actually, Coleman Hawkins, too." Not a bopper himself, Prez could play with them and was an indirect influence on those who laid the foundations

---

8   Except Little Richard, T-Bone Walker, Memphis Slim and all his disciples, Muddy Waters, Ruth Brown and Fats Domino. But this was 1954. The great James Brown, Howlin' Wolf, much less Leon Russell, Dr. John, Janis Joplin, the Moody Blues, Joe Cocker, Kris Kristofferson, Johnny Cash, Merle Haggard and other authentic artists had yet to appear on the scene. Still, when Johnny Mercer later categorized all the music emanating from the rock and roll, country, and country-rock scene to be "all the same song," Aiden agreed.

9   It was not lost on Aiden that bebop, a music so complex and so representative of the period in which he lived, should have such a demeaning name, but he knew that "jazz" means "fuck," so it didn't bother him. In his fourteenth year, he had stolen a copy of Leonard Feather's *Inside Bebop* from the Evanston Public Library and learned that "bop" or "bebop," was a diminutive for the nonsense phrase "a-klookie-mop," as in "Ooo-Bop-Sh-Bam, A-Klookie-Mop" which was a way of spelling out in letters that Dizzy Gillespie's big band drummer, Kenny "Klook" Clarke, one of the inventors of bebop, was playing on his drum kit. The tune is based on "I Got Rhythm."

of the new music at Minton's Playhouse, in Harlem, beginning in 1940, four years after Prez's recording debut in Chicago, with a small component of Count Basie's band, the year Aiden was born.

Foremost among those at Minton's were Charlie Parker, trumpeters Dizzy Gillespie and "Little Bennie" Harris, pianist, Tadd Dameron, sometime house pianist, Thelonious Monk, who began his career accompanying gospel groups and rhythm and blues touring bands, and guitarist, Charlie Christian, made popular by his presence in Benny Goodman's Sextet. Through amplification Christian had revolutionized his instrument, making it sound more like a tenor sax.[10]

The marriage of Broadway show tunes and worthy popular songs with jazz had begun years ago and was formalized with musicals like the Gershwins,' *Girl Crazy*, in which jazz greats like Gene Krupa, Benny Goodman, Tommy Dorsey, Jimmy Dorsey, Red Nichols, Glenn Miller and Jack Teagarden, before they became household names in the swing era, played in the show's pit band. The original score included two songs that became jazz standards: "Embraceable You" and more importantly, "I Got Rhythm."[11]

It seemed to Aiden that this modern phase, in which the melodies of masterpieces like "What Is This Thing Called Love" and "All The Things You Are," were extended into complex works more inventive, charming and evocative than the works of all the so-called "serious" composers of the day, was the greatest period of all.

As he reaches his destination, Aiden, it must be said, may not have thought all these things at once, but they were generally on his mind, and he promised himself once more, as he done so many times before, that he would someday produce a jazz musical.

****

---

10 Bebop developed, in part, in order to bar unwanted participants from joining the Minton's sessions. Harmonic progressions were developed in private or whispered on the stand. Flatted fifths and minor sixth chords were unexpectedly interpolated, wrecking the unwelcomed musician's improvisation. Old tunes were revised with progressions involving chord substitutions and complicated thematic variations, such as Tadd Dameron's "Lady Bird," based on "Lullaby in Rhythm," and Benny Harris's "Ornithology" based on "How High the Moon."

11 A countless number of songs are referred to by musicians as "Rhythm" songs, and are based on the chords of "I Got Rhythm," such as Duke's "Cottontail," Lester Young's "Lester Leaps In" Monk's "Rhythm-a-Ning" and Dizzy's "Salt Peanuts," while a number of others merely follow its same A-A-B-A 32 bar pattern. Charlie Parker's felicitous version is called "Dexterity."

The Open Door was located close by Washington Square Park, on the corner of Third Street and Washington Place, a block away from the Triangle Shirtwaist Factory. It had been a speakeasy, then a strip club and, now, in the last few years it had become a small jazz venue where Parker, Monk, Charles Mingus, Roy Haynes and others participated in disorganized sessions. But Bird was the main attraction.

Aiden arrived to find a dozen seedy-looking men lined-up around the corner of the club as if it were an audition. Some carried horn cases; one powerful fellow stood guarding his conga drum. One squat cat, carrying a trumpet case, looked like Moe from the Three Stooges. Under his pulled down blue fedora he was balding and his simian-like face was badly pockmarked. He walked back and forth nervously puffing on a Pall Mall, same as Prez smoked. Perhaps he was thinking of what to play, something in C, for sure, maybe "Undecided," or "C-Jam Blues." That is if Bird would allow him to play at all. It depended on how Bird felt, what mood he favored, what he, Bird wanted to play. He could, of course, play anything. All of these men, Aiden was to discover, were waiting for Bird to arrive in the hope he might allow them to jam.

Aiden entered the club to find it barely occupied.

It must be understood that the most important question in jazz at this time was: "What's up with Bird?"

His records were selling voluminously, but because of his heroin habit he seldom retained the profits. People in big cities searched for veins in which to stick needles in celebration of his greatness, some in the hope that doing so might make them play as well as he. Cab Calloway, in a well-publicized *Downbeat* article, opined that bebop had spawned a generation of dope-addicted jazzmen.

In his last formal engagement Bird had swallowed iodine in a suicide attempt. He was hospitalized twice at Bellevue in episodes characterized as mental breakdowns. His infant daughter had died. He was separated from his wife and was living with a friend. Devoid of a cabaret card, he played "pick-up" sessions in storefront joints. A new gig was scheduled with strings. There had been two such successful recording sessions and a brief, troublesome tour, all arranged by Norman Granz. But the new tour was cancelled because of Bird's troubles with Local 802, the musician's union.

Bird was shooting dope regularly. In recent pictures he looked like a bloated Buddha, but he was only 34, and had been, for nearly a decade, the most influential modern source of sound, not only for those who played jazz in America, Europe and elsewhere, but for arrangers worldwide who scored for movies and television. Dizzy Gillespie would tell Aiden: "He gave us the style, Charlie Parker gave us the style."

Now, it was after 11:00 P.M. and there were only two tables occupied in the room, which accommodated 150 and had a very small bar off to one side. The stingy, half-moon of a bandstand faced the door. Tiny, but large enough to accommodate a female taking off her clothes, it was decorated overhead with a scalloped, red and white striped border circus motif and the art of the ecdysiast was celebrated in a lascivious, reclining nude, ineptly painted on a panel, which served as background for a set of drums.

Acting like a big shot, Aiden took a table near the piano, ordered a drink and waited. A good deal of time went by and a young African-American with a pencil moustache emerged from the kitchen and approached the piano, a battered, Baldwin upright, missing the upper panel, so that the hammers and sounding board were exposed. He sat down before the keyboard, flexed his fingers and began playing blues-tinged tunes, with quotations and progressions associated with Bird. Aiden later learned the pianist was Hampton Hawes, in from L.A.

By midnight, the place was packed and all the tables filled. Among the customers were two gray-haired men who accompanied a woman in her late 40's. As the evening ensued, musicians patronized them, sitting at their table. Aiden surmised them to be celebrities of some sort, and would come to know them quite well as Francis Wolff and Alfred Lion, German Jews, (bankrolled partly by a third, silent, partner, Max Margulies, a Marxist writer) who founded the prosperous jazz label, Blue Note Records, which began recording folk and rhythm and blues artists in the early Forties, and later became a pioneer in issuing the work of stellar bebop artists, such as Monk and Bud Powell.

And the woman was the Baroness Kathleen Annie Pannonica de Koenigswarter, née Rothschild, nicknamed Nica, an heiress to the legendary family fortune, which bankrolled Napoleon. She was linked with and said to be bankrolling Monk, too, as Aiden was to learn, because all of them, as the reader will discover, were frequent visitors to the Palace of Audible Dreams.

The musicians who had waited outside now entered the club and lined-up against the uptown side of the room while a band formed onstage. Hawes was on piano, Charles Mingus, on bass, and Tony Scott, on clarinet. Aiden had never seen Mingus before but knew of him from his recordings with the Red Norvo Trio, which included the renowned Tal Farlow, on guitar. Because he was not ofay, Mingus, whose previous base of operations was L.A., had had problems touring with Norvo. He joined Duke Ellington, briefly, a year before and, though he had gigged with Bird, he was still relatively new to the Apple. Scott (Anthony Sciacca) played a whispery clarinet like Prez. Charming and dapper, he grew up on 52nd Street playing with Ben Webster and Oran "Hot Lips" Page. Roy Haynes played frequently at the Open Door, but a series of drummers played that night.

Bird finally showed up around midnight using the same entrance used by patrons. It was the Open Door and anyone could enter. He was wearing an arrogant grim and a rumpled suit and bowing decorously, like royalty, to scattered applause and cheers of "Hey, Bird!" Excitement came in the door with him, along with more musicians and a cadre of groupies. The latter followed everywhere in his wake, unless you saw him when he was broke and desperate, alone and in need of a fix or a quarter "to get home on the subway."

But tonight he was serene and in charge and, Aiden guessed, for he was not THAT naïve, that Bird had undoubtedly gotten high. Parker crossed the barely existent dance floor before the stand with composed grace and a practiced smile that said "I am the King of England and you are my loyal subjects," a far cry from the sniveling schizophrenic eventually seen on celluloid. And he didn't keep the audience or the other musicians waiting; no messing with reeds. He asked for an "A" and launched into an avalanche of sound and ideation which most alto players had abandoned all hope of emulating, while the rest of the world woodshedded his every articulation.

He started fast and stayed that way, playing "Ko-Ko" and a very pulsating "On A Slow Boat To China" and he never played a note, never composed a phrase which didn't enthrall and elevate Aiden. But there was no gentleness from Bird that night. He played savagely; years later they would say that at this time in his life he played without warmth. But to Aiden he sounded great. As a kid, Bird practiced playing along with Lester's solos on Basie recordings and he listened to Buster Smith, Pete Brown, Benny Carter, Johnny Hodges, even Jimmy Dorsey, and some said, initially, he sounded like Lester playing alto. However, he was too innovative to be imitating someone else.

But on that particular Sunday night, after having played one brilliant set, Bird began playing games. Assuming the role of genial master of ceremonies, with a perpetual gleam in his eye, he began inviting the musicians who lined the walls, most of who resembled candidates for the hangmen's noose, to join him on (verily, before) the stand.

He ate them up, one by one. One of these so consumed was the diminutive trumpeter, with the funny puss. Aiden would learn this man dressed habitually in the same uniform of worn blue suit, white shirt, with frayed collar and plain, black tie. The fringe of hair surrounding the pate of his oversized head gave him that look of a small ape, and there may, indeed, have been a trace of the Mongoloid in him. Yet, he was most appealing because he constantly smiled and was gentility itself. His name was Nat Lorber, but everyone called him "Nat the Face" and he was, it turned out, a fixture at the Palace of Audible Dreams, appearing there almost daily, usually tagging behind one of his heroes, Roy Eldridge.

He lived with his mother and sister in Brooklyn and, supposedly, received his nickname from Louis Armstrong. All trumpet players loved Pops, but Nat, who was fanatical about Louis, somehow wheedled his way backstage at one of Pop's Town Hall concerts, and got a choice spot in the wings in order to closely observe his idol. When Armstrong gave the downbeat and they launched into "When It's Sleepy Time Down South," Nat, who, let's face it, wasn't all there, could contain himself no longer and took a step, edging onstage, a hand outstretched toward his deity, a silly grin upon his goofy mug.

Pops stopped playing, executed one of his patented bug-eyed stares and declared to the audience and those on, off and backstage,

"Man, what a face!" "Face" became Nat's name from then on, so goes the the story as told, later, to Aiden, but it never occurred to him that evening that this seedy little man, this authentic free soul, would become one of the characters in his gallery of Broadway boppers and bandits. Nat was kind and, often, wise, and unlike most people Aiden met, Nat was not greedy. All he wanted out of life was the chance to blow, sit-in and to hang out with, and run little errands for, immortals. Nat claimed that all he needed was, "a half to make you laugh and a place to take a shit." The fifty cents was carfare to and from Flatbush and he had many friends who, because of his sunny disposition, were happy to let him use their john.

In the second set that evening, Bird, with an arcane smile that seemed, to Aiden, wicked, invited "Face" to the stand. Nat's specialty, Aiden then learned, was to play a solo containing one chorus in which he held one note for 36 measures. He was terrible.

After "Face's" performance, Bird summoned the conga player to the stage area and ripped into an impossibly fast tempo, which only the expert rhythm section could maintain. The conga player was left in the lurch from the get-go and strained to keep up. But when they reached the end of a chorus or two, Bird signaled the rhythm section for a stop-tempo break, then turned and yelled to the conga player: "Blow, Baby!" denting the man's false pretensions and self-esteem forever. The man, who was tall and powerful, played a figure, then repeated it in order to establish a pattern and, reaching for another idea, flaying the skins unmercifully, watching Bird watch him with Buddha-like patience, the galloping tempo inevitably defeated the would-be Candido and he faltered and soon defaulted altogether in a complete rhythmic collapse. There was a total silence in the club while Bird smiled sadistically at the conga player, then, resumed the break-neck tempo and brought the number to an end.

The "cutting session" deteriorated from then on. Bird called for the group to play "Papa Loves Mambo," a popular hit of the day, but hardly a song at all, and, due to the fiasco of "Nat the Face" and the conga player, Mingus, who astounded Aiden with his enormous sound, packed his bass fiddle and left soon after.

Aiden was sophisticated enough to know that Bird played rubbish occasionally to show that, like Fats Waller and Billie Holiday, he could make lousy songs sound good, but, as was the case with Mingus, "Papa Loves Mambo, " was too much for Aiden and he left the Open Door and headed back to the Y.M.C.A. for shut-eye.

He had driven cross-country and secured his ideal job, and to top it off, had finally seen the great Charlie Parker, he mused, as he crossed the street and began traversing Washington Square Park, the persistent echoes of the ascendant chromatics of "Slow Boat To China" still sounding in the night air, serenading his joyful spirit.

Then he saw, for the first, the beautiful arch designed by Stanford White! He knew nothing of the famed architect, who copied the Arch de Triomphe and placed it in Washington Square Park, but seeing it for the first time that particular night would be a never forgotten epiphenonon. And, knowing he had the job and was on his way in the theatre, like so many young men and women who had come to Gotham before him, having heard the hoped-for knock of opportunity, he was infused with fervent optimism. When he reached Sixth Avenue it was past 2 A.M. He hailed a cab and returned to 33rd and Ninth, where he had parked his car. It had been burglarized and everything inside stolen.

2

"The Great Hotbed
Of Human Power"[12]

Aiden moved into Charlton Heston's old apartment, at 433 West Forty-Fifth Street, next to the playground that, in five years, would become infamous as the scene of "The Capeman" murders, a turning point in the degradation of civilization. A "railroad," walk-up apartment in Hell's Kitchen, just off the Theatre District, with the Martin Beck Theatre a block away, was most desirable. Fellow alumni of Heston's, a married couple who were actors, and who inherited the pad from the man who played Moses, sub-leased it to Aiden.

Autumn drew on, McCarthy's censure by the Senate was passed, Dave Brubeck appeared on the cover of *Time* and, on his nights off from working at the Palace of Audible Dreams, or on matinees, Aiden saw *By The Beautiful Sea*, starring Shirley Booth, with a score by Arthur Schwartz, and Montgomery Clift, in *The Seagull*. He saw *Fifth Season*, starring Menasha Skulnik, a college education in comedy, mastermind George S. Kaufman's *Solid Gold Cadillac*, and, at a time when memorable revues still graced Broadway, *John Murray Anderson's Almanac*, with Hermione Gingold, Billy de Wolfe and a mesmerizing Harry Belafonte. A top ticket cost six dollars for musicals and three bucks for plays. One could sit in the balcony for a dollar and eighty cents.

---

12 Sir Humphry Davy (speaking of his arrival in London as a young man).

But for Aiden, who had seen so much, Maurice Chevalier's one-man show at the Bijou was the most powerful theatrical experience of all, better than seeing Martyn Green play a different role in Gilbert and Sullivan, one night after another, or watching the way Henry Fonda simply stood still, or the way the Lunts reached the back of the house and still seemed real (despite Holden Caulfield's opinion in the matter). In the first place, seeing Chevalier in person had little to do with Chevalier on screen. Each song was a three-act play; every gesture conveyed a meaning that every eye obeyed.

In the second place it was not a one man show, it was a two man show because the great singer was aging and, at the very last minute, requested some other performer of his choice be hired for interludes so he, Chevalier, could rest between numbers. The "other" (a man previously unknown to Americans until then) was a tall mime in whiteface, dressed like Jean-Louis Barrault as Jean-Gaspard Deburau, in *Les Enfants Du Paradis*, who performed skits that were profound, but hilarious, morality plays. The unheralded "other" was Marcel Marceau, who, like Chevalier, astonished the audience. Two giants on the same bill were electrifying.

Aiden continued the affairs he began with the three women he loved at the Great Playhouse, blonde, redhead and brunette, all beautiful, and superb actresses. And he patronized the old whore who stationed herself at Forty-Fifth and Ninth and who, rendezvousing with him in his walk-up apartment, preferred bending over the toilet bowl, bracing her hands and face against the wall, and taking it up the bum. In high school, Aiden and the most beautiful girl in his class had been in love but when she mentioned marriage Aiden quickly disengaged.

He enjoyed working nights and walked to work around dinnertime to labor beside the zanies who worked in the store and the screwballs and celebrities who frequented it. Unlike the record emporium on Randolph and State in Chicago, which had eight sound booths where potential buyers sampled recordings before buying them, in the Palace of Audible Dreams there were no sampling booths at all, everything – except the stock – was out in the open and the word of the day was: "Two-ten this guy," a fellow clerk would warn, which meant: "Keep your two eyes on this guy's ten fingers 'cause I think he's a thief."

One never knew who the next customer would be. The most important person in the store, aside from the owners Ziggy and Bunky, was Dean Romanoff, Aiden's new "Brudder." Dean taught Aiden to smoke pot and play the horses and Ziggy, Bunky and Dean brought Aiden to the racetrack for the first time in his life, the old Aqueduct Racetrack. And the track, he discovered, was the second (or was it the third?) most exciting thing in the world!

He did not win that day, but his first bet had come earlier in his employment, when Dean told him to put up four dollars to bet on a "sure thing" at the trotters that night. The horse won and paid $64 and Dean gave him $128 back and Aiden was hooked forever, imagining how much *gelt* he would have acquired had he bet his week's salary on the tip, or a month's, or so on, ad infinitum.

Beautiful women went in and out of the store from minute to minute; faded madams and gorgeous young call girls were regular patrons. Aiden knew nothing of female procuresses except for *Mrs. Warren's Profession* and those he had seen in movies and, as far as prostitutes were concerned, there were, as a point of reference, only the two or three with whom he dallied in seedy Chicago hotel rooms, along with his high school buddies. So, it was Dean who pointed out the fallen women to the young man.

Romanoff identified a greedy, deeply tanned woman, with her raven colored hair in a bun. Busily, she selected LP's from piles of audible dreams, while, with urgent whispers, she bossed around a suntanned, brunette teenager whom Aiden thought so ineffably beautiful he nearly swooned. When Dean told him she was the older woman's slave and, that on a trip to Miami, in the Cadillac of his friend, "Poughkeepsie Joe," the younger woman, with the older woman's approval, succumbed to Joe's urgent demand he engage the teenager in anal sex, then and there on the side of the road, Aiden's stomach experienced a nauseous twinge.

His attention was also directed to a tired woman of forty, whose pouty lips were painted beyond their boundaries, and whose legs were slightly bowed, all indications she was past her prime. And yet she was truly sexy and had attracted, as her sexual partner and escort, a young man nearly half her age, a man so handsome, with his sapphire blue eyes and golden hair, he could have been a beautiful woman had he primped more and worn a dress. This madam's name was Carol and Dean claimed she was the most successful in her trade, at the time. Aiden never learned the young man's name or the nature of their sexual practices, though it gave him pause for thought during those first months of employment in this sweet, but thoroughly poisonous, climate of corruption.

Some ladies hit the street only at 4 A.M., when the clubs vomited their patrons and the Palace of Audible Dreams shuttered for a few hours of rest. Among these were the Twomey Twins who always arrived only as the store was closing. Then, Tina, the eldest, no more than two years older than Aiden, her skin an exquisite shade of a tannish hue for which there is no adequate name, would enter the thick, glitzy, shatter-proof glass doors, while her lookalike "twin sister," who was really her cousin, waited on the sidewalk outside. All curves and long legs, she would sashay slowly, but directly up to Aiden, wherever he might be standing, grab his crotch, put her shapely body and her slightly-parted, painted lips close to his and whisper "You're arrested and you're coming home with me and my sister. Now! "

She would buy a record, or Aiden would buy one for her, and the three of them would take a cab to her sleeping grandma's house, off Lennox Boulevard, in the hundred and teens. There, she and her harmonious "sister" would take off their clothes, turn down the lights, turn on soft music and assume postures of prayerful supplication, one kneeling before, the other aft of Aiden, whilst Grandma Twomey, in an adjoining room, dreamed away the early hours of the morning, content in the knowledge her lambs were safe from sin which lurked outside and that they had arrived home intact, for she had heard them enter and close the latch behind them, softly, with hardly a sound.

And whilst Aiden stood in a posture of benediction in the still minutes "'fore the crowing of the cock," the knowing Twomey Twins, with the calves of their slender legs stretched behind their undulating derrieres, far from a process of expiation or a state of atonement, would investigate the crevices and protuberances of Aiden's body with their adventurous mouths and acrobatic tongues, their sweet asses swaying rhythmically in contrapuntal disunity. And with the benison completed, concerning that of which he knew not, Aiden received impassioned tutorials from the talented Twomey Twins.

"Put the boy in the boat," Tina's "sister" moaned in the direction of his head, as he performed cunnilingus on her quivering vagina.

"Whaaaa???" Aiden asked, in a muffled voice, from between her thighs.

"Put the boy in the boat!" Tina urged enthusiastically but with a touch of irritation. "Put her clit in your mouth, sugar."

It was the first time Aiden had heard the expression, or, in truth, knew of the practice. If, and when, Grandma Twomey, from her bedroom, would call out inquiringly: "Is everything all right?" they would laugh and Tina or her "sister," would call back, "Everything's fine, darlin', go back to sleep."

And when Aiden left the Twomey Twins and walked into the dawn of a cold morning, he saw a world he barely knew, but about which he had heard and read so much - Harlem before the riots.

****

Only slightly bedazzled at the start of his stay, it did not take long for Aiden's attitude toward the metropolis to become a trifle jaundiced. The saturnine part of his being, an enemy of parades and circuses, responded negatively to the perseverant sound of sirens and collisions of metal and steel upon concrete, the roar of the subway, the stench of refuse mingled with the smell of money coming from Park Avenue and Riverside Drive, and like Dreiser, he was struck by the fact that "the strong were so very strong and the weak so very, very weak and very, very many." These imperfections contributed to the inculcation of an ambivalent relationship, despite its gilded glamour, between the new New Yorker and the island that had become home. Cognizant now of the dangers of Times Square, he habitually looked behind and way ahead wherever he went and walked faster than anyone in any crowd. Constitutionally indisposed toward the wealthy, he despised the ostentatious flaunting of, no doubt, ill-gotten gains, and this, combined with the indisputable cliché-fact New Yorkers were not as friendly as Chicagoans, made clear these severe defects dictated that if not for the Theatre he would not live in New York City or its environs.

Initially shocked by the profligate use of the word "mother-fucker," seldom said back home, he finally succumbed to its over-use himself, realizing the epithet to be a profane declaration Cholly Knickerbocker was a demanding master, that there was frustration attached to NYC if one were somehow lacking, a crude reminder "Life itself is 6 to 5 against," as Damon Runyon said, even though a cup of coffee still cost five cents, except at "Horny Hardon," where it cost a dime.

As for the gaggle of geese with which he toiled, the "zanies," his fellow record clerks at the Palace of Audible Dreams, every race and nationality was represented on the store's employment roster and an expert hired for every category of music. Eliminating for a moment those who had recently left the ranks of the imprisoned and had been hired by the empathetic Ziggy, who wisely believed in affording everyone a second chance to screw up, the staff consisted of two categories of strictly male employees: non-performers and performers, the latter mostly has-beens, ageing chorus boys from flop musicals, or wanna-be, mediocre jazz musicians and half-baked thespians.

Billy Delahanty was rightly called the "The Duck Salesman" because he was a ventriloquist who played straight man to a duck. He frequently brought the duck, which he had trained, to the store, to the amusement of some and the annoyance of his employers. Billy claimed he was an octoroon, had a pompadour and a pencil mustache, and, similar to a number of well-known jazz musicians of the day, ran a couple of beautiful "working girls," who provided him with the gains of their travails, so that Billy could boast he had not only a duck but a couple of hookers turning tricks on his behalf.

Yet some succeeded in their quest for fame. Aaron Banks was a lanky six-foot, two, with a prominent nose, beady eyes and bushy hair. Small boned and non-muscular despite his height, Aaron was a Method actor who got into character by banging his head against the wall in the store's stockroom. When aroused, he displayed a very bad temper. He played bit parts in two Broadway plays and a couple of minor films, but ended up with his own academy on Broadway,[13] his name in king-size letters, the result, presumably,

---

13 New York Karate Academy.

of a horrendous physical skirmish with a customer in the Palace of Audible Dreams. According to the world-wide web, the cops were called and, though Aaron fought with all his might (they say "six men in blue pulled the fighters apart"), the customer, who was the smaller of the two, won and Aaron suffered a humiliation so severe he was motivated to take ten lessons from a master, give up booze and the evil weed, earn a Black Belt and become the prime progenitor of Karate in America, breaking boards on national TV talk shows and presenting two decades of televised events from Madison Square Garden.[14]

Similarly successful was Howie Thomashefsky, a black man and a member of the famous Yiddish theatre family. Howie worked at the store during the Borsht circuit's off-season and, a couple of decades later, had a successful act (and recording) called "It's Tough To Be Young, Gifted And Black."[15]

That was just before the near-blind violinist, Reuben "Ruby" Levine, without the owners consent or knowledge, made the Palace of Audible Dreams his official headquarters, booking sports and horse bets on the store's public phone, a small-time operation. Ruby played outside Broadway theatres at show time, then cabbed it downtown to perform a peregrinating standup act at a Rumanian restaurant, wandering from table to table saying, "I'll ruin any song for you. You name it, I'll kill it." Ruby, became the subject of a twenty-seven-page profile in *The New Yorker*.

Then there was a white man of indeterminate age who bore the strange antebellum slave name of Hudy, which rhymes with Judy, a name the uninitiated pronounced as "Hootie," thinking it was a pejorative comment on the comical strangeness of the man, that Hudy was a hoot. Barely five feet tall, his hair shorn like a prisoner from Dachau, he resembled an emaciated jockey from the Gran Guignol sans silks, cap, breeches, boots and whip, yet his job was to trundle, lug and schlepp the phonograph records from their delivery point

---

14 Ed. Note: Apocryphal, like much on the Internet, the real story is Banks' motivation stemmed from his losing a fight with the less physically imposing Aiden, at the front of the store, witnessed by Dean, and co-owner, Bunky. But their mutual fondness for Nat "The Face," who both [but esp. Aaron] protected, eventually united the actor-fighters in friendship.

15 The title being a takeoff on *To Be Young, Gifted And Black*, a theatre piece based on the diaries and writings of *A Raisin In the Sun's* author, Lorraine Hansberry, and crafted by her husband and literary executor, Robert Barron Nemiroff, who took credit for coining the phrase, when it was she who first used it and at a time when the word "black" was considered improperly impolite.

on the side street entrance, down to the basement stock rooms, only to later trundle, lug and schlepp them back upstairs, in order to file them in their appropriate place in stock.

Unshaven for days, he was missing most of his teeth and the remainder was black with decay. But the most striking feature of his appearance was the short-sleeved shirt he inhabited for months at a time. Originally beige, or yellow, or even white, it was thickly caked, now, with layers of *shmutz*, and his dirty, brown trousers, held in place by a thin strip of tied-together leather shoelaces, only added to his shocking presence. No explanation was given for his abominable condition and he smelled awful, yet nothing would deter him from the supremely idiotic belief that he was a great pop singer just waiting to be discovered, his signature song being the all too familiar:

"Beautiful Dreamer, Wake Unto Me.[16]
Starlight And Dew Drops Are Awaiting Thee."

A hit, six years before, as sung by his idol, Al Jolson, the abominably unsanitary Hudy sang this over-performed chestnut in a unique arrangement of his own, mixing a "doo-wop' opening vamp with operatic gusto befitting "Pagliacci," employing unseemly hand gestures with unabashed bravado in the genre of florid declamations associated with Delsarte and 19th century acting, placing them together and nestling them beneath his tilted cheek in imitation of slumber each time he came to the word "dreamer," and peppering his emotive stew with a grotesque flamboyance unwarranted by the simpleminded ditty, so that it seemed to be a burlesque, only it wasn't.

And though the vocalizing of the little unshaven man with wretched teeth lacked merit, he was uniquely musical and could identify the key and call out the chords of almost any popular song as it played on the radio or phonograph. "F Major, B-Flat Seventh, E-Flat Minor Seventh, A-Flat Major Seventh," the idiot savant would intone, as the harmonies progressed, and, when Aiden learned the half-demented man possessed a scholarly grasp of the

---

16 It was also a big seller, too, for Bing Crosby; written, of course, by Stephen Foster.

chronology of the history plays of Shakespeare and could rattle off the batting order of every Yankee team back to Murderers' Row, Aiden and Hudy became friends.

The teenager learned Hudy was hired through the largesse of Ziggy, who had read about the strange story of Hudy's father, a menial laborer on a building site who, while playing around with fellow workers, swung a bucket of cement around and around, unintentionally decapitating a colleague who carelessly came within the boundaries of the whirling vessel turned weapon.

(Ed. Note: Aware of George Orwell's comment that Charles Dickens throws characters into the plot like logs on a fire, though not intending to compare himself to that master, the author has chronolgically introduced players who return for further development in Book II, "Rise and Fall in the Age of David Mamet," for though The Palace of Audible Dreams will move to another location it will remain an ongoing part of this story.)

In the college named in honor of the beloved president who defeated Hitler, and which soon occupied the glorious Chicago Auditorium Building, Aiden's sister, Betty's closest friends were a white girl, Lorraine, and the man with whom Lorraine had fallen in love, Mel Williamson, a fellow student on the G.I. Bill, a black man from the South Side of Chicago, whose father, a red cap porter, was a follower of A. Phillip Randolph. A talented artist and writer, bespectacled, mustachioed, of average height and great charm, Mel, who had studied with the social realist artist, Charles White, dressed immaculately and insisted others on the Left behave similarly. All disciples of Robeson, Mel, Lorraine and Betty graduated together from the school around the time that Lorraine Hansberry, the future playwright, and Oscar Brown, Jr., the singer-composer, briefly attended the same college.

Then, Mel (who was a great advocate of Duke Ellington's music) and Lorraine married. Her father was dead but her mother rejected Mel, and they left for New York City, where miscegenation was tolerated, to a certain extent, in certain neighborhoods. Aiden idolized Mel, sat on his knee as a child, and looked forward to seeing the couple, then, living in Brooklyn. Mel was working at Viking Press; Lorraine had become a teacher at a prestigious school, and they would soon be moving to a new development called Central

Park West. They were Aiden's best and most reliable friends in New York and Mel would, in the future, make an arrangement on Aiden's behalf that would change Aiden's life forever.

****

Despite the fact he was from Rogers Park, Aiden had never seen so many Jewish people before. Many spoke Yiddish, or used Yiddish phrases pungently in conversing in a language with which the *shaigetz* was only barely familiar. Aiden was accustomed to people telling him, "But you don't look Jewish!" Now they would say, "If you're Jewish how come you don't know no Yiddish?"

It was a question Aiden was embarrassed to answer when queried by one of the store's high-powered salesman, a pie-faced man named Tex, who boasted a Keystone Cops moustache, spoke with a heavy Brooklyn accent, and whose only connection with the Lone Star state was serving at Fort Bliss and getting laid in Juarez. Tex was the store's country and western expert.

"Stop *haken* me a *tsheinik!*" (Stop annoying me; especially with long-windedness, or, more correctly: *"hah mir nit kain tsheinik."* Lit. To bang on the tea kettle), Tex said constantly to customers, his fellow salesmen and even the bosses, Ziggy and Bunky. Almost everyone at the Palace of Audible Dreams spoke Yiddish to some degree, even the non-Jews, so Aiden purchased a Yiddish dictionary in order to learn words and phrases.

He decided this atmosphere of *yiddishkeit* is what triggered an unpleasant repetitive dream he had not dreamt since his arrival in October. In order to rid himself of the burden, and to understand the meaning of the dream, for Proust said: "Our memory of dreams may become lasting if they repeat themselves often enough," and because he remembered with perfect clarity the locales which corresponded to their real-life counterparts, he decided to write about the dream. The frightening part was the beginning; the setting was an all-too familiar schoolroom. Here is what he wrote:

"'Dirty Jew! Dirty Jew!' cried the children of the Tiny Tots Academy of Elmhurst, Illinois and, though I had no idea what a Jew might be, I realized I was one according to them and had to pay for it. I am beginning to think that my payment, and the blow which followed, served as predicates to my future conduct and

proclaimed my destiny as both victim and perpetrator. A playable play is often one in which rituals are repeated and I am frequently replaying the events of that fateful year when another World War became reality.

The Tiny Tots danced and jeered as I stood there in the winter of Poland's discontent, bare-legged, too young for knickers, much less long pants, a smiling, compliant, small-boned but well-formed, handsome child, of fair hair and complexion, pampered and much-loved (especially by my doting mother), trusting, oblivious to self-defense or pre-emptive action.

Born during the diphtheria epidemic of 1936, according to literate notations in 'Baby's Treasures,' a thick, now-begrimed and dilapidated, hollowed-out "dummy" volume of the Depression period, a memento collecting book for storing baby's rattle, a curl of hair and first birthday party invitations, on a page reserved for data on baby's progress, entitled 'Baby's Illnesses,' transcribed in a precise hand by my Russian immigrant father, who spoke impeccable English, read Edith Wharton, Herbert Gold and the essays of Francis Bacon, and stayed up nights battering an ancient Underwood portable, writing countless unpublished stories for the pulps in the style of Dashiell Hammett:

> 'Almost immediately after circumcision,
> diphtheria of a local nature, centered
> around the penis, took place; a pediatrician
> was called in after the original
> physician failed to properly analyze the
> symptoms. Almost five weeks passed before
> the child was on the road to recovery.'

My life struggle thus began with a vicious attack upon my organ of procreation, that mercurial appendage which recklessly waxes, indifferently wanes, but remains at the core of Whitman's 'Urge, urge, urge.'

Now, back in the dream in the Tiny Tots Nursery School nearly four years later, here I stood, healthy, sweet-natured, angelically good looking, friendly and, though circumcised, having no idea what was a 'Jew,' the word my four year old classmates continued yelling in more ominous tones, though some thought it hilarious, too. I should have remembered the only other time I had heard the word that I heard now and would come to know so well.

'They don't want Jews!' my cagey, usually un-demonstrative father angrily mutters, as my dream shifts locale. He grabs my hand, now, and hauls me from out the courtyard of an immaculate, white-marbled residential structure nestled on the serpentine road that hugs the lakeshore, memorializes a ruthlessly effective Union general, and forms a boundary where Chicago becomes Evanston, a world apart. It is before the schoolroom confrontation; I was three.

We lived, my sister Betty and I, with our parents in a semi- bucolic western portion of Rogers Park, north of Devon Avenue, adjacent to a vast open field dominated by a towering silo. Tractors and mobilized hoers dotted the landscape. It is the pleasant northwestern boundary of the Windy City. But my father wanted a larger place, in a different neighborhood and this particular day, he takes me along with him on his quest.

'What's wrong,' I peep as he hustles me away, but though visibly upset, he fails to explain. This cryptic, some said 'slippery,' poker-faced atheist from Odessa, this well dressed, intelligent, European-turned-modern-American, a Levite and a Mason, who claimed, also, to have been a Russian sailor and a follower of Kerensky, this man who derived from a family renamed under Austrian rule to a cognomen that translates to 'precious stone,' then, expelled to the Pale, this sly man, who, like his older brother and father, had been a jeweler, then, a traveling salesman, an executive and an entrepreneur in the automotive parts business, was keenly observant of eye but not of faith and the only things Jewish about him were his name and the way he looked.

My sister, who took great pride in me, though jealous of the excessive attention I received, was born in Charlotte, South Carolina, her diminutive, following the Southern custom, was 'Betty,' and the three of them settled in Rogers Park, Chicago where I was born. That's all I know, but I suspect it may conceal...I know not what.

In time for the Fourth of July, my father mysteriously moved us into a comfortable house, in the Chicago suburb of Elmhurst, famous for its stately trees and formerly restricted to those of the Hebrew persuasion, making my father one of a handful of groundbreakers.

In my dream I find myself with my sister, mother and father on the lawn of our new home, as my father leads us in celebration of the nation's birthday by deploying sparklers and other uncooperative small explosives on the newly seeded front lawn, scampering bandy-legged across the budding firmament, frustrated by unruly rockets. But my father failed to inform us the town had only recently reversed its restrictive policies and (in my dream) the memory of our precipitant celebration is marred when fall begins and anti-Semitic classmates, on the way to school, enthusiastically throw rocks at my sister as I stand by helplessly.

Then, in my dream, back in the Tiny Tots classroom, finding myself before a sputtering radiator that stands before a frosted windowpane, my classmates are still taunting me, I remain the object of contemptuous merriment, unsure, as the shouts became a chant, of the nature of the game, or if it is a game at all. My childish companions, propelled by naked, dimpled legs, the boys in short pants, the girls, in dainty skirts, hopping like bunnies, flying, arms outstretched like airplanes, skipping in circles, running nowhere over the wooden floor of the overheated, single room of the Tiny Tots, in a downtown business building of a small Illinois town formerly barred to Yids, still crying 'Dirty Jew!' until it gains liturgical proportions. And something tells me I am on the threshold of an event that will affect my life and shape my character forever.

I was accustomed to being the center of attention within my family circle when I stood on the tabletop to perform my vocal repertoire, but that required preparation. The second floor landing of our spacious house formed a 5 x 5 platform, which I, now, in my dream, transform into my personal stage. The only audience, hanging on the wall in muted propinquity, is an imposing portrait, in oil, of a 17th century cavalier, a popular decoration in upwardly mobile middle-class homes of the pe-

riod. And now, before this austere Jacobean, this 17th century upholder of all that I would learn to detest, namely orthodoxy and inherited privilege, with dedication and an eye toward the perfection so essential to a true artiste, I rehearse my spiel.

But when I commence my declamation I am suddenly speechless and propelled, somehow, back into the schoolroom. And the tots who surround me now as I stand before the steaming radiator, are not interested in hearing me give my speech; they want to hurt me for some reason related to the word "Jew."

Two of them step forward, a boy and a girl, and without any warning except sudden looks of hatred, the boy pushes me onto the radiator and, then, I am sat upon by both. Joined by like-minded classmates, the bastards simply will not allow me to get up until my screams alert the teacher, who, finally, intervenes. The burns are of the third degree, my legs smeared with sticky ointment and wrapped in bandages for weeks to come.

Back in the dining room goes the dream, but the dining table is no longer the stage upon which my cousin-brother, J.D., placed me in the past, for it is surrounded by men and women in black, and one of them is my mother. Awash in tears, she takes me by the hand, and I accompany her down a street of stately homes before which stand towering elms, and, on this sunny afternoon, beneath the umbrageous canopy and with no one else in sight, my tiny hand in hers, she bids me look to the verdant scrim above and gently says: "Your daddy's up in heaven now." I lean back and stare straight up at the firmament, but all I see is a pretty, blue sky and fluffy, white clouds, and the sun is in my eyes and I know it is a lie.

The nightmare usually ends with my father crashing into a truck, or visa-versa, though sometimes, with the funeral that followed, a ceremony I was not allowed to attend. My sister later told me my father's older brother, who flew in from New York City, and who had held my father's tiny hand in his when they fled Odessa, broke down hysterically when his mysterious sibling was lowered into the ground. There would be no more J.D., No singing or reciting or dancing on the table.

The Tiny Tots taught me to be alternately wary and pre-emptively aggressive. And when my father died, I like so many others in a similar situation, decided I would be my own father.

****

At the Palace of Audible Dreams, Nica de Koenigswarter, the youngest daughter of Charles Rothschild and his wife, Hungarian Baroness Roszika Edle von Werthimstein, and an heir to what was then one of the world's greatest fortunes, had become one of the store's best customers. The nickname "Nica" derived from the "Pannonica" which followed her given and middle names. It took courage for her to flaunt convention, as she did, by championing the black musicians whom she had chosen to support, but others were not so kind and attributed malicious and fictitious motives to the attractive, now matronly, brunette, who, along with her husband, a French diplomat and Underground hero, fought with the Free French. Aiden liked Nica very much and formed the opinion, soon after coming to work at the store, that anyone who slandered her should be shot.

During the war she was able to send her five children to America. Staying behind to fight Nazism, she served as a lorry driver, radio host and decoder and was awarded by the Allies at war's end. Then, only three years before Aiden arrived in the Apple, in her late thirties, Nica left her husband, eventually being disinherited by the Rothschild family.

You wouldn't call her a cover girl, given her age and multiple childbirths, but she had lovely, dark eyes, gentility and a musical laugh, among her attributes. In New York, she established herself at the Stanhope Hotel, across the street from the Metropolitan Museum of Art. There she entertained great boppers and they her with memorable sessions lasting hours. She had done all this she said, because when she first heard Ellington's "Black, Brown and Beige" she determined that it was fated she do so. She was not a silly woman. Duke changed Nica's life as he changed Aiden's.

And when Nica first heard Monk's "Round Midnight," she determined to meet its composer; having met, they fell in love, and in 1954 it was a budding romance that would last through her being arrested and taking the rap for him on a pot charge, to living with him, in propinquity with three hundred Siamese cats, in Wee-hawken, in moments both happy and triste, to the end, when she sat next to Monk's wife, Nellie, at the funeral. The Baroness was an artistic soul with an understanding of, and an urge to nurture, great-ness, so that, as Aiden surmised, if ever there was nurturing muse it was she.

Aiden as a budding egotist and opportunist of the first water (how could he be otherwise, fatherless and bereft of familial influ-ence as he was?) liked Nica, liked Wolff, who had a gentle, Huck Finn look, and he liked the wavy-haired, world-traveller, Lion, because they all were deferential to him. Had they not said "Hello," and beckoned him to their table at the Open Door, had they not smiled and greeted him nicely when he delivered piles of records to Nica's daughter's apartment on Park Avenue, even though they might not have known his name and regarded him merely as Dean's "Kid Brudder," had they not performed these niceties, Aiden might have given them the "dead hand."

Instead, he realized these three wandering Jews contributed much to the wellbeing of others, Nica by "sponsoring," and Wolff and Lion by copiously recording, a range of artists. Each deserved approbation without suspicion of motivation. They should have been voted a Presidential Medal by Congress.

The two men were boyhood, jazz crazy chums in pre-war Ber-lin, and they individually escaped Hitler (Lion left for Argentina in 1930), then met up in New York in 1939 and founded their record-ing company, specializing in folk music, later recording boogie-woogie pianists Albert Ammons and Meade "Lux" Lewis. Quick to appreciate bop, they possessed the foresight to record Monk, who, previously, soloed only a chorus or two, on acetate, under the lead-ership of Coleman Hawkins.

To Aiden, the thrill of working at the Palace of Audible Dreams derived from those occasions when Nica's gray Bentley, body by Mulliner, parked outside the store at closing time of 4 A.M., when Birdland had shuttered, likewise the penny arcade on the corner. Nearby Rudleys and the Ham N' Egger, always had early morning stragglers and a band might be recording in Nola's Studio's, above the closed arcade, but the bars had let out and the "working girls" repaired to lesser boulevards in search of trade.

And at this irreverent time of the morning, Nica arrived accompanied by Art Blakey (whose Muslim name was Buhania), Lion, Wolff, sometimes, the smiling, handsome, twenty-six year old pianist from Connecticut, with the lock of brilliantine hair hanging down in his eye, who sounded great with Stan Getz and was, now, with Blakey, Horace Silver. But, though he spoke little, the center of the group was the tall, slow-moving, monosyllabic, largely uncommunicative, but not unfriendly, just very shy, Thelonious Monk. Dean would lock the doors to public entry, turn off the outside lights, and most of the ones inside the store, and Aiden would show off by playing recordings he knew Nica would want to hear and, probably, buy.

One night he surprised the outgoing Blakey, by playing an ancient 78-RPM recording, on the blue National label, of "Dr. X," with Billy Eckstine's band, Art's first recorded solo. The short, muscular Blakey (1919-1990), who had switched from piano to drums in the early Thirties, played with Fletcher Henderson and Eckstine. Though influenced by Chick Webb and "Big Sid" Catlett, who were a decade older, Art was an original and his style had not, as yet, been copied by others. Aiden admired his slightly back-beat hi-hat work, his thunderous, quick press rolls, unexpected snare and bass drum accents, the great push he gave trios, small groups and large ensembles, powering them into life. All present listened to the recording with beaming faces. Everyone loved Buhania, whom Monk favored above all other percussionists.

It would be ten years before Monk's elegiac ballads and jagged, rhythmic excursions landed him on the cover of *Time*, propelled by music profoundly evocative of the Twentieth Century and its attendant anxieties. Stiff-legged, hardly a showman, when his quartet struck a groove that pleased him, he danced around the stage, twisting from side to side, in a jubilant, seemingly semi-hypnotic trance. He flexed his arms, shuffled his feet and shadow boxed, occasionally springing forward to throw a treacherous punch. Watching him later at the Village Gate, Aiden learned this was Monk's way of conducting his band and maintaining a groove.

A silent sufferer, not a drug-taker, he had been arrested, the year Nica came to town, while parked in a car with Bud Powell, his friend of a dozen years, who was four years his junior. Bud was carrying, it was his dope, but Monk took the blame and, for years, was denied a cabaret license which forbade his employment in New York City nightclubs and was still in effect in 1954.

Aiden had a surprise in store for Monk. "Monk, Monk, Monk, I got something for you," he cried, rushing to the front of the store, an LP in his hand. Everyone called him "Monk," you couldn't call him "Thelonious;" it was inconvenient to articulate; some referred to him as "Sphere." He seemed always to be looking off in space. Trying to get his attention people called him simply "Monk" and Aiden followed their example. "Monk, I got something you gotta' hear," coaxing the tall, lumbering man in the blue overcoat toward the counter and a phonograph. "It's 'Ruby, My Dear,'" one of the pianist's greatest compositions, a song of songs, it enchants, no matter the rendition. But this was one of the song's first recordings. Under the leadership of drummer Stan Levey, it featured trumpeter, Conte Condoli.

In all his years of pedantically parading his musical knowledge before friends in attempts to educate them and before customers in attempts to convince them to purchase audible dreams, never before did Aiden find a more cooperative listener than Monk, who slowly and awkwardly, bent his formidable frame close to the speaker of the phonograph. Monosyllabic? Surely, but his facial reactions were reflexive and the intense concentration on his expressive face showed Aiden that Monk embraced the matter seriously. At the end, like a man who speaks seldom but, who, when certain, uncontrollably blurts out the truth, Monk, raised himself from his bent position, stood to his full height and declaimed, with poison in his low-pitched voice, "They played that one note wrong!"

He was right; Condoli muffed the bridge. "They played that one note wrong!" Monk muttered the phrase to himself, sternly, sotto voce, once more, as he wandered his solemn, tentative way back to the group, the nexus of which, shuffling through record covers, gabbing with the music makers, was the woman with whom he had recently rather publicly conjoined. Their public behavior was subtle and mature, still, it was the kind of love books and movies are made of.

Harold Arlen[17] never sang a song, his own or anyone else's, the same way twice, and he encouraged other singers in this practice. But Monk, the great improviser, did not want even one note changed both in the initial and terminal choruses of his compositions. His saxophone players, Sonny Rollins, John Coltrane, Charlie Rouse and Johnny Griffin, all learned Monk's complicated melodies note for note; Monk tolerated no deviations and his melodies were complex.[18] He possessed a vast knowledge of popular and gospel songs, but, like Charles Mingus (who played more than passable piano) could not orchestrate at all and had neither the time or inclination to learn to do so.

The reader might think that Monk and Nica, Frances and Alfred, Blakey, Dizzy and Bird, because they were preoccupied with bebop, were divorced from the struggle gathering steam since the May Supreme Court ruling that separate was not equal, that, because they stayed up late and did not read *The New York Times*, they were apolitical, but the reader would be wrong. Aiden knew.

As a Red Baby he realized that, even if they never voted, these people were consciously engaged in political acts. Nica, with de Gaulle, Francis in the U.S. Army, Alfred by fleeing, all fought Nazism and now they, and the musicians they fostered, were engaged in a war in which convention, Jim Crow, McCarthyism, "How Much Is That Doggie In The Window" and "Rock Around The Clock" (at least Bill Haley's version) were the enemy.

Bird played for a 1952 rally in support of Communist New York City Councilman and lawyer, Benjamin J. Davis, who had been convicted of conspiring to overthrow the government under the Smith Act, which had abolished the American Communist Party. Davis, a graduate of Morehouse, son of a Republican politician, through a particular trial in the Deep South in which he defended a young, innocent, Communist, black man, was exposed to such brutality and corruption that he himself became a card carrying Red. He was a pal of William Z. Foster, Chairman of the ACP, and both were fighters for the working man. But they loved (and were duped

---

17 The immortal composer of "Over the Rainbow" (lyrics by E.Y. "Yip" Harburg), a footnote unnecessary in any era but the present.

18 It took years for Aiden to realize one of Monk's first and most complicated inventions, "Four In One," is based on "Please Don't Talk About Me When I'm Gone." (w. Sidney Clare, m. Sam H. Stept.)

by) Stalin and, while they, like Claude Lightfoot, in Illinois, were never a threat, as alleged by the government, they were sent to jail for years. Davis, who also ran for office on the People's Party ticket, was a popular leader in Harlem, not a grafter.

Lorraine Hansberry, who, in a couple of years would write "A Raisin In The Sun," and become the first black woman playwright to "be produced" on Broadway, had just been hired as a clerk, then, became a reporter, and would, inevitably become associate editor of Paul Robeson's Harlem-based publication, Freedom whick sponsored the rally. Hansberry, too, must have been present at the affair for Councilman Davis, whom she had only recently interviewed.

Bird rallied in favor of the councilman that evening, as did Billie Holiday, Ella Fitzgerald and Teddy Wilson. Bird played five sets, some with strings. When Paul Robeson sang "Water Boy," Bird trotted up to the platform and offered a cup of water. Bird was known to do shocking things. He borrowed a horse from a policeman and rode it up to his future wife, Chan's, apartment house on 54th, off Fifth Avenue, or, depending on who told the story, to Charlie's Tavern, the musicians' hangout, on Seventh. Was it even true? Bird, like Zapata, Robin Hood and King Arthur, was made of myths.

But urinating in the phone booth at Chicago's Argyle Lounge because the stingy manager was a prick, throwing his sax out of a hotel window, missing concerts, dissing critics, wearing a new suit into the sea, downing 16 double whiskies, eating 20 hamburgers, going to bed with almost any ofay chick who offered herself, all these acts of defiance of the establishment were not inventions, they were true!

There was no Martin, yet, no Malcolm, no Eldridge Cleaver, or Angela Davis. Bird's blues-based, insurrectionary jazz and his iconoclastic behavior were seen, especially to black people, as blows against white oppression. A put-on artist who never even voted, Charlie Parker was a warm-up act for the militant figures about to appear. Aiden realized bebop evolved because certain black musicians reacted against the white attitude that African-Americans were supposed to merely entertain. Aiden did not want to be a jitter-bug; he wanted to listen (or play). Though you could (and some did) dance to it, it has been said by certain critics that bebop was declaring, "Sit down and listen to what I'm playing, or skip it."

****

Lester Young was the only other person accorded "after closing" privileges at the Palace of Audible Dreams. "Prez," or Pres," or "The President" would sit on a chair, before the rear counter and play along with recordings he selected, sometimes until 6 A.M. (See frontispiece) A photographer, Jerry Lee, who frequented the store, was allowed to stay on one of those occasions in order to snap a picture of Prez and Dean and the other record salesmen who willingly complied to appear in the shot. But Aiden, in accord with Katherine Hepburn's warning to would-be, future celebrities to avoid impromptu photos, remained outside the frame.

Prez walked sideways, played his sax with the mouthpiece at a 45-degree angle, and wore an oversized, wide-brimmed pork-pie hat, which he contorted into an extraordinary, squashed shape. Except for the brief years when he married his third wife and lived in Queens and fathered a boy and a girl, he was a nomad with only a portable phonograph, his horn and one small piece of luggage. Aiden had known many characters but Prez was the most interesting person he had ever met.

The saxophone, invented by a Belgian named Adolphe Sax, around the end of our Civil War, popularized, in Roaring Twenties jazz, by Adrian Rollini, on an offshoot of Sax's bass saxophone, and by Frankie Trumbauer, on the C-melody soprano, became a staple of jazz worldwide largely through the powerful playing of tenor saxophonist, Coleman Hawkins. Known as "Bean" because of his intelligence, his style became the model for others. Typified by a heavy vibrato, often caressing, capable of deep emotion, his playing was essentially forceful and hot.

Then, along came cool, laconic Lester. Early on, while he was in high school, Aiden learned that, in 1934, the famous bandleader-arranger-pianist, Fletcher Henderson, auditioned Prez to fill the vacant chair of his star soloist, Coleman Hawkins, who was leaving to form his own band. But because of his singular style the band laughed Prez off the stand. Another version is that Henderson liked him and hired him, but Prez lasted only a short time because Henderson's wife conspired against him. Though Prez discussed this with Aiden, Aiden was never sure which story was true. But in 1936, Prez found a home with Count Basie.

Prez's floating sound, original phrasing, and unexpected swinging syncopations immediately captivated both the public and musicians alike. In the future it would be said that only three other people so influenced the playing of jazz– Charlie Parker, John Coltrane and Louis Armstrong.

Prez frequently stayed at the Alvin Hotel, adjacent to the store, and he played across the street at Birdland on a contract basis, so his visits to the Palace of Audible Dreams were frequent. And because Aiden, like so many others, idolized Prez and had seen Prez in appearances with JATP and at bust-out joints in Chicago, and knew all his records from Basie to his most recent releases, Aiden would, with Dean Romanoff's assistance, allow no one else but Aiden to tend to the President's audible dreams. Aiden was too young to realize Prez was lonely and needed people with whom to converse.

Prez invented his own language in which ordinary words assumed new meanings - "a taste" was a drink of alcohol. "I feel a draft," meant he felt the presence of racial intolerance or, generally, bad vibrations. He also employed epithets and nicknames that had relevance for him alone, and it was sometimes difficult, even for hipsters, to understand what he was saying, especially since he called everyone, male or female, "Lady," like "Lady Day," "Lady Webster," and "Lady Sweets, " the latter for Harry Edison. His worst terms of opprobrium were "Doctor Wiggins," or "Mrs. Wiggins," or "Lady Wiggins" all of which, Aden would, eventually, hear him say.

"Bob Crosby" meant the police. "Bells" meant something good and was often enlarged to "ding-dong," meaning especially good, no sexual connotation intended. "Gray boys" were white musicians. Prez always purchased 78's, single recordings by singers, Bob Manning and Kay Starr, among hem. He liked Joe Derise. He never bought instrumentals. He would often ask to hear Kay Starr's "Wheel Of Fortune," a commercial, pop hit.

"Why you like that one so much, Prez?" Aiden would innocently inquire.

"Next to Lady she my favorite lady singer, kiddie," he replied in his curious, high-pitched voice.

At first, Aiden prompted Prez but when he saw that the older man was not reluctant to speak about himself revealingly, Aiden shut-up and felt flattered. Prez spoke of his childhood.

"My daddy was a teacher. We moved around 'cause he had a band; with the circus. After awhile, he taught everybody. Taught Lee to play violin-"

"Your brother-"

"And Lee, he switch to drums. Then Ben Webster come along, daddy teach him, too."

"I never knew that!"

"My daddy teach Ben Webster everything he know and the motherfucker end up sounding like Coleman Hawkins!" he told Aiden, a touch of fire in his watery, green eyes, the heavily-lidded eyes of a forty-five year-old alcoholic.

He was strong in his dislike of Bean. He told Aiden that his inspiration was Frankie Trumbauer, Bix Beiderbecke's partner on the famous Bix and Tram recordings. Sounding like Tram, who played a different instrument than he (the C-melody saxophone), using him, not Hawkins, as his model, was an odd choice to almost everyone, but not to Aiden, who listened to Bix and Tram constantly, though boppers would look at him sideways because of it.

Aiden knew much of Lester's story already. Prez lived all around the South and Midwest, too; New Orleans, Mississippi, Minnesota. Aiden knew about Henderson and that there were two Lesters, one who played with Basie's band in the Thirties and one that suffered a painful military service in WW II, which left him sounding differently. A buoyancy was gone, the optimism and joy of the Basie years had vanished. He was still "cool," still floated in his solos, still wore blue suede shoes and glided when he walked. But it was a different Lester now, somber, sad and bluesy. Most critics called this his "second phase." Or was it the third phase; was it the ending? (Noted jazz historian, D.J., Phil Schaap points to three periods, the second beginning in 1942, when Prez left Basie.)

What bothered Prez was that most young saxophone players were imitating his style: Stan Getz, Zoot Sims, Allen Eager, Brew Moore, Phil Urso, Bill Holman, Al Cohn, Dexter Gordon, Ira Sullivan and Illinois Jacquet, among them, though there were countless others. Paul Quinichette, who worshiped Prez and played just like his idol, and had been dubbed the "Vice-President," was booked at Birdland, on the same bill, "Prez versus Vice-Prez" and as a consequence, Prez felt he was losing his identity "If they're all playing me, then who am I?" he was quoted as saying.

There were jazz magazines that widely reported Prez's activities and criticized and/or praised his playing. He took a *Downbeat* "Blindfold Test" in which he refused to say anything disparaging about the music played by the interviewer, quite unlike the bitterly opinionated attitude he adopted with Aiden. The jazz journals mentioned Lester's unpleasant sojourn in the then Jim Crow U.S. Army, but never in detail and Prez had no reason to speak about it with Aiden, who only discovered the following later in reportage by others.

Inducted into Army service in the Deep South, Prez fell from a barrier in a forced calisthenics drill. He was an overly sensitive child, his mother said. She said they taunted him and called him "sissy" because he was so different and always marched to his own tune, conked his hair to hide his ancestry. Hospitalized and psychoanalyzed after the training accident, he admitted to drinking daily and smoking pot whenever available, and this shy, fragile, unique man, beloved throughout the world, was court-martialed and sentenced to one year in the brig, followed by a dishonorable discharge. These unforgettable indignities indelibly influenced his future. He played differently thereafter, although the change was equally attributable to his growing older and wearier of the world.

Aiden came to know all the players in Prez's current group. Jessie Drakes, who played trumpet, and also managed the band, taking care of details with which Prez could not cope. One night, between sets at Birdland, Jesse, pianist, Gildo Mahones, drummer, Connie Kay and bassist, John Ore, brought Prez into the Palace of Audible Dreams, and steered him to the sheet music department, where they conspired with Aiden to show their leader new tunes he might incorporate in their performances, instead of the tired ones he played repeatedly. But Prez would not capitulate; innovation, at that point, was unlikely, at least in live performances, though his work in the recording studio, with other musicians, was, it turns out, another matter.

Aiden's relationship with Prez grew in the months to come, when both were on the road, practicing their respective forms of human expression, in Cleveland, the following summer.

3

Bird On The Loose

When Aiden started working at the Palace of Audible Dreams that fall, the hottest ticket on Broadway was *Pajama Game*, directed by George Abbott and presented by the new producing team of Robert E. Griffith and Harold S. Prince, who had been production and assistant stage manager, respectively for the old hit-maker.[19] Rosemary Clooney's rendition of "Hey There" blared constantly from the speakers outside the store. They were illegal, under the law, but, for the privilege of their use, Aiden was delegated to pay "Joe the Cop," the policeman on the beat, the grand sum of $5.00 every Sunday morning. Bright lights and venality were ever present and con men, legal and illegal, everywhere.

No longer a neophyte but steeped in deception himself, sometimes selling ninety-nine cent records for five dollars and ninety-nine cents to rich Argentines in vicuna coats, Aiden attracted a faction of that brethren dedicated to fleecing the common folk who frequented Times Square, the seat of skullduggery and scams. On occassion he assisted the deceivers in their pitches; words were at the heart of their crimes, petty crimes devised in order to eat and stay alive. Preferring to dine at the Forum Of The Twelve Caesars instead of walking the streets in hunger, it would be Aiden's misfortune, in the future, to adopt their methods, from time to desperate time, since he was living in the belly of the beast now and preferred his own belly be adequately appeased.

---

19 Frederick Brisson, husband of Rosalind Russell, joined them.

In November, President Eisenhower warned the country against involvement in a place they, now, called Viet Nam, known formerly as French Indo-China, Senator McCarthy was finally censured by the Senate in early December, and the jazz scene in the Apple was strictly Eastern Hard Bop, with momentous Latin accents coming from Tito Puente, Tito Rodriguez, and the mighty Machito at the Palladium, just kitty-corner from the store, on 53rd. And the real "Killer Joe" (Pyro), the one for whom they wrote the song, and who could kill you with a single look, M.C.'d the show at that palace of Latin jazz dance and came in the store with a pretty partner every other hour trying out dance steps, artfully flinging females across the floor; never killed a soul but earned his homicidal name from the frenetic manner in which he wore out his partners, so on fire was he, he danced himself into disco.

Soon after the New Year, one evening, at the height of Broadway show time, with gaggles of hayseed tourists gawking down the once-Great White Way, Charlie Parker, leading a motley entourage of grinning, young, white hangers-on, entered the Palace of Audible Dreams as if he owned the place.

He travelled the length of the store, like a mother hen with her chicks in tow, to Aiden, who was standing behind the rear counter of the establishment, near the spot where Lester sat on the folding chair and played along with the phonograph, from time to time. Bird smiled a fake smile and said: "Say, baby, lemme hear 'Four' by Miles."

There was no condescension in his manner but no "please" or "thank you" either; he asked simply, as if it was his right. Aiden said, "Sure, Bird," and the master and his collegiate gathered around the phonograph, as Aiden retrieved the 78 RPM recording, which was very popular at the time.

Bird watched the record as it spun on the turntable and his followers watched him watch it. When he broke into a smile, they followed the lead of this chubby man in a European duffle coat, with imitation shark's teeth for fasteners, who, no doubt, was high as a kite or he wouldn't be hanging with these nudniks. When the record finished playing, Charlie Parker said, "Say, lemme have that record, baby."

Sometimes, customers wanted to inspect the label; 78's had no covers; all the information was on the label, and, for a moment, it occurred to Aiden that Bird might have remembered his face from that night at the Open Door. Aiden was sitting close up and he was the youngest person there. Before Aiden knew it, Bird took the recording of "Four" and put it under his coat. It was okay with Aiden, but the cashier saw the maneuver and stopped Bird at the door, as he was leaving with the groupies. Bird protested loudly.

"Man, don't you know who I am? Don't you see that place across the street," as he pointed to Birdland, all lit up, now. "That club is named after me."

"We know that, Bird," said the cashier, "but we can't let you steal the records."

In anguish, his head raised in appeal to a higher authority, Bird loudly announced, so that pedestrians on Broadway and everyone in the store could hear him: "Man, don't you know you can't get blood from a turnip?"

This imperfection in nature was decried with great sincerity; there was no joke involved; it was not meant to be funny and Laurence Olivier or Al Pacino couldn't have said it more convincingly. The phrase was cliché, but in Bird's case it was absolutely accurate. Everyone had stolen from him and life had wrung him dry.

Aiden, who had rushed to the front of the sore, paid for the record. A single 78 cost seventy-nine cents then, but at the Palace they cost ninety-nine. On his dinner break, Aiden often ate at a diner on 52nd and Eighth, where four courses, consisting of meat loaf and potatoes, soup, salad, and desert, cost a buck and a quarter and ten cents was a decent tip, a quarter sheer big-time. But it was an honor to pay for Bird's record, though he sped off in the chilly night with no "thanks" and the white kiddies in tow.

Charlie Parker came back alone a couple of times before that winter was over. He was desperate and demanded carfare money to get home, which meant Brooklyn, where he was staying at the time. He wasn't living with Chan. Most of the men with whom Aiden worked were older than he and had more respect for money. They were disgusted to see Bird in what they regarded as a self-induced state of debilitation. But Dean Romanoff gave Bird the carfare. Aiden was embarrassed for Bird's sake, and too callow to comply with his request, so he stiffed him, as the Holy Apostle stiffed Jesus, the Christ.

Bird's situation deteriorated rapidly. In February, he played the Bee Hive, in Chicago, and he spent his nine hundred dollar paycheck for a week's worth of dope. Aiden did not read this in a magazine; he had a better source. Morris Levy was too big a shot to speak with him. Aiden only observed him when he rarely came in the store and spoke with the cashier, or to Ziggy and Bunky.

Levy (along with his brother, Irving, and a couple of lesser investors) owned Birdland and Roulette Records – Count Basie, Sarah Vaughn, other major jazz artists – and he was mobbed up. You don't walk up to Arnold Rothstein and start a conversation. Well, maybe you do. You could do it with Frank Costello, they told Aiden, but not with Morris Levy.

Oscar Goodstein was Levy's right hand man and the manager of Birdland, and, according to some, a part investor. Jazz critics describe both men as *"shtarkers."* Balding, long white hair slicked-back on the sides, in his late 40's and dressed like George Raft, he was the only man tough enough to boss the treacherous midget, "Pee Wee" Marquette, Birdland's knife-wielding doorman. "Pee Wee" and Oscar hated each other passionately.

Oscar was energetic and outgoing, a necessary requirement in his trade for he hosted celebrities constantly. And he liked Aiden and played an avuncular role to Aiden's inquisitive interest in Birdland's affairs. Aiden was Dean's "Kid Brudder" and Dean was god at the Palace of Audible Dreams, so Oscar kept both abreast of what was transpiring in the ongoing saga of Charlie Parker.

One night in March, Oscar rushed into the store smiling broadly, and yelling like a happy barker, "We're bringing Charlie Parker back to Birdland!" A proud showman, he had engineered a coup here in the nexus of the jazz world which would reverber-ate throughout the planet he told himself. The Palace of Audible Dreams was a haven for Oscar because Birdland was dark and full of smoke, while the store was ablaze with fluorescent light, and, in Gene and "Brudder," Oscar had a hip and interested audience. Evi-dently, he had just sewn up the deal and wanted someone to know about it.

"And get this," he said dramatically, "Bud is going to be the leader!" Aiden and Gene exchanged wide-eyed looks of incredulity, thinking Oscar might be joking. Bud Powell came in the store frequently, sometimes escorted by Elmo Hope, but often alone, because he played across the street on a regular basis. Oscar was Bud's manager and "held" his contract because he was also his court-appointed legal guardian. "Madness in great ones must not unwatch'd go" was jake with Oscar, but it should not interfere with making money, he had reasoned to himself, or of presenting a once-in-a-lifetime show, slice it either way you want to.

Once Aiden bumped into Bud near the newsstand on the corner as they were both about to cross the street. Earl (Bud) Powell, the world's most important bop pianist, stood on the corner of 52nd and Broadway howling to the skies, like something out of Frank Norris; like a wolf. Aiden lacked the experience to understand and empathize with this genius who was inflicted, by nature and at the hands of others, with unfathomable horrors (including electro-shock treatments a lá Randle Patrick McMurphy).

When Aiden waited on him in the store, Aiden, in his ignorance, often struggled to keep a straight face. Sometimes it was like waiting on a zombie; lycanthropic one moment, inarticulate the next. Because of Oscar, employees of the record store were permitted to enter Birdland free and sit in the "bullpen," to the side of the bandstand. Aiden had done so a number of times to see Bud. The great pianist kept falling off the piano bench, and frequently babbled to the crowd, making strange faces at certain customers and laughing to himself weirdly. It would be impossible for him to lead a group, any group. Oscar said, "Bird can't be the leader because he owes the union money, so Bud's gotta front the band. We're gonna try and get Dizzy."

Diz said "No" and Kenny Dorham was signed, instead. The Massey Hall concert of May, 1953 reunited Bird, Bud, Diz, Mingus and Max Roach for an historic recording but it was well known that Bud and Bird did not get along together. No one knew this better than Oscar. Bud's beating by nightstick at the hands of a Philadelphia policeman, and subsequent shock treatments in mental hospitals, plus the negative effects of alcohol, were poisonous to his condition, and both he and Bird were in awful shape for the proposed engagement, *vai iz mir!*

Fifty-Second between Fifth and Sixth was no longer filled with jazz clubs; that was a thing of the past. The undistinguished buildings that now line Broadway from Times Square to the Broadway Theatre on 53rd had not yet been erected. The Rivoli and the Capitol still stood. Lindy's was Lindy's, not McDonalds. The Royal Roost and Bop City were extinct, but the Band Box was still next door to Birdland and, though frayed at the edges and no longer great or white with gaudy lights, as in the Twenties, the Main Stem was not nearly as ugly and elegant as it has become.

Still, Birdland, as far as the jazz world was concerned, was the equivalent of the White House and nothing could be more compelling than the return of Charlie Parker to Birdland on Saturday night, March 5th of 1955. Aiden was nineteen now and he had been involved in many opening nights, but this one felt quite unlike the others. This one had everyone guessing because there was no rehearsal, so no one knew what to expect, except Oscar, who had a positive attitude…up until the last few minutes.

He reserved a table for Aiden in the middle of the room, at the very point where the famous comings and goings, which were about to happen, took place. Aiden was the only employee of the Palace of Audible Dreams who was present. The club held but 250 patrons. Some jazz critics were present; others were not. The setting was tense, the room was packed, and anticipation hung heavy in the smoke-filled air. The engagement was scheduled for a two-week stay. Oscar hoped for an extension beyond that, but that was a pipe dream and the group did not get through a single number.

It took a long time for them to appear, but they finally *schlepped* onstage. In retrospect, they *schlepped* because they were already unhappy. Bird stood over Bud, who seated himself at the piano downstage. He whispered something to Bud. Bird looked around at Mingus, Dorham and Buhania and counted off a tempo and they launched into "Out Of Nowhere" for a measure or two. And suddenly Bud arose from the piano bench, stepped off the stage and, eyes glazed, mouth half-open, walked right past Aiden's table to the stairway leading up and out to Broadway, exiting the premises. Bird, laughing at first, called after him, but Bud kept going. Becoming angrier each time, Bird said, "Bud Powell, Bud Powell, Bud Powell! Come back here!"

Then, Bird left the stand following Bud's route, likewise going past Aiden's table. He was pissed off, but he was smiling in embarrassment, aware he had misjudged the situation, that he had made a fool of himself and everyone on the stand. Mingus, furious at both men, grabbed the microphone and loudly called after Bird, "Charlie Parker, come back here! Charlie Parker, come back," and then, Mingus announced, disgustedly, to the audience, "These people are ruining jazz! Please don't associate me with any of this. This is not jazz, these are sick people."

Then, he walked off, too, with his bass, leaving Blakey and Dorham alone on the stand. These two burst into a ragged version of "52nd Street Theme," at a breakneck tempo (a fact which has never been set in the historical record, but which Aiden remembered vividly because of the ironic choice) and, then, they too left the stage. Aiden assumed this was done in order to fulfill a union requirement of some sort. The crowded nightclub was in a state of bewilderment and Aiden exited soon thereafter. It was the last time Charlie Parker ever played and he would be dead in a week.

Kenny Dorham later explained that, when they came out on the stand to play, Bird said to Bud: "Let's play some 'Out Of Nowhere.'" And Bud asked: "What key, daddy?" And Bird, who could play everything in every key, said, "The key of S, motherfucker." And that's what motivated Bud to split the bandstand, in a slightly delayed, spastic reaction, that is, after playing the intro and a measure, or so.

Many years later, Aiden read the liner note to a Bud Powell recording written by jazz writer-critic, Ira Gitler. In his article (he does not say whether or not he was present at Bird's final performance) Gitler set the stage for the historical night:

"Lennie Tristano tells of sitting at a table in Birdland with Parker when Powell walked by and said, 'You know, Bird, you ain't shit. You don't kill me. You ain't playing shit now.'…In another conversation…Bird said of Bud, 'You think he's crazy? I taught him to act that way' … Parker wasn't the only musician to make this claim. Thelonious Monk, Powell's main mentor, said that Bud picked it up from him; and Powell's boyhood friend, Elmo Hope, said that he instructed Bud in (as Dexter Gordon put it) 'playing crazy.'"

According to the liner note, Oscar Goodstein told Bird to go out and play and Bird, pointing to Bud, said:"You expect me to play with this?"

****

The following Sunday evening, Oscar Goodstein entered the Palace of Audible Dreams. Sunday nights weren't busy; Dean was on the register. Aiden saw there was something bothering Oscar; he was not his usual gung-ho self. He walked solemnly up to Aiden, in the LP department, drew a deep breath, sighed and said, as if re-lieving himself of a heavy burden, "Bird is dead. He died at Nica's pad in the Stanhope, last night; it'll be in the next editions. The coroner said he had the body of a fifty-five year-old man."

"Whaaat?"

"He was watching the *Dorsey Brothers Show*. Can you imag-ine?" Oscar said, twisting his lips, the wrinkles in his chin rising to his earlobes. "Listening to Jimmy Dorsey!" And he related to Dean and Aiden, the ugly details that have become part of jazz lore. It was not an overdose but a matter of Bird's body giving out and he had, according to the coroner, expired principally due to a heart at-tack. He had not been shooting-up during the three or four days he was lodging temporarily at the Baroness's digs. Oscar had the story straight and the newspapers reflected his account, the coroner's comment in particular.

Aiden asked to be dismissed from work early. He knew his ultimate destination, but first, he went next door to Rudley's. The counter was half-filled with diners, the window seats, facing Broad-way's downtown path, were vacant. It was quiet except for the polite noises of eating coming from the eight or nine men seated on the tired, leatherette-covered stools.

Coleman Hawkins, wearing a gray, pork pie, hat and a tweed overcoat with raglan sleeves, sat in the middle of the line of men, drinking a cup of coffee. Kenny Clarke, eating a piece of pie, sat next to him. Everyone wore a hat and most wore overcoats. Bean and Clarke had a tight relationship. Klook was Bean's regular drummer, big band or combo, and he had followed the saxophonist to Paris, after the war, where Hawkins was third in popularity to Louis Armstrong and Duke Ellington. Clarke would soon be a permanent escapee from America, forming his own band in Paris, with Francey Boland.[20]

Bean (also known, because of his masterful, musical flights as the "Hawk") was dignified, reserved, not what you would call "easily approachable," not for a teenage white boy. He was a distinguished leader of men, not a braggart, but he could be vulgar, and he had a justifiably high opinion of himself. Once, going down the stairs to Birdland, where Getz was playing (with Bob Brookmeyer, Johnny Williams, and Frank Isola), Aiden fell in step, quite accidentally, behind Bean, who was catching up with Dizzy Gillespie, who had reached the bottom of the staircase. Hawkins yelled to Diz, loud enough to be heard by everyone within earshot: "Get that motherfukin' white boy off the stand, Coleman Hawkins is here!" which both men found hilarious.

When Aiden sold Hawkins a copy of Brahms's Third Symphony (with its haunting *"poco allegretto"*) the saxophonist barely looked at the boy, who was probably too much in awe of the dapper patrician and showed it, embarrassing both himself and Hawkins.

This was the nadir of his career, because the band biz was dead, because he had been superseded by others, including Sonny Rollins and Coltrane, both of whom had recently come on the scene, and, perhaps, because he was, as was rumored, involved in a hopeless affair with a younger woman. (No other instrument speaks of love as well as the tenor saxophone). But Granz administered adrenalin, featuring Hawkins on JATP tours and recording him copiously.[21]

It was a no-brainer as to whom Aiden should first convey the bad news. He stood at Hawkins right hand and said, "Bird died; in Nica's pad, last night." Bean hesitated minutely, the cup of coffee poised at his lips, and looked straight ahead. He said nothing, but began shaking his head grimly, from side to side. It seemed he

---

20 When confronted with the chart of John Carisi's (who was of Sephardic lineage) "Israel," at Miles Davis's "Birth of the Cool" session, Clarke, reportedly objected saying, "Hell, I ain't playin' no Jewish music."

21 Though Hawkins and Bird played together in JATP events, many of which are recorded, the only time they specifically made a recording in tandem was for a compendium album, *Jazz Scene*, produced by Norman Granz. The four minute side is entitled *"Ballade"* and is based on the changes of the Arlen-Ted Koehler standard, "As Long As I Live."

had been sitting there waiting for the news and, then, he carefully replaced the cup in its saucer.

Aiden did not go down the line telling each man. He just told Kenny Clarke. Klook summarized the situation better than anyone else, better than Oscar, who seemed exhausted, or Dean, whose eyes glazed with tears. Klook, shook his head, as did Hawkins, hardly acknowledging Aiden's presence, and said softly, and with deep feeling, "Man, what a drag!"

Aware that imparting this news to the older men in Rudley's was a form of showing-off, telling these cats he was "in the know" and hip, Aiden hopped a cab and went to the Open Door. The first people he spotted were Nica and Francis and Alfred, sitting at their usual table. They were laughing. It did not seem like a funeral. Aiden was shocked to see them engaged in frivolity, and he looked puzzled when they waved to him with smiles on their faces. Perhaps they did not know Aiden knew of Bird's passing. Few, if any, present, excepting the musicians on the bandstand, had heard the news; the papers had not yet hit the stands. Nica must have been up all night speaking with the police. "But how could she be laughing at a time like this?" Aiden asked himself.

Soon, "Bird lives!" began appearing scribbled on Village walls.

****

Though he knew every Charlie Parker record ever made, the four occasions on which he observed Bird were insufficient to evaluate the man's true worth as a human being.

Aiden knew that Bird could be silly, funny and mean and that he was intellectually inquisitive. Heroin and alcohol and the death of his young daughter gave him license to debase himself, but he bore little resemblance to what became the celluloid Bird. Aiden agreed with those who said Bird died of racism but he was not looking for arguments and kept his opinions to himself.

Ross Russell, who recorded Bird's famous session on Dial Records, said Bird saw "no future for the music he played, or for his race in America. To live once, and to the limit, was his game plan." Hampton Hawes said Bird was deeply aware of the plight of his people and profoundly depressed by his inability to do something about it. "So he stayed high."

The doctor who examined Bird's corpse said he died of advanced cirrhosis of the liver, a corrupted ulcer, and a possible heart attack, but, just as sure as Monk's unjustified persecutions by police, and the vicissitudes of being black in the USA brought on the state of inactivity in which he whiled away his final years, Bird, too, died because of a society that failed to value his worth and provide him with the respect that should have been his reward. The innovations of Bird's tortured but fecund mind were copied, as already noted, during his lifetime, and without payment, throughout the world, wherever modern music was arranged or played, and the most he ever earned was $900 a week, which was just enough to pay for drugs, in order to forget the life he painfully endured.

Years later, Aiden became friends with Joe Albany, the legendary pianist who played with Bird in the mid-1940's, at the Spotlight, in New York, and the Finale in L.A. Joe not only played with Bird, he was incarcerated with him at Camarillo when they were both confined to that California prison for heroin offenses.

Interviewed for his first major recording after years in Europe, Joe was asked what kind of man was Charlie Parker and Joe said: "He was a humble man," and the interviewer, in an attitude which assumed a forthcoming positive reply, said, "Humble in the face of music," without a question at the end. And Joe, in a soft, but contradictory voice returned, "No, humble in the face of God."

****

Only months before Bird's death, on a break between shows at the Great Playhouse in Ohio, sitting in the "death" seat of a 1953 Hudson Hornet convertible, going 100 miles an hour, on the way to Chicago for a brief holiday accompanied by his paramour of the time, a beautiful brunette actress, who nestled in the back seat while Aiden remained awake to watch the speeding "Barney Oldfield" at the wheel, Aiden confronted death.

Of a sudden, the three of them (which includes the owner-driver of the car, a crazy guy who played Turk, in *Come Back, Little Sheba*) looked with horror as there appeared before them a hairpin turn at a straight right angle, clearly non-negotiable at the speed at which they travelled. As Aiden's life passed before him and the phrase, "died at seventeen," sounded within his fatalistic mind, he murmured, "Shit!" and the lights when out.

Then, he was thrown twenty feet in the air and awakened a half hour later, lying in a cornfield, wrapped in the arms of his girlfriend, looking up at the night sky, through a circle formed by a ring of curious Hoosiers, an ambulance driver and a state police-men, as in a 40's film noir.

Instead of jamming on the brakes, the "crazy guy" stepped on the gas and drove straight ahead, over the turn in the road, and, now being airborne, the metallic green monster sailed beyond the road which turned so precipitously and landed in a farmer's field with a thud that made the canvas top fly off. Aiden was ejected far from the once shiny convertible, which ended up a topless heap. Taken to the hospital and laid on an operating table, everyone agreed that, with only semi-severe scratches and bruises, Aiden had survived what ordinarily could have been curtains.

As the reader knows, Aiden was no stranger to death. Back home, the downstairs neighbor he adored drowned on the York-town; in the adjacent building, the Mizerney brothers' mother lost a baby at childbirth, and Aiden saw the man who owned the tavern on Clark Street, stumble home, steeped in blood, to die, the victim of a beer casket exploding in his face, an awful thing for a nine year-old to see. Death was all too familiar.

But, just as Bird's departure from the scene was a crucial turn-ing point that posed the question "What's next in the world of mu-sic?" so, too (perhaps because of his proximity to the event) Charlie Parker's death coincided with a turning point in Aiden's life.[22]

He did not understand why Nica was laughing, at the Open Door, the night Bird died. He could not conceive, until many years later, that Bird's death was just another trial to them, another hor-rible death. But Aiden's depression extended beyond the fact of Parker's premature departure.

---

22 And he knew he was not alone in this. Many musicians felt likewise. Tony Scott, who, in 1958, emigrated to live and die in Rome (in 2007), said: "Everybody I love died…Bird was the big shock, then Prez…I wanted to get out. New York was a big cemetery." At the time, jazz led the way musically. Miles replaced Bird, then, came Miles Electronica, endorsing machine-made music by non-entities who neither read nor play a note and parade themselves as "sound designers." With the uninformed, everything begins with John Coltrane, who was truly great but not the "be-all and end-all."

The point has been made that Aiden thought he was sophisticated. He had read Krafft-Ebing, parts of it, at least. In the acting group back home there had been a middle-aged barber, an African-American with a shop on State Street where hookers and lowlifes dwelt, including the top black detective on the vice squad, a square-jawed, hefty man, with steel-gray hair, tough but affable, especially when he knew you knew his obsession, which was drinking the piss of prostitutes. "Gimme some tea, baby!" the lawman would beg, on his knees, while the woman urinated in his mouth, as Aiden and his friends watched through a secret peephole.

But five and a half months at the Palace of Audible Dreams taught Aiden that when it came to so-called "worldliness," he was a second-rater; until just now, he had been nothing but a piker. He disliked bribing "Joe, the Cop" and was sick to his stomach every time he thought of "Poughkeepsie Joe" demanding anal sex on the roadside with the beautiful teenager. He even hated himself for selling LP's at marked-up prices, without any prompting from the bosses.

Mencken called it "the biggest hick-town in the world," but temptation, degradation and failure were all around him and, though he realized he was "a lover of pleasure more than a lover of God" he was unhappy with the transactional nature of the life he was leading, where everything had a price, especially love, which really wasn't love at all.

In short, he was certain he had been corrupted by his surroundings, and when, one night, he traversed the patch of sidewalk outside the Metropole on Seventh Avenue, between 47th and 48th, after work at 4:15 A.M., when all the bars closed up, and he was on his way to Toffenetti's for breakfast, he saw a scene hitherto unknown to him, one which he had never stumbled on before, and which he would never forget: dozens of prostitutes traversed the pavement, up and down, some pretending not to be whores until approached by a john, others making outright solicitations to passersby. And there among them, walking straight toward him, was Carol, the high-priced madam with the pretty boy boyfriend. Aiden knew immediately that she had fallen from her perch, that somehow she had lost everything to the shylocks or to the pretty boy or the Mafia, perhaps. Carol saw Aiden, then looked away quickly. It was clear that her fallen state was a transparent fact to the boy who had waited on her and her Hollywood-handsome boyfriend in the store, and she was humiliated beyond words.

****

Except for Sunday meals with Mel and Lorraine Williamson, in their pad, Aiden had no family life and learned New York City could be a lonely place. For a while, he moved in with Dean and Dean's ninety year-old grandmother, in their apartment near Lewisohn Stadium. A distant cousin of the Czar, she fascinated Aiden with tales of the productions of Constantin Stanislavsky and the Moscow Art Theatre, which she had seen as a young girl.

And the political climate was worsening.

McCarthy was in disgrace, but back home in Chicago, where the first Daley had been elected Mayor, Claude Lightfoot was sentenced to jail under the Smith Act, and the Supreme Court upheld the conviction of thirteen U.S. Communist leaders, despite Harvey Matusow's admission that he had lied at their New York trial. Matusow testified, days later, before a Senate Sub-Committee, that he had, all along, calumniated in conspiracy with McCarthy and the HUAC'S Chief Counsel, Attorney Roy Cohn.[23] He said "every one" of the 244 people whom he had accused were innocent of being Reds.

Then, four days shy of two months after Bird died, Aiden was arrested for boosting a summer suit from Gimbel's. It was the day Swaps won the Kentucky Derby, as Dean, who had backed him heavily, had predicted, and Aiden spent a night in the Tombs, his ears assaulted by the incessant tintinnabulation of improvised bongo drums, the polyphonic competition of anti-social percussionists creating a cacophony evocative of Vachel Lindsay, a frenetic beat pierced by the cries of a boy who, they told Aiden, was being gang raped in the bathroom down the hall.

Aiden never stole anything again. His matriculation under authority of the Chicago Board of Education had taught him the subtle differences between Nihilism, Hedonism and Existentialism, and

---

23 Drew Pearson, "The Washington Merry-Go-Round," *Washington Post* and *Times Herald*, February 5, 1955

under the guise of the latter (for he rationalized he was deprived of his patrimony and the world owed him a living) he had stolen before, once, at the May Co., in Cleveland, a fine navy blue cashmere overcoat for Dom De Luise, who paid him sixty bucks. But after the Tombs, Aiden never stole anything, from anyone, ever again.

Ziggy and Bunky bailed him out and a *pro bono* attorney wrangled a suspended sentence and, upon Aiden's release and appearance back at the store, the next morning, Tex played Jimmie Rodgers record of "In The Jailhouse Now" on the loudspeakers, while everyone applauded. They gave Aiden a new tag: "The Little *Goniff* from Chicago," which only added to Aiden's state of depression.

Still two years shy of his majority, a New Yorker for nearly six months, he no longer considered himself a hayseed and believed he 'knew it all." And then he met Buff Barrow.

As summer approached, one early morning, at closing time of 4 A.M., "Brudder" Dean, who was counting up the money in the cash register and turning off the lights preparatory to closing the store, summoned Aiden to the front of the store with a nod of his head.

"Say, Brudder, you like Doris Day?"

"Gee, who doesn't like Doris Day?"

"Do you have to go right home or could you deliver a package?"

Dean Romanoff sent Aiden to deliver a stack of records to the apartment of someone with the name of Buff Barrow. Dean gave Aiden a smile and a wink before the boy left the store, but Aiden did not know what to expect. It was a nice building on the East Side and Aiden announced himself to the doorman and ascended in the elevator.

Blond Buff Barrow opened the door wearing a see-through nightie and stiletto heels – the kind that strippers wear – and invited Aiden into her studio apartment, where her girl friend, a brunette, similarly dressed, was draped on a couch. Aiden thought to himself: "How could they, in diaphanous nighties and titillating footgear, nearing 5 A.M. In the morning of an ordinary weekday, be anything but high-priced prostitutes?"

After a few minutes of flirty conversation, sexy Buff Barrow (her real name) rose, strode across the room on her high heels, stood near a doorway to another room and beckoned Aiden toward her. She looked so good, Aiden arose, compliantly, and, following her, found himself in her incommodious bathroom, where she turned suddenly, shed her nightie, displayed her lovely body, lay on the floor in a highly provocative pose, lasciviousness incubating in her eyes of blue, which stared intently from beneath her bleached blonde bangs, and invited Aiden to conjoin with her on the cushioning carpet.

It probably wasn't the first time she made this more. Aiden, in his callowness, enjoyed her selfishly, without bringing her to a climax, for, when they broke apart and Aiden travelled downward, toward her nether parts, she took his face between her hands and said, "I want more of that dick."

Disengaging herself, she rose on slender legs, still wearing heels, and took the few short steps toward the shuttered toilet seat. Perching on its edge, hunching forward, balancing on her scrumptious bum and the balls of her manicured feet, with the same wicked smile and crooked finger with which she lured Aiden into the cramped room, she bade him come forward, and when Aiden was close enough, she grabbed him by the scrotum and pulled him until he stood within the V formed by her parted thighs, which half embraced him.

And, caressing Aiden's testacles with one hand and sedulously manipulating his spent member with the other, she brought forth, by her obdurate efforts, a regeneration they both greeted with lustful satisfaction. Aiden was well-aroused by her ample cleavage, which jutted above her dimply knees, but Buff Barrow, in order to assure the robustness of Aiden's resurrection, with both mouth and forefinger and thumb formed in the shape of two perfect "O's," flicking her tongue like a snake at the hole in his prick and looking the spitting image of the biggest box-office star of their generation, with the face of an angel and the body of a pin-up girl, she assured Aiden's rebirth. The boy figured it took many years of practice to achieve such perfection.

Clutching it and never letting go, she arose from the seat and brought Aiden to the same spot they occupied before, where they positioned themselves and copulated, to the woman's full gratification, on the bathroom floor. Again, it seemed clear to Aiden that to do all that which she did required more than imagination and talent, it took a wealth of experience.

She could have sat on Aiden's face all night it would have been okay with him. He liked her, but, presently, they returned to the living room and she chased her girl friend and they deployed to Buff's open daybed, where she and Aiden went to sleep around 6 A.M. But before that, she told him she was being kept by an older man named Frank and that he came around only once a month, if that. Aiden imagined this was to deter him from thinking she was a whore. They fell asleep and she snuggled up to him. He guessed he was her type.

He awoke with a hard-on around noontime and found her staring into his eyes and smiling, her face an inch or two from his. Her resemblance to the actress-singer he so admired was uncanny. She did not look like a whore. There certainly was a disparity between the way she looked at noontime and her sexual behavior in the incommodious commode in the wee hours of the morning and, for moments at time, Aiden imagined she was too wholesome to be a professional prostitute.

With a little giggle she reached down and grabbed Aiden's boner. Then, she pushed up and maneuvered herself into a crouch between his legs and, to assure, maintain and further promote his member's efflorescence, increase its lubricity and maintain its rigidity, she spit on it, and jerked it and smiled wickedly, again. And, then, showing him her ass, she mounted Aiden reverse cowgirl-style, and they engaged, once more, in coitus. A kept woman or a real pro, what did it matter?

Aiden returned two days later. And Buff, when she opened the door, with slow discretion, was buff naked - except for the stiletto heels. He told her to wear them. On this second visit, Aiden made love to Buff's alabaster backside, doggie-style. All his problems and insecurities congealed and their concomitant frustrations were subjugated on Buff, or that surrogate part of her whose succulence she perfectly positioned, boldly exhibiting her soft spot.

Afterwards, she began discussing getting an apartment together, saying of the initial fuck-fest, and, this, equally erotic encore, "It was 'love at first sight' when we met," or some such shit, and, "Say, why don't we get a place together? I'll pay the rent, baby."

"You mean 'Frank will pay the rent.' Isn't that what you mean?" Aiden replied with a hint of irony and an air of dissatisfaction.

"Now, look, baby, don't start that. How do you think people make it in this town? How do you think anyone makes it? Do you think they all have talent? Come on," she implored, "how do you think Marlon Brando got to play Stanley Kowalski?"

"Talent."

"Yeah, sure" she shot back sarcastically. "He went to bed with Tennessee Williams," she nearly shouted. Then, lowering her voice, "That's how. I'll bet half…no make that seventy-five per cent make it on the casting couch. Boys, girls it doesn't matter."Aiden was silent. She continued.

"Come on, honey, get hip. I could take care of you."

"With Frank's money?"

"You're so naïve," she insisted and began massaging him, then caressing him and finally, making love to his member, and the subject was dismissed for the remainder of the visit.

Was she lying to herself? Aiden couldn't tell. She was very forward, in the sense that she was outgoing, but one hesitates to foster the notion she was vulgar. Not only was there nothing vulgar about her, no more than Swann's Odette, she was well spoken, not an attic wit, but not a dummy, either; incisive, full of jokes, she had even read a book or two. If one saw her on the street with clothes on, as Aiden did when she came to visit him in the Palace of Audible Dreams, you'd think she was in the Junior League, she looked so East Side, so chic.

Aiden liked seeing her come to the door *en dishabille* in towering heels, with a ribbon in her hair, looking like you-know-who. He was tempted to purchase, for her, some black patent leather stilettos, like he saw Tempest Storm wear in an advertisement in the entertainment section of a Chicago newspaper when he was a boy.

But soon Buff began, what they now call, stalking the boy. She came into the store when he wasn't there and left, with Dean, literate and funny, but silly, love notes, hinging on the racetrack and the mating of fillies and studs, or some such, indicating that Dean was acting as intermediary. After the first of these, Aiden agreed to come see her. But when he arrived, she was out walking her poodles. Aiden left and stood her up, using her absence as an excuse.

As June, and summer stock, came near, and he had been resident in the city for eight months, despite the occasional stirrings of affection directed at the very attractive Buff, he concluded that he had had a surfeit of lust, but of love not a jot, and feeling unclean about Buff's "relationship" with Frank, reckoning she was what they called a "kept woman" and that, every time he visited her he was invading Frank's love nest, he ended the affair with the same cowardice he had shown before, and would in future show, in terminating other love relationships. Aiden was left with only the memory of Buff' sexiness and her love of his youth. It had merely been another transaction, or, better still, call it a "proposition."

The Tombs internment, learning how difficult it was to get a role on Broadway - or even an audition much less an agent - and the dark episode of Bird's demise, renewed, to a painful point, Aiden's inherent awareness of the fragility of life and the immediacy of death. And these experiences coalesced with the unhappy termination of the affair with Buff Barrow, leaving Adien as blue and disheartened as a New Yorker of eight months could be. Now it was time for summer stock.

Three memorable things awaited him that summer in Cleveland: his first wife, a beautiful brunette jazz dancer from New Jersey, the role of "Nathan Detroit" and the broadening of his relationship with Lester "Prez" Young, but Aiden was Aiden no more.

4

LESTER LEAPS OUT

I had come a long way since my arrival in the Apple the previous October and, after Bird's death and the Tombs, I sincerely believed I was nowhere near as naïve as before.

In late spring, I was cast as Nathan Detroit in Cain Park's production of *Guys & Dolls*.[24] This best of all musicals was to lead off the coming four show, eight-week summer season at the huge, outdoor amphitheater[25] where the large cast, composed of actors from the Cleveland Playhouse and from New York, backed by a sixty-piece orchestra, employing members of the Cleveland Symphony Orchestra, performed full-scale revivals of Broadway hits.

The previous summer, following my apprenticeship at the Cleveland Playhouse, I had appeared in the chorus there, playing bits, including the skeleton, Tibia, to June Squibb's[26] Wicked Witch of the West, in a spectacular revival of *Wizard Of Oz*. Dom De Luise was an audience favorite as the Cowardly Lion. It was the first time I had received a salary for my efforts as an actor, though I had by now appeared in a couple of dozen plays.

That first year, 1954, just before I came to live in New York City, the largest of my small roles was that of the French Ambassador in *Call Me Madam*, the Irving Berlin musical about a thinly disguised Ambassador Perle Mesta (1889-1975) "The Hostess With

---

24 Music & lyrics by Frank Loesser, book by Jo Swerling and Abe Burrows.

25 Subject of the 1980 Frank Langella cult movie *Those Lips, Those Eyes*, directed by Michael Pressman, who was a young member of the stage crew when I worked there.

26 Academy Award nominee Best Supporting Actress, *Nebraska* (2013) and Jack Nicholson's wife in the 2002 film, *About Schmidt*.

the Mostess On The Ball," which originally starred Ethel Merman as Mesta. Dom (whose landlady berated him summer long, saying he used too much toilet paper and left empty tuna fish cans under his bed) played the Italian Ambassador, and I made a fool of myself, mustachioed, dressed in tails, top hat, striped trousers and diplomatic sash, announcing, before 3,500 people, to the blare of trumpets and the role of kettledrums, the imminent arrival of:

"The Duck and Doochess of Lichtenberg!"

(FOR MORE RE: CAIN PARK & CLEVELAND PLAYHOUSE/ SEE APPENDIX #5.)

Now, a year later, I was playing the leading character in the opening show and it was a boost to my career as an actor and to my ego as well. To be the centerpiece of a carefully choreographed, meticulously rehearsed major production number (Frank Loesser's "The Oldest Established") before an audience of thousands, accompanied by an ensemble of skilled musicians, while surrounded by the entire male chorus, and principal male characters all praising in song my virtues as Nathan Detroit, the only man in Manhattan who runs a trustworthy crap game, was heady for a *nudnick* of nineteen. Fortunately, I had just seen Walter Matthau play Nathan in the New York City Center revival of the show and copied his every gesture and line reading. It would never get me into Actors Studio.

Like Nathan Detroit, Sam Levene (who created the role) and Matthau were both gamblers. By this time, so was I and I soon discovered I had an unusual ability to pick winners, at long odds. I was told, that it might be a valuable asset someday[27] a prospect I found frightening and associated with poor old men on Social Security.

What aided me in playing comedy *shtik* such as Nathan and Lippman, in *Of Thee I Sing* was working in the store with the salesmen and customers and Broadway characters with their strong

---

27 That fall, after the season at Cain Park, and before going back to work at the Palace of Audible Dreams, playing selected stakes races in different cities, flying there in person to place the bets, since there were no OTB's or an Internet and I did not trust bookmakers, I amassed $6, 000, a year's salary then. My mother discovered the boodle of cash among my belongings when I visited her on the holidays, and, when I explained how it was acquired, as we watched Nashua beat Swaps on television, she divulged the fact her grandfather was a Kentucky "hard boot" trainer, operating out of Churchill Downs, who "run" third in an ancient, pre-turn of the century running of the Derby. My winning streak, for equine historians, began with Dean Romanoff betting $40 for me on Flower Bowl, in the Delaware Park Handicap, then, St. Amour II (sp.) trained by Bill Stephens, brother of Hall of Fame trainer, Woody Stephens, in the Randall Park Handicap then, the fall races of famous mares Rare Treat, Blue Sparkler, and Calumet Farms' Miz Clementine, Eddie Arcaro up, and finally the winner of Belmont's Sysonby Handicap, Elizabeth Graham Arden's, Jet Action.

Yiddish accents and inflexions. And despite the way I looked, and the fact I was only nineteen years old, I had become a Broadway character myself.

I spent some time with Lester Young that summer after Bird died, while I was appearing as Nathan. There were three jazz clubs in operation in the ofay section of Cleveland then. Two of them were dives and one was high class and served good food. That is not where Art Blakey and Prez played; they played the dives. All three were Mafia joints; Willie Bioff didn't die until November.

I read in the *Plain Dealer* that Prez was playing at the dive on Euclid Avenue, near 125th Street. Blakey was playing at the other, smaller club near the downtown area. One of Prez's biographers reports Prez was the victim of a nervous breakdown that summer (1955) and was hospitalized at New York City's Bellevue mental facility, then, released to travel in a Jazz at the Philharmonic European tour, in the fall of that year. But I must contradict that reportage and say I saw Prez on three occasions during the Cleveland engagement, in the early summer of '55.[28]

He did not look well but I was thrilled to see that Buhania was also present. Remembering me from the Palace of Audible Dreams, he, too, welcomed me hospitably. We had independently gone to the racetrack (the now defunct Randall Park) that day and bet on the same horse, Mrs. X. M. Carter's, Betty Barr, which won the Imp Handicap. Art told me he bet the mare, a 17-1 shot, because his wife's name was Betty ("Along Came Betty").

Unless the reader is as old as I, and a devotee of jazz, it will mean little to say how anointed I felt to be sitting at the same table with these immortals. Surely I have shown the importance of Lester Young and the idolatry heaped upon him by all races, his walk, his dress, his language and his manner of playing being aped by black, white, yellow and tan. Art Blakey is renowned as a musical mentor to a long list of famous players. He was not only one of the great innovators in jazz drumming but also an inspirational leader and teacher. That these celebrities treated me as an equal says more for them than for me. To be the recipient of such kindness, I had to have proven myself in past conversations back home at the Palace

---

28 I sorely dislike contradicting Prez's excellent biographer, Dave Gelly, to whom I am indebted for reminding me of things Prez told me when I was a teenager.

of Audible Dreams. When I told Art I was sitting in the front row of the Civic Opera House (as a 15 year-old) the night "Big Sid" Catlett died backstage, at the intermission of D.J. Al Benson's concert, my connection to the music was secured.

The disreputable establishment in which we sat served as a speakeasy during Prohibition and was typical of Midwestern taverns of the period presenting jazz. It was located on the city's main stem, between the 86th Street headquarters of the Playhouse and the movie district a few blocks below Case Western Reserve University. Beat up booths surrounded a horseshoe bar in the midst of which stood an elevated bandstand that forced the musicians to ascend and descend it by an insecure, narrow staircase. A few dozen high stools stood before the curved bar and there was abundant room for standees. It was larger than, but similar to, the joints on Chicago's Northwest Side in which I, reluctantly, played requests for polkas with Tunis and Tino. An ugly place with high ceilings and dirty walls, you could be certain that when it closed up and folks went home the rats came out to play. It smelled bad, as such places always do, predominantly of beer, with an admixture of perspiration, smoke and urine.

Art was dressed for the track; Prez wore his usual uniform - gray sharkskin, single-breasted suit, white shirt, and black tie. The suit needed pressing. And he wore his dark blue suede shoes, in which he glided sideways. His eyes narrowed as he drew on his Pall Mall and he wore a small ring on each hand. Art, a Muslim, did not smoke or drink, while Prez did not stop.

Prez's "kiddies," Mahones, Ore, Kay and Jessie Drakes, were still with him and he played as laconically and as little as possible. It is true that Prez chose these men as much for their compatibility as their musicianship. The most talented of them, Connie Kay, who would soon become the regular percussionist of the Modern Jazz Quartet, was approaching thirty and, like his compatriots, was reserved and quietly friendly, but not overly outgoing. Prez liked it that way. The congenial Drakes made up for the reticence of the others, which, in part, accounts for his position as road manager and general factotum.

Prez's playing with his "kiddies" did not display him at his best, but his recordings for Norman Granz, with other personnel (pianists

Hank Jones, Teddy Wilson, and John Lewis, drummers Buddy Rich and "Papa" Jo Jones) during this period were among his last great efforts despite novelist Chester Himes' description of Lester's playing at this time:"It was like listening to someone laughing their way toward death."

That night, as usual, aside from their cordiality, there was little to discuss with Prez's quartet except tunes. Blakey had departed, and the smoke, heat and watered-down booze made socializing nearly impossible. Prez was shy and engaged in conversation only when agitated, intrigued or feeling humorous, all of which were anomalies, and which makes memorable what happened in a later visit. And this is a man who, according to his biographer (and I don't dispute this), checked into Bellevue a month, or so later. I stayed awhile longer, that first night I saw him in Cleveland, but went home before closing time because I was rehearsing another show the next day.

When I returned a few days later, Prez was lolling in a different location, facing the Euclid Avenue entrance. His legs were stretched out and he leaned his head and back against the grimy, plastic upholstery of the half-circular booth. I went directly to him and he indicated I should sit down and join him. The band was on a break.

He looked even wearier than before and still wore the same gray suit with a handkerchief squared in his pocket. He asked me how my show was going; I asked after his health. Again, there was not much to talk about. I already was acquainted with the milestones in his career; to badger him with questions would make me an interloper. I was flattered to just be with him and he was content to merely sit and smile in his laid-back style.

Then, of a sudden, I saw a stern look develop in his heavily lidded, green eyes. Then they narrowed. He was looking over my shoulder at someone who had entered the club. Still seated in the booth, my back to the door, I turned around. It was a blind African-American man, my age, wearing shades, no suit, no tie, and a tired jacket. He was tapping a white stick, with a tip painted red, and he came to a stop at our table. He carried a tenor sax in a soft case and had another tenor around his neck on a string of twine. Crosswise, on another strap, he wore a cylindrical instrument which, one later learned, was a stritch. Overall he bore the aspect of a tramp-like street performer. "Lemme blow, man," he addressed Prez, when he reached our table.

Lester knew him, it was clear, and, after a long pause, and a look of sullen disdain, which was wasted on the compromised musician, Prez, in his weird voice, grudgingly consented. As the young man slowly tapped his way to the other side of the high-ceilinged room, which encompassed the horseshoe bar with the performing stage in its midst, I did not ask Prez questions. I watched him as he, over his shoulder, still semi-recumbent, and with a look of disgust pasted to his wan façade, watched the blind man, while he repeatedly muttered, "Motherfucker," and "Dirty motherfucker!" to register his displeasure and show me he did not like the blind man at all.

The eyeless reed man, though he wore dark sunglasses, navigated the geography of the premises unimpeded and without incident, around the bar, to the flimsy staircase that led to the island-like bandstand. I did not see Prez's group greet the sightless saxophonist. Eventually, all but Jesse Drakes assembled on the stand, the trio set a tempo, and suddenly there erupted sounds from the incomplete sax player unlike any I had ever heard before. He had two horns in his mouth and was playing them simultaneously!

I could not control myself from smiling with glee and wonderment. What the unseeing man played made me happy, but Lester thought it somehow dishonest. He did not approve, yet he continued watching with gelid hatred on his face. But the gazeless man swung. His musical vocabulary was diverse and he quoted from various sources, some swing, some bop, all set to unexpected syncopations, occasionally producing continuous sound through a technique of breathing which allowed him to hold notes for an extended period.

Discovering a unique musical treasure in Cleveland was not a new experience for me. The previous summer, walking through a middle class black neighborhood, I had heard a remarkable sound emanating from a tavern, again, a sound unlike any I'd ever heard before. It was Jimmy Smith, from Norristown, PA., Playing the Hammond B-3, in his revolutionary way. Francis and Alfred heard about him almost simultaneously and he made his Blue Note debut within months.

Tadd Dameron came from Cleveland, Art Tatum from Toledo, and the blind man on the stand, giving Prez such pain, came from

Columbus and his partly given, partly self given, name was Rahsaan Roland Kirk (1935-1977). He played in Cleveland for another year or two and, when he finally came to New York he quickly developed a cult following. Women threw themselves at his feet.[29] Coltrane, Mingus and Eric Dolphy became his musical and philosophical colleagues, but he left Prez cold.

My last meeting with Prez that summer in Cleveland was disastrous.

Cain Park is still one of America's great outdoor theatres and, at the time when the entire summer was devoted to musical comedy, no show was insurmountable or too ambitious for production. The orchestra had as one of its outstanding features, a remarkable pianist, an independent contractor, whose name (for these purposes) was Marianna Harmony, and she could swing a band not just as well as May Lou Williams, but as well as anybody you might name, including Basie, Duke, or Earl Hines.

A singular woman, she was volatile, dynamic, and proud. I stayed with her and her son that summer at their home not far from the theatre. Of Scandinavian extraction, a blonde with electric blue eyes, she was conducting an affair with the stage director of the season's shows, an equally intense artist. Irish-American, dark-haired and quick-tempered, he was an adept farceur and an authoritative *metteur en scene*, and could do takes and double takes with the best of them.

She, chain-smoking non-filtered Kools, and he, lighting one Lucky Strike after another, alternately coached me in the role of Nathan Detroit and argued passionately, into the wee hours, as to who had more schmaltz in their vibrato, Joseph Szegeti or Mischa Elman. They allowed me to listen in because I had seen Elman, and other great violinists, at Orchestra Hall, and had become their protégé, at nineteen, while playing near middle-aged, Nathan Detroit.

Marianna was tough and profane, with intense demons, and she could drink men blind. Consequently, she usually became belligerent, a recipe for disaster with someone as super-sensitive as Lester Young. But I did not consider that when I invited her, one night, to see Prez, after a performance of *Guys & Dolls*.

---

29 He even interjected tributes to Paul Robeson in his worldwide performances.

Before we got to Prez's club, we, unfortunately, made a few stops and Marianna was sozzled by the time we sat down with Prez, at his table, along with his quartet. Prez and the band members were happy to meet my lady friend, and we sat through sets and intermissions, until near to closing time, both Marianna and Prez drinking and talking steadily. Then, looking at me, but speaking to Marianna and the group as well, Lester announced, in his semi-soprano voice, "I'm gonna get me another taste," and rose unsteadily, travelling to some special stash behind the nearby horseshoe bar. My attention was diverted momentarily and I began speaking with another member of the group. A few minutes passed and Prez returned to his seat at the table, adjacent to Marianna.

The noise from the jukebox made conversation difficult. You spoke directly into someone's face as loudly as possible. Everyone was smoking and yelling and drinking. I looked over at Marianna and Prez and their faces were only inches apart. Both narrowed their eyes, not only because of the smoke but, because of the intensity of expression engendered by whatever it was they were discussing. It had developed into a heated argument. Marianna seemed to be yelling, but only stuttering monosyllables emerged from her mouth above the sound of the blaring jukebox.

Suddenly, squinting her exquisite blue eyes through the stifling smoke, her Kool, a burning nub in one hand poised aloft, she swiftly drew back her other, "good" hand, and delivered a roundhouse slap to the center of one cheek of Prez's anemic looking face. He, nor anyone at the table, could believe it, so horrified and mystified were we all. Why had she done it? Was it something sexual that was said? Why did she slap this sweet, famous man? What was it all about?

Then, for everyone to see, Prez held both hands before us, one after the other, saying, in his queer voice, "I got one Mary on this finger and one Mary on this finger; I don't need no more Marys."

It is true; two of his wives bore that name. But Marianna was not finished. She continued needling him until he began calling her "Mrs. Wiggins," and the evening deteriorated unpleasantly. When we drove back to Shaker Heights, after a long silence in which no explanation of the slap was offered, Marianna asked me to stop the car while she relieved herself on someone's lawn and I never mentioned the subject again, attributing the incident to the gap in communication between ofays and African-Americans.

Prez was not forgiving. He never forgave Fletcher Henderson's wife for standing in his way when he needed a job; never forgave the Brute (Ben Webster) for being like the Bean, or, Bean for being Bean.

He went on tour that fall, and when he returned to the Apple, eventually checking back into the rundown Alvin, he came in the store early the following year. I rushed to take care of him as he entered the store, but when I greeted him he gave me the same look of rejection he gave the sightless Roland Kirk, then, muttered "Doctor Wiggins," under his breath, and averted his eyes, acting as if I weren't there. I knew our friendship was over. Dean took care of him instead. It was a monumental rebuff. I stayed at the Alvin, occasionally, and I saw him on the street in the early hours, lugging his case, wearing the flattened pork pie, but he never spoke to me again.

The manner of his death is sad to relate. At the breakup of his marriage, no longer wanting to live too far from the "Jazz Corner of the World," where everyone knew he was "The President," he moved into the Alvin, permanently. Then, he fell into a deep depression lasting months.

A younger woman, a friend, who recorded his ramblings and watered down his booze, took care of him, and through other friends, a caring physician was secured. Staying off alcohol and eating properly, Prez gained weight, according to his biographer, Gelly, and felt good enough to accept a gig in Paris. Once there, he began drinking again and said he "felt a draft" with the band, even though they were acclaimed musicians.

He began having stomach pains, couldn't get out of bed, and three weeks into the eight-week engagement, decided to take a plane back home. Once in the air, he began vomiting blood profusely; the cause was eventually determined as a rupture of the varicose veins of his esophagus. Deplaned, he returned to the Alvin and continued drinking, through the pain, and died that night, leaving $500 in travellers' checks, his wallet, a ring and a worn, Selmer saxophone. He never took good care of his horn.

The sound of Lester's horn (and clarinet, too)[30] was one of the most profound expressions of the human soul. Lester Young, Charlie Parker and Thelonious Monk gave much to the world and received little in return. Lester Young, blindsided by indignities suffered at the hands of the military and white society in general, died at the ripe old age of forty-nine.

I never figured out what it was that Marianna said to Prez, or visa-versa.

****

Mel Williamson was moving up in the publishing ranks, becoming Art Director at Viking Press.[31] At Christmas of 1960 he said he had something important to discuss with me and it turned out to be a new musical that was headed for Broadway and involved friends of his. The musical was Oscar Brown, Jr.'s *Kicks & Co.*, and though it has been all but erased from memory by someone's determined efforts, and references to it obliterated from biographical works, it was a production of some significance in the history of musical comedy, the African-American Theatre, and a turning point in my life.

---

30 On the movie set of a film he was shooting on the campus of Columbia University (*A Midsummer Night's Sex Comedy*), at the insistence of José Ferrer, I played a cassette of the 1958 recording of Lester's clarinet solo on "They Can't Take That Away From Me," his last great recorded statement, for Woody Allen who said, "He plays the clarinet like he plays the sax," a true statement, if ever there was one.

31 The famous blue cover for Saul Bellow's *Herzog* is one of Mel's well-known covers jackets.

KICKS & CO.

5

GOOD INTENTIONS

Yes, Mel Williamson opened the door that got me in the mess that put me in the Big Time.

Robert "Bobby" Barron Nemiroff, the husband of Lorraine Hansberry, author of *A Raisin In The Sun*, contacted him about Oscar Brown, Jr.'s Broadway-bound musical, which he, Nemiroff, was producing in partnership with his boyhood friend, Dr. Burt D' Lugoff, research doctor, concert promoter, and part-owner of the famous Village Gate nightclub, operated by his brother and business partner, Art.

But when Mel told me the story line of *Kicks & Co.* a sinking shock of the recognition of failure coursed through my cynical self, a fancy way of saying I knew it was in for a shitload of problems if ever it got to Broadway and I wasn't sure it would.

A Raisin In The Sun, a "well-made" play with real people and events,[32] fertilized many careers for African-Americans in every aspect of the theatre and "changed the American theatre forever." [33]But *Kicks & Co.*, Brown's legendary, full-scale, 1961 musical,

---

32 An African-American family, living in a cramped apartment on the South Side of Chicago, inherits $10, 000 in insurance money.

33 Frank Rich, in *The New York Times*, in 1984 on the 25th Anniversary of the play's opening. Three Off-Broadway plays, contributed greatly to the changed atmosphere: *Simply Heaveny* (Langston Hughes, 1957), *The Blacks* (Jean Genet, 1960), and *Only In America* (Martin Duberman-1961). I saw the last two and would soon direct Claudia McNeil, the standout in *Simply Heavenly*. In recent years, revisionist critics who weren't present at the time have misunderstood and improperly scoffed at Rich's accurate statement. A vast pool of talented African-American theatre artists had expanded to a point of explosion, but *Raisin*, a beautifully written play about real black Americans, was THE catalyst that created a new reality throughout the theatre and provided inspiration for belief, on the part of black actors, directors, playwrights, scenic artists, etc., that there was, indeed, a place for them on American stages. Theatrical unions soon turned a new cor-

about integration, segregation, miscegenation (interracial fornication) and *Playboy Magazine* (or a facsimile thereof), as told through the fustian Faustian prism of Goethe's 150 year-old shopworn legend, was, as we shall see, the first direct beneficiary of the success of Hansberry's play.

Nemiroff, who, upon his wife's death, became her literary executor, is listed in the opening night program of *Kicks & Co.*, as co-author of the show's book, and Lorraine Hansberry had replaced Vinnette Carroll as director though *Playbill* was late in updating the changes. Yet all biographies written about Hansberry make no mention of *Kicks & Co.* or, even, of Oscar Brown, Jr.! These omissions are by design. Someone wanted *Kicks & Co.* obliterated from print. To some the story of *Kicks* may be a footnote, but it is a historical footnote and since someone wants it swept under the rug it becomes all the more compelling to tell.

Through the years, knowing of my involvement in the production[34] people have asked me: "Was *Kicks & Co.* any good, or was it 'before its time,' too hot for critics and audiences to handle? Was *Kicks & Co.* suppressed by racist critics because of its left-wing ideas? Or was it "warmly received"[35] as *Jet Magazine* declared, and 'riveting' as Internet postings, now, claim?" Finally, when filmmakers Tracy Heather Strain and Randy MacLowrey, who were producing a PBS documentary about Hansberry, contacted me, and MacLowrey interviewed me in person, I decided to write about it.[36]

After I finished writing this book, and while it was being formatted for publication, I was contacted by noted literary biography, Charles J. Shields, who has signed with Henry Holt & Co. to do a new take on Hansberry. Being the one living survivor of the

---

ner, hiring black office personnel, AEA initiated the Paul Robeson Award as its highest honor and elected long serving Frederick O'Neal as president. I cite these powerful facts and could name others to support Rich's claim. This new play by a clearly left-wing, black woman, who gave articulate interviews and looked lovely, had a powerful, and, as it turns out, lasting effect on the American Theatre.

34 I raised one-third of the budget and am listed on the title page of the opening night program as "Production Supervisor" and "Casting Director."

35 Larry Still in Jet Magazine, 10/12/61 Johnson Publications. Publisher, John H. Johnson, gave me a check for an $8,000 investment in *Kicks*, in his Michigan Avenue office, arranged, not by me but by both Oscar, Jr. and Sr. Mr. Still is referring to the only preview of the show, a benefit performance on behalf of the Urban League. It was closed to the general public and critics.

36 Strain's excellent PBS film *"Sighted Eyes/Feeling Heart"* debuted on January 19, 2018 and, following previous protocol, made no mention whatever of *Kicks* or of Oscar Brown, Jr., though Oscar's song "Brown Baby" was a significant feature of the soundtrack.

production, I have divulged certain, but hardly all, of the following facts to him but am uncertain whether, or not, they will see the light of day.

Kicks and *A Raisin In The Sun* are joined at the hip. Oscar lived near Lorraine, on the South Side of Chicago. Their parents (progressive Black Republicans) knew each other. Before opening on Broadway, *A Raisin In The Sun* played the Blackstone, in Chicago (after successful tryouts in New Haven and Philadelphia) and Oscar visited Hansberry and Bobby Nemiroff as they were reading the first published Chicago reviews.

At that time, then and there, backstage, at the Blackstone, before a Broadway theatre for *A Raisin In The Sun* became available, but with positive reviews already on the street for only hours, Oscar presented Lorraine and Bobby with the script of *Kicks & Co.* and sang some of the songs from the show. Bobby was immediately enthused and decided to represent Oscar as a performer, get him a record and publishing deal, and produce *Kicks & Co.* on Broadway.

Bobby followed through, obtaining a manager for Oscar (Al Hamm) and a recording contract with Columbia. According to Oscar, in an interview years later, Lorraine did not like *Kicks* on first hearing, but, it didn't matter, Bobby, as you'll see, was like a steamroller and, contrary to anything Phil Rose may have said in his autobiography, for he is the only person to have memorialized her involvement, Hansberry soon became enthusiastic, and then, deeply enmeshed in *Kicks* throughout the pre-production period, beginning at the end of 1958 to the fall of 1961 - what amounts to a goodly portion of her creative life, a life tragically cut short. To be truthful, *Kicks* should be included in any biography of the playwright. But I am now the only living person privy to what happened; the only one who has survived and can tell the truth.

The reviews they were reading when Oscar came in the door were sensational, especially that of the powerful critic, Claudia Cassidy, of the *Chicago Tribune*. Then, the Shuberts gave *Raisin's* producer, Phil Rose, the Ethel Barrymore Theatre, and *Raisin* (which we'll, for the most part, call it, but NOT to be confused with Nemiroff's 1973 musical version of the play, entitled *Raisin*, just as we'll refer to *Kicks & Co.*, merely as *Kicks*) opened in New York, on March 11, 1959, to rave reviews. My telling of the saga of *Kicks* begins and ends with *Raisin.*

Two years had passed since the death of Lester Young and, after appearing with Kay Ballard, at Herb Rogers' Music Theatre, in suburban Chicago, obtaining my Equity card and good reviews as Frank Lippencott, in *Wonderful Town*, I directed fifteen musicals at two theatres which would become well-known incubators of musical comedy talent: Guy S. Little, Jr.'s Grand Theatre, in Sullivan, Illinois, and Victoria Crandall's Brunswick Summer Theatre, at Bowdoin College, renamed the Maine State Music Theatre. It was the first Equity season for both.[37] At these last two theatres I directed talent that ranged from Anna Mary Dickey (in *Song Of Norway*), whom Noel Coward, in his published letters, dubbed "the epitome of everything awful in operetta" to a young and adept Alan Alda repeating his father's performance, as Sky Masterson, in *Guys And Dolls.*[38]

By the winter of 1960, I had appeared as an actor-singer (often as a chorus boy and bit player) and/or had directed, twenty-seven musicals, some more than once.[39] Though I was only approaching twenty-four, I had become a whiz at casting, organizing and mounting productions, especially musicals (though I appeared in and

---

37 Planning to return to Chicago, ostensibly to go to college (one semester at U. of I. at Navy Pier, another at Roosevelt), Sheila F. and I were married in a cold-water flat at a friend's apartment, on 44th and Ninth Avenue, by a rabbi provided by Sheila's father. My mom and Sheila's dad (her mother was dead) and friends from Chicago and New York were present. There were no speeches, no ephithalmium, no *chupeh*, no stomping on a glass. Required to repeat, after the rabbi, a series of Hebrew words, Shelia and I broke-up throughout the ritual. Our laughter was contagious and, soon, everyone but the rabbi, joined in. It was indicative of the seriousness with which Sheila and I would conduct our marriage. We bought a car from a used car dealer who was a relative of Dom De Luise's and headed for Chicago. But the pull of the Theatre was too great, I obtained work acting and directing, in Chicago, and we divorced.

38 My choreographer at both theatres was young Joel Schnee, from Los Angeles, who went on to a productive career with some of Europe's top dance companies. In between directing for Guy and Vickie, I briefly wrote and directed industrial shows at Fred A. Niles Film Studios, in Chicago, where Haskell Wexler was top dog and we auditioned Bob Newhart, doing his Abe Lincoln skit, and I, stupidly didn't think him funny.

39 *A Tree Grows In Brooklyn, Gentlemen Prefer Blondes, High Button Shoes, Wizard Of Oz, Guys & Dolls, Vagabond King, Of Thee I Sing, Wonderful Town, South Pacific, Sing Out, Sweet Land; West Side Story, The King and I, Student Prince, Say, Darling; Song Of Norway, Kismet, Naughty Marietta, Roberta, Fanny, Desert Song, Call Me Madam, Carousel, Plain And Fancy, Kiss Me Kate, Paint Your Wagon* and *Bloomer Girl* (which ran for 17 weeks at the Cleveland Playhouse) but with time off to play Tom in *Tea & Sympathy* and Mother in *Hatful Of Rain*, at the Chagrin Falls Playhouse. Partly under the influence of H.L. Mencken (*American Language*, Fourth Edition, page 501) and, though there are many well-known scientists, producers, directors, philanthropists and even a critic bearing the well-honored name, because it was easier to fit on the marquee, to the dismay of my mother, I shortened my name from "Edelstein" to "Eden," and proceeded, thereon, to appear onstage and conduct business with that name, not changing it legally until years later.

directed straight plays, too). It was my métier. I was authoritative and dictatorial. Pursued rather than the pursuer, I bedded chorus girls and leading ladies alike and acted as if I were the next George Abbott. Some people liked me and some hated me and, engendered by the "radiator" incident of my childhood, the humility so emphasized in my upbringing by my mother was entirely lacking in my behavior.

Back to *Raisin*; for many years before its debut, aside from the exceptions listed herein, despite a rich heritage dating to the early 19th Century, and later in the black film industry, black actors, in white films and stage plays, had been confined to playing mostly maids and butlers. But *Raisin's* characters were real people in a believable situation. Those not old enough to know the film and stage history of African-American performers and playwrights in the United States are invited, at this point, to visit my brief summary of the subject. (SEE APPENDIX #6.)

Raisin won the Critics' Circle Award for Best Play of 1959, four Tony nominations and became an international hit, translated into nearly 40 languages, produced all over the world and made, the following year, into a Hollywood movie. Since then, it has had two major revivals on Broadway, the last in 2014.[40] In 1960, Lorraine Hansberry had become, partly because of her associations with Robeson, Du Bois, James Baldwin and Langston Hughes, a celebrity and, according to some, "the most popular girl in town."[41]

Both *Kicks* and *Raisin* were inspired by the political events of the day. Discussing either requires setting the historical background against which they took place. My view is characteristic of that of the people involved in *Kicks*, which came at the dawning of a new day, a time when "kicks" signified the exhilaration of riding a famous highway in a song by Bobby Troup, or something you didn't get in champagne in a song by Cole Porter, because, in those innocent days when a President hadn't been shot for sixty years, "kicks" were not at all what they are now.

---

40 The 2008 production starred Sean "Puff Daddy" Combs and Phylicia Rashad. The latter became the first African-American woman to win a Best Actress Tony, for her portrayal of Mama Younger. The 2014 showing starred Denzel Washington and won the Tony for Best Revival. Two plays that are inspired extensions of *A Raisin In The Sun* are the 2011 Pulitzer Prize-winning *Clybourne Park*, by Bruce Norris and *Beneatha's Place*, by Kwameh Kwei-Amah.

41 Biographer, Susan Linnot.

But for the aware and semi-aware hipsters, beatniks, peaceniks, lefties, pinkos, most people of color and those who were oppressed and knew about Jim Crow, HUAC and McCarthyism, the times were far from innocent and not much different from my arrival in New York, six years earlier. After eight years of Ike's tortured syntax and gray-flannelled flummery we had, thanks to the candied corruption of Richard J. Daley, a new President who shunned three button sack suits, hung out with movie stars, championed African independence, suggested the formation of what became the Peace Corps and promised an end to segregation (though he knew not how to achieve it).

An estimated one-third of the earth's population was starving on the cold, sunny Friday morning in January 1961, when this hatless, handsome man John F. Kennedy was inaugurated as our thirty-fifth President and nearly upstaged by an ancient, purblind poet from New England. People on the Left had scant confidence the Cold War was going to end and that racial discrimination would be legislated out of existence simply because of this rich war hero with a Back Bay accent.

My incipient pessimism and hatred of the rich led me to believe Americans had been hoodwinked once more. But Nixon was an odious alternative. In his initial appointments, JFK threw a sop to my beloved Adlai Stevenson, making him U.N. Ambassador, where he'd be out of the way, and appointed a confirmed Cold Warrior diplomat from Georgia, Dean Rusk, as Secretary of State. And, as Secretary of Defense, he picked the new President of Ford Motors, Robert McNamara, he of the slicked-back hair and rimless glasses. These latter two designees were meant to deploy the policy the new President enunciated on the Senate floor before his White House run - more munitions and an even tougher stance against the Russians, especially in Central Europe and the Balkans.

Relations with Cuba were dangerously tense. Fidel Castro had visited the U.N. in September of the previous year and stayed uptown, in Harlem, at the Hotel Theresa, where he entertained the young minister and spokesperson for Elijah Muhammad's Nation of Islam, Malcolm X., who achieved national prominence with the Mike Wallace - Louis Lomax, "The Hate That Hate Produced," television broadcast of the previous year.

As far as civil rights were concerned, the powerful racist coalition in both houses of Congress, the coalescence between most Republicans and all Southern Democrats, stood in the way the of the new leader succeeding with legislation outlined in his campaign in the Wisconsin and in other primaries, where he defeated Hubert Humphrey, the most vocal civil rights advocate of all the Democrats who had competed. JFK, Robert F. Kennedy and their savvy father knew passage of legislation for African-Americans was a losing strategy and the South would reject his future candidacy if he pushed too hard in what was an impossible legislative situation.

To begin with, the Kennedy brothers knew very little about people of color and nothing of poverty and oppression. James Swanson and other historians are correct in saying JFK was "a reluctant supporter of civil rights." Two years later, when King, of whom JFK was "suspicious," spoke at the Lincoln Memorial, the President was absent. Had he been there and had he addressed the gathering he would have lost the South in the next election, had he run (which was his intention).

While I admired the Chipp & Co. suits (designed by Paul Winston) he wore, I thought the knots in his narrow ties to be too fanatically small, the collars too conservative and, in the show I wrote for the Independent Voters of Illinois the year before, to be performed in the Golden Ballroom of the Hilton, in which I gave each Democratic candidate a parody song to sing, I assigned Kennedy, whom I thought inconsequential, a bunch of patter to the tune of Rodgers and Hart's "Everything I've Got Belongs to You."

"I've a background that is steeped in eastern wealth, And I'm full of boyish charm and vibrant health"

(SEE APPENDIX #7.)

Left-wingers, such as I, were doubly suspicious of JFK's campaign manager-brother Bobby (who he had appointed Attorney General in January, via a shifty, "Yea" or "Nay" voice vote, conducted by Senator Russell of Georgia), for RFK had been an ally of the notorious lawyer, Roy Cohn, and a friend of the verminous Joe McCarthy. There were ever more ominous rumors in circulation regarding the new President's father, Joe (Joseph P. Kennedy, Sr. [1888-1969]) who owned the Merchandise Mart in Chicago and who had been FDR's Ambassador to England, as well as the first

Chairman of the Securities & Exchange Commission (SEC) and who was supposed, by some, to be an anti-Semite.

However, there was a soupcon of cautious optimism, even among intellectuals of the Left, if only because the future President called Coretta King in order to comfort her when her husband was jailed at the Georgia State Prison, during the presidential campaign the previous October. Ike had taken forever to silence McCarthy (through influencing the Senate to impose censure) and, though the General sent federal troops to Little Rock, he advocated a very gradual granting of full rights of citizenship to people of color, while JFK said he wanted them here and now.

The first sit-in demonstration at a lunch counter, on February 2, 1960, in Greensboro, involved four African-American students. Nashville's lunch counter protests began on the 13th and an estimated 50,000 people had participated similarly throughout the South by April of that year.[42] Rosa Parks had become a legend; leaders like Shirley Ann Jackson, Andrew Young, Wyatt Tee Walker, Bayard Rustin and Ella Baker came into prominence. The struggle for racial equality was the main concern of all intelligent artists and *Kicks*, I was told, was aimed exactly in that direction. And, because I wanted to be among the optimistic, when Mel Williamson related to me the outline of the book of Oscar's musical, as I've said, I went queasy in my stomach with profound disappointment.

Mel was no musical comedy maven, but he knew that Oscar's book (the spine, the show's engine, the dialogue that comes between the songs) needed work. And the manner in which he said it "needed work," implied it needed a whole lot of work and woe to the musical with a book that needs a "whole lot of work."

That elusive phantom, "the book," when properly finagled, diddled with and devised, drives a successful musical; when faulty it makes paupers out of tone deaf producers, uninventive songwriters and intransigent librettists who are so enamored of their own words they think they know more than the audience, critics and, or their own collaborators, and refuse to revise a book that stinks; and when a book "stinks," it impoverishes unsophisticated investors

---

42 According to Professor Henry Louis Gates, Jr. on PBS Special *And Still I Rise*.

(and, sometimes, even the producers, themselves) who can't afford the loss.[43]

That Oscar's book involved the student sit-in demonstrations underway in the Deep South was much to my liking, but the device he chose to hold his show together was a rehashing of Goethe's worn-out Faust legend – already exhaustingly employed by numerous writers from Christopher Marlowe to Thomas Mann; from Orson Welles to Comden and Green, with Gounod thrown in between. Mr. Kicks was really Mephistopheles in disguise.

"Oh, no!" I thought to myself, as Mel related the story line to me, this sounds like a takeoff on *Bandwagon* (1953), the classic Fred Astaire, MGM, Technicolor extravaganza about the staging of a flop musical, the plot of which is, likewise, based on Goethe's stale tale, with English musical comedy star, Jack Buchanan, making a buffoon of himself as the Evil One. It sounded awful, but I had not seen a copy of the script as yet, and, the fact is, Mel had kept his promise by involving me in "something important."

After hearing of my left-wing credentials and musical comedy experience, Bobby Nemiroff told Mel he was interested in meeting with me to discuss my possible involvement with the show and that, even though I was already scheduled to direct that summer in Chicago, at Herb Rogers' Tenthouse Theatre, I should call him in order to arrange a meeting.

Mel was certain he had brokered an ideal relationship: I, a Red Baby from Chicago, knew all about musicals while *Kicks'* producers, though a few years older, were fellow left-wingers in pursuit of a hit Broadway musical. Instinctively, Mel knew they were inadequately informed and would see the efficacy of harnessing my knowledge. Mel was scheming for me to be the show's director, though I did not realize that until later.

Also in my favor was the fact I was from Chicago, a city Bobby considered "lucky." He and Hansberry were married there, *Raisin* became a solid hit in its first Chicago engagement, and the city

---

43 I write about *Kicks* even though it may cast iconic people, whom I greatly admire and who are rightfully idolized for their works and personal virtues, in a something less than glowing light. I was fortunate to have been involved with Oscar and Lorraine, both of whom persevered in the struggle for equality and freedom and, in my opinion, would never have compromised their ideals in today's world. Perhaps, the day will come when everyone may speak critically without giving offense or being falsely accused of anti-Semitism, racism, anti-Islamism or for simply telling the truth.

was both the setting and the inspiration for Lorraine's play, for, in 1937, her father, Carl J. Hansberry, graduate of Alcorn College and a successful South Side real estate agent, moved his family into the all-white Woodlawn area, near the University of Chicago (6140 S. Rhodes, now a national landmark) with terrifying consequences. The neighborhood association called for their eviction. Angry whites protested outside the home, bricks were thrown through their living room window, one just missing the 8 year-old Lorraine. Her mother, Nannie Hansberry, grandchild of slaves, a college graduate, a black Southern Belle and a school teacher and Ward Committee-woman, was forced to carry a loaded Luger in order to protect her four children, two boys, two girls, Lorraine being the youngest of all.

Mr. Hansberry, represented by Earl B. Dickerson, brought suit which, though denied in Illinois, eventuated in the victorious but hollow landmark 1940 U.S. Supreme Court decision (Hansberry vs. Lee) which said whites cannot bar blacks from moving into white neighborhoods. But the ruling was unenforceable at that time and the Fair Housing Act was years in the offing.

Carl Hansberry died of a cerebral hemorrhage in Mexico City, in 1946, at the age of 50. The family had visited there, and Hansberry intended moving them to that metropolis permanently. Lorraine felt her father's death was the result of his strenuous efforts on behalf of civil rights and his awful dismay at what he considered a dearth of results. The 1948 Shelly vs. Kramer case, knocking down racial covenants, was the key decision leading to fairer housing, but Carl Hansberry's previous efforts figured greatly in that outcome.

It is universally agreed that these events were part of the subliminal and conscious inspiration behind the writing of *A Raisin in the Sun*.

But there are two different versions about how the initial production came into being: the official version rendered in all of Hansberry's biographies and the version given in the autobiography of Phillip J. Rose, the show's producer.[44] The versions differ be-

---

44 Rose, Phillip *"You Can't Do That on Broadway:" A Raisin In The Sun and Other Theatrical Impossibilities,* Limelight Editions, NYC, (2001). The only person (aside from me) to have written about Kicks, Rose knew little about the production once it was auditioned for him and he passed on it, which insulted Nemiroff.

cause of a falling-out between Nemiroff and Rose and that bitter disagreement was because of *Kicks*. The saga best begins with the partnering of Bobby and Lorraine.

6

DIFFERENT VERSIONS

Ralph Ellison's *Invisible Man* won the National Book Award in 1953, the year Lorraine and Bobby were married in the living room of the Hansberry home in Chicago, the day after they protested on behalf of the Rosenbergs, at the Federal Building, in the Loop. Preacher Archibald M. Carey, who later became a delegate to the United Nations, conducted the ceremony. The courtship began with Bobby and Lorraine meeting two years earlier in a picket line in Washington Square Park, while protesting alleged racial discrimination in the non-utilization of African-American students on the basketball team of New York University.

Lorraine idolized her father, Carl, the grandson of a black slave who was fathered by the white master of a plantation. He emigrated North and provided well for his family, by way of the real estate market, became importantly active in the NAACP and the Urban League, and, opposing the Democratic Party politics of ward-heeling Alderman William Dawson, ran unsuccessfully for Congress on the Republican ticket, in 1940.

Politically progressive, Carl Augustus Hansberry, was the friend, confidant and, with his family, the host for guests such as Paul Robeson, Duke Ellington, Joe Louis, W.E.B. Du Bois and Langston Hughes (1902-1967), whose poem, *Harlem*, yielded the final title of Lorraine's play, originally called *The Crystal Star.* But Carl Hansberry was also known as the "king of kitchenettes" because, as the result of decreased home ownership during the Depression, and the unaffordability of large apartments, he pioneered in the butchering of spacious apartments into one room with-offshoots-fits-all variety kitchenettes - a contributing factor to the decline of the African-American family unit (See St. Clair Drake's *Black Metropolis*).

After attending Betsy Ross Elementary and Englewood High, Lorraine enrolled, briefly, in the University of Wisconsin, Roosevelt and Howard, where Uncle William Lee Hansberry (1899-1965) was an eminent scholar in African-American history. But she left Howard, too. Having seen and been influenced by the beauty and power of the Theatre (in high school she had attended first-run touring companies of Broadway shows), a college performance of Sean O'Casey's *Juno And The Paycock* influenced her greatly (it is said) and, hearing the call of her muse, she came to New York to study writing at the New School for Social Research. She worked as a waitress in Greenwich Village. All biographies have her in Mexico during the summer of 1949.

But - and this is where two versions diverge - according to Phil Rose (1921-2011) Lorraine, in the summer of 1949, waited tables at a summer resort, Camp Unity, in Wingdale, New York, 100 miles from Gotham. It was a haven for liberal folk, one of who was Bumpy Johnson (1905-1968), the African-American who cornered the numbers racket in Harlem over the opposition of "Dutch" Schultz (1901-1935). The entertainment director at the camp was Herschel Bernardi, who would become the longest-running Tevya on Broadway, in *Fiddler On The Roof*. A veteran of the Yiddish theatre, he would play *Zorba* (1968) in the unsuccessful Broadway musical adaptation of the same name, presented and directed by Harold Prince.

And on Bernardi's staff, hired as the leading vocalist for that summer, was a would-be opera star, a veteran of Gilbert and Sullivan and opera touring companies going back to 1945, Phil Rose. A slender, bespectacled man of medium height, with thinning hair, Rose was drawn to singing at an early age and performed at Bar Mitzvahs and weddings on Manhattan's Lower East Side, where he was born.

At the age of 19, he became a rent collector in the black neighborhoods of Baltimore, where his father, Max Rosenberg had moved the family. He developed an interest in the culture and struggle of African-Americans and, in the mid-1940's, returning to New York, he sang with the Gilbert & Sullivan company at the Provincetown Playhouse, in the Village, where he met and married his wife, fellow Savoyard and lifelong companion, the actress, Doris Belack. And they became politically active in the struggle for racial equality.

Rose met William Marshall, who played De Lawd, in *Green Pastures,* Marshall introduced him to Paul Robeson, Rose's idol, and actors from Frederick O'Neal's American Negro Theatre, including a young actor just returned from a tour of *Anna Lucasta*, Sidney Poitier, who would become his enduring friend and collaborator and the star of *Raisin*.

According to Rose, he and Lorraine, who was nearly a decade his junior, became pals that summer of 1949. At staff discussion groups though the summer, Rose was impressed by the opinions and wit of the young waitress. Lonnie Elder III (1929-1996) was also on the entertainment staff that summer, both as actor and as writer of short plays, skits and sketches. He would create the important role of Bobo, in *Raisin*, and write the play *Ceremonies In Dark Old Men*, as well as the Academy Award-nominated screenplay for *Sounder* (directed by Martin Ritt).

Phil and Lorraine promised not only to stay in touch when they returned to Manhattan but agreed that, if the budding young waitress-writer wrote something of value, she would let the more theatrically-experienced Rose have a look-see.

In August of that same 1949, a little closer to the Hudson River, but not too far away from Camp Unity, there occurred one of the ugliest events of the postwar period – the Peekskill Riots. A benefit concert by Paul Robeson and Pete Seeger brought forth the Ku Klux Klan, and their affiliates, in anti-black, anti-Communist, anti-Semitic displays of reckless violence. The riots were triggered by Robeson's recent HUAC appearance and by remarks the singer had recently made in a Soviet-sponsored World Peace Conference in Paris:

> *"We in America do not forget that it was the*
> *backs of white workers from Europe and the*
> *backs of millions of blacks that the wealth of*

*America was built. And we are resolved to
share it equally."*

Phil Rose and Lorraine Hansberry saw each other often in the metropolis. Rose, in order to supplement his performing career, was employed by a record distributor on 52nd and Tenth, and eventually learned that racket, ending up as distributor for the hugely successful Atlantic Records, owned by brothers Neshui and Ahmet Ertegun. And he learned the song publishing business, where filthy lucre could be attained with a modicum of smarts and no real talent at all. He started his own recording company, Glory Records, eventually taking an office on 57th Street, where singers and actors were welcome to visit for possible employment, to audition, or simply to *schmooze.*

Back in New York, it wasn't long before Paul Robeson, because of his friendship with her father, hired Lorraine for an office worker-type gig at his small but outspoken Harlem newspaper, *Freedom*, of which he was the publisher. Lorraine rose to the position of reporter, then, associate editor, coming into contact with the variegated life of Harlem and receiving encouragement from Representative Adam Clayton Powell, Jr. (1908-1972) and Communist New York City Councilman, Benjamin J. Davis, Jr. (1903-1964). And she enrolled in a seminar on African history taught by W.E.B. Du Bois.

In 1951 she met Bobby. In 1952, Robeson, who was denied a passport to travel, chose Lorraine to read a speech of his at the Conference for Peace, in Montevideo, Uruguay. Then she married Bobby, the son of Russian immigrants who suffered through the Depression but prospered, now, in the restaurant business.

Bobby was a young, would-be man of letters; an editor, for a time, at Avon Books, a part time songwriter versed in music publishing, mainly through the good services of Phil Rose, who, at Lorraine's insistence, first gave Booby office space and, then, hired Bobby as an assistant to his partner, Lou Sprung, in that division of Phil's business.

All of what I've just told you is missing from all of the biographies and television presentations to date concerning Lorraine and her monumental play.

Under the pseudonyms Robert Barron and Burt Long, Nemiroff and his lifelong chum from youth summer camp, D'Lugoff, had written a 1956 folk-type pop song hit, based on a Georgia sea chantey, called "Cindy, Oh, Cindy." They pitched it to Phil and he recorded it with his "discovery," Vince Martin, whom he coupled with a trio called the Tarriers, which included a guy named Alan Arkin (who later won an Academy Award) and they recorded the song on Glory Records. E.B. Marks, a prominent firm, published it and it rose (no pun) to number one on the charts and stayed there for weeks, even got a "cover" by Eddie Fisher, the last time that singer would have a hit. Bobby, reportedly, made $100,000, which provided a cushion for Lorraine to stay home and write. And Bobby worked for Phil in Phil's office.

The product of Lorraine's efforts was *A Raisin In The Sun*. Supposedly, Bobby and Lorraine were at a loss as to how to proceed. Supposedly, they knew nothing about the process of getting a play produced. I say "they" because, Bobby, in months to come, would look me in the eye and, speaking metaphorically, I assume, say, with great dramatic significance, "I wrote every word of that play."

The emphasis with which he spoke amounted to: "I'm not kidding," but I told myself he was speaking metaphorically; after all, he was an editor. But subsequently, I have doubted my initial reaction. Did he not add additional dialogue over Phil Rose's objections when *Raisin* was published? Did he not take Lorraine's diaries and make them into *To Be Young, Gifted and Black?* Who knows what he added of his own? What about *Les Blancs*, which he developed from rather sketchy material? Without a doubt, both, in future, attempted to re-write *Kicks*, during final rehearsals in Chicago, though only Bobby took credit in the *Playbill.* There is no question he worked diligently with his wife on both *A Raisin in the Sun* and the *Sign in Sidney Brustein's Window.*

With the play completed and, again, supposedly, not knowing where to turn, Lorraine cooked a spaghetti dinner, invited Phil and Bobby's friend, Burt, and read the script for them. Phil went home, couldn't sleep, and called Lorraine at 6:30 A.M. of a Sunday morning to say he wanted to produce the play on Broadway. Lorraine agreed at once and people in the show business began telling Phil he was nuts and would lose his shirt, and any money he might raise; blacks didn't go to the theatre and whites wouldn't support a play about blacks in which whites were the mocked antagonists.

Phil Rose was a novice at producing, but he was better positioned than he makes out in his memoir. Sidney Poitier was a close friend. Lorraine and Bobby knew this. Sidney, after *No Way Out*, *Blackboard Jungle, Cry, The Beloved Country* and *Edge Of The City*, was a star and perfect for the supposed starring role of Walter Lee Younger, though Mama turned out to be the play's dominant character. And it eventuated that if they (Phil and Lorraine) agreed to cast Ethel Waters in the role of Mama Younger they would easily raise the necessary capital for the production. But that was a choice they were not prepared to make.

Phil persevered, rather unsuccessfully, in raising the operating budget. Kermit Bloomgarden, the most successful producer in New York at that time, with *Music Man*, etc., offered all the money and co-billing for Phil if Phil and Lorraine would agree to casting Waters and firing their choice of director, Lloyd Richards, an African-American actor-director who taught at Paul Mann's Workshop, and who was an acting coach and friend of Poitier's. They refused both of Bloomgarden's requests. They thought that hiring Waters "would be," to quote Rose, "adding another easy choice for the audience to love and thereby do a disservice to the play," which shows the immense power, magnetism and popularity of Ethel Waters.

Instead they hired Claudia McNeil who was known mainly for her musical ability, though she had appeared as a replacement in the small role of Tabitha, in Arthur Miller's *Crucible*, which Bloomgarden produced in 1953. When Claudia read for Rose and Hansberry, they felt she would be the perfect Mama Younger.

The role of Beneatha, who is based on the playwright, herself, went to Diana Sands, who was appearing, along with Phil's wife, Doris Belack, in the off-Broadway production of *World Of Scholem Aleichem*, directed by Howard Da Silva. Lorraine was, initially, opposed to the choice and thought Diana would play up the comedy in the role to excess.

The Roses, the Poitiers and the Davises (Ruby Dee and Ossie Davis) were all good friends, so Ruby was the logical choice in the role of Ruth Younger. Future Academy Award-winner (in 1982's, *An Officer And A Gentleman*), Louis Gossett, Jr. was cast as George Murchison. Ivan Dixon, who would appear as a regular on TV's

Hogans Heroes, played the role of the African "warrior," Joseph Assagai.

The role of the youngster, Travis Younger, was given to Glynn Turman (1967-) who went on to a long career as an actor, director, and producer. John Fiedler, who had recently completed his role as juror number two (the most *nebbishe* one of all) in Sidney Lumet's *12 Angry Men,* played the role of the lone white character, Karl Lindner, who attempts to bar the Youngers from inhabiting his neighborhood.

When Rose struggled to raise his budget, his general manager, Walter Fried, told him to abandon the effort, but Phil eventually joined forces with another novice, an accountant and money manager who had dabbled in investing before, David S. Cogan (1924-2002). He raised $30,000 for Rose but was uninvolved in artistic decisions. A Detroit showman and theatre operator, Ken Schwartz put up ten grand. Eventually, Rose assembled a total of 147 investors and, after the rave reviews from Chicago's and, then New York's critics, the play became a sellout on Broadway in two weeks, with the investors receiving the return of their initial investments in five weeks.[45] After its 200th performance at the Barrymore Theatre, the play returned a 343 per cent profit in twenty-five weeks, closing after 538 Broadway showings.

The story of that Broadway opening night of the great play, the emotional and heartfelt standing ovation, at a time when standing ovations had meaning, the story of how Sidney Poitier leapt off the stage, as everyone cheered, and brought Lorraine up onstage before the wildly appreciative full house, has been told more than once, but most vividly by Phil Rose in his autobiography.

He says he was seated next to Lorraine, of which I have no doubt. But Rose makes no mention of Bobby Nemiroff being there and Bobby was, certainly, with Lorraine at the previous opening in Chicago, when Oscar came in the door with *Kicks.* How could Nemiroff not be present on the occasion of this premiere? Who escorted Lorraine? Phil? Does it matter? Does the truth matter? The reader will be the judge, and the person who sat on Lorraine's other

---

45 According to the Schomburg Library.

side, on that famous opening night, will presently appear in coming pages.

The truth is that the night *A Raisin In The Sun* opened on Broadway, Bobby, Burt and Oscar were in Las Vegas, attempting to convince Sammy Davis, Jr. to play the role of Mr. Kicks. Bobby was no longer working for Phil and he and Burt flew Phil to Chicago to see Oscar perform a condensed version of *Kicks*, in the junior Brown's living room. Phil liked Oscar's performance and some of the songs, but thought the book was weak and said so to Bobby and Burt, who were insisting he join them as co-producer. Rose later wrote he was about to suggest they involve Lorraine as co-author of the book, when Bobby jumped in to say Phil didn't understand Oscar's libretto and it was "Better and more profound than anything I was accustomed to reading."

****

In the winter of 1960-61, *Raisin* had shuttered on Broadway and gone on national tour with some of the original cast, minus Sidney Poitier, who returned to Hollywood. Ossie Davis stepped in for him on Broadway and was, himself, replaced for the tour by Douglas Turner Ward, while Diana Sands and Claudia McNeil remained.

Though Lorraine and Bobby now lived a few short blocks apart in Greenwich Village and conjugal relations were, at least by the time I met them in early 1961, nonexistent, and it was intimated to me that Lorraine was a lesbian, they were not yet divorced. But their professional relationship was solid and now, Lorraine had grown to like and believe in Oscar's script.

Fulfilling his contract with Columbia Records, Oscar's first album was *Sin & Soul* and it was a hit.[46] The success of his singing on that debut recording was understandable and it turned out to be a classic in African-American expression, but if all the songs in *Kicks* were sensational they could never, I surmised, counterbalance the book's three tortuous acts in sixteen scenes, nearly three hours long, all hinged on the tired Devil device and a scatter-shot story.

---

46 Reissued by Columbia on compact disc, it now includes three numbers from *Kicks*, including the title song.

But the neophyte producing team of Nemiroff and D'Lugoff, sounding like a special brand of Russian vodka, thought otherwise. They had never really tasted defeat. Lorraine's play was a hit, the Village Gate was packin' 'em in, and "Cindy Oh Cindy" was still churning shekels. So, at Mel's behest, I called Bobby Nemiroff.

In his quiet but urgent fashion, he invited me to a presentation of the show to be performed by Oscar, at the Johns Hopkins Club, on the coming Sunday afternoon. This was the first time I heard a voice that has become unforgettable. Ethereal but mesmeric, his soft-spoken sing-song seduced the famous into giving him written testimonials of approval for a show which hadn't, as yet, been produced. Wispy, but not feminine, the voice was insistent.[47]

When I met him I found him to be a good listener, always assessing what you were really thinking. But because of his personal prejudices he had the unfortunate habit of over-looking what others thought obvious, all in the cause of what he, personally, believed proper. I didn't know all this from our first phone conversation, nor that my life was about to turn upside down.

---

47 It droned on till it wore you down, which was, famously, the case in 1975, when *Resim* won the Tony Award for Best Musical. That acceptance speech seemed as if it never would end. Nationally televised, it was so long it drew frustrated laughter before finally eliciting jeers of anger from many in the audience of theatre professionals.

7

"A Sea of Green"

Two days later, around 1:45 P.M. on a cold Sunday afternoon, I checked in at the first floor reception desk of the venerable Johns Hopkins Club, in Manhattan, and ascended the century old staircase to the second floor. There, I was checked in on the list of those invited and passed into a wood-paneled presentation room where a few dozen folding chairs had been arranged upon a parquet floor. A podium on a platform with six feet of depth behind it was all the stage area in which the presenter, who I understood was to be Oscar, would perform, and there was a piano off to "stage right." The show was to start in a few minutes.

The first person who struck my eye, among those assembled, was a bow-tied Dave Garroway. Naturally, he was also wearing his trademark horn-rimmed glasses that I, and a million others, not just in this country but also around the world, had, for a few years, imitated. I took a seat in the last row, as is my practice.

On each seat was an 8x10 pamphlet that included a facsimile of the cover of Oscar's album, *Sin & Soul*, and, ensconced behind soothing blue legal covers, sheets of paper devoted to quotations from celebrities praising the musical.

As previously noted, with Bobby everything began with the word; he was an editor. I soon learned (as will the reader, by turning to the ILLUSTRATIONS) these extravagant statements (this puff-sheet being the second version) were generated mostly through private, living-room presentations; certainly that was the case with the well-meaning Reverend Martin Luther King, Jr., Sammy Davis

Jr., Rosa Parks, Harry Belafonte, Dave Garroway and Steve Allen, a frequent customer at the Palace of Audible Dreams, as was Dorothy Kilgallen, sometimes with her husband, Broadway producer, Richard Kollmar, who owned the Left Bank, around the comer from the store, on 50th off of Eighth, other times, accompanied by young, gay escorts like Ben Bagley, though she was deeply in love with singer, Johnnie Ray at the time. Smarting painfully, because of Sinatra calling her "the chinless wonder" and making it part of his act at the Copa, she was the most important woman reporter of the day, a Broadway columnist who could make or break a reputation with a word; a radio and TV (*What's My Line?*) personality known to millions. (Despite her poisonous reputation, she was a very amiable lady, as far as I was concerned.) I believe Irv Kupcinet, Chicago's famous reporter-columnist, alerted her about *Kicks*.

Tonite Show initiator, Steve Allen had long been, a cultural icon. These were potent endorsements. To this list of illustrious names there was to be added that of the woman about to enter the room. As I studied these documents, thirty or forty people assembled about me. It was showtime.

And in walked the woman on whose head the Ku Klux Klan had long ago placed its greatest bounty, Mrs. Eleanor Roosevelt (1884-1962), all five feet eleven of her, the "World's Most Admired Woman" (according to *The New York Times*). Personally, I do not believe it would be an exaggeration to cll her the Most Important Woman in the World, for, among her many accomplishments, it was publicly assumed by everyone but the worst people in our society that she had saved her husband so that he could save the world.

After bearing him six children and, then, discovering his infidelity with her own social secretary, Lucy Mercer, and after, with sober resolve and the acquiescence and support of Franklin's influential mother, laying down the law to FDR and re-arranging their marriage, she helped restore him back to a kind of health when he contracted polio and she was instrumental, in his campaign for governorship of New York and, inevitably, the White House.

As First Lady, she used her power to do immeasurable good for the defenseless coal miners, the poor everywhere and African-Americans, North and South, often working behind her husband's back in order to goose him in the right direction, as was the case with her support of the Tuskegee Airmen, of A. Phillip Randolph's efforts to desegregate the defense industry, and of Marian Anderson's right to appear at the Lincoln Memorial despite the protestations of the Daughters of the American Revolution.[48] (Of course, man of these facts were unknown to the general public, much less historians, at the time.)

If I run the risk of providing a surfeit of biographical material concerning Eleanor Roosevelt, it is because she is important to the story. For, having perused the 9 x 10 pamphlet in my hand, it did not take long to conclude that Mrs. Roosevelt had been invited to this presentation in order to attempt to add her name to the list of those celebrities who had already endorsed the musical; only her name meant more than all the other names.

Today, her secretary, Maureen Core, accompanied Mrs. Roosevelt. They spotted Garroway and went directly to him. The tall ex-First Lady walked purposefully to the folding chairs which had been allocated adjacent to the television celebrity. Things were pre-arranged and stage-managed and there was no time to greet the assemblage, nor was it appropriate, or incumbent upon her to do so. The entire audience would have happily lined-up to shake her hand, but that required a self-centeredness she did not possess, and once they were seated, the lights quickly dimmed and the show began.

Oscar Brown, Jr. entered, script in hand, and met a spotlight at the center of the platform. He had assumed the character of the hip, Mr. Kicks, which was the way he carried himself, anyway - loose limbed, balletic sort of a swagger, moving as you'd expect a nightclub singer, or a tap dancer, a Sammy Davis, Jr. or a Bobby Darrin would move. The beam of light focusing on his upper torso disclosed his red hair, light complexion, freckles and large, humorous, green eyes, as he snapped off a funky medium tempo and the

---

48 Although she had suffered a defeat when her candidate, Adlai Stevenson, succumbed to the Kennedy steamroller, and, though she disliked JFK's father, as did her husband, though he appointed him twice to important posts, Eleanor Roosevelt remained a force in the Democratic Party, still wrote her column, "My Day," the third most syndicated in the world, and initiated and still had an agenda vital to her constituents and the country, which was immediate civil rights for African-Americans and equal pay for women (with Equal Rights for Women Amendment to the Constitution to follow later). The new president, who counted on her support and visited her at Val-Kill, her upstate New York home, deferred to her when she requested the White House for a spring of 1961 conference on these important women's issues. Some say Mrs. Roosevelt's 1948 Declaration of Rights, which led to the U.N. Human Rights Commission, was her greatest achievement, though others feel her financial committment to the Legal Defense Fund of the NAACP, which eventuated in the 1955 Brown decision and other historical rulings, was the most significant.

pianist, who had snuck into position when Oscar entered, and who looked very familiar to me, as if I should know him from the Palace of Audible Dreams, now, began a vamp.

Oscar continued the finger snapping almost throughout the singing of this opening number, a minor key, eight-bar blues with extensions and interludes of additional patter. He sang:

"Permit me to introduce myself. My name is Mr. Kicks" and, then, came the quatrain ending with the very obvious da, da, de, da, da, de, da, da, - you guessed it – "around the River Styx!"

This first number was catchy and effective as performed by Oscar. It was just a simple blues with add-ons, but was it enough to open a show, no matter how great the star singing it might be?

In truth, it wasn't the opening of the show at all, yet it was instrumental in raising over four hundred and forty some thousand dollars in 1960's coin. Four years in the future, producers David Susskind, David Merrick and Joseph E. Levine, of Embassy Pictures, and their investors, would lose the, till then, record amount for a Broadway musical with their flop *Kelly*, about Steve Brodie, who claimed to have jumped off the Brooklyn Bridge. It closed in New York in one night at a loss of $400,000, the same amount *Kicks* was mandated to raise. A $400,000 budget in 1960 is the equivalent of six million dollars today. That would not be enough to produce a comparable musical today; it would require an additional four million dollars. A show such as *Kicks* would cost ten million dollars in 2014 dollars, attributable to rising advertising and production costs.[49]

The "opening," that simple blues sung so strikingly well by Oscar in backers' auditions, didn't occur until page four of the script, a long way to go in a musical. The real opening, the one which audiences were destined to see, was a morality play/dance pantomime involving a burglar, a policeman and Mr. Kicks, the Devil, hanging from a moon of *papier mache.*

Then, the scene shifted to the offices of Orgy, a girlie magazine, and the Devil sets up a plan with the magazine's editor to destroy the lunchroom sit-in movement on a the campus of a southern black college. Oscar's presentation worked because it included

---

49 (According to theproducersperspective.com)

only the songs and but a smattering of the story, without revealing its weaknesses.

I still had not as yet seen a script but I did not care for what I heard. The Devil bit was silly and the lyrics mediocre. I could see one of the songs, "Hazel's Hips," being a crowd-pleaser. Oscar's 30-minute presentation was an effective solo backers' audition, the con man in me could see that, but I could also see through it and what I smelled was turkey. They had conned themselves into thinking they had a hit.

This Hopkins Club presentation was not formally a backers' audition because the necessary SEC filing, giving approval to solicit funds, proffer limited partnership agreements and accept checks, had not yet been obtained. I soon learned that other "backers' auditions" had been held, the quotes from the big shots told me that, but what good are such presentations unless one can legally accept investments?

A meaningless stunt, it would have been insidiously clever if they had held those previous "auditions" merely to solicit big name endorsements to be used in garnering funds from future investors, but that was not the case; there was no intended deception on the part of the producers. When it came to producing on Broadway they were inexperienced enough not to know there was anything untoward in presenting words of praise by famous people to potential investors.

After Oscar said "Curtain," the presentation ended without a pitch of any kind because Bobby didn't want Mrs. Roosevelt to escape the premises without his talking to her first. When Oscar finished, Nemiroff appeared at my shoulder briefly, saying, "Sidney, don't go away, I'll be right back," and darted off to catch Mrs. Roosevelt, who stood on the second or third step from the top of the antiquated, curving staircase, her right hand poised on the bannister, about to descend to the first floor, her secretary having preceded her. But Bobby, pencil and pad of paper in hand, politely accosted her, engaged her in conversation, scribbled energetically upon the tablet of paper he held in his hand, as she spoke.

Matching the face with the voice I heard on the phone, Bobby was a pleasant looking, even handsome, brown-haired man, of average height, with an intelligent forehead. He was friendly, not overbearing, and his main features were his assessing brown eyes and, what Phil Rose referred to as, a persistent, open-faced, wide-eyed "look of wonder."

By now, I had identified the pianist, who accompanied Oscar, as Alonzo Levister, Jr., a composer whose album, *"Manhattan Melodrama,"* had been released earlier by Charles Mingus' Debut Records. Now in his mid-thirties, Levister was a confidant and friend of Mingus, Miles Davis and John Coltrane, pals with the "Baldwin Brothers," step-brother Billy and James, and knew just about everyone in the jazz world. I would later learn Lonnie had been introduced by James Baldwin to Lorraine as a potential composer for her projected opera about Haiti's Toussaint-L'Ouverture. Phil Rose was to be the producer. Lonnie told me in 2014, from Portugal:

"I pushed Phil Rose to give me a fee to secure my role in Toussaint. He refused. Lorraine then gave me a check for $1,500 (1960 $$) to go to Haiti to do music research. All I learned was that they had a brand of rum from one to seven stars. After considerable research they all tasted the same to me. Also, I was her front row tux guest at opening night for Raisin. Standing ovation by entire audience. A young playwright's dream. Like a movie! When Raisin ended and the curtain went up and down, Sidney jumped down off the stage, grabbed Lor. sitting next to me. Handed her with both hands up onto the stage for bows. People flooded up onto the stage. Including me. I gave her a strong bear hug and she quietly said:

"'There goes my expensive gardenia.'"

Levister also revealed:

"No memory of Bobby at the opening or the after party. Jimmy Baldwin introduced me to Lorraine sometime before Raisin opened and have no memory of Bobby at the Bleecker Street apartment before the Kicks trip started."

A handsome, solemnly cool African-American wearing dark glasses, which he rarely removed from his face, Levister walked with composed deliberation and spoke with well-modulated bluntness. Always his own man, he possessed a keen sense of humor, but was often too outspoken, so that the combination of his good looks, the mysterious dark glasses, the laid-back manner combined with caustic barbs, could become ominous to the uninitiated. He and his, then, first wife, a buxom redheaded white woman with a sulky mouth and lucious lips, came into the Palace of Audible Dreams with Mingus frequently to listen to recordings, though I only observed them from afar. I later learned he had attended the Julliard School of Music, where he met Miles Davis, while they both studied music theory and became lifelong friends, and he had arranged for John Coltrane and been praised by Leonard Bernstein, among others.

"What," I wondered, "was he doing here?"

It took me awhile to discover that Lonnie was, then and for a time thereafter, Oscar's scribe. It was notable that the most successful songs on *Sin & Soul* had melodies written by someone other than Oscar, and that Oscar was the lyricist, not the melodist, on Bobby Timmons' "Dat Dere" and Nat Adderley's "Work Song" and Mongo Santamaria's "Afro-Blue."

Oscar could not read or write musical notation. He hummed the tunes, Lonnie wrote them down. This is not an uncommon practice. Nor is the inability to write and read notes, i.e., relying on someone else to do so, a matter of ethics. It is perfectly legitimate.[50]

I did not approach Lonnie Levister after the showing; I was waiting for Bobby to finish with Mrs. FDR and, when he did, and she descended gingerly down the staircase on her way back to her brownstone on the East Side, Bobby returned to me and said, "Let's go get something to eat." He was smiling with satisfaction.

We got a cab and drove to the corner of Perry and Eighth, in the Village. In a four-story, brown building, designed in the 1870's to accommodate the block's strange shape and house a restaurant with a professional kitchen in the rear, we ordered something to eat.

---

50 Knowledgeable readers need not be reminded Charlie Chaplin couldn't read music, yet he scored many of his films and wrote the lachrymose standard "Smile," with the help of someone who could write the notes onto manuscript paper. Bobby Short, the café singer, played the piano from the age of six but never learned to read notes, ditto, the great Erroll Garner. Another example is Johnny Mercer, considered by many to be the greatest lyricist of all, a man who could memorize a song in one or two hearings, go home and come back (albeit, sometimes three months later) with a finished lyric, couldn't read music but he wrote words to the cadences of composers such as Harold Arlen, Hoagy Carmichael, Jerome Kern, Vernon Duke, Richard Whiting, Harry Warren, Duke Ellington, Henry Mancini and others, never being able to read notes but relying on his memory of the melody. Mercer also "wrote" some extremely good songs "by himself," inventing melodies in his head, picking them out with one finger on the piano, eventually learning elementary triads (his m.o. for "Dream") and depending on a scribe to annotate the melody onto music manuscript paper and fill in an appropriate bass-line.

It was evening by now and, as folks were watching the news and looking forward to the *Ed Sullivan Show,* Bobby hunched forward and said, confidentially, "I'd like to ask you some questions." We had spoken without restraint in the cab and I thought him likeable and I believed he liked me.

"Sure," I said and he pulled out a piece of paper and, in the dim light of the restaurant, began reading.

"What are props?" he asked.

I thought he was kidding and I smiled and waited. But he wasn't kidding. I realize this is hard for readers to believe; everyone becomes confused at one time or another, and he had a perfect right to be confused about anything at all. Nevertheless, I'll take an oath on it that that is the first question he asked. I replied, "They're the items the actors handle or items which are part of the scenery." He squinted back at the paper, holding it close to his face in the pale light. "What's the difference between a stage manager and a general manager?" he rhetorically proposed and I knew for sure he wasn't quizzing me just to see if I knew the answer; he truly didn't know and I realized I was in a screwball situation.

"A stage manager runs the show in rehearsal and in performance on-stage and all the time the cast and crew and band are in the theatre. On Broadway he's called 'production stage manager' as opposed to his underling and assistant, who's called 'stage manager,' the guy who gives the 'calls,' you know, 'Ten minutes!' or 'Five minutes' till the curtain goes up. The general manager is a different union altogether. He's the guy who runs the whole business end of the show. He makes the budget and pays the salaries and disposes of the scenery when the show closes; he writes most of the checks, though you end up signing them."

When he asked, I showed him how sets moved on and offstage on wagons and what it meant to play "in one" while the scenery was being changed behind a "traveller" curtain and other elementary procedures germane to staging musicals. Our food came.

"What about a director?" I asked, not thinking of myself, not wanting the job of directing a potential flop. His face became blank and he stared at a faraway somewhere in the distance of the cozy restaurant. This pose, this technique of avoidance, I would come to know, was a main trick in his repertoire, at least at this point in his budding career.

"You know, you really need a director almost from the beginning when you're doing a musical. And you need it for the prospectus when you're raising money. You owe it to the investors."

I was referring to the pages of celebrity endorsements and the cover of *"Sin & Soul,"* which I brought with me from the Johns Hopkins Club.

"Have you spoken with anyone?" I asked. He snapped out of it.

"We spoke with Elia Kazan and Josh Logan."

"And?

"Kazan said 'No' and Logan said he'd do it if we played it in one set with the actors in whiteface."

"WHITEFACE!"

"He said 'the Negros in whiteface and the whites in blackface,' something like that. He's crazy, of course. Nice man, though."

"You and Burt went to see him?"

"In his apartment."

"What about George Abbott?" I suggested.

He made a sour face and shook his head.

"That's what you need," I subtly urged, as his eyes glazed over, "someone who knows how to structure the story and make the show move, make it fit together," I said, but he shook his head and began eating.

He didn't want George Abbott (1887-1995) because Abbott would take over. "Mr. Abbott," (as he was called, by everyone except his most intimate friends) was 73 years old in 1961 and extremely active onstage and on the ballroom floor. He began his career on Broadway as an actor, in 1913, after studying playwriting at Harvard, with George Pierce Baker. He wrote his first play under that great mentor's tutelage and the first play of Abbott's own authorship to open on Broadway was *The Fall Guy*, in 1922. He developed a reputation for spotting what was wrong with a play and fixing it. He did so, and received co-authorship with Phillip Dunning, in his first great hit as a director, with the 1926 production of *Broadway*. In the 1930's, listing only straight plays and in no particular order, he directed these legendary hits: *Three Men On A Horse, Boy Meets Girl, Chicago* (the original source of the musical), *Twentieth Century* and *Room Service*, among others, before concentrating, for the next quarter of a century, on musicals.

During that time, George Abbott directed these musicals, editing, developing and helping construct a workable book: *Jumbo, On Your Toes, Boys From Syracuse, Too Many Girls, Pal Joey,* all by Rodgers and Hart, *On The Town* and *Wonderful Town,* both by Leonard Bernstein, *High Button Shoes, Where's Charley?, Call Me Madam, A Tree Grows In Brooklyn, Pajama Game, Damn Yankees, New Girl In Town, Billion Dollar Baby* (a flop, but a favorite among those who saw it), *Tenederloin, Fiorello, Once Upon A Matterss* and *Take Her, She's Mine* (that same year of 1961). The following year he would direct *A Funny Thing Happened On The Way To The Forum.* [51]

I didn't expect George Abbott to agree to direct *Kicks*, but, just as Josh Logan had volunteered his concept of doing the show in whiteface, so, too, I thought, could Abbott give a word of advice, some tangible idea with which the producers and Oscar could make improvements. Abbott was formidable, but approachable. As Cole Porter, when asked to evaluate Irving Berlin's place in American music said, "Irving Berlin IS American music," George Abbott WAS musical comedy.

And then, it became clear to me that Bobby and Burt (probably Lorraine and, maybe even Oscar, himself) DIDN'T LIKE MUSICAL COMEDY! Their intention was to meld the political content of *Kicks* with the commercialism and apolitical nature of most musicals in order to create a didactic, Brechtian kind of statement and NOT a show that merely sought to delight and entertain, a concept which was anathema, as far as they were concerned.

As we ate Bobby revealed the fact that a production meeting for the show was about to convene at his office, closeby, and Burt and the staff would be there. Would I join them, he offered, even though I was committed to directing in the coming summer stock season in Chicago? (Hal March, of *$64,000 Question* fame, *Gazebo*, and two

---

51 Trim six foot-four, gray-haired, patrician, blue eyed, wearing clear Lucite frames, he returned to the stage as Mr. Antrobus, in the U.S. State Department Tour of Thornton Wilder's *Skin Of Our Teeth,* directed by Alan Schneider, (who began his directing career at Cain Park) with Helen Hayes as Mrs. Antrobus and Mary Martin as Sabina. The greatest honor given to a member of Actors' Equity (AEA) is the Paul Robeson Award. In the directors union, SDC (Stage Directors and Choreographers) it's the George Abbott Award. Mr. Abbott, who made a practice of writing for at least 15 minutes each morning, was active until his death at 108.

other "straight" plays with stars.) I accepted the offer and asked for a salary of two hundred dollars a week. We agreed we would worry about my summer commitments as they approached. It was, after all, the cold of winter.

Then, in the chilly night, we set off across Seventh Avenue, walking toward Bobby's office, three or four blocks away, just around the corner from St. John's Lutheran, which abided by a delicatessen-diner frequented by Alger Hiss, who lived in the neighborhood and who had been employed, by a benevolent sympathizer, as a brush salesman. It was the Sheridan Square neighborhood I knew so well from Café Bohemia, Café Society Downtown and Ted Mann and Jose Quintero's original Circle in the Square.

Our destination was the second floor walk-up of an ancient residential building on the corner of Bleecker Street and Christopher, above a grimy tobacco store and a laundromat. It was a small, no bedroom apartment with a linoleum floor, a couch and a recliner, from Castro Convertibles. Previously, Lorraine and Bobby lived there. This is where Lorraine's famous play was written.

There, in a dwelling which, today, rents for thousands a month, on a street featuring one couturier after another, I met, for the first time, Bobby's producing partner, Burt D'Lugoff, and the others who were assisting them. Burt was lumbering, a bit overweight, teddy bearish, wore horn-rimmed glasses, had unruly, curly-hair. And he had wise eyes and was most affable. He and his brother were great appreciators of the arts and friends with a long list of famous performers. Only months before they had transformed a mens' flophouse on Bleecker and Thompson, albeit designed and built in 1896 by Chicago School architect, Ernest Flagg, into the hottest jazz club in town.

There were two ladies present. One was Bobby's secretary, Janet, an African-American woman in her late thirties who wore her hair in an Afro before it became popular and had a son at home. The other lady was Edith Gordon, a blonde in her forties, who was the manager of the Village Gate, where Nina Simone currently held sway.

And there was a young African-American in his early twenties, an outgoing go-fer who ran errands between Lorraine Hansberry's apartment, two and one half blocks away, at 112 Waverly Place, and the "office" in which we met and Bobby slept. His name was Frank Dandridge and he soon became a well-known photojournalist for *Life*, covering MLK's March on Washington in 1963, the Birmingham Bombing in 1963, and the Harlem Riots, the year following, eventually becoming a film and television writer and producer.

It was a congenial group and I was warmly received and formed an immediate bond with all four. Then, Bobby convened the meeting by throwing me a curve ball.

"Well, Sid. What would YOU do now?" and they all looked at me.

"I'd get Mrs. Roosevelt's quote and print it up and put it in front of all the other quotes and go out and find the investors." So you see, I was just as guilty as they.

"Could you raise money in Chicago?" he asked.

"I think so," I answered, wildly guessing. I was thinking of the left-wing rallies I attended as a child and the manner in which they solicited donations at the Chicago Stadium, just as in the 1955 MGM film, *The Trial*, starring Glenn Ford, wherein a crooked Arthur Kennedy, in a stadium seating thousands, holds a bill above his head and, inciting the crowd in frenzied solicitation, screams,

"I wanna see a sea of green out there, I said, A SEA OF GREEEEEN!!!!!"

What I had in mind was tracking down those major contributors whose names I remembered from rallies years before, when I was a child.

"You know we're waiting for the SEC approval we need in order to go ahead and raise the money."

"Yes."

"Would you be willing to fly down to Washington and bring some papers to the SEC in order to speed up the process?"

"Sure. When?"

"Tomorrow or the next day," he answered quickly. "Let's get the authorization for the quote from Mrs. Roosevelt first. I'll call her tomorrow and you go pick it up. You can go to Washington the day after."

The next day, a Monday, I met Maureen Core, at the door of the townhouse on East 74th Street, which the ex-First Lady shared with Dr. and Mrs. Gurevitch, and we exchanged envelopes. When presented with a prospectus, her endorsement would be the first words seen by potential investors. Mrs. Roosevelt's statement made reference to Rodgers and Hammerstein's *Oklaholma*, comparing *Kicks* favorably to the long running hit.

The following morning at 6 A.M., on a frigid day in February, I flew to Washington and read the wretched script… in its entirety… fifteen thousand feet in the sky. It was awful. And it couldn't be fixed. When something is that bad, where do you start? But I was enervated; I did not question my motives; I was involved with a Broadway-bound production with people who were influential and decent, though naïve.

I took a cab to the SEC Building in D.C., exchanged papers with officials there, cabbed it back to Washington National and returned to LaGuardia. Armed, now, with approved limited partnership agreements which would allow us to accept investments in the show, along with a recording of the show made by Oscar and Lonnie, and a checkbook with a dozen blank checks with Bobby's name affixed and to be spent as I saw fit (they had that much confidence in me), I booked a reservation for a suite (certainly, not just a one-room closet but a suite) at the Palmer House. So, one could accurately say the "front money" for *Kicks* was made possible by *Raisin*, for from where else would this expense money have come? Answers to this question would be deposed in the not too distant future, but right now, I had in hand the third incarnation of the prospectus, this time with Mrs. Roosevelt's words of praise on the leading page, by its lonesome, along with others gathered by Bobby (as previously noted) and, optimistically and enthusiastically, I flew to Chicago at the end of the week.

8

LOVE AT THE PALMER HOUSE

Let me tell you about Oscar. Hip, charming, articulate, slangy, nobody's fool, he was, like Lorraine, the product of an upper middle class home and knew of deprivation and poverty by observation only. But what he saw was enough for him to commit himself to making a better world. His impulse and gift for writing songs and poems became the vehicle for achieving his altruistic ambitions.

After Willard Elementary and, then, Englewood High School, the same school Lorraine attended, Oscar[52] "bounced around colleges (University of Wisconsin, Lincoln U., in Pennsylvania, Columbia College and Roosevelt University here), but it was no use: songwriting was what he wanted to do. 'Even in high school, every time a girl would break my heart, I'd write a heartbreaker.' Oscar's father tried to interest him in the real estate business. 'If I'd spent all my time in real estate, I'd have a whole colony of buildings by now. Sure I wanted everybody to live indoors, but I didn't care where. I would look at a song and then a six-flat and the song would always win.' Oscar was defeated for political office (State Legislature, 1st District, Progressive Party, 1948; Congress, 1st District, Republican Party, 1952); held a job as an advertising copywriter; and was a radio announcer (WJJD), but this wasn't enough. His friends wife and relatives, who would remind him of the bleak prospects for success in songwriting, got up $1,000 to try to publish his songs. 'We were going to storm the citadel head on. It didn't work.

---

52 From an article by Lionel Lindner, *Chicago Daily News*, 10/7/61.

But this kind of thing would keep me going for a while'...Oscar never had formal training...He would hum the melody...and have a friend write down the notes. He learned how to create pictures in songs 'because people accept the truth if they think they see it.'.... One day Oscar was gossiping with a friend...about an acquaintance...who lived only for kicks – a thrill seeker who would do anything for excitement. This gave Oscar the idea for a song called 'Mr. Kicks.' The material built around this character was written much later after Oscar had recorded many of his songs, including 'Brown Baby,' for Columbia Records on a disc called *'Sin and Soul.'*....The theme of; 'Kicks' is exploitation and corruption."

Expanding on this autobiographical account: Oscar's mother was a schoolteacher. His comfortably middle class upbringing distanced him from the struggle of his fellow African-Americans. He was talented and Chicago was a hotbed of productivity in the world of radio, second only to New York City.

In his first venture into show biz, Oscar auditioned for and obtained work as a radio actor at the age of 15. One year later, in the middle of WW II he enrolled in college, but dropped out, enrolled in another – his father wanted him to reject show biz and study law – and in 1947, he won a job writing and delivering the news on the radio show "The Negro News-Front" on the old Blue Network. This show contributed to his knowledge of the Struggle, he grew politically aware and, around this time, joined the Communist Party. "It was the only outlet available to participate in the struggle for black people," he later wrote. He was eventually booted out of the party in 1952 for being "a black nationalist."

He was 21 when he began running, unsuccessfully, for office. He performed his Army service and, while enrolled, started writing songs and, though he considered himself to be primarily a writer, performing in a singing duo. Honorably discharged, married, divorced and married again, the father, now, of five children, he gravitated to working in ad agencies, wrote more songs and ended up in his father's real estate office where, while married to wife Maxine, he wrote *Kicks*. It should be noted that some of Oscar's best and most original compositions are about children.

Here is a review of the stand at the Music Box Theatre, in Los Angeles, by John A. Tynan, in *Down Beat*, dated August 2, 1962.

Though it appeared the year after *Kicks*, it is reflective of Oscar's reception in the early 1960's. Meant to be a review of Miles Davis, at a point when the trumpeter's popularity was at its zenith and his Columbia LP's selling in the millions, it turned out to be a valentine to Oscar, who was merely the opening act.

"While Davis got top billing during this nine-day concert series…the star – from the stand point of audience reaction – unquestionably was 35-year-old Brown.

Night after night, performance after performance, Brown's presence, repertoire, and almost uncanny rapport with his audience added up to a unique entertainment experience and, in this reviewer's conviction, the certain knowledge that in Oscar Brown, Jr. we have the most exciting entertainment figure in decades…

Brown's impact was instantly electric. He opened with his own 'Humdrum Blues;' followed by Bobby Timmons 'Dat Dere;' the tender 'Brown Baby' with its message of human dignity; the humorous 'Signifyin' Monkey;' Nat Adderley's 'Work Song,' which was delivered with powerful impact; 'Rags and Old Iron;' the hilarious 'Hazel's Hips;' a profoundly moving memorial, 'Hymn to Friday;' 'Mr. Kicks;' 'A World Full of Grey;' (ed. note: both from *Kicks*, as is 'Hazel's Hips') and the satiric and extremely funny 'Don't Blow Your Cool.'

Brown is not merely a highly effective singer but also a consummate actor who co-ordinates body movement with facial expression and gesture in the manner of Yves Montand.

He draws his material – which is largely original – from urban Negro life with a perception and sensitivity enabling him to range from political social comment to satire and humor that is essentially Negro - rich, full and warmly rewarding. And because of the universality of his grasp of the material and the power of his own theatrical personality he drives home these aspects of Negro culture with frequent stunning force.

Brown therefore, is possibly the first Negro performing artist to project a whole Negro Concept to wide audiences outside that milieu and to make it stick on its own terms. This is his gift, and this is why he appears destined for a remarkable future in theater. – Tynan."

Why didn't Oscar perform in *Kicks*, why didn't he play the leading role? He had written the book, the music and the lyrics, too, and it might have seemed like he was hogging things if he took on a fourth responsibility, that is, if it didn't seem that way already, which it did to theatre professionals. Even Anthony Newley (1931-1999) had his Leslie Bricusse (1931-   ).

I was twenty-four, good-looking, well dressed, living it up at the Palmer House, on State and Monroe, with a dozen blank checks signed by Bobby. My mother, sister, brother-in-law and friends were impressed. I had not yet met Lorraine Hansberry. Nor had I met Oscar, or Lonnie, either, but I had their recording of the show, on acetate, and it was up to me to unearth backers. I was alone, but in my bailiwick – the heart of the Loop. I knew the terrain from one end to the other, from Lake Street to Van Buren, from Fritzel's and the State & Lake to Goldblatt's department store and Minsky's Rialto, at the other. And Henrici's, the Sherman House, Brass Rail, Erlanger Theatre, Garrick Building, even the Great Northern Theatre, were all still standing.[53]

Eight years had passed since I worked in the record store and appeared in plays at the Chicago Musical College, but both were nearby.[54] A couple of blocks north, Randolph Street, the main drag and center of vice in decades past, with bordellos and gambling halls lining the east-west lane, and where many a man lost his life in a shootout,[55] was still aglitter with marquees.

One of *Kicks* "firsts" is that it was the first time someone by-passed New York City and came to Chicago instead to make a con-

---

53 So, too, were the Selwyn and Harris on Dearborn and the movie theatres the Woods, United Artists, Roosevelt, McVickers, and the Oriental, though stage shows at the latter were long gone. Around the corner from the record store, The Loop, a small film emporium, featured newsreels, then the space was converted to selling records and appliances. Separated from the Chicago Theatre by a wide alley, it was sandwiched between baseball player Mort Cooper's Menswear and a small shop that had been, at various times, a jazz joint, a donut shop and a stand-in-line steak house featuring inferior cuts of meat. This site is, at time of writing, scheduled for construction of a retail-residential complex. Walgreen's flagship store was on the corner and its basement cafeteria lured headliners such as Ella Fitzgerald between performances next door, at the Chicago Theatre. On the other side of the record store, on Randolph, was the old bus station. Both faced Marshall Field's department store.

54 An 11-story building at Van Buren, between Michigan and Wabash, originally founded by Florenz Ziegfeld, Jr.'s father, the Chicago Musical College is now a part of Roosevelt University. The great pianist Rudolph Ganz, whom I saw in concert, was its president at the time of my matriculation, as a teenager. I studied singing and then acting, with Anna Helen Reuter, who taught the Method.

55 Herbert Asbury, *"Sucker's Progress: History of Gambling in America"* Thunder's Mouth Press, New York (1938).

certed fund-raising effort for a Broadway show through the device of multiple backers' auditions. Bobby and Burt were in New York and never came to Chicago while I was raising money there.

Which raises the ethical question:

"Why raise money for a show you think will fail?"

Reminiscent of selling wealthy Argentinians one dollar and ninety-nine cent LP's for nine dollars and ninety-nine cents, or of the deceptive salesmen, at the record store on Randolph, foisting appliances on African-Americans for inflated prices, selling, as is the case with most every red-blooded American, was in my blood. And when you sell records, or ladies shoes, you sometimes receive a bonus, a "p.m.," they called it, for getting rid of hard to sell items the bosses no longer wish to keep in stock. But in this case, it was different because the producers loved the show and believed it would be a hit.

So, absent the assistance of a shrink to aid me in further cogitation leading to an indisputable truth, my lonely lucubration inclines me to say: "I did it for the experience," which sounds pretty weak, once I say it, but it's true. How else would I learn the mechanics of producing? I had come to the conclusion it would be necessary for me, as it had been for other directors, to learn to be my own producer. And I was obligated to the producers. Even though they were inexperienced they considered they were affording me an opportunity and it's true they were. "But was it ethical?" you insist.

Though the Kennedy Center was in the near offing, in 1961, the government was disinterested in producing theatre and "Arts Councils" didn't exist. A Broadway drama could still be mounted for $35,000. Producers raised money from other people; ordinarily, they didn't invest their own. Also, I was kidding myself that I might make a contribution in rearranging the script; that Bobby and Burt, and others involved would recognize my knowledge and seek my aid; that there was a possibility of my being listened to in the process of selecting the creative team. Again, I did not want to be the director of *Kicks & Co.*

Inevitably, the political concepts inherent in the script compelled my involvement and that is also why I proceeded. The producers put up the "front money," I figured out a pitch and found the Chicago (and subsequent Cleveland) investors, all but three of them, by myself, while the producers were pursuing other angles back East.

At least three investors were directly connected with the Hansberry and Brown families and I merely collected their checks.[56] As for the others, I received no other assistance from the producers and proceeded strictly on my own, having devised a cold-call phone pitch which went like this:

"Hello, Mr. Jones," I'd say, if I were lucky enough to get past their secretaries, "my name is Sidney Eden and I'd like to invite you to a backers' audition for a Broadway show, which really has a chance of making it big."

"A Broadway show?" they'd usually say, hopefully with a note of curiosity; it was that novel a notion, back then.

"At the Palmer House. I'm calling on behalf of Robert Barron Nemiroff, husband of Lorraine Hansberry, author of the prize-winning Broadway hit play and Hollywood motion picture *A Raisin In The Sun*," and I was hard to resist and, what the hell, they came to the Palmer House, it was no toilet, after all, and the good service and food and drink it promised were on the house. I had a two-room suite to which I could invite individuals, or small groups of investors and play them Oscar and Lonnie's record (which I soon tired of hearing).

I remembered names from past Progressive Party rallies and one name led to another until I found someone with many contacts - Lois Solomon, whose family owned a well-known drugstore on Rush Street, just around the corner from her home. But first I had to learn the elements of a limited partnership. For those interested: (SEE APPENDIX #8.)

I loved the historic grand hotel from which I operated. My affection for the majestic establishment dated back to childhood shop-

---

56 Earl B. Dickerson (1891-1986) "Dean of Chicago's Black lawyers," legal counsel for the largest African-American insurance company, a founder of the N.A.A.C.P. Legal Defense Fund, he, also, ran against the powerful William Dawson for alderman and won. Dickerson, who represented Lorraine's father in Hansberry vs. Lee, gave me the fish-eye when he delivered to me a check for a unit or a half unit, and a signed limited partnership agreement, under the Wabash Street entrance of the Palmer House, on a brisk Chicago evening. I have already mentioned meeting with John H. Johnson, founder of Johnson Publications (Jet, Ebony, etc.) in his Michigan Avenue office. I met Oscar's father, an attorney and successful real estate agent, in my suite at the Palmer House. A man of medium height, stout and serious, he seemed out of place dealing with anything connected with show business when he proffered a signed contact and a check for a unit in the partnership. Johnson, Dickerson and Oscar Brown, Sr. were eminent Chicagoans.

ping excursions with my mother. Originally the site of robber baron
Peter Palmer's sumptuous mansion, a gift to his bride and, later, an
oasis for the wealthy, it was less than a mile from the lakeshore and
a short walk from the bastions of trade on La Salle Street. Many
Presidents stayed there, as did Sarah Bernhardt, Eleonora Duse,
Mark Twain and Oscar Wilde.

It was like the proverbial shot of adrenalin each time I entered
its mammoth second floor lobby, ornamented with chandeliers
fitted in gold by Tiffany, dominated by grand, elevated ceilings
painted by Italian craftsmen and, at the northern end of the lobby,
an inviting, crimson carpeted stairway with wide, marble banisters
which led to the swank Empire Room where appeared the biggest
names in show business, accompanied by a perennial favorite of
that "great big town on a great big lake," the orchestra of Maestro
Ben Arden.

The bandstand was placed against the northern wall of the
oblong-shaped room so that, when one entered, the orchestra leader,
who doubled as master of ceremonies, could turn around, look
directly over the heads of the couples assembled on the dance floor,
spot the celebrity who had just arrived, and announce:

"Ladies and gentlemen, we have with us this evening the star
of that long-running hit just across the street, Miss Bea Lillie, from
Inside USA," or whomever, because the key theatre in town, the
Shubert, was right out the door and down the street, a half block
away, and the Empire Room, which seated around 350 people,
played the top acts – Jimmy Durante, Darin, Belafonte, Liberace,
Peggy Lee and Maurice Chevalier, and if they had rented it to me I
would have raised all the coin for *Kicks* in one fell swoop, one big
backers' audition.

The block long corridor in the Palmer House, a glittering
throughway with polished floors of Carrara marble, had wonderful shops, jewelers, couturiers and fancy haberdashers, with fancy
prices, even shops selling Scottish kilts and one known worldwide
for its collection of arts and crafts of the American Indian. It was
a "grand," not an ordinary, hotel, and though I knew, by then, the
amenities and cuisine of many fine hotels in Chicago, New York
and Miami, one of the greatest delights I had experienced in American hostelry, up until that time, were the creations of the Palmer

House's Creole chef in its New Orleans-style restaurant, just off a wing of the ornate, main floor corridor. My mother and I loved shrimp and we dined there with one of her boyfriends when I was twelve years old.

I took my mother to a late afternoon lunch in that establishment, in between money-raising activities, and something strange occurred which I have never forgotten and, though I am not altogether aware of its significance, it is part of the pattern of my life, as will be seen, and reckons back, I suspect, to that radiator incident of so long ago.

There were only four or five tables occupied within the commodious dining room for it was late in the afternoon. I had consumed my favorite dish, shrimp *de Jonghe*, and became aware that there was now only one other table in the whole joint at which people were sitting. It was a couple; a not unattractive, blue-eyed, washed-out blonde, with crazy eyes, the same age as I, and a much older man, her father, or uncle, or sugar daddy, I knew not which, but he was uncomfortable, I knew, because she was staring at me incessantly and with clear intent. I felt ludicrous. She was flirting with me, or at me, across the room.

My mother and I were sitting on a raised platform looking directly down at their table, approximately forty feet away, on a direct line with our own. People who ate there weren't exactly on the dole and these people, clearly, had some cash, some old time conservative money. I could tell from their clothes they were Republicans.

The man was in his late fifties, early sixties, wore glasses, was undistinguished but well dressed, not flashy, not well-tailored, but well-fixed, maybe Abercrombie, but definitely off the rack, expensive, but not tailor made. And she, I don't remember what she wore but it was very expensive, very, what they now call, "yuppy" and they showed her off pretty good, as they say in Westerns, and after a while, after a long time of staring at me and making goo-goo eyes, which all of us including the waiter could see, were meant to see, she rose from the table, to her partner's somewhat dismay, and showed exactly what she had by going to the john. I was, clearly, supposed to follow her, but my mother understandably chimed in, "She sure is making a play for you," and I took it as a cue to inaction.

Someone cleverer than I would have known what to do, and my Hamlet-like inaction, it soon occurred to me, was unbecoming to an Existential Man of Action. Reticence to commit to involvement and possible adventure is, in my chosen field, a failure. I did not boff the babe in the bedroom of the upstairs two room suite and fleece her and her avuncular paramour of their well-inherited boodle. She looked like trouble this young nymphomaniac did, or else she was vindictively "getting back" at her aging lunch mate. But trouble though she be, trouble can sometimes be fun if it comes in the right package. My unwillingness to improvise, my insistence in taking the path of Hitchcockian pre-planning as opposed to Felliniesque improvisation, my hesitancy in acting on impulse, my cowardice troubled me, as if I were fearful of the unknown, of being pushed upon a steaming radiator. And similar troubling episodes were to follow. [57]

I continued collecting money at the backers' auditions. I induced my friend, Irving J. Rosenbloom, the advertising man who had headed the Independent Voters of Illinois, to buy a share in the show and, then, dug up a whole group people of whom the producers had never heard a word before. I compiled a list of Chicago investors, wealthy, politically liberal citizens with an inclination for the arts.

And always staying within the confines of the Palmer House, I played the record and I gave a pitch and I was, as my sister who, with her friends and husband invested a total of $8,000, "dynamic." I was hard to resist.

The subject of the show was so important it was not that difficult to sell, but inducing people to affix their signatures takes talent, for people are reluctant to commit themselves. Within two weeks I collected $100,000, 25% of the budget, the equivalent of $2,500,000 in today's money, considering that a similar show would cost $10,000,000 today. By the time I had the 100 thousand g's, Bobby and Burt, back in New York, having made a money-raising trip to Philadelphia, had collected under $20,000.

And then I met Diana Sands and we fell in love.

---

57 Perhaps, I had a surfeit of "dangerous" love, forced departures down rust-ridden, fire escapes, naked, clothes in hand, and other transgressions of the Tenth Commandment, though I be not the seducer but the one seduced.

****

A Raisin In The Sun was making a triumphant return to the Blackstone Theatre, in Chicago, where it became a hit three years earlier. I am not certain if I fell in love with Diana the woman, or Diana, the actress.

We met at a party I hosted at the Palmer House. I did not meet Claudia McNeil, the star of the production, that night. I spoke at length with Bobby Dean Hooks (Robert Hooks), who was playing the role of George Murchison, and Douglas Turner Ward (future author of the plays *Day Of Absence* and *Happy Ending*), who was replacing Ossie Davis, in the role created by Poitier. In 1967, Hooks and Ward, along with director, Gerald Krone, would found the celebrated Negro Ensemble Company. And I met Frances Foster, who had replaced Ruby Dee, after being her understudy from the start, and Ed Hall, who was now playing the role of Assagai, after being one of the moving men on Broadway and, likewise, understudying, from the production's inception.

When Diana and I met we were spontaneously attracted to each other. She was an eloquent artist onstage; offstage, she was funny and, often, caustic. I went to the show every night and when I picked her up afterwards we went nightclubing on Rush Street. Mixed couples in public were a rarity and people couldn't stop staring wherever we would go. We were all over the Palmer House together; people stared like mad. We saw Frances Faye in the biggest Outfit joint on Rush Street. They never stopped staring. The hatred directed toward us, everywhere but on the South Side, was tangible, and I experienced, first hand, why Mel and Lorraine Williamson had chosen to live in the Apple instead of their hometown.

Diana and I were present opening night when Dinah Washington took over Roberts Show Lounge, renaming it Dinahland. Redd Foxx opened for her, with spates of hilarious obscenities. Then, Red Saunders and band struck-up an overblown fanfare, and Queen Dinah entered drunkenly, wearing an off-kilter tiara and a gauzy, chiffon gown. She made no visible effort to conceal her inebriated state, and, attempting to seat herself on a high stool, she comically slipped-off nearly to the floor, but Saunders cleverly stopped her fall. Her sixth husband would find her dead from sleeping pills in two years time.

Diana never spoke about the hostile stares that followed wherever we went, but they troubled her. Anti-miscegenation laws were still in force in border-states and in the South. When we returned to New York we could be comfortable only in Harlem and Greenwich Village.

Sometimes, when I picked up Diana after the show, we would pile into the backseat of a car with Howland Chamberlain, who was playing the lone white actor in Lorraine's play. The car was driven by Roy Glenn (Roy E. Glenn) who was playing the role of Bobo, in the show. Roy began his career in radio, on "Amos & Andy," and in Duke Ellington's *Jump For Joy*, but his best-known performances are as Rum Daniels, Pearl Bailey's beau and the manager of the heavyweight champ, in Otto Preminger's *Carmen Jones*, and as Sidney Poitier's father, in *Guess Who's Coming To Dinner*.

Roy Glenn was one heavy dude. He sat at the steering wheel, examining me through the rear view mirror as I scrunched between Howland Chamberlain and Diana. Roy scowled the patented scowl he was so good at scowling throughout his film career, and thought to himself, "What's she doing with this white boy? They'll never make it; she's wasting her time."

Howland, the blacklisted, rat-faced, brilliant Howland, was jovial, happy to be working after suffering the ravages of McCarthyism. He's best remembered as Dana Andrews' oily, pre-War boss, in *Best Years Of Our Lives*, who, in the gut-wrenching scene in the cubbyhole office overlooking the drug store floor, refuses to rehire the ex-G.I. Howland also scored as the desk clerk, in Stanley Kramer's, *High Noon*, and as the corrupt CPA, in Abraham Polonsky's anti-capitalist, film-noir *Force Of Evil*, starring John Garfield. I liked him best and as Burt Lancaster's crooked mouthpiece in Jules Dassin's, *Brute Force* (1947).

Howland got along amiably with his fellow actors in the, otherwise, all-black cast. But there was great friction between Diana and the woman who wowed Broadway as Mama Younger, Claudia McNeil. Claudia, in each performance, as part of her role as Mama and at a key point in the play, slapped Diana, who was playing the role of her daughter, Beneatha. According to Diana, Claudia was hitting her harder with each showing. So, Diana decided to bring Claudia "up on charges" of "unprofessionalism" before the Chicago branch of Actors' Equity.

In his memoir, Phil Rose relates: "In our cast we had a built-in discontent mechanism in the person of…Claudia McNeil. I could be fairly certain that few weeks would go by without getting a call from our stage manager…that Claudia, again in a dispute with one of our actors, was threatening to quit if the other actor wasn't fired." Rose goes on to say McNeil was careful not to cross swords with Sidney Poitier.

I knew about slapping and getting slapped onstage, but Diana was not an easy person. She was certain she could handle the situation. And it had become necessary at one point in my money-raising activities that I return to my employers, in New York.

When I arrived, I met Oscar and Lonnie, finally, and established good relationships with both. Why not? We were the only hipsters involved in the project. It occurred to me that I should go to Cleveland with them. Again, I courted black leaders, did especially well with wealthy matrons, and booked the main hall of a lovely landmark Cleveland hotel, the Park Lane, where Lonnie and Oscar performed in person. I raised $36,000. When I came back to the office on Bleecker Street, I was in sweet and received thanks and compliments from Lorraine, Bobby and Burt. This was my first meeting with Lorraine, who spoke with me independently.

"I hear you're knocking them dead in Chicago! You're doing a great job!" she said.

I don't know if she knew about my relationship with Diana. I did not realize, at the time, how much of the character Beneatha was Lorraine, herself. I inarticulately accepted her compliments. Although her public words were militant, her replies in televised interviews were delivered in well-modulated, carefully chosen words. She was refined and articulate. Her thinking was flawless on social and political matters. And she was attractive with her coal black eyes, lovely complexion and short bob hairdo.

Also complimentary of my efforts was Walter Fried, who had been hired as general manager. Short, liver-lipped, with wavy gray hair, and accusatory eyes, Wally was wise and tough. He studied to be a classical pianist and began each morning playing Chopin

Etudes on the grand in his office, near Steinway Hall, then, haggled on the phone the remainder of the day with scene shop owners, ticket brokers, union reps and numerous other suppliers. Wally, having started as a company manager, progressed to being a general manger and, then, producer. With Kermit Bloomgarden, he co-produced *Death Of A Salesman* and *All My Sons*. The show he general-managed after *Kicks* was *Man Of La Mancha*.

In mid-March, without warning, Bobby announced Dave Garroway had agreed to devote an entire morning of his NBC *Today Show* to a backers' audition of *Kicks*, with Oscar performing and Lonnie accompanying him. A few months earlier, Joe Glaser had booked Oscar on Garroway's show to sing a couple of songs. Dave was so impressed he went, with his daughter, to see Oscar perform at the Village Vanguard and, now, offered Oscar an entire two-hour spot. No one realized the implications of doing so without approval from the Securities Exchange Commission, but Oscar and the producers jumped at the offer. Garroway's importance as a cultural influence for good in the pre-assassination, bicentennial year of 1961 needs retelling.

He began his career in Chicago radio as a disc jockey for WMAQ, the NBC affiliate, after returning from service in WW II, at a time when Chicago radio was in its heyday and WMAQ was heard throughout the Midwest and beyond. His easy-going personality camouflaged a politically aware intellectual who loved and promoted good music, jazz in particular, and who, privately, suffered from severe depression.

When introduced to national television audiences on *Garroway at Large,* telecast from Chicago, he proved so appealing that Sylvester "Pat" Weaver, President of NBC, appointed him host of the brand new *Today Show*, in 1951, a position he retained until he voluntarily retired. He was one of the inventors of the talk show, introduced a new conversational Chicago-style, typified by Studs Terkel and Hugh Downs, and his trademark sign-off was to say "Peace" and hold up two fingers, a gesture which became ubiquitous.

On March 28, 1961, while I sat by the phone in the tiny "office," where *A Raisin In The Sun* was written, waiting to field calls from possible investors and with Bobby sitting in Lorraine's apartment doing likewise, Oscar and a very nervous Lonnie Levister, assisted only by the great drummer Elvin Jones, John Coltrane's regular percussionist, (brother of Hank [piano] and Thad [trumpet & leader]), performed the trimmed-down backers' audition of the show. Lonnie was blotto. He had been drinking for 30 days straight. He wrote me recently saying, "Went to sleep at 4 A.M., up at 6 A.M. Trying to get myself together I drank 12 cups of coffee in 2 hours. Left me with my hands shaking so bad I couldn't play the piano to work on finishing the arrangements, laying on the bed groaning, 'I pushed it too far, this time, I'll never be able to do this.' But, I did and I swore I would never do that to myself again. The punch line was the *Daily News* review: 'The whole show was presented in a calm and confident manner.'"

Over the airwaves they were giving out our phone number to millions of people and, as I stretched out in the Castro convertible lounger Bobby favored, the phone, with its many lines, began to ring continuously. People were calling in from all over the country, and before the *Today Show* was over we had raised $440,000!

This included the money I brought in from Chicago and Cleveland and money that Bobby and Burt had secured in Philadelphia. Like Zero Mostel in *The Producers*, we were over-capitalized!

But as soon as the Garroway show ended a telegram arrived from the SEC saying "Cease and desist." It had never been tried before. No producer had ever gone on TV or radio to solicit money for a Broadway show, but, according to the SEC it was against the law and, as a result of *Kicks*, it has never been done since! Because of the *Kicks* broadcast, the number of people whom producers can solicit before being required to submit extensive filing papers to the SEC, for approval, would eventually be limited to thirty-six (later expanded to forty-five). But even more serious consequences were to follow.

I distinctly remember seeing, on that particular date, that the producers had received a contribution from Republican Attorney General of the State of New York, Louis J. Lefkowitz. Within a day or two, the main lawyer for *Kicks*, Clarence Jones of the firm of Kinoy and Rossmore, straightened out the SEC squawks and the overcapitalized monies (some $40,000) were repaid.

We now had the money with which to produce the show. But, in the effort to raise that budget, a great deal of money (again, approximately $40,000) had been expended on hotels, airline tickets, backers' auditions and other incidental items.

Soon after the Garroway show I flew back to Chicago to see my family and indulge in more nightclubbing with Diana. *Raisin* was shuttering and, soon, we would be together in New York. I told Herb Rogers I would not be able to direct for him that summer.

While I was in Chicago, The Bay of Pigs fiasco occurred. In my mind, it further confirmed the warlike tendencies of the Kennedy Administration. Little did I know the reality of the situation. I was happy to be working in the theatre. I was in love and, as far as *Kicks* was concerned, the next move was to find a star to play Mr. Kicks and someone to direct the *shmeer*.

9

Paging Mr. Abbott

But Bobby did not want to hire a director; he did not want to relinquish control. He knew it was the most important decision he would make, as important as signing a star to play Mr. Kicks.

Put yourself in his shoes; what he had accomplished was nearly miraculous. He made a moneymaking hit song out of thin air, contributed greatly (if only through inspiration) to an enormous Broadway hit and he and his famous spouse were in the forefront of an historical and righteous movement. He had "discovered" Oscar and made him an up-and-coming recording star. And now, he had amassed a record amount of money for a Broadway show and achieved a much-publicized nationwide television showing, on a major venue. I cannot imagine he was happy that his marriage had detonated, but other than that he was on a lucky streak.

And he hired me. Could he have raised the money without me? Absolutely. But without the Cleveland and Chicago money – for which I was responsible – the capitalization effort might have been halted with the SEC "cease and desist" order. Dissemination of the encomiums that were given out with the prospectus might have been more severely debated. Having nearly a third of the budget in tow, prior to the *Today Show* and the SEC stoppage order, was certainly beneficial to the enterprise.

Now, though I told them it didn't make sense, the producers wanted to proceed with casting and hiring the other members of the creative team before hiring a director; just the opposite of how it's supposed to be done. I exerted as little influence on Bobby as did Kennedy on Khrushchev, that same June, in Vienna.

They were not only ready to commit to a choreographer without having a director in place, they decided to hire two. They liked two guys, couldn't decide which, and hired both. I told them it was unheard of and meant paying two salaries, but both Donald McKayle AND Walter Nicks were signed. Puzzled by the idea initially, they worked well as a team when the time came. It turned out to be one of the best decisions the producers made.

I took Bobby and Burt to meet famous set designer Rouben Ter-Arutunian and, then, William and Jean Eckert, who won Tonys regularly, but the producers opted for Jack Blackman. For costume designer, they chose Edith Luytens Bel Geddes (1893-1958), widow of the noted architect and industrial and stage designer, Norman Bel Geddes (1893-1958). Her moniker, the Bel Geddes part, would be one of the few, "recognizable" names in the opening night program.

Since the choreographers had been hired, it was obvious a musical director must be hired immediately in order for casting to proceed. I could have taken this opportunity to meet, say, Lehman Engel or Jay Blackton, or others, and feather my nest by making valuable future contacts, but I decided to militate on behalf of my friend, brilliant, fun-loving, Jack Lee, with whom I worked at the Cleveland Playhouse, Cain Park and, then, the State Music Theatre of Maine, where we did a smart production of Jerome Kern's *Roberta*, with Jack playing the Bob Hope part and Ethel Smith (1902-1996), the organist who sold millions of records for Decca, in the title role.

Getting that first big Broadway break is the tough nut for designers and musical directors, in particular. There was no question in my mind that Jack was headed to the top and I was glad to do him this *mitzvah*. As musical director, he would also be choral arranger and orchestra conductor. Bobby and Burt quickly gave him the nod. Jack's appropriateness for the position, despite his being white, was apparent. He had worked at Karamu's inter-racial theatre in Cleveland and had been musical director at the Cleveland Playhouse. The producers knew from speaking with him that Jack was committed to the same principles as they. Donnie and Walter were excited to be working with him, and Jack and Oscar went on the

Mike Wallace Show together, a platform Lorraine used effectively months earlier.

Jack hired Joe ("Big Joe") Benjamin as the show's AFM, union contractor (the man who hires the orchestra), making him the first African-American in such a position in the annals of legit theatre.[58] Jack, and the choreographers, selected Dorothea Freitag to be the rehearsal pianist. She would score the dance arrangements, too. The musical and dance elements of the show were in place and the designated participants, though inexperienced except for the very talented Ms. Freitag, would come through admirably despite the *tsores* and *meshugass* ahead.

We were, then, ready to audition principals and to look for a star to play Mr. Kicks, while we continued searching for a director. These important details became my main concern. The Ambassador Theatre (as seen in Bob Fosse's *All That Jazz*) was booked for auditions and squadrons of talented African-American dancers, singers and actors poured forth; there were so many gifted people of color who, for years, had had no outlet, no permanent, well-funded theatre, or venue in which to perform! Word of the content of *Kicks* had reached the theatre community and the public at large.

All this occurred at a time when James Farmer's Freedom Riders left Washington, D.C. on their initial journey through the South. On Mother's Day, members of the Ku Klux Klan, in Birmingham, Alabama, attacked them. Bull Connors, the local Commissioner of Public Safety, conveniently delayed arriving to protect them and, in so doing, became a notorious national figure. John Lewis, of Georgia, was a victim of that brutal attack. The Rides continued southward through those weeks.

****

In my copy of *Kicks*, from that summer of 1961, are casting notes made opposite the names of characters in Oscar's script. This is an appropriate place for a brief synopsis of the show, one, not entirely free of occasional commentary. I am quoting from the original script which I have before me.

---

58 Joe, a great bassist, with Joe Malichi (piano) and Roy Haynes (drums) comprised Sarah Vaughn's backup trio for years.

Kicks, as mentioned before, began with a prologue, a mini-morality, anti-capitalist play-let in which everyone, Burglar, Disc Jockey, Policeman, Teenagers and just plain folks, it develops, are all crooked and can be bribed. They, along with Mr. Kicks, who has appeared "perched in mid-air" on the Moon, urges them on, singing "Take The Money."

"Take the money, use your head;
Supplement your daily bread."

A madcap ballet ensues in which everyone runs around crazily. They all exit, leaving Mr. Kicks, who, then, sings:

"Permit me to introduce myself.
The name is Mr. Kicks"

The very next scene takes place in the executive offices of Will Wenchin ("wenching," get it?) of Orgy Magazine, a thinly disguised Hugh Hefner. There's a buxom blonde pinup girl (Laurie Lee) on the make for Will and anyone else who'll pay the rent. She sings "What's In It For Me?" after *Kicks* (The Devil) has materialized magically upon the scene. Having served little purpose advancing the plot, Laurie Lee exits.

Will, it turns out, has sold himself to Kicks long ago in order to become pre-eminent in his field, but now, with rival rags like "Stud Monthly" competing with him, Will's continued preeminence is in jeopardy. Kicks claims Orgy needs more controversy and he asks:

> "What's the most controversial subject in this country today?"

> "Birth control? Creeping socialism," Will guesses.

> "Inter-racial sex," Kicks answers.

And he commands Will to launch a Crusade for Brotherhood with the emphasis on inter-racial sex. Kicks champions the utilization of innocent Negro college beauty queens as cover girls and inside-the-fold pin-ups.

For starters he has chosen one at Freedman University in the Deep South, a girl who comes from a prominent family and who has been arrested in a dime store sit-in demonstration. Says Kicks:

"There's something sickeningly healthy about this sit-in business that just rubs me the wrong way."

Will, succumbs (after pages of endless dialogue) and sings "Cutthroat Competition." In this long scene there have been jokes about false patriotism, the Cold War, foreign aid and Jack Paar.

The next scene finds Kicks secreting himself in the bushes on the campus of Freedman University while, "the all- Negro student body spills out of the building, books in hand," to perform a major production number, "Hooray for Friday."

"Today is Friday, bye-bye books and classes
'Cause Friday is my day to swing where all the jazz is."

Enter June, whom Kicks has targeted. She begins distributing leaflets for the upcoming sit-in, as Kicks reveals himself and engages the students. He, The Devil, gets a big laugh when they ask him where he's from and he answers, *Chicago.*

Soon, student sit-in demonstartors make an unceremonious entrance and Kicks uses his wiles to convince the students he's there on a special assignment connected with the sit-in movement.

Left alone, he lures June into accepting the offer of becoming "Negro Orgy Maiden of the Month," in his scheme to promote inter-racial copulation. She sings "While I Am Still Young"

"My frolicking heart feels
like doing some cartwheels…"

The Students have re-entered, during her song, to provide the choral background. Kicks even joins in and they all, conveniently, and without motivation of any kind, exit after the song (according to the script).

June's beau, Earnest Black, a composer, enters to initiate a lengthy love scene, alternately vacuous and coy. Earnest, being earnest, is naturally resistant to Junes's cooperation in Kicks' scheme and let's June know it in page after page of dialogue, only terminating when, left alone, he turns to self-flagellation because of his lack of finances.

Torn between the Scylla and Charybdis of the spiritual rewards of a pure life devoted to art versus the iniquities of the capitalist system so dependent on wherewithal and dumb luck, and slightly jealous of his girlfriend's impending fame, he sings "Opportunity, Please Knock."

> "Don't land in my room
> With a treacherous boom…
> No, Opportunity, just knock."

The following scene finds us at lunch counter in a dime store near the University campus, where we discover a broadly comical, white Waitress who picks her teeth and coughs on the food as she serves it to a comical white Travelling Salesman, who turns green at the drop of a hat. This newcomer is seated adjacent to swinish white Townspeople and they are soon joined by leather-jacketed Policemen who behave in a Gestapo-like manner.

In walk Freedman University Students and one of them, Eggy, orders a hot dog and an orange drink. But they are confronted by young, local white Hoodlums, who come upon the scene and, inevitably, Kicks, who mockingly admonishes the Students (in song) to "Turn The Other Cheek."

Enter our hero, Ernest, who turns out to be a boyhood chum of one of the Hoodlums and, after a momentary and unconvincing confrontation, a defiant Ernest orders a hot dog and an orange drink and "BLACKOUT," we don't know if he is served them or not.

Scene 5 – by now, 50 some minutes into the show – finds a grimacing Kicks hanging from the moon again, this time eating a hot dog, washed down with an orange drink and not liking either of them at all. He tips the cup over disdainfully. He seems to have emptied it, but a shriek comes from the audience and the spotlight reveals an outraged Woman, doused with orange juice. She grabs her coat and stomps up the aisle, yelling for the manager. The spot returns to Kicks, who jokes:

> "And who said theatrical realism is dead?"

Kicks picks up a phone and calls a character about whom we've previously heard nothing whatever, Silky Satin. Kicks wants a special woman for a special task and this slick dude, Silky, without any preamble but a vamp, now sings about someone else about whom we've known zilch – Hazel, a lady who, he rhapsodizes in song, will fill the bill for "Negro Orgy Maiden of the Month." And soon, lo and behold, she materializes in the campus soda grill, of which, conveniently, she is the manager.

Earnest Black, it also happens, works jerking sodas at the grill and Hazel, to complicate matters, is in love with Earnest, who is in love with June. Kicks nixes Silky's Orgy candidate because he knows Hazel from another picture, it develops, and the fact that he knows her corrupted past makes her an inappropriate candidate. Kicks wants someone who is "a real credit to her race."

Hazel, who, in truth, has already decided to reform and wants no further part of the fast talker from Down Below, now sings the lovely aria "I'll Get You Killed," a helluva sentiment to introduce in a musical comedy, and a ragged contrast to what's come before. Sondheim and Bernstein, in *West Side Story*, can get away with Anita singing of death, in "Your Own Kind," but in the theatre imitation is rarely an effective form of flattery.

Earnest asks Hazel for the night off so he may attend the prom with June, but June sees Hazel in Earnest's arms, takes offense, and decides to go to the prom with, of all people, The Devil, himself, Mr. Kicks!!

CURTAIN
(End of Act One)

Three act musicals went out with Rudolph Friml, but no one told Oscar, or Bobby until the script was circulated. When things were falling apart in the final rehearsals, Bobby reworked the script after delaying the opening, reduced it to two acts and the opening night program read:

Book by Oscar Brown, Jr.
in collaboration with
Robert Barron Nemiroff.

But even two acts turned out to be three and a half tedious hours of floundering gags, endless, vapid love scenes, *Hellapoppin'* pranks between comical students and nutty professors, a mimicking of Thomas Mann's *Doctor Faustus* where the Devil plants tunes in a composer's head, Brechtian posturing and mediocre lyrics, not to say the show lacked merit. Nichelle Nichols, Carols Arthur, Jack Lee's arrangements, Donnie and Walter's choreography, Dorothy's work in rehearsal, were admirable, but let the reader decide, for every review written of the show is included herein. The remainder of the long synopsis of the play is contained in Appendix #9.

Jack Lee (and others associated with the production) suggested to me that, in addition to Bobby's having revised some of the script, Lorraine Hasberry re-wrote sections of the final presentation. Jack said this over the decades and reiterated it to me in his final years. He was there during those rehearsals when both Bobby and Lorraine came in with pages of rewrites, daily, before the Chicago opening.

10

"Tell Me About the Rabbits, George"

While the casting without a director continued, Diana returned from the national tour of *Raisin* and moved back into her Manhattan apartment on 22nd Street, between Ninth and Tenth Avenues. It was the pits.

We seldom went out as we did in Chicago. The stares continued most everywhere we went. But there were pleasant evenings when we saw Nipsey Russell, at the Baby Grand, and sat with him between sets. We ate at Tony's in the Village, bumped into Godfrey Cambridge and sat on a stoop off Sheridan Square for a visit. They seldom stared in the Village. At that time, few really knew who Diana was and I believe that bothered her.

So most of the time she stayed in the small, dimly-lit pad and bemoaned her lack of work; there were no parts for her; no one was writing roles for black girls; her agent was ineffective, she said. So, we fucked and, then, went to sleep, or argued – incessantly - about nothing. But it was, really, about the fact she had no work. The apartment was dingy. The floor was covered with linoleum of a putrid pattern and hue and caked with dirt. Cleaning up a shit hole of a pad in a crummy neighborhood, such as it was then, was no oc-cupation for an out of work genius of an actress.

The actor-director, Harold Scott, who would understudy the role of Mr. Kicks (and play the role in one portentous performance) and who, later, became the Artistic Director of Philadelphia's Playhouse-in-the-Park, lived across the street. He was available to console her and was no threat to our romance. I welcomed the solace he afforded the temperamental Diana.

We engaged in an ugly imbroglio that summer in which she attacked me with a broom, the one with which we swept the dirty, linoleum floor. I hate being hit with a broom. It's undignified. And it happened more than once. The first time may have been when I teased her with rumors of her supposed lesbianism, which she protested with unconvincing vigor. She was sitting atop me, about to be self-impaled, her apple-sized knockers alert as was my attentive pecker and she looked me in the eye and said, flippantly, but seriously, "Baby, I ain't no lesbian, I'm all woman," and she mounted me and posed, hands on hips, challengingly.

There had been rumors, often from fallen woman who knew about such things, that Diana engaged in what is known Uptown as "girl talk" with a famous woman writer and I thought at the time, "The lady doth protest too much." Her reading of the denial bothered me; it was unconvincing to an expert liar such as I.

Whatever it was that started the argument that led to the implementation of the beat-up broom, the weapon left no mark upon my body. But on the cognitive and judgmental recesses of my mind, which contemplated, that summer, the continued worth of our relationship, it left a considerable dent.

Her appearances on stage and in film show Diana to be a real sexpot and that's the role she would excel in when she played the prostitute in *The Owl and The Pussycat,* opposite Alan Alda. Julian Barry stage-managed that show, and his experience with her is illuminating. Initially, I asked Julian for his recollections of Phil Rose, the show's producer, and he volunteered this story about Diana, which is in his autobiography *"My Night With Orson."* To quote Julian:

"For a few months I replaced Lenny Auerbach as stage manager on the show (*Owl & The Pussycat*) I got to know Diana slightly. First about her. She was difficult. Some nights didn't feel like acting and said she was sick. One night onstage, she exited into a bathroom and signaled to me that she was finished. Since she had already warned me that she wasn't likely to play the whole evening I dressed the understudy (Rose Gregorio) and had her standing by. So Diana exited into the 'bathroom' of the set and on cue Rose emerged in the same costume. It threw Alan Alda for a loop, but oddly enough there was little disturbance in the audience considering the abrupt change of ethnicity of the main character. I learned a lesson that night. Audiences sitting in the dark watching a story unfold are like kids. They just want to see the story unfold. As for Phil Rose…He showed up from time to time to kiss Diana's ass to make her behave. With little result. She was fun."

Perhaps, the disease that led to her early death was already affecting Diana's state of health (and mind) at the time.

****

The process of casting the roles in *Kicks*, in advance of a director being signed, continued.

I asked Johnnie Ray to audition for the Devil role and it was okayed by his agent, but only on a hush-hush basis. Ray's star had faded and hits such as "Cry" and "Little White Cloud That Cried" were faded memories. Wally Fried lent his office and his piano, on 57th Street, and I greeted a nervous, but outgoing ex-pop idol and his accompanist. I ushered them into the inner sanctum of Wally's office where the plans for many a hit were made. Sounds like crazy casting, but I thought my idea had possibilities. Johnnie Ray's audition did not impress anyone. I felt sorry for the singer and responsible for putting him to the trouble. The producers probably thought I had lost my mind.

Though I had certainly acted as a co-producer, or an associate producer, at the least, my current title was "Casting Director," and it was beginning to dawn on me that I should have received a "finder's fee" for all the money I had raised, a finder's fee of something like $10, 000.

And, in my position as casting director, I thought Roscoe Lee Browne would be fine as Mr. Kicks, but he couldn't sing it. Godfrey Cambridge auditioned for the role, as well. Among those seen for Ernest were James Earl Jones, Ernie Andrews, Ivan Dixon, Brock Peters and Robert (Bobby Dean) Hooks. My choice was Billy Dee Williams, who had returned to the stage after a long absence.[59] But

---

59 He first appeared as a child actor in the 1944 Kurt Weill-Ira Gershwin, *Firebrand Of Florence*, a musical about Benvenuto Cellini. A few months earlier Williams had returned to Broadway, now, a grown man, in the 1960 play, *Cool World*, co-written and directed by filmmaker, Robert Rossen.

the role went to Lonnie Satin, which was confusing, especially for press agents, because Al Freeman, Jr., who understudied in *Cool World* (he listed it as his Broadway debut) was everyone's choice in the role of "Silky Satin."

The role of Hazel Sharpe, the subject of "Hazel's Hips," a decision crucial to the show's success, occasioned a strange turning in the course of the production. Lorraine Hansberry, to the surprise of the staff, was present at, and became part of, the crucial auditions and the discussions that followed. Some of these occurred without my presence and I was the casting director. I wondered what I had done wrong or whom I had offended.

Was it because Bobby felt he no longer needed me, that he did not need me in the first place, that if he had waited and merely used the Garroway show he could have capitalized *Kicks* on his own? Or did Lorraine have something against me? Was it because of my affair with Diana? The discerning reader will know sooner than I did by careful reading.

Typical of Bobby's suddenly excluding me from important discussions after the money was raised, was his delegating me to handle, on my own, the "open" calls, where non-union performers were seen. Bobby asked me to do so without any other member of the artistic staff, much less he and Burt, being present, providing merely an assistant to handle the flow of traffic. Such events can be tedious and even depressing, but it's part of the business and a good way to find new talent, but Bobby and Burt did not attend. I believe they were with Lorraine, seeing principal actors that agents had recommended, thus eliminating my input.

With a couple of hundred or more performers lined-up outside the door, in a long gone rehearsal hall on 46th between Broadway and Eighth, I saw, on my own, the most exciting person of the hundreds who auditioned for *Kicks*. A tall, thin, toothy, twenty year-old, fronted by a personal manager and accompanied by a jazz trio, sang "Lover Come Back To Me," the Sigmund Romberg-Oscar Hammerstein II operetta oldie, performed by the very square Jeanette MacDonald in movies, subsequently swung into life by Billie Holiday. This young woman's swinging rendition, performed with such a warm, individual sound, and great musicianship, reminded everyone present that the technique and creativity of the jazz singer deserves a high place in our culture. She was a knockout. I told Bobby, Burt, Jack, Donnie and Walter Nicks, even Dorothea Freitag, who was a helluva musician, but the producers declined giving her a "call-back" and the young woman, whose name was Dionne Warwick, waited a few more months before becoming an "all time great," as they used to say at the Palace of Audible Dreams.

Diana worked with Jack Lee in his apartment in the Village and, then, auditioned for the Hazel role. She was, according to Jack, "brilliant." Many women had been seen for the role of Laurie Lee Southern, who belts "What's In It For Me," a number meant to be a showstopper. For that role, Jack worked with Kathryn Damon (1930-1987).[60]

Then, in a hush-hush conference held in the Bleecker Street office-apartment, of which I was not informed, and over the strenuous objections of Jack, Donnie and Walter, Lorraine rejected both Diana and "Skipper" Damon. Additionally, Lorraine insisted a personal friend of hers, someone who Jack Lee called "an opera singer," be hired as the boffo-type gold digger, Laurie Lee. As a consequence, in performance the song became a dud.

But when Nichelle Nichols appeared onstage to audition for the role of Hazel, she became everyone's selection. She had appeared as a singer with Duke Ellington and Lionel Hampton and went on to fame and stardom in TV's *Star Trek*, but this would be her major stage debut. A less experienced Vi Velasco, who recorded with Zoot Sims, would be cast as the beauty queen, June.

Buck Henry (1930-2020) was considered for Will Wenchin, but he took a pass. His star was on the rise. Other casting notes regarding Buck, who wasn't cast, and Carol Arthur,[61] who was, are listed in Appendix #10., which also includes a complete listing of chorus members.

Still, no director had been hired, so I continued to suggest and, then, implore the producers to see George Abbott. It became an annoyance to Bobby, so I began calling directors I wanted to meet. Since childhood, one of my idols was Burgess Meredith (1907-

---

60 Kathryn Damon was a gifted actress-singer who wowed every audience before which she appeared and ended up a star in sitcoms until her premature passing.

61 In a bit part – *The Waitress* - that elicited both critical commentary and big-time laughs from the audience.

1997). What a career! Born in Cleveland, making his debut in Eva Le Gallienne's production of *Romeo & Juliet*, in 1930, a lifetime member of Actors Studio, the revered actor's nickname was "Buzz."

In 1935 he appeared opposite Katherine Cornell (1893-1974) in *The Barretts Of Wimpole Street*, directed by Cornell's husband, Guthrie McClintic (1893-1961)[62] In September of that same year, McClintic directed him in a landmark of the American Theatre that catapulted Buzz to the top of his profession – *Winterset*, by Maxwell Anderson (1898-1959).[63]

Anderson, then, wrote two more plays in verse in which Buzz starred: *High Tor* and *Star Wagon*. With the production of these three plays in particular, even though the last two were commercial failures, Burgess Meredith advanced to the front rank of American actors. Great hopes for our stage were invested in his future career. But he went to Hollywood, instead. I was very conversant with the Anderson plays and, as a young actor, memorized Mio's speeches diligently. As late as 1952, Buzz and Margo (1917-1995), wife of the actor Eddie Albert, repeated their roles in *Winterset* in a radio adaptation, to which I listened with avid interest.

I was three years old when my mother took me to see Buzz and Lon Chaney, Jr. in the film version of John Steinbeck's novel, *Of Mice And Men*. As we left the movie theatre, and for weeks thereafter, we would play a game in which she cued me to ape the beetle-browed Chaney, and I would respond by saying:

> "Georooorge, oh ,Geooorge, tell me about the rabbits, George; tell me about the rabbits, George."

Throughout the 30's and 40's Buzz was a major Hollywood star, adept at both comedy and drama.[64] His appearance as the correspondent and wartime hero, Ernie Pyle, whose reporting was read daily by millions, soldier and civilian alike, in *Story Of G.I. Joe* (1942), was a great success, but, after the War, he fell afoul of

---

62 A union generally considered to be a "lavender marriage"

63 The cast included Margo and Eduardo Cianelli. It was filmed the following year, directed by Alfred Santell.

64 He married and divorced actress, Paulette Goddard (he had been married twice before) and, then, wed Kaja Sundsten, to whom he remained married for 46 years. I saw Buzz at the Studebaker Theatre, in 1953, when he played the title role in *The Remarmarkable Mr. Pennypacker*. Buzz lost this juicy role to Clifton Webb, who starred in the 1959 film version. Buzz was still steaming from it, with good reason, as he was the one who made a hit of Liam O'Brian's play. He directed *A Season In The Sun* (1950), written by theatre critic and humorist, Wolcott Gibbs.

HUAC, which summoned him to Washington, and his testimony before that insidious body resulted in his being blacklisted in Hollywood for seven years.

In 1958, Buzz directed blacklisted Zero Mostel (1915-1977) in an adaptation of James Joyce's *Ulysses*, called *Ulysses In Nighttown*, which travelled from off to on Broadway. I did not see *Thurber Carnival*, which he also directed a year before, though it ran for over two hundred performances (88 of them with the poorly-sighted James Thurber, himself, in the cast), but both productions showed his ability to deal with source material and translate it into theatre.

By 1961, Meredith was no longer a leading man. Because of his short stature he had always been what they called an "eccentric" leading man. Now he was a character actor, whose last appearance on Broadway, as an actor, was in the 1956, all-star revival of George Bernard Shaw's *Major Barbara*, playing the Cockney, Snobby Price. But my having so recently seen Zero in *Rhinosceros* and connecting it with Burgess Meredith was why I suggested Buzz to Bobby.

With the latter's approval, I set up a dinner date at the Seafarer Restaurant, on Eighth Street, between Waverly and Sixth Avenue, in Greenwich Village. Given over now to emporia hawking souvenirs and T-shirts of a once sinful city, featuring hookahs and crack pipes, futons and foam rubber, the art of tattooing and the piercing of ears, eyebrows, noses, tongues, mammilla, genitalia and almost any other portion of the human anatomy, male, female, bi-sexual and transgender, at almost any time of the day or night, by appointment only, it was a classy block, then, in 1961, where book and record stores thrived and well-dressed New Yorkers lined up to see art movies. I waited for Buzz, at the appointed time, in the anteroom of that long gone, genteel fish house.

It was a chilly evening, spring, as usual in Manhattan, was late in arriving, and Buzz walked in wearing a navy blue overcoat, similar in design and fabric to my own. But this unsmiling, gnome-like figure, this short, graying man who would be swimming in a thirty-six suit, was not the comical fellow I had seen making love to Ginger Rogers, in *Tom, Dick & Harry*. He was a worn, grumpy man of 54, who was pissed there was only me, an underling, a kid of 24, to greet him at the appointed time and not Bobby, the husband of Hansberry. I'm thinking: "He don't know he's dealing with dummies and I'm the one who duked him in!"

Buzz was pissed-off. Then, I made the mistake of being complimentary and telling him how much I admired him and what an inspiration he had been to me, and this annoyed him even more.

Finally, Bobby, who was forever late and harried, arrived and we sat down in the dining room. No one in the crowded fishery noticed the star; no one made a fuss; no one recognized him or asked for his autograph and here he was in the heart of Greenwich Village! The man never smiled the entire night. We finished eating and walked back to Bobby's office-apartment so that Buzz (we never called him by that appellation and he never gave us permission to do so) could get a script. So many people had, by this time, told Bobby how lousy the book was, that Bobby was not anxious to distribute copies to potential directors.

We took off our coats, I gave Buzz a script and the three of us spoke for a few more minutes. Approaching midnight, he rose, shook hands with his small, limp paw, got his coat and script in hand, and went home. I remained to speak with Bobby, but when I went to get my coat I realized Buzz had left mistaking it for his own, even though mine was a size 40 and would be like a tent on Meredith's small frame. I was able to run home the two long blocks to Washington Street, where, I had moved into a floor-through apartment, in an ancient two-story building in the meatpacking district. Julian Barry (who would write the play *Lenny*) had the floor-through, above mine.

When I related what had happened to Julian he told me he played a small role in the recording of a play in which Buzz participated and, just when Barry's cue was approaching, the great, small man, at a point when his character was offstage, beckoned to Barry whose own cue was approaching and whispered authoritatively, "Hey, kid! Get me cup of coffee, two sugars, light on the cream!" According to Julian, Buzz was very absent-minded and, to boot, could be mean.

I retrieved the coat from Buzz's maid the following day. He read the script and turned down the directing assignment. Actors (and directors) are complex people and, when, after they are lucky enough to achieve a measure of Fame but are subsequently, for some reason or other, targeted and defeated by Fate and duplicitous talent agents (as happens when they lose a coveted role to someone else), when they are not treated as they wish to be treated and are not as famous as they think they ought to be they become ornery. Being nice becomes a liability. Some people are so talented their orneriness is tolerated. But there is a rare breed, too, among which both talent and kindness abide.

I immediately contacted another blacklisted director. I traced the Connecticut-born, expatriate, Jules Dassin (1911-2008) one of eight children born of a Russian-Jewish barber, to the apartment he shared in Paris with his wife, the actress, Melina Mercouri (1920-1994), and their children. Director of *Brute Force* (1947), the beautiful and authentic, *Naked City* (1948), *Cantorville Ghost* ((1944), *Rififi* (1955) and, among many others, *Never On Sunday* the previous year, Dassin was as gracious as Meredith was unfriendly. He was flattered to be considered and apologetic in refusing.

"What a shame" he wailed. "I am so deeply sorry I will be unable to involve myself in such an interesting project," he said, with genuine sincerity, and he went on to film *Phaedra* and *Topkapi*, later, with his missus. Bobby refused to see Charles Friedman, who directed *Carmen Jones* and *My Darlin' Aida*. He was not opposed to my seeing Gene Frankel (1920-2005), director of *The Blacks*, on his behalf, but, later, Bobby nixed him, too.

I called Martin Ritt (1914-1990) who, after years on the blacklist, was securely established as an important Hollywood film director with *Edge Of The City* (1957), *The Long Hot Summer* (1958) and *The Black Orchid* (1958).[65]

In his late forties, wisely rabbinical, almost self-effacing, charming but clearly not a bull-shitter, Marty came by the office in a rumpled raincoat, carrying a folded-up newspaper. He was known to be an expert handicapper, an avocation on which he was forced to rely for upkeep during the blacklist days, and the paper under his arm, no doubt, contained the racing entries, which, I fancy, he had been studying with Talmudic insightfulness.

Beginning his career in FDR's Works Progress Administration (WPA) a highly-respected teacher, a superb actor (his rare appear-

---

65 *Hud* and *Sounder, The Spy Who Came In From The Cold, Norma Rae, Cross Creek, Ryan's Hope*, and others, were in the future.

ance supporting Jon Voight, in *End Of The Game* [1975], is proof enough), Kazan is credited as being Marty's mentor when both were in the Group Theatre. Marty was in the first show I had ever seen, *Winged Victory*, and friends of mine who knew, or worked with him, told me that as a racing expert his skill, and his teaching at Actors Studio for five years, is what kept him going during the time he was blacklisted and unemployed in Hollywood. *Edge of the City* (1957) with John Cassavetes, Jack Warden and Sidney Poitier, was his comeback film. Five years older than Ritt, Kazan was at the heart of a lengthy story Marty unfolded attesting to the vagaries of the Theatre, which I have never forgotten. (SEE APPENDIX #11.)

No doubt to get rid of me temporarily, Bobby asked me to attend a seminar at the New School to be given by the producing team of Robert Griffith and Harold Prince. They followed their hit, *Pajama Game*, with *Damn Yankees*, *Tenderloin*, *New Girl In Town*, *Fiorello!* and *West Side Story*, all but the latter directed by George Abbott, who had been been mentor to both when both stage-managed for him.

The "seminar" was called "Producing On Broadway" and turned out to be the two producers, one tall, reserved, with eyeglasses, the other younger, shorter and, as yet, beardless, and three wannabes, including me, sitting in a small room overlooking 12th Street, swapping stories and discussing budgets. Hal Prince (1928-2019) was nothing like the flighty elf Bobby Morse played and Richard Bissell wrote about in the 1958 musical, *Say, Darling*. Griffith died a short time after this meeting. Nemiroff should have come; he would have learned something. (SEE APPENDIX # 12.)

It was a fun job meeting and speaking with such talented people as Prince, Marty Ritt, and Buzz Meredith and having as employers, Bobby and Burt who were benevolent. At Burt's instigation, Bobby and Burt took me on a boat excursion to Monmouth Park Racetrack where we met Jack Price, the trainer of that year's Derby-winner,[66] who came by to visit us in the box Burt had taken for the day. I believe this jaunt was a payoff for my fundraising efforts.[67]

---

66 Carry Back, a horse which almost magically closed from dead last, race after race, winning far beyond his negligible breeding. (Saggy out of Joppy by Star Blen).

67 I did not win that day.

That July, Whitey Ford threw a home run pitch to Willie Mays in the All-Star game and Mickey Mantle, playing center field, watched the ball sail out of Candlestick Park. He and Roger Maris engaged in a duel to break Babe Ruth's record for home runs in one season, while relations in Berlin between the East and West were worsening and the Wall was soon erected.

And then Bobby said he had found the right director - an off- Broadway actress-director, Vinnette (Justine) Carroll (1922-2002). She would be the first African-American woman to direct a show on Broadway. Currently, she had a production running at the Y.M.C.A. of the old play *Dark Of The Moon*.[68] The cast included a group of relative unknowns: Cicely Tyson, James Earl Jones, Harold Scott, Clarence Williams III and the Alvin Ailey Dancers, which had been formed three years earlier.

"The idea of hiring Vinnette," I told Bobby and Burt, "is ludicrous; it's like throwing the $400,000 out the window; not because she's a woman and not because she's black, but because she's never done anything similar before, and she'll be unable to handle the logistics of the production. You don't learn how to do it until you've done it - on a smaller scale, in stock or in university theatre, or by being in many musicals as a performer, and by being in a position to study the structure of the genre and learn how to mount a show. And there's the problem of editing and arranging scenes in a...well, let's face it, a very bolloxed-up script."

They did not like what I was saying. Knowing the irreparable state of the book and the inability of anyone present to fix it, I was certain that hiring Vinnette meant failure. It is true I believed the show would fail with any director at the helm, but I also felt, on behalf of the investors, the more experienced the director the greater the chances of somehow transmogrifying *Kicks* into a non-failure. But Bobby gave me Vinnette's phone number and I called her, got tickets to see *Dark Of The Moon*, and set an appointment to met with her, at her apartment, the next morning.

Phil Rose, in his autobiography, claims credit for the idea of hiring Vinnette. I saw *Dark Of The Moon* and it was well-directed and

---

68 Written by Howard Richardson and William Berney, and a favorite of university and amateur groups (the play featured the folk song "Barbara Allen"), it was first produced on Broadway in 1945.

acted, but, good as it was, it had not changed my mind about her. That was my attitude when I arrived that sunny, summer Monday morning at her loft-like, floor-through apartment on lower Broadway, off Union Square, where I was greeted by Ellis Hazlip (1930-1991), co-producer of the play series he and Vinnette were giving at the "Y."

With his slight frame draped comfortably on a curved sofa, set against the background of low-lying buildings on Fourth Avenue, Ellis, who would become famous as an interviewer interviewed me prior to my interviewing Vinnette.

"So, you're a director?" he asked, his wizened face puckered with friendly interest, his eyes lively behind heavy bottom glasses.

"Yeah, been doing stock n' stuff like that, a show every week or two. Started at the Cleveland Playhouse…."

"The Cleveland Playhouse! Well, then, you must know Karamu!"

I had recently seen a production there of *Volpone*, directed by the German, Benno Frank.

Somehow, I didn't mind being grilled by Ellis because he was congenial and knowledgeable. That accounts for his becoming a successful television interviewer.[69] But Vinnette soon made her entrance and Ellis departed. Earlier that year, I had seen her play Dido in the Phoenix Rep's revival of Dion Boucicault's 19th century melodrama, The *Octoroon*. Meeting her in person that day is a pleasant memory hovering in my ungovernable subconscious. She was a glowing soul who gained my immediate respect, if not my approval, and it became easier to account for Bobby's enthusiasm.

She wore her straight black hair a lá Bloody Mary in *South Pacific*, that severe style whereby a bun is pierced by what looks like two knitting needles, and even though she was not yet 40, her deep bass voice, her piercing eyes, behind thick spectacles in black plastic frames, her empathetic warmth, which bordered on the avuncular – she had been a child psychologist for NYC Child Protective Services – all these qualities made her seem older than she, in truth, was.[70]

---

69 *Soul.* WNET, Channel 13 PBS

70 Born in New York City, her father was a dentist. She grew up in the West Indies and the lilt was in her voice. Returning to Manhattan, she obtained her master's in psychology from Columbia Uni-

When I discussed my trepidation at the producers hiring some-one to manage a musical extravaganza who was without prior experience, she could say little to assuage my fears, but it was all friendly, and while we spoke, Cicely Tyson appeared from another room and whispered in Vinnette's ear, then, departed.

I returned to the office and reported to Bobby that Vinnette's, *Dark Of The Moon* was very well done, but bore no relevance to *Kicks* in terms of her ability to stage a Broadway musical. I said that I thought her to be a swell person, but that it was suicidal to hire her. Still, Bobby was determined to proceed with his choice.

And then, as of a sudden, completely out of the blue, Bobby said he was going to sign Burgess Meredith to play the Devil and star in the role of Mr. Kicks.

****

I was wrong about Vinnette. She commanded the respect of everyone and the cast loved her. Burgess was very cooperative. The choreographers and Jack Lee performed the job of organizing the staging and scheduling of rehearsals. My work was done. There was nothing I could do to save the ship because the script remained a mess.

Approximately one week into rehearsal, as I was sitting in a vacant room of the rehearsal facility, Donald McKayle and Walter Nicks and Oscar interrupted my afternoon meditations by making a hesitant approach. They were not happy about the way things were going and asked, "Can't you step in and do something?"

I laughed. I said, "I don't have the option. You know that. There's nothing I can do."

I guessed they were speaking of the script, but I was not sure because, at this point, 1.) I was beginning to lose interest because things were happening behind my back, when I had been responsi-ble for a large part of the capitalization and 2.) Bobby was suddenly unhappy with Vinnette.

More importantly, I have neglected till now to disclose the hor-rendous fact that during this entire period the producers and their

---

versity and, after working for CPCS, entered the acting profession in her mid-twenties, enrolling in the famous workshop of Erwin Piscator (1883-1966). She also studied with Stella Adler and Lee Strasberg.

general manager had failed to secure a theatre in which to open the production – not only for the Broadway run, but also for the out-of-town tryout. Some other show on Broadway would have to fail in order to create a vacancy. And that's how the Shuberts and the other theatre owners left it with Bobby, Burt and Wally Fried.

I was upset when they hired Vinnette and blindsided when they hired Buzz, but I threw in the towel altogether when I was informed they had decided to open *Kicks* in the new 4,200 seat Arie Crown Theatre, at McCormick Place, in Chicago. The facility, at that time, was unsuitable for theatrical presentations. Those tough Chicago critics will kill the show in a sec I thought. That's one reason musicals tried-out in Philadelphia and Boston, not Chicago; another was proximity and the attendant travel costs. It was a foolish move.

So that's how it was going to end! Well, I wasn't going to stick around. I liked Burt very much and Bobby most of the time, frankly, less and less, but now I was bailing out. Never mind whether or not I was going to lose their friendship. I was mad my advice had been ignored. I devised a plan of attack and confronted them in the office on Bleecker Street.

In August, while the show was in rehearsal in New York, just at the time when Vinnette was desperately trying to get hold of Oscar's material, the East Germans, with Soviet help, began harassing U.S. and Allied troops when they crossed the boundary called "Check-point Charlie." They soon encircled what became the Berlin Wall and halted unhampered travel between East and West, starting from August through September. International tension between the U.S. and Russia mounted and whatever little good had been achieved in the meetings in Vienna between JFK and Khrushchev melted away.

Sympathy for anyone or anything on the political Left became non-existent; suspected Communist sympathizers were in big trouble. The subject was on television, the radio, the front page, and in every gossip column of every newspaper in town.

"Give me a check for $2,500 or I'll go to Earl Wilson and every other columnist in town and tell them you're a bunch of Reds," I despicably demanded of the producers. "I want a guarantee of my credit as Production Supervisor on the title page of the show's program and on any subsequent sheet music or promotional material of any kind where the director and choreographers also appear. And in the back of the program where stage manager and other listings appear, I'm to be listed as Casting Director." (And so it was) Though I had no intention of carrying out the threat, it was just a successful ploy. Don't ask me how I arrived at the sum of $2, 500; I deserved more compensation than that for my efforts. A finder's fee was ten per cent.

Oscar speaks, in his Internet interview, of raising the money, but he was never even present, except as I have reported. I was the person who played his record, made the pitch, and collected the checks. It's true he came to Cleveland, but that was my project, my idea; I arranged it on my own, found each investor on my lonesome. Oscar raised the reminder of the capitalization monies on the Garroway show, and I, sitting on Bobby's recliner from Castro Convertibles, and Bobby, in the next room, or at Lorraine's apartment, nearby, fielded the calls, all of which has been clearly reported herein previously.

Bobby gave his patented, wide-eyed stare when I made my demand. Burt said, resignedly, "Give it to him."

Bobby's bio in the opening night program read:

"With the combined effort of co-producer D'Lugoff, they (Bobby and Burt) raised the requisite budget of $400,000 in just six months, a remarkable feat for a new producing team."

That really pissed me off.

11

Down the Drain and Then Some

Diana and I agreed we should go to her mother's house in White Plains for a Labor Day barbecue in order to meet her, her sister and others in the family. This for me was, ostensibly, to acclimate them to our impending nuptials, for despite the termagant battling and the concomitant smacks on the butt with the beat-up broom, we were contemplating marriage. Maybe it was a matter of convenience, or convention but it was 1961 and people thought differently, then, about getting hitched.

First though, I took the train to Belmont Park to bet on a horse called Beau Prince. Nowadays they race at Saratoga on the day that honors the working class, but that year they were at Belmont and, to make things more confusing (because they were remodeling Aqueduct) they were running the Aqueduct Handicap at Belmont Park.

My horse, a heavy favorite, was, I thought, a predictable front-running winner. So I took the Long Island express to the "Queen Mother" of racetracks to increase my dwindling bankroll. But the trainer of C.V. Whitney's rateable Tompion[71] fooled me and most of the 40,000 present by instructing his jockey, "Gentleman" John Rotz, to smack his mount from the first step out of the gate, an unusual tactic for a patient horse in a long race. Beau Prince and the others in the field were so surprised they gave up and Tompion, having taken the initiative, found himself alone on the lead, hence, victorious in the winner's circle, and I was a few hundred dol-

---

71 By Tom Fool out of Sunlight by Count Fleet, trained by British-born, champion, polo-playing, socialite, Ivor G. Balding.

lars poorer and on the train back to the beautiful Penn Station of McKim, Mead (and forget about White, who had scandalized his partners by then with his obsessive behavior). Upon arrival, in order to get to Diana's mother's house, I took a cab cross-town to Grand Central and the train to White Plains. By the time I bought my return trip ticket, I had a mere forty bucks remaining in my pocket.

"What a lovely little town!" I thought, when I de-trained. Ten per cent of the town's population was of African-American decent, among them, then as now, many prominent upper and middle class folks.

Diana's mom was well groomed, dignified and worried for her daughter. She tried to put a valiant face on the situation, but with composed resignation she subtly conveyed to me that she thought a marriage between Diana and I would not materialize. Diana's sister was fun and friendly and so was everyone else. So was her lovely mom. Don't get me wrong.

The household was admirable and had a grand backyard and a comfortable recreation room in the basement. So often through my young life, in auditoriums, living rooms, bar rooms, bawdy houses, barbershops and bust-out joints, I found myself to be the only white person present and I never felt uncomfortable in any way.

Nor was it any different that Labor Day of 1961.But it was hot in the backyard sun. I realized I was jobless and poorer than the day before. And, with only $40 at hand, instead of a wad in my pocket from betting Beau Prince, I separated myself from Diana and the group in the yard and gravitated to the basement where I knew a poker game was in progress.

It was a small affair. A friend or relative of Diana's or her mom's (I know not which, though it is over a half a century ago and I recall, vividly, as you see, so many other precise details), a woman of grand proportions held forth at a folding card table set to one side of the immaculate cellar. She was attended by two men of the same age – they were around 40 – and, all smiles, she invited me to sit in.

"Hey, handsome, won't you join us? Take a seat," she invited in her forthright, brassy manner, smiling and shifting her weight on the seat as the folds of fat which hung from her face, neck and torso jiggled like jellied jam.

I abhor games of chance, but I sat down anyway. Could I have been thinking of winning back the money I lost at Belmont? I was introduced to the two gentlemen, one of whom soon departed, so that there were, quickly, just three of us. The man who remained seemed to hold cards just as crummy as mine, while the woman of girth collected nearly every pot. We were playing with chips, of course, and with only $40 in my pocket it was paramount I be able to "settle up" when the game concluded or I'd appear to be the asshole I already knew I was.

Luckily, I won a pot and it was clear we were neglecting the people upstairs and had best conclude. It all boiled down to one hand, a situation in which, after the man dropped out, I had two three's, the "call" was $36 and it was, "Up to you, baby," she said to me.

Never play scared. Everyone knows that. But I froze. Arriving back in Manhattan, with no cab fare to get home, to have to walk all the way from Vanderbilt and 42nd to Washington and Christopher, or even go by public transportation, was repugnant. I chickened out. I didn't call. I threw in my cards and, with arms abundant with dangling flesh, my opponent raked in the pot, as she chuckled and teased me with a, "Shoulda' called, you know," as she threw down a hand in which no card matched another. She had nothing. She had bluffed me.

We traipsed upstairs where pictures were being taken, one of which I have before me now. It shows me reclining in a deck chair surrounded by Diana, her sister and a quintet of other similarly smiling faces. The stout woman is missing, as are her, probable, confederates. Diana is smiling the most and rather nervously. Because she is not in the picture and, because mothers love pictures more than anyone, I imagine her mother is the person taking the picture, the picture in which I am the only one not smiling. It was not the happy, positive day Diana and I had anticipated and that was my fault.

We were unemployed, but I still had remaining some of the money given to me by the producers, so, at my suggestion we went to Aqueduct in a limousine to see Globemaster win a stakes race and the limo driver stared at us in the rear view mirror all the way there and back with 1961 style hatred, which escaped neither Diana or myself.

Gielgud said that in order to be a star in the theatre you must retain the child in you and never let it go. Diana was an adult politically and intellectually, but she remained a child in significant ways and that was too great a test of my fealty. Again don't get me wrong; I'm probably worse.

Later that fall, she came to my place on Washington Street and we had a serious talk in which I told her we were incompatible, and, nonsensically, she took it badly. Is it possible she loved me? She lapsed into silence and I volunteered to take her home. I'm no good at these things. What man is?

We walked up Christopher Street in midafternoon on a cold, sunny Sunday and stopped at Hudson to hail a cab. She was wearing a blue formal coat similar to the one Oleg Cassini fashioned for Jackie Kennedy and her feet were shod in matching pumps. I hailed a cab and we self-consciously waited for it to stop. And when it did I opened the door for her but didn't try to kiss her goodbye she was so mad. She stooped a bit to get into the cab and, as she did, from the side of her mouth and in her best possible Diana Sands reading, she said, "Well, now, I guess you've had your colored girl," and drove away.

In retrospect, I am ashamed of my behavior and wish I could have ended our romance more gracefully and in a manner less hurtful to her, for Great Ones deserve special treatment, something I otherwise afforded her. I remember the good times but I remember the broom, too. It was the end of our sexual, but not our professional, relationship.

****

In late September, his *"ich bin ein Berliner"* speech two years in the offing, JFK appointed General Lucius Clay to straighten things out in Deutschland's capitol and the Yankees beat the Cincinnati Reds in five games. And in Chicago, Carol Channing headed the show in the Empire Room, *My Fair Lady* continued its long run at the Shubert, Gore Vidal's *Best Man* was doing a "take-in" at the Blackstone, and *Bye, Bye, Birdie* was selling out at the Erlanger. In the *Playboy* Jazz Poll for 1961, Stan Getz won in the tenor sax category with 10, 258 votes, while Coleman Hawkins placed second, with 5, 633 (Charlie Ventura was fifth); the new vocal group Lambert, Hendricks & Ross topped their category (and were in town, at Mr. Kelly's); and the country's best-selling girlie magazine, still headquartered in Chicago, was flourishing with worthy authors, and, because of its interest in good writing and music, developing into a positive cultural influence. A black Chicagoan named Dick Gregory, "discovered" by Hugh Hefner at Roberts Show Lounge, on the South Side, now replaced Professor Irwin Corey at the Playboy Club. (Bill Cosby, who had been playing clubs in Philly, was a year away from his New York debut.)

And *Kicks*, rehearsing at the huge Arie Crown (its elephantine proportions were later modified) was in deep doo-doo. Vinnette had been unexpectedly fired as the show's director and replaced, without warning, by Lorraine Hansberry. The star, Burgess Meredith, the production staff of Jack, Donnie and Walter Nicks and others, and the large cast of principals and chorus arrived in Chicago to find their beloved Vinnette gone and the famous playwright and wife of one of the producers as her replacement. The company of *Kicks & Co.* was stunned. (Almost simultaneous with my departure, the firm of Kinoy, Rossmore and Brown withdrew as attorneys for the show saying Bobby refused to take their advice.)

The way I see it, once the play was "put on its feet" and Bobby heard the endless pages of dialogue he panicked. Subconsciously, I believe, the editor in him made him realize that if he couldn't sit through it, how could an audience? Weaknesses in the casting became evident, too. Nichelle Nichols' great talent and looks set a standard that overshadowed lesser performers. On the other hand, Buzz was having problems with his role.

Bobby thought his wife's name would lend legitimacy to *Kicks*, that the Chicago public would associate the two plays, *Raisin* and *Kicks*, in their minds. Some might think Lorraine's playwriting skills would save *Kicks*. Put bluntly, Bobby thought Lorraine could save the show; more realistically, that her name could save it.

Lorraine's relationship with Phil Rose was ongoing, so when Bobby decided to fire Vinnette and he asked Lorraine to take over, she called Rose for advice. "She sounded very stressed," according to Rose, and he told her it would be a terrible mistake, that to return to the town in which she had had such a great success and in which she had become such a potent figure, would be a bad choice, that, should she want to play Chicago with a future play of her own, she would, if she succumbed to Bobby's demand, be relinquishing the good will she had built with *Raisin*. Rose says he kept to himself the belief that Bobby's request was exceedingly self-serving. But Lorraine took over as if she knew what she was doing. She asked that certain prominent cast members be fired. That did not happen; it would have cost a great deal of money. Besides, Jack Lee and others objected.

Mounting a show on that mammoth stage was akin to directing at outdoor amphitheatres such as the St. Louis Municipal Opera Theatre or the Kansas City Starlight, 11,000 and 7,000 capacities, respectively, or Cain Park, with its 3,500 seats. Lorraine positioned herself in the huge auditorium on the right side of the audience, which is stage left, and flew in from New York a young friend as an assistant to direct the actors on stage right. Buzz, who was very upset at the firing of Vinnette, stood in the very middle of stage center and said, belligerently, to Lorraine, "Okay, who's directing me now?"

Then Buzz started directing Lorraine's direction, standing onstage, telling her what to do. And he was a very good director; that's why I dragged him into the project in the first place. But it was too late. Stage manager, Nathan Caldwell (1929-2013), who knew and respected Lorraine, and who joined *A Raisin In The Sun* in its final days in the initial Broadway run, played Bobo, and, then, stage-managed the national tour which followed, and would soon work with Vinnette, on *Black Nativity* before the year ended, told me months before he passed away in 2013: "It was a joke! A MESS!"

In an emergency production meeting at the Croydon Hotel, Lorraine, via a flurry of notes, made certain artistic demands of the amiable, but opinionated and very knowledgeable, Jack Lee. A genius of the lyric theatre, he didn't agree with many of the things Lorraine said. He thought her notes showed inexperience. Jack, who walked with a swagger, feet turned-out, head protruding, arms swinging with each stride, all the result of tap dance lessons in his youth, had put on many shows, and he politely refused to accept the requests of the adamant new director. Lorraine angrily picked up a glass ashtray, filled with cigarette butts, and threw it at Jack.

"Did it hit you?" I asked, decades later.

"You're damn right! She hated me! Because I represented 'Musical Comedy!'"[72]

Lorraine was trying to save Bobby's ass, but to think she could handle a company of 70 or more (counting the musicians and stage-hands) was presumptuous.

In the meantime, Chicago's press, greatly focused on the product of homegrown Oscar, learned the show was in dreadful condition. The opening had been scheduled for October 7, but postponeitis set in. One of the delays was ascribed, by the show's press agent, Alan Edelson, to Burgess Meredith's fulfilling a commitment to the filming of Otto Preminger's *Advise & Consent*. Buzz did go to Washington and shoot some scenes for the movie. The opening was, now, set for the following Wednesday, but a very rough benefit performance was given for the Urban League, a largely African-American audience.

On Sunday the 7th, the date on which the show was originally scheduled to open, the very favorable and extensive piece by Lionel Lindner, with photos of Oscar performing alone on the stage of the Arie Crown, appeared in the magazine section of the *Chicago Daily News*. It was a nice spread and, along with positive blurbs, elsewhere in the paper, by its first-string critic, Sydney J. Harris, it was clear that, like the partisan audience at the Urban League, at least one local paper was pulling for Oscar, Lorraine and the producers.

Kicks opened at the 4,200 seat Arie Crown McCormick Place Theatre, on Wednesday, October 11, 1961, and closed on the following Saturday night, with a total loss of its entire budget of $400,000 plus, which was a record, PLUS an additional 40 to $50,000 - money that the general partners, the producers, didn't have.

---

72 Jack Lee reminded me of this incident in a March 22, 2014 interview. No slur on Hansberry, even icons have tempers. Still, her admirers will question its inclusion, as would champions of MLK, the reporting of his infidelities. Q.- Why write about it? A.- It is true. It happened. Everyone has frailties. Truth should be the only standard.

The reviews were withering. In the *Chicago Sun-Times*, Glenna Syse began:

"What KICKS & CO. needs is a play doctor."

Then, beginning paragraph two, set in the only bold face in the entire review:

"GEORGE ABBOTT would do nicely...."

Claudia Cassidy, in the *Chicago Tribune*, started:

"More as confirmation than information this morning, Kicks & Co. is a poor excuse for a show."

Roger Dettmer in the Hearst paper, the *Journal-American*, under a banner "Kicks & Co. A Shambles" began:

"Kicks & Co., the victim of a first performance Wednesday, is amateur night in, not out of Dixie....

The Chicago critics, writing in the tradition of Ashton Stevens, were not only tough but also learned and Sydney J. Harris's review in the *Daily-News* was respectful: "It would be a pleasant civic and dramatic duty to report this morning that the first legitimate venture in the new Arie Crown Theatre at McCormick Place was a rousing success. But despite the tantalizing promise of better things to come from young Chicago composer, lyricist and librettist, Oscar Brown, Jr.,... *Kicks & Co.*, which made its delayed opening Wednesday evening... has pathetically little to recommend it."

Unanimously negative, thoroughly devastating, the reviews, which were soon to be publicly labeled "racist," by Nemiroff, are reprinted, in their entirety, in APPENDIX #12.

Two movements began now almost simultaneously. First, the producers decided to re-capitalize the show (which is their prerogative as general partners in a limited partnership) by reassembling the cast in New York in the coming week for a "performance" of the show before potential investors, as Herb Lyon, reported in his "Tower Ticker" column, in the *Chicago Tribune*, the morning after the closing:

> *"The cast of "Kicks & Co." got a week-end shot of adrenalin. Broadway Kingmakers Dave Merrick and Dave Susskind, and star Harry Belafonte ordered the show to New York for a personal audition later this week. The boys may take it over, revitalize things and launch it on Broadway later. "Kicks" writer-composer, Oscar Brown, Jr., of our town may get the Burgess Meredith role."*

The African-American press, a euphemism for the venerable *Chicago Defender*, erupted in a storm of controversy concerning the worthiness of the production. In an interview years later,[73] Oscar said, "The critics in Chicago hated it, but the *Defender* loved it."

Unlike the four major dallies, the *Defender* did not have a theatre critic per sé, so they carried no review the morning after the premiere. The myth of the excellence of *Kicks* and its butchery by four white critics was initiated by two entertainment writers on the *Defender* staff, Bob Hunter and Al Monroe, in articles that appeared five days after the opening. The drumbeat began with, a quasi review, by Hunter, under a headline: *"'KICKS' TOO MODERN FOR MOST"*

"Now that most of the reviews for *Kicks & Co.* are in – and all of them bad, it appears that the Faust opus is in for the fight of its life – even in Chicago. (Ed. Note: The show had already closed.) Although the show played to a packed house, which seemed to have gotten a kick from the yarn, most critics, or (rather) experts, turned thumbs down. Possibly, it's because the theme of Oscar Brown, Jr.'s attack on segregation is all too true…..Interracial sex is certainly not something to be taken lightly…*Kicks & Co.* is much too forward for stagnant minds."

(AGAIN, SEE APPENDIX #11, FOR COMPLETE ARTICLE; AND THE FOLLOWING *Chicago Defender* ARTICLES IN THEIR ENTIRETY.)

---

73 1996 *ROCTOBER*, online.

On the same date, in the same paper, Mr. Hunter's colleague, the popular entertainment columnist, Al Monroe in his "So They Say," said:

"The 'experts' were a little rough in their reviews, in fact, they were down right nasty and short sighted, in this corner, Oscar Brown, Jr. came home with a winner. ...Miscegenation is going on. Maybe behind closed doors but still going on."

In the next edition of the *Defender,* dated the following day, October 17, Monroe, in the same "So They Say" venue, declared:

"They say two sides to every story - at least there used to be. So let's look once more at the life and times of Kicks & Co., which should be entitled The End of Oscar Brown By The Knives of Four Critics. It is considered well known that ....Kicks & Co. stresses miscegenation, and brother, that hurts down to the white. Nuff said."

Kicks opened on Wednesday, the 11th, and bombed, but from Thursday morning through Saturday, the night the show was closing, the movement was launched by the producers to keep the show alive. On Saturday night, at the same time that, according to Tony Weitzel in the *Tribune,* "Burgess Meredith, a great trouper, shucked off his Mephisto suit after the last performance... and headed straight for the Gate of Horn where he had a ball listening to Leonard Bernstein's *Trouble In Tahiti,*" I met with Jack Lee and members of the cast at the Croydon Hotel, on Rush Street, where Sammy Saddler held forth in the large horseshoe bar, playing show tunes on the piano, while cast members from *Kicks* and other national touring companies, then in town, performed as soloists.

The next afternoon, I drove my mother's car to a gathering at Lois Solomon's house. Lois had been a major contact for me in finding investors. Jack and a few others from the show were there. Annie Ross and Dave Lambert, of Lambert, Hendricks and Ross, were also present. I was introduced to Ross and went off to the side to speak with Jack. I noticed Burgess Meredith was there, too, but paid him no attention. He was not looking happy. Who would with reviews such as Roger Dettmer's?:

"Burgess Meredith, as the villain from Down Below, resembles Chinese Og from the Shanghai company of Finian's Rainbow."

or

Claudia Cassidy's referring to his being: *"the painfully miscast Burgess Meredith… a sort of sulfuric leprechaun."*

I felt sorry for the little man, avoided looking at him, and continued speaking with Jack. Then, I must have said something funny, or at least I thought so, and I laughed, when, suddenly I heard Buzz nearly screaming and saw he was looking at me but speaking to Lois Solomon, who stood beside him.

He said "Where the hell does he get off criticizing? Who the hell are these people who come in off the street with their fucking opinions? God damn…." (mutter-mutter-mutter)" he trailed-off, under his breath, but he was furious and fighting himself not to give way entirely and explode even more violently.

Lois moved slightly toward me with a benign smile, as if to say, "Forgive him, don't make a scene," but Jack stood there like a deer caught in the headlights, looking slightly quizzical, as if to say, "Hey, what's going on here, I thought you knew each other?" Jack did not come to my defense, nor was there anyone else to help me, and Annie Ross and Davey Lambert, both of whom I admired, looked at me with suspicion. I did not know how to reply; I was insufficiently experienced to simply say: "I'm the one who duked you in, asshole, I'm the catalyst that brought you all together." Instead, I left in silence and drove off toward Lake Shore Drive.

The next morning, Tony Weitzel flashed:

"ITEM: Oscar Brown, D'Lugoff, Nemiroff, Hansberry & Co. are trying to set up a full-scale run through of *"Kicks"* in New York Thursday. They hope to interest such potential angels as David Merrick, David Susskind and Harry Belafonte…."

Bob Hunter, in the *Defender*, belatedly, on the 21st, treated the story under the headline:

"KICKS & Co. GET CHANCE TO 'LIVE IT UP' IN NEW YORK"

"The assassination attempt on the life of *Kicks & Co.* by Chicago's four 'expert' critics, was a damaging blow to integration and the play but…'Oscar and I are not angry at the critics for causing the flop of Kicks here,' said Mrs. Brown,[74] 'but we are displeased at their failure to face the fact that times have changed…For the first time they have seen the true spirit and determination of today's young Negroes and they are afraid of them. They saw *Porgy & Bess* and *Raisin In The Sun*, but both are concerned with bygone times.'" And the article concluded by saying: "*In the play miscegenation is rammed home with all the force of a jackhammer. Kicks is much too modern for the decrepit.*"

With a waiver from Actors' Equity having been effected, that Thursday, the 19th, Merrick lent the stage of the Imperial Theatre, which he was leasing at the time, to the producers, and with the entire cast, and understudy, Harold Scott, filling in for Burgess Meredith, an abbreviated run-through performance of the show was presented to very tepid applause at the final curtain.

Afterwards, with Lorraine sitting alone behind him on a bare stage, Bobby made a speech in which he decried the Chicago critics and called them "racist." He droned on as people exited, though some remained out of respect for his wife. Phil Rose said he felt embarrassed for Lorraine; that she was being used as an exhibit. But it was to no avail and no *gelt* was forthcoming; no *tsdokeh; zilch*. Rose said: "It turned out to be one of the most unusual afternoons… I ever spent in the theatre, not because of the show, but the one that followed after."

After his curtain speech/pitch, Bobby, with Lorraine following, came off of the stage, into the house, and rushed all the way to the rear of the orchestra in order to shake hands with the embarrassed audience members, who sheepishly exited, heads down. But the controversy continued and, on October 23rd, Al Monroe, in a long entry in his column "So They Say," in the *Defender* (THE FULL TEXT OF WHICH IS AT THE END OF APPENDIX #13) wrote:

---

74 Maxine Brown, Oscar's then wife.

*"If by chance I'm beginning to bore you with these bits on
KICKS & Co. then kick me. On the other hand, if you aren't,
then read me loud and clear.*

*Until convinced otherwise, I will always believe that its debut
in our town was deliberately butchered because some people
are not ready to open their eyes and see what the new world is
like... A second-class citizenship is slavery itself. Therefore, the
emancipation proclamation of 1863 freed the Negroes in theory
but not in practice. If it had, there would be equal rights. Oscar
Brown, Jr.'s, the originator of Kicks & Co., is the first Negro
play with guts and imagination to conceive a musical bearing
such a message, so powerful, that not even Western Union can
not deliver it."*

The morning after the opening, reporter, gossip columnist, and
future talk show host, Irv Kupcinet, who, with his wife, Essie, attended the opening of every legit offering in Chicago, reported in
his "Kup's Column" in the *Sun-Times*: *"E.B. MARKS Music Corp.,
one of the oldest and most successful picked five of the tunes by
Oscar Brown, Jr. in Kicks & Co. for immediate publication. The
entire score will be published eventually."*

But it wasn't.

And on the 18th of October, he opined: *"PERHAPS if Oscar Brown, Jr. had listened to the advice of an old pro, Bob Pol-
lack, the La Salle Street broker and drama critic, "Kicks & CO."
wouldn't have been the $450,000 fiasco.[75] But youthful Oscar was
surrounded by too many 'yes' men."*

****

OSCAR BROWN, JR. Oscar, in the *Roctober* interview in
which he says the white critics hated *Kicks* but the black press loved
it, attributes the show's failure to "pelvic choreography."

Oscar said, "It was the Twist before the Twist had broken out!
In fact, the Twist didn't break out until like two weeks after *Kicks
& Co....*" Oscar goes on to say the show "probably ran out of

---

75 Kup already knew that, in addition to the entire budget being blown, an additional $40 to
$50,000 (big money, then) was also lost.

money. The budget was $400,000, but by bringing the show here to open, they spent, they gambled, and they thought by being successful in Chicago, they would be able to recoup their initial $400,000 and go into New York sittin' pretty. However, the cost of flying all those people here to Chicago and putting them up in hotels, and rehearsing them and finding rehearsal halls and all that depleted the money so that before we opened in Chicago, they were broke."

Oscar finally got to Broadway in 1969 when he developed Joseph Dolan Tuotti's protest play, *Big Time Buck White*, which started in California, then played off-Broadway, into a musical. Oscar also wrote the lyrics and provided the direction. A singing Muhammad Ali, who had temporarily been barred from boxing, played the title role, in the cast of eight. It lasted 7 performances.

Previously, Oscar's collaborative efforts with drummer Max Roach eventuated in the "Freedom Now" Suite and with Alonzo Levister in the opera *Slave Song*.

According to Lonnie:

"Phil (Rose), as well as Frank Loesser, wanted to produce *Slave Song*. He (Rose) had Ossie Davis write a script for *Slave Song* that ended with hero walking/striding uphill with a burning torch toward the big house. We laughed at it. And he offered to send Oscar/ me to Fire Island with a director to work on a script. Oscar refused Phil and Frank Loesser after we auditioned *Slave Song* for him, and I think Stuart Ostrow (producer of the original *Pippin* and others), in his living room immediately wanted to do a B'way (production) saying at least it would be a *'suces d'estime.'* Oscar nixed it fearing 'loss of control in production.'" *Slave Song* may have been Oscar's best work and it has been produced at Howard University. Lonnie also said: "Phil proposed me/Oscar first do *Purlie*. We didn't. I don't recall why."

Jean Pace was the costume designer for *Big Time Buck White* and, in 1971, after divorcing Maxine and marrying Pace, who was also a singer, and teaming up with Brazilian accordionist, Sivuca, Oscar wrote the show, *Joy*, an Afro-centric small scale, hippy-type revue which, ultimately, as in its closing number, says the world would be a better place if only President Nixon would learn to say "shit." Oscar's body of recorded work (twelve albums) is considerable and he published 125 songs. His work is much admired throughout the world. His "Between Heaven and Hell" album with Quincy Jones is among his best efforts on record. Jean and Oscar produced a son named Oscar. A couple of years after *Kicks*, Lonnie brought me to a suite in the Marlton House, on Eighth Street, across from the New York Studio School. There I met with Oscar and Al Hamm, his manager, and some of Oscar's friends, who wanted me to produce a show Oscar had written. I liked Oscar and the feeling was mutual, but I did not know if we could work together, and we never did.

At some point after *Kicks*, Bobby and Oscar stopped speaking with each other. Oscar passed away in 2005.

ROBERT NEMIROFF remarried (Jewell Handy Gresham) after Hansberry's death and devoted his life, as literary executor of Lorraine's estate, to editing, promoting and producing her works. As a theatrical producer, Bobby was an insurrectionist. The Broadway theatre and insurrection (*Waiting For Lefty* aside) do not mix, but fighting for your show is an attribute and protest was his métier. When Broadway's critics failed to embrace *Sidney Brustien*, Bobby fought back by arousing friends – filmmakers Frank and Eleanor Perry (*David And Lisa*), Mel Brooks and Anne Bancroft, the playwright William Gibson (*Two For The Seesaw, Miracle Worker*), actresses Viveca Lindfors and Madeleine Sherwood, and others, to make contributions of $2,500 and upward to launch a campaign to keep the show on the boards. He wrote an open letter to *The New York Times* and, with Ossie Davis (not in the play) making curtain speeches, sufficient money was raised to keep *Sidney* alive and transport it to another theatre, to complete a run of 101 performances. Also, Bobby added two scenes, previously excised in rehearsals, to the printed edition of *A Raisin In The Sun*, maddening Phil Rose and others.

Aided by Charlotte Zaltzberg, who would become his associate and close collaborator until her death in 1974, Bobby devised an evening based on Lorraine's letters and other writings entitled *To Be Young, Gifted And Black*. The show was a hit off-Broadway in 1969, then toured 41 states, was recorded, filmed, televised and translated into 34 languages and has inspired people through productions all over the world. Nemiroff adapted Lorraine's *Les Blancs* material into a 1970 Broadway production, starring James Earl Jones, Cameron Mitchell, Lili Darvas and Earl Hayman. Produced by Konrad Matthaei and directed by John Berry, it ran for 30 previews and 40 performances.

In 1965, Bobby devised a theatre piece based on letters written by German soldiers during the siege of Stalingrad and presented it on Broadway with Burt and Franklin (Frank) Fried, a Chicago concert promoter. The play, entitled *Postmark Zero,* lasted 8 performances and was later presented on British television.

Along with Zaltzberg, Bobby, then, developed the musical *Raisin,* out of his wife's famous play, with songs by Judd Woldin (music) and Robert Brittan (words). Premiered successfully at Washington's Arena Stage, it opened on Broadway and won the 1974 Tony, as Best Musical of the Year. It had an extended, but troubled Broadway run of 874 performances. Bobby insisted on keeping the musical open despite dwindling business and dipped into payroll taxes in order to pay salaries and keep the show alive, as reported copiously in *Variety,* toward the end of two production runs. He was 61 years old when he died in 1991. Bobby told me he was writing a long essay on Theodore Dreiser, his favorite author, at the time Oscar walked in the door with *Kicks,* that night after *Raisin* premiered in Chicago.

LORRAINE HANSBERRY's first project after her immensely successful first play was a teleplay for CBS commissioned by Dore Schary (1905-1980), former head of MGM, commemorating the bicentennial of the Civil War, called *The Drinking Gourd.* Her subject was slavery and, while Schary was all for it, the network's execs thought it too controversial and it was scrapped. Then, came *Kicks.*

Lorraine died of cancer at the age of 34. She had written two other plays, *The Sign In Sidney Brustein's Window* (1964), produced by Bobby and Burt, which shuttered the night of her passing, and *Les Blancs*, a play set in Africa, which she did not complete. The material was subsequently adapted by Nemiroff.

But one wonders how much of it is Bobby's, how much Lorraine's and when she had time to write it. I have studied the play over years, even worked with actors on scenes in classes, before small audiences. I did this because I had students who seemed right for certain roles. I found, still find, the play stiff, but I believe in its politics.

If Nemrofff, as a producer, was an insurrectionist, Hansberry, as a playwright, was a propagandist in the best sense of the word. Shakespeare was one for the House of Tudor, Brecht for benevolent communism. Lorraine stood for justice and everything good, the things Robeson, Du Bois, King, and Malcolm X. advocated for: world peace, civil rights, economic and social justice. Her prose, her letters and diaries, her public statements that articulate these policies are superbly phrased and uplifting. That is how her former husband (aided by Zaltzberg, one assumes) succeeded in assembling her words into an evening in the theatre - *To Be Young, Gifted and Black*. But while it has glorious moments, it is a theatrical presentation, not a play and to a high degree should be credited to Bobby efforts - an editor, in such cases, being almost as responsible as the source.

Her first play evolved from, was inspired by, personal experience – the fury of the whites that attempted to prevent her and her family from moving into a neighborhood was the catalyst. The "apartment" in which the Younger family dwells is a creation of the "king of the kitchenettes," her father; Hansberry is Beneatha, take my word for it. Loathe to associate myself with politically conservative, revisionist critics who dispute Frank Rich's claim that *Raisin* "changed the theatre forever," right-wing naysayers who claim she wrote one good play and one bad play, the good one being old-style Ibsenism, the other being didactic in the most pejorative sense. Writing a good play is a difficult achievement; writing a second one is even more difficult, the usual example cited for the failure to do so being Thomas Heggen, who adapted his novel, *Mr. Roberts*, for the stage, albeit with the assistance of the production's director, Joshua Logan (who profited greatly from the effort), but could not write another play, as detailed in *Esquire* after he committed suicide, supposedly because of his creative failure. Countless others have written one play that worked and never written another, or failed with their second try and went cold thereafter. And some who fit either category usually flee to Hollywood or became novelists, even non-fiction writers, such as Robert Ardrey, who wrote successfully on anthropological and philosophical matters. "Talking about an opera based on Toussaint Louverture is one thing; writing it is another," Lonnie Levister remarked.

Yet the plays' prominent publisher advertises *Raisin* and *Brustein* jointly as "two masterpieces." I saw *Brustein* on Broadway and enjoyed it, but a masterpiece it was not. I am a professional and enjoy risk-taking, which is a component of the play, switching, as it does, at one point, from a realistic setting to abstract projections of a sudden. And I have enjoyed re-reading it. But it was a dud with New York critics and received consistently poor reviews. Forget about the New York critics; this is more telling: When it came to Chicago (presented by Sherwin Robert Rodgers and Laurence Feldman, not Bobby and Burt) with most of the original cast, Claudia Cassidy, the same Claudia Cassidy who (some say) made *Raisin* a hit with her rave review in its Chicago tryout, tough, fair, but always pulling for Chicago artists, unprejudiced and almost always right, wrote, in the *Tribune*, under the headline, "The Sign in Sidney Brustein's Window is a Long Slow-Moving Garrulous Play: It must have been an extraordinary welling up of admiration and affection that subsidized the New York run through Lorraine Hansberry's fatal illness. It is more difficult to understand what prompted reopening the play for a tour which opened Friday night at the Studebaker Theatre…For not only is it not a good play it is quite desperately dull…the play talks and talks and just keeps on talking…but most of the time the evening is as dull as the people it had the misfortune to drop in on." Personally, though flawed and sometimes boring, the play's premise (that we should get off our butts and try to save humanity) was appealing and the acting first-rate, often moving. But when queried by me as to his opinion of the work, even Hansberry's new biographer, Shields, without elaboration, replied in a single word:"didactic."

Lorraine Hansberry was much more than a playwright. She was perhaps the most articulate woman of her generation, able to stand up to Bobby Kennedy (as she did) or anyone else, and better than anyone else, including even James Baldwin, and that is saying something. *A Raisin in the Sun* is a masterpiece of American literature. One masterpiece is enough to be among the most honored American writers. I am not saying that she could not have written another next time out or sometime down the line. She had the ability and she had the experience. The great tragedy is that she did not have the opportunity.

Finally, with reference to *Kicks*, it is interesting that no critic has anything bad to say about the director. I was too young then to understand that when it comes to flops, most critics seldom knock directors, blaming the author instead for the whole shebang. Had I known that at the time, I might have promoted myself for the position.

Lorraine Hansberry would never have "sold out;" ditto Oscar. They would be appalled by the great disparity in wealth throughout the world. Paul Robeson spoke at Lorraine's funeral. From her Croton-on-Hudson home, shortly before her death, as PBS's "Sighted Eyes/Feeling Heart" reported, she made a diary entry: " Made love with D.S."

BURGESS MEREDITH directed Diana Sands and Al Freeman, Jr., among others, in The Actors Studio 1964 production of James Baldwin's, *Blues For Mr. Charlie*, at the ANTA Theatre. He played the Penguin in TV's *Batman*, a portrayal of surer similitude than his simpering Satan of *Kicks*. His career gained new impetus when he won the Academy Award for Best Supporting Actor in the film, *Rocky*, starring Sylvester Stallone, in which he played Rocky's trainer-mentor. As one might expect, his 1994, 277 page, memoir-hagiography, detailing his distinguished career, makes no mention whatever of *Kicks*, Oscar Brown, Jr., Lorraine Hansberry or Robert Barron Nemiroff, but does contain an admirable and frank admission of his mood swings. He was one of the preeminent stage and film actors of his time and a very able and educated director.

JACK LEE, who slept on my living room floor the first night he came to live in New York City, became one of the most important musical director/conductors on Broadway and, generally, in the wide world of show business, working with stars such as Burt Lancaster, Gene Kelly, Jerry Lewis and Tommy Tune, to name a very few. The subject of a PBS documentary, *Conductor*, he finally worked with George Abbot in the Broadway flop, *Fig Leaves Are Falling* (1969). Jack died in 2017.

NICHELLE NICHOLS, an octogenarian, became immortalized as Lieutenant Uhura, on the television series, *Star Trek*. ALONZO LEVISTER, JR. (1925-2016) came to music late in life, after WWII, and studied with Nadia Boulanger, in Paris, before returning to the Apple and Julliard and extirpated his demons many years ago. He told me, before he died in Portugal where he had retired with his wife the former Gloria Bleezarde: "I didn't stop drinking, I just turned against it."

VI VELASCO and LONNIE SATTIN, continued working in recording studios and nightclubs. BERNARD JOHNSON, who danced in the chorus and played the role of Eggy, developed his skills as a costumier, formed his own dance troupe, and was the costume designer for the musical *Raisin*, on Broadway.

MERCEDES ELLINGTON, a member of the *Kicks* chorus, daughter of Duke's son, Mercer Ellington, continued her career as a dancer and is an active force, today, behind the Duke Ellington Center for the Arts. CAROL ARTHUR, who received the only "house" laughs in *Kicks*, and positive critical notices as the white waitress in the redneck café, has a resumé too dense to include here and appears, therefore, in the APPENDIX #10. AL FREEMAN, JR., is a continuing character in my saga.

BURT D'LUGOFF (1925-2016) returned to medical practice in the Maryland area, first as an internist then as a psychiatrist, in charge of the Johns Hopkins Addiction Center out-patient clinic. A true friend to Bobby and Lorraine, you will never hear an unkind word about Burt because he was a *mensch*. Neither Bobby nor Burt,ever intended violating SEC rules in the raising of funds for *Kicks*.[76] A kind man with wide interests, considerable knowledge and accomplishments, it is difficult to associate Burt with Bobby's occasional bending of the truth.

---

76 When I began writing this book, I contacted Burt D'Lugoff by telephone after 50 plus years, apologizing for the manner in which I left his and Bobby's employ. In a brief letter I later told him I was writing about *Kicks* and hoped he might answer some questions, and I followed through, but never heard from him again. I last saw Bobby in D.C. on *Raisin's* opening night.

VINNETTE CARROLL, who was the founder of the Urban Arts Corps and won the Obie for Best Actress of 1962, the year after *Kicks*, for her performance in *Moon On A Rainbow Shawl*, became, with the musical revue, *Don't Bother Me I Can't Cope* (1972), the first African-American women to direct a Broadway show. She followed that with the gospel-infused *Your Arm's Too Short To Box With God*, which played the Main Stem on three separate occasions. Neither was a "book" show; both were revues and major successes.

PHIL ROSE, a few months after *Kicks* closed, met with Bobby and Burt in Phil's office. Phil excoriated Bobby, relating a long list of ugly grievances relating to calumny in and out of Phil's office with Phil's employees and associates and with the whole Broadway show business "industry," the sabotaging of Phil's relationship with Lorraine, Bobby's steering of Lorraine's career in the wrong direction, citing her helming *Kicks* as a prime example and, throughout, Phil said, Bobby smiled with his patented eyes wide open stare. Bobby retaliated by obliterating the record of the Phil and Lorraine friendship.

Phil believed that he, not Bobby and Burt, should be producing Lorraine's second play. But she severed her relationship with Rose, claiming, Rose said, that she said he was better producing musicals than he was at doing straight plays, which, he claims, was stupid, as he had just had a flop with *Bravo, Giovanni*. Lorraine was pissed when Phil criticized her for directing *Kicks*. He said she said "something about her right to direct, sing, produce, or dance in the theatre if she chose to, cutting the meeting short…" Ruby Dee averred her husband, Ossie Davis's *Purlie Victorious* (1961) would probably not have been produced it if not for Rose. And it was Rose who used what was then considered innovative casting when he turned Joe Manhoff's 1964 comedy *Owl And The Pussycat* into a hit with Diana Sands playing opposite Alan Alda. In 1970 he made Ossie's play into a musical, *Purlie*, with Robert Guilliame and Melba Moore and, in 1975 won a Tony Award as co-author of the musical *Shenandoah*, which he also directed, showing he acquired theatrical smarts through experience. He flopped with *Does A Tiger*

Wear A Necktie? in 1969, which introduced Al Pacino to Broadway audiences, and *Nobody Loves An Albatross*, starring Robert Preston.

LOUIS J. LEFKOWITZ (1904-1996), a moderate, Rockefeller Republican, who served as "the peoples" Attorney General of the State of New York longer than anyone else, and who was, a small investor in *Kicks & Co.*, brought suit in New York questioning the handling of the finances in the raising and expenditure of the budget of $400,000 and additional claimed losses incurred in producing the show. He did not win the action but he codified and helped promulgate and win passage in the New York State Legislature of measures which became known as the Lefkowitz Laws. Administered faithfully buy New York State's SEC, these laws have established the rules by which producers solicit funds for Broadway shows.

My experience with *Kicks* left me feeling exploited but grateful for the opportunity of learning so much in so little time. But I knew about deception from the time my mother pointed to the sky and said "Daddy's up in heaven."

The ability to dissemble is prerequisite to becoming a Broadway producer. Seventy-five percent of Broadway shows fail, so telling an investor a particular play is sure to succeed is a fib. A producer juggles investors, stars, lawyers, authors, agents, cast, crew, conductors, arrangers, ad execs, theatre owners, unionists, media mavens, box office treasurers, people in the seats, and through his or her general and company managers, musicians in the pit. How far do you think an impresario can go without a bit of malarkey, a dash of what makes Sammy run and a number of little white lies? In a world of make believe facts and fantasies conjoin; the play's the only thing that really matters and duplicity is ofter the means to an end.

Feigning self-effacement in his "P.S.," pretending he attended "a lecture" that never took place (see my previous account), finally, Bobby heeded my insistent imprecations he contact George Abbott, or at least attend the event at the New School with Mr. Abbott's stage-manager protégés, Harold Prince and Bobby Griffith, which wasn't a lecture at all. He sent this telegram (the product of research on the part of Charles J. Shields) to Prince, inviting him to attend the debacle of an "audition/run through" performance at the Imperial Theatre, with Harold Scott as Mr. Kicks.

"Invite you to see, just for yourself, bare stage show "Kicks & Co." First musical to try out Chicago 45 years, derailed there. Significant show, dance, music, excellent potentialities. Major partiipation for first call monies. Imperial Theatre, Thursday, October 19, 2 P.M. sharp. P.S. Sat in your lecture New School. Unfortunately didn't learn enough. Can we get private tutoring?"

****

A couple of months after the show's demise, quite unexpectedly and without any finagling whatever on my part, I was given the exclusive opportunity of directing and producing a summer stock tour of *A Raisin In The Sun*, starring Claudia McNeil (and what turned out to be a cast of future stars).

ILLUSTRATIONS

Herald for L.A. stand of *Hughie* following Chicago and St. Louis openings and prior to Broadway.

Tableaux from Cleveland Playhouse 1954 revival of Arthur Schwartz-Dorothy Fields/George Abbott-Betty Smith musical adaptation of *A Tree Grows in Brooklyn*. Eve Roberts is seen stage center, Dom De Luise and author stand upstage right before barroom doors.

Alan Alda as Sky Masterson in *Guys and Dolls*, in 1959 summer stock production directed by author.

ABOUT
THE WORK

"I have just had auditioned for me a musical that I think is truly unusual and absolutely top-notch. The name of it is 'Kicks & Co.' For whatever it is worth... I am sure that the combination of a star and the property itself would absolutely guarantee its Broadway success."
—STEVE ALLEN, in a letter to his
business associates

"Personally, I regard this as a major work that should mark the emergence of a truly major talent in our theatre.

"It offers an astonishing succession of brilliantly entertaining and illuminating songs embedded in a work which startles by successfully wedding the already potent vitality, high theatricality and rousing entertainment value of American musical comedy, to the blistering traditions of classical satire from Lysistrata to Three-Penny Opera.

"Perhaps its most remarkable achievement is that it does so with a fidelity to American idiom which is as current and true as the disorders it assails and the possibilities it projects. For me, it is therefore high art."
—LORRAINE HANSBERRY

"Get ready for a new genius in the theatre. He's young Oscar Brown, Jr., of Chicago, who has written the book, music and lyrics for a show titled 'Kicks & Company,' in which Sammy Davis, Jr. may star."
—DOROTHY KILGALLEN, in her
syndicated column

"A great work.. profoundly moving... moving... mirrors with extraordinary perception the conflict of soul, the moral choices that confront us today. Wonderful humor... It will in its own special way affect vast numbers with the moral force of our young people today."
—DR. MARTIN LUTHER KING, from
his comments after a reading

In the light of the above, it would be superfluous to essay further comment, other than to indicate the producers' own conviction that "Kicks & Co." represents an historic moment in musical theatre.

Copy of testimonials for *Kicks. & Co.* The names of Sammy Davis, Jr., Rosa Parks, Dave Garroway, Harry Belafonte and Mrs. Roosevelt would be added, all contrary to SEC law.

Stagebill for *Kicks & Co.*, starring Burgess Meredith as Mr. Kicks (The Devil)

ARIE CROWN THEATRE

McCormick Place • 23rd St. and South Lake Shore Dr. • Phone 225-4350

CHICAGO STAGEBILL • OFFICIAL THEATRE PROGRAMS • 53 W. JACKSON

Week of September 24, 1961 Eves. at 8:30 P.M.

BURT CHARLES D'LUGOFF • ROBERT BARRON NEMIROFF present

BURGESS MEREDITH

in

"KICKS & CO."

Also starring LONNIE SATTIN

with VI VELASCO, NICHELLE NICHOLS,
AL FREEMAN JR., WILLIAM DWYER, LYNNE FORRESTER

ZABETHE WILDE

Carol Arthur   Miriam Burton   Gino Conforti   Bernard Johnson   Nancy Ray Noel
Caryl Paige   Paul Reid Roman   Gus Solomons, Jr.   Ella Thompson

Music and Lyrics by **OSCAR BROWN, JR.**
Book by **OSCAR BROWN, JR.**
in collaboration with ROBERT BARRON NEMIROFF

Choreography by **DONALD McKAYLE & WALTER NICKS**
Settings and Lighting by JACK BLACKMAN
Costumes by EDITH LUTYENS BEL GEDDES
Musical Direction and Vocal Arrangements by JACK LEE
Arrangements, Orchestrations, Additional Music by ALONZO LEVISTER
Dance Music and Additional Arrangements by DOROTHEA FREITAG
Production Supervisor, SIDNEY EDEN
Production Stage Manager, MARVIN KLINE

| Production Directed by |
| **VINNETTE CARROLL** |

Title page for *Kicks & Co.*
Vinnette Carroll was fired and replaced by Lorraine Hansberry.

Snapshot of author with Diana Sands and family, Labor Day 1961.

Chicago Daily News, October 7, 1961. Oscar Brown, Jr. onstage, Aire Crown at McCormick Place, just prior to opening of *Kicks & Co.*

Stagebill for author's 1962 tour of *A Raisin in the Sun*.

Stagebill for
You Can't Take It With You,
starring Edgar Bergen

Stagebill for
High Button Shoes, starring
Larry Parks and Betty Garrett.

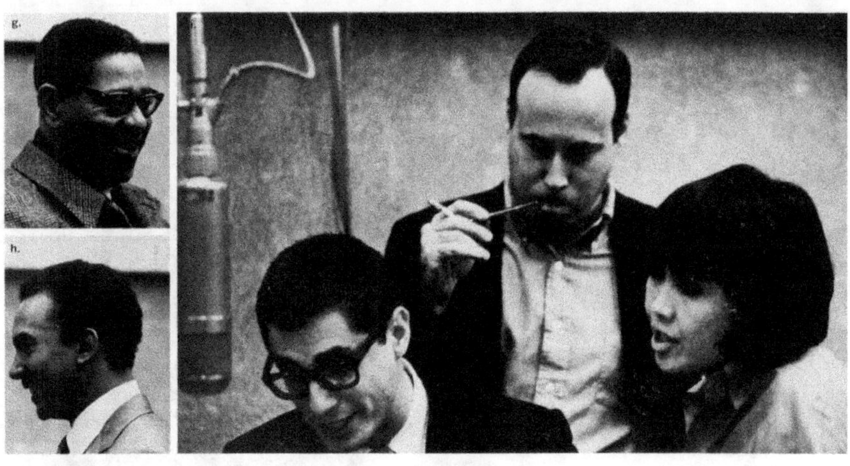

Upper left: Dizzy Gillespie and others at recording session of
Lookin' For The Man.

Lower left; Al Freeman, Jr.

Upper right: Warren Meyers, at piano; Julian Barry, standing, and Pat Suzuki.

Left: Julian Barry and José Ferrer.
Upper Center: José Ferrer and Dizzy Gillespie.
Center left: Warren Meyers.
Center right: Carl Lee.
Seated: Al Freeman, Jr. and Pat Suzuki.
Far right: José Ferrer.

LOOKIN' FOR THE MAN

Cover (purple) by Mel Williamson for LP record set of *Lookin' For The Man*.

$166 check for purchase of copy of *Lookin' For The Man*.

RAISIN ON THE ROAD

12

DEBASEMENT

This is about debasement. Death cheats all; failure, in some form, is inevitable. The "high-blown pride" we feel "when goodness is a'ripening, nips the root," and when we fall, we "fall like Lucifer." Respect, not superstition makes us honor the departed, so, speak truth to posterity.

I knew Claudia McNeil was a ball buster. Diana told me so. Lonnie said she could be "evil."[77] In my ignorance, I thought I could charm her. But from the moment I met her I knew I was in deep shit through Labor Day, and it was only early April, an evening in 1962, when I stood on the top step of the stoop of her Harlem brownstone, one of a row of historic, four-story, single-family dwellings, in the heart of Sugar Hill.

I was meeting her as the producer and director of a summer stock tour of *A Raisin In The Sun*, in which she was to repeat her famous performance of less than a year past, as Mama Lena Younger. The tour was to last through Labor Day.

Claudia knew of my involvement with *Kicks*, that I had had an affair with Diana Sands, who played her daughter, Beneatha, throughout the Broadway run and national tour, and she knew I knew what the general public didn't know: that Diana brought her before a Disciplinary Committee of the Chicago branch of Actors' Equity on the charge of unprofessional behavior due to Claudia

---

77   In a 2014 e-mail, Levister stated he 1.) did not know McNeil, but 2.) he heard she was "evil" that that was the reputation which proceeded her. See Phil Rose's previous comments.

slapping her with (according to Diana) too much force in performing the play. The charge didn't stick.

Producer, Herb Rogers wanted *Raisin* for the upscale suburban Chicago audience at his Tenthouse Theatre, in Highland Park, where the tour would end, and offered to make me his partner if I could sell it to other theatres. It was a nice credit and a challenge to produce and direct a production that could come close to the original.[78] Lorraine would be watching. So would Bobby and Diana. The film of the play had received only moderate praise and receipts for Columbia Pictures; incipient racism in high-line Eastern resorts, where most successful summer stock theatres operated, and the fact that some theatre owners were prejudiced, made the play a hard sell.

But I managed to convince six of them, making for seven stands in all. Each would advance a portion of pre-production costs of my casting (with Claudia's approval), rehearsing and directing the show, and each would build a set to my specifications. I would be the advance man, arriving at each theatre before the cast and insuring things would run smoothly when they opened. Claudia was to receive $1,500 a week and the actors worked for scale. I saw no obstacle except the task of dealing with Claudia.

As I stood on the top stoop of the turreted townhouse designed by Stanford White, two alike on either side, my concern was: would things run smoothly with the "difficult" Ms. McNeil; would she behave? Diana told me Claudia had had a tantrum involving Glenn Turman, who played 10 year-old, Travis, son of Walter Lee, played by Sidney Poitier. Glenn was well mannered and respectful of his fellow cast members and, at an appointed time each day, called his mom on the backstage phone. While speaking with her one day, Claudia passed by on the way to her dressing room and said in her booming voice, "Get off the damn phone!"

And Glenn's mom, who knew Claudia from their neighborhood and recognized her voice, asked Glenn, "What did she say to you?"

And when Glenn told her she got mad and said, "Tell her to kiss my ass!" and Glenn said to Claudia's departing back, "Kiss my ass!"

---

78 As seen before, the original production had closed its post-Broadway tour in the summer of 1961.

Claudia immediately informed stage manager, Lenny Auerbach, that either Glenn would be fired or she would quit the show. It happened at intermission and the two were hustled back to their dressing rooms. Phil Rose and Auerbach, eventfully, convinced Claudia that by insisting on her demand there would have to be a hearing by Equity against Glenn, that witnesses could be called against Claudia and she eventfully, settled for an apology from young Turman.

In another incident,[79] Claudia accused Glenn of stuffing the commode in his dressing room with too much toilet paper, causing it to flood through the ceiling into the fancy "star" dressing room she, soon, occupied after the show's opening. This time Ruby Dee refereed on Turman's part. Some insiders knew this stuff, but for the public, Claudia was the personification (as the playwright intended) of African-American matriarchal society – and she knew it. She almost won the Tony; she won the Golden Globe, the Cannes and the Foreign Film Critics' Best Actress Awards. She was bigtime and, in all likelihood, becoming more difficult by the day.

"Was I masochistic?" I wondered, as I stood on that doorstep, confronting a venerable door of goodly design, awaiting the woman who would be the prime focus of my attention all summer long. Scratch a masochist you find a sadist, but I detected neither in myself. I was still somewhat naïve, but these were pre-Assassination times. Civil rights and banning of the Bomb were all consuming. Sexual freedom was parenthetical and late in arriving.

Yet, I knew that eating shit, be it that of star, producer, or, even, playwright or composer, is endemic to the life of a young director. I walked out on Vicki Crandall, in Maine;[80] then, *Kicks*. Now, it was important I learn to control my temper. Throwing fits, as did David Belasco, Jerry Robbins and Toscanini, may aid one's colorful image, but it can also destroy a budding director's reputation. Collegial collaboration is the goal in theatrical endeavors, but getting a show

---

79 Reiterated by Turman at the televised September 20, 2014 memorial service for actress, Ruby Dee, at the Riverside Church.

80 Vicki, Rodgers and Hammerstein's longtime rehearsal pianist, insisted I stage *Carousel* exactly as had Billy Hammerstein, a couple of years before. It was the third time I had done the show and I never liked *Lilliom* in the first place. Except for Fritz Lang's 1934 film. I did not have to, but I walked out and was replaced by "Larry" Lawrence Kasha, who along with Harold Prince coproduced *She Loves Me* and *Applause*, before dying of AIDS. Earlier, I had offended Vicki when, on opening night of *Kismet,* I stayed backstage to greet composers Robert Wright and George Forrest but, instead of waiting a few moments longer, departed for an encounter with a chorine rather than remain to meet Bette Davis. I regret not having met the great actress.

on can often be a choice between throwing a tantrum and eating shit. I was good at one and needed improvement in the other.

When I was four, my father, about to depart on a sales trip, inquired what present I wanted upon his return. "A Russian sailor," I replied, because he said he had been one (which was untrue). But when he returned with a substitute of some other derivation, I threw a fit worthy of a John Barrymore impersonating Belasco. "IT'S NOT A RUSSIAN SAILOR!" I screamed. "But it's still a sailor," my father reasoned uneasily. "THIS IS NOT A RUSSIAN SAIL-OR!" I bellowed to the full capacity of my cherub lungs and, in my heart, I believe my father looked at me askance from then on.

Humility at this point in my theatrical journey was a necessary requirement. Only to that extent did masochism bring me to the doorstep of the site built by McKim, Mead & White, for whites, before being inherited by upwardly mobile African-Americans and becoming the subject of a lowdown Cab Calloway blues refrain in a minor key: "'Cause I'm a Striver, from Striver's Row, Vo-do, vo-do, vo-do."

I was greeted at the door not by Claudia but by the owner of the house, a slight African-American in his mid-sixties, Herman Mc-Coy, Claudia's new husband, the proprietor of a successful beauty parlor, who had been widowed only months prior to his marriage to my star. He smiled shyly, ushered me into the hallway, and, after introducing himself, said, "She's downstairs."

And he began leading me through the narrow house, a couple of dozen feet wide, a good part occupied by staircases and accompanying hallways. The fourth story of the landmark masqueraded under the euphemism employed by hyperbolic sellers of Manhattan real estate and was, in fact, nothing but what we Midwesterners call a basement. That's where we were going.

Polite but strangely out of place in his own home, uneasy perhaps playing host to a white boy in a Brooks Brothers suit, shepherding him through the wainscoted hallway, past the open sliding French doors of a high-ceilinged parlor whose three bay windows fronted the street, allowing the young visitor with the trained eye of an experienced con man, *goniff* cum budding producer-director, right hand glances at a wood fireplace with a marble mantel and a crystal chandelier, McCoy said nothing, just led the way.

Walking on inlaid wood floors, I slyly ogled, on the hallway walls, faded pictures from an earlier time competing with dainty, new decorations of a celebratory nature, as if a party had recently occurred, a party perhaps in recognition of the current reign of Queen Claudia, for she aspired to nothing less than becoming the successor to her late-in-life mentor and co-religionist, the great singer-actress, Ethel Waters, till then, the highest-paid star in the history of the Broadway theatre.[81] Claudia showed her mastery of the Pearl Bailey style in *Simply Heavenly*.[82] At that time she was a svelte "Good Old Gal" (the song she sang in that production) but, since playing Mama Younger, she had ballooned to well over 200 pounds and now wore mostly Lerner's oversized dresses.

Having shown off-Broadway that broad comedy and brassy singing were within her compass, because of her Broadway triumph in Lorraine's play, her goal of being recognized, like Waters, as master of both comedy and tragedy, was now within reach. With her ascendancy, one could sense that husband Herman was dazed by his forced entry into the realm of celebrity at so late a time in his life, and just after the death of a loved one, his previous mate.

As he led the still confident me (confident of my charm, knowledge, diplomacy and cunning in winning over his new wife) to the basement recreation room where his bride awaited my arrival, let me tell you she was born in Baltimore on August 13,1917; her mother was Apache, her father black and they divorced when she was six. Her mother, whom she did not like, brought her to New York, placing her, at the age of twelve, with the Heckscher Foundation for Children where she began working as a mother's helper. Adopted from there by a Jewish family, she learned to speak fluent Yiddish but became a Catholic.

She started singing at the age of six; sang "Pennies From Heaven" at the Apollo Amateur Night and bandleader, Chick Webb, the great hunch-backed drummer, took an interest in her.

---

81 $5,000 weekly, supposedly unequalled until Jackie Gleason played Uncle Sid in *Take Me Along*, for David Merrick, receiving $5001. BIO FOR ETHEL WATERS SEE APPENDIX #14.

82 According to critic, Frances Herridge in the *The New York Post*, "With the earthy comedy and timing of a Pearl Bailey, plus a mature wisdom of her own, she can put over a wisecrack or a song with enormous effect..." Herridge also compared Claudia to the immortal Bessie Smith, saying "The rave reviews were for every facet of her (McNeil's) performance – her marvelous sense of comedy timing...and her big, bold Bessie Smith type voice..." and the 1957 Off-Broadway hit by Langston Hughes was swiftly transferred to Broadway and recorded by Columbia Records.

This led to her being tutored by the immortal Eubie Blake. At twenty she joined the chorus at the *Black Cat* club, in Greenwich Village, at $13.50 a week, and later toured with Katherine Dunham's Dance Troupe.

I do not know how they met, but biographies say she was advised by Ethel Waters to turn to acting and studied with Maria Ouspenskaya (1876-1949), best known as the fortune-telling gypsy Cassandra to Lon Chaney, Jr.'s *Wolfman*.[83] Claudia played in stock in Roxbury, Massachusetts for a season or two, and then was accepted at Actors Studio. She auditioned successfully for producer Kermit Bloomgarden to understudy the role of Tabitha in Arthur Miller's *The Crucible*, and eventually went on in the role herself. When Waters declined recreating her *Member Of The Wedding* (directed by Harold Clurman) role for television, McNeil replaced her. Then came *Simply Heavenly*.

In 1958 she appeared on Broadway in the 13 performance, flop production of the adaptation, by Christopher Sergel, of Sherwood Anderson's *Winesburg, Ohio*, as well as in the film *The Last Angry Man*, with Paul Muni. That same year, Elia Kazan offered her a role in poet Archibald MacLeish's eventual Pulitzer and Tony Award-winning play, *JB*, but she turned it down for *A Raisin In The Sun*. Through the careers of Waters and McNeil you see the fine hands of both Clurman and Kazan (who directed Waters in *Pinky*, starring Jeanne Crain). The official biography[84] omits years of "straight" jobs and attributes years of unemployment at her true calling to the dearth of good roles available to women of color. She spent time writing publicity and overseeing a radio station in the Caribbean.

Her first marriage, her bio states, had been to "a wonderful man" who died in World War II and she had two sons who died in Korea. No names are given. If true, these are devastating facts. Her suffering must have been enormous and partly accounts for her artistry in credibly portraying Mama Younger's torments. But this "official" bio was about to be contradicted by something she would

---

83 Even more rewarding is her performance as Charles Boyer's mother in the 1939 film *Love Affair*, with the exquisite Irene Dunne. The almost documentary-like mother-son relationship so credibly created by these remarkable actors (replete with Ouspenskya's actual piano playing) are a paradigm for future such familial on-screen bonding.

84 Schomburg Center for Research in Black Culture, papers of Claudia McNeil.

say to me momentarily, for now, Herman McCoy, the bearer of a seemingly heavy load, led confident me to the summit of the stairway and we descended into a very palpable hell.

The setting was eerie, a space between a shiny linoleum floor and a ceiling of a caramel color which failed to conceal ugly overhead heating pipes. The linoleum floor, unlike the tatty one in Diana's small apartment, was newly laid. I wasn't sure what was bothering me, the slipperiness of the floor, the harsh lighting in the confined space, or the ugly pipes overhead, but I was uneasy then and it haunts me now.

I viewed Claudia McNeil on stage and off at the Blackstone, in Chicago, while I waited for Diana after the show, but now here she was, looking, as the *Time* critic cruelly wagged, "like a man in a fright wig." And the creases and contours of her chubby face blended with the diabolical twinkle in her piercing eyes as she summoned all the warmth and fake humility in her venomous arsenal acquired over years of maltreatment and hard knocks. Highball in one hand, she shook my hand firmly with the other and declared, "Oh, Mr. Eden, I am so looking forward to learning from your knowledge and wisdom."

It was said without sarcasm. "What a joke!" I thought! I was twenty-six, she was forty-seven. She created the role, made the movie and played it on national tour. How could a summer stock, white boy like me impart anything to a woman who wowed Broadway and the world in creating the role? I immediately insisted there was nothing I could do which would improve her great performance and said it was my job to honor the play by mounting it well and casting it with care. We were standing facing each other. Herman went to the far side of the room, behind a bar along the uptown wall, in order to fetch me a drink. And then, completely out of the blue, Claudia announced to me, "You know I had a son by Adam Clayton Powell." It was a statement, not a question.

I mean no disrespect to the outspoken Congressman and minister, or to his descendants, but that is what she said; cut out my tongue for repeating it, but it's my life and that's what she said.

I don't know if Claudia even knew Adam Clayton Powell, Jr. (1908-1972), Minster of the Abyssinian Baptist Church and Congressman from Harlem (1945-1971), the first African-American to so be elected from the Empire State, but Claudia knew something about me from Diana, or Bobby, or even Lorraine herself. You don't agree to a tour, repeating your famous role, unless you've checked out the director. She was putting me on, testing and taking pleasure in making a fool of me, biting the hand that fed her. Because that's what I was doing; feeding her for the summer, increasing her fan base. I booked the tour in first-rate summer theatres; I "sold" the, often, reluctant theatre-owners.

Herman, polite, never uxorious, but still acting dazed, made, and we consumed, more whiskey highballs, sitting on a couch before a coffee table adjacent to the bar, and Claudia and I smoked cigarettes. But what little else was said that spring evening escapes my unfailing memory for I was stunned by the falsity of her initial greeting and the Adam Clayton Powell, Jr. remark. But I remember that when I spoke, I was heir to a vast repertoire of stares from her strong, but squinty, regal-eagle eyes, stares ranging from suspicion to wonderment to fake benevolence and, after this bizarre beginning, I went home, by cab, feeling uncertain I could handle this wily woman. I had met my match.

Oh, how I wish I could return to the basement of the house built by Stanford White. I felt silly, as if I'd refused to call the bet in the poker game with the lady in Diana's basement, because, being the person I am now, knowing what I now know, I would have taken her *meshugas* in stride, played it cool, played her along, asked her about crippled Chick Webb, who took up the drums because his doctor recommended it as a way to "loosen up" his bones. And Buddy Rich called him "The Daddy of us all." I would have told them with the confidence and pedantry that permeates my personality, the dwarflike, crippled man would never have played at all had he not suffered from tuberculosis of the spine since childhood!

Maybe Herman was hip. Living in this 60 year-old house, running a popular business in the neighborhood for his former wife for many years, surely, he would have tales to tell of the days and locales and people of Harlem that interested me so. But Claudia screwed up everything by putting me on.

Awakening the next morning, I was even more determined to assemble a cast that would do the play justice. A week or so later, I heard from someone that Herman and Claudia had met the previous fall after the death of Herman's fourth wife, Madeline, who hung herself from the overhead pipes in the basement.

I told you this was about de basement.

****

The first day of rehearsal went smoothly, especially the morning, when we simply read the play. It was clear I had assembled a powerful cast. This put Claudia in a swell mood, so we hopped in a cab (we were rehearsing in a dance studio-rehearsal hall on Broadway and 56th) and went to lunch together, a few short blocks downtown, at Sardi's. We were joined by a lady whom she introduced, that morning, as Velma, her hired companion, an African-American woman of the same age as her employer. She would be with us until the end of the tour.

Slender, well coiffed, but plain of feature and dress, Velma never expressed an opinion unless asked to do so. She developed friendships, over that summer, with members of the cast, but, whether by nature or because of some tragic event, she was a lady to whom self-abnegation and non-assertiveness came naturally. I sensed she had something valuable to offer, but because of "her position," whose boundaries were clearly established and adhered to by both parties, I made a weak effort to prompt her participation at that lunch at Sardi's, but not much thereafter.

From time to time before, during and after the meal, for these were the days of coffee and cigarettes in the world in general and the theatre in particular, Claudia would ejaculate these terse commands, accompanied by a loud snapping of the fingers, just like the Emperor Jones: "Cigarette," in this case grandly proffering a slightly outstretched palm, as queens might do. This would be followed by a well-modulated bark, "Light!" and Velma would similarly comply.

Like most everyone else, I smoked cigarettes throughout my waking hours and carried matches and lighter on my person, but it was clear that no one but Velma was allowed the honor of lighting her mistress's coffin nails.

Initially, sophomoric trouble maker that I am, I felt uncomfortable with Velma's silence at table and tried to bring her into the conversation from time to time, but Claudia brushed my egalitarianism aside with a stern look of disapproval. This judgmental look had became integral to her playing of the role of Mama Younger, as reflected in publicity photographs chosen as the best representation of her character. Mama Younger remains the center of a drama, which says: Integration is valueless if it means joining the Rat Race and remaining clueless to one's ethnic history and its higher values, though the author summarized her intent succinctly saying it's about "human dignity." Mama knows what's what before the others do, although the African, Assagai has already "gotten it," and transmitted "it", to her daughter, Beneatha. Claudia played Mama as world-weary but blessed with an intrinsic fount of knowledge, a woman who never lost sight of her values. (SEE APPENDIX #15.)

And these same characteristics now invested Claudia's offstage persona as well. Mama could do no wrong and neither could Claudia. She was a star now and she wanted things her way. Velma had her position; the supporting cast had theirs. We were her satellites; like Herman, who was not far away. Indeed, he sat with us at table, the "star" table in the midst of all the lunchtime commotion, as the saucy waiters, dressed in red bolero jackets and black tuxedo pants, scurried about, a hubbub of chatter and a clatter of dishes for a sound track. And portraits of Broadway actors, covering every inch of space from ceiling to chair rail, stared down upon the assemblage whilst you wished you were one of them, too.

Only the Herman who sat with us in the famous eatery, where business was booming even on a Monday, was a small toy pet dog, six inches high, of a tannish color with a red felt tongue and a black cotton nose. He, too, would be with us until Labor Day. He was placed at table so there were four of us: me, Claudia, Velma and the dog… Herman. And Claudia would address the dog throughout the meal executing, in her best Pearl Bailey manner, such "house laugh" lines as, "How do like that B.S., Herman? " or "Shut up and eat your food, Herman!" or, she would pick him up and spank his bottom, saying, "Herman, you're a bad boy," or "bad dog!" It was semi-humorous, though curious, so I took it for the gag it was. It was all part of eating shit till Labor Day.

I said the morning went well because we only read the play, we didn't start blocking and staging it, and the remarkable cast of near unknowns, four of whom progressed to stardom and another two had long and successful careers, were well-prepared. They had much to live up to; the original cast and initial replacements included: Sidney Poitier, Ossie Davis, Ruby Dee, Louis Gossett, Lonnie Elder III, Ivan Dixon, Robert Hooks (Bobby Dean Hooks), Douglas Turner Ward, Diana Sands, Glynn Turman, Frances Foster, Beah Richards, Roy Glenn, Howland Chamberlain, John Fiedler among them. Only Ed Hall, who played the small moving man bit the first night on Broadway and, then replaced Ivan and went on tour as Assagai, and, of course, Claudia, remained from the original ensemble. Even though Diana and I had broken up, I asked if she would like to repeat her role as Beneatha and patch things up with Claudia, but she declined and I had difficulty finding someone who could match her performance.

Gail Fisher, a New Jersey girl whose credits were limited to small roles on television and a commercial for a soap detergent and who, her bio claims, was the first woman of color to appear in a TV ad, won the role. She was in *Simply Heavenly.* Later as Mike Connors' secretary in the TV series *Mannix,* she was rewarded with an Emmy, the first black woman to be so honored.

Gloria Foster had played the role of Ruth Younger in a Syracuse production[85] and Rose signed her for *Purlie.* She was a Chicagoan who attended Goodman and had a classical background, playing roles such as Volumnia, Jocasta and Hecuba. In years to come she would star on Broadway in *Having Our Say,* the play about the Delany Sisters, win three Obies, and give birth to two sons with husband, Clarence Williams III. She is best known, by some, for playing the Oracle in *The Matrix* and *The Matrix Reloaded.*

On Broadway and on tour, Ed Hall replaced Ivan Dixon in the role of Joseph Assagai. Ed became a star in residence at the Trinity Repertory in Providence, and, later, appeared on Broadway in August Wilson's, *Joe Turner's Come And Gone.* Ed was my Assagai.

I cast Al Freeman, Jr. in the role of George Murchison. After *Blues For Mr. Charlie,* in 1964, he appeared with Frank Sinatra, in *The Detective,* later, with Fred Astaire, in *Finian's Rainbow.* He starred in *My Sweet Charlie* and gave an indelible portrayal of Elijah Muhammad in Spike Lee's, *Malcolm X.* When the film *Lilies*

---

85   Phil Rose released the stock rights to the play earlier than usual and a pick-up production played a two week stint at the Bucks County Playhouse the previous summer, too.

Of The Field was made into the musical *Look To The Lillies* (1970), Al starred in the leading role opposite Shirley Booth. For 15 years he had a major role on the soap, *One Life To Live*, and portrayed Malcolm X., in *Roots*.

I saw Raymond St. Jacques in the role of the Judge (a part he would assay years later on the daytime TV court room series, *Superior Court*, long before *Judge Judy* and Judge Joe Brown) in Jean Genet's *The Blacks*, in whiteface, at the St. Marks Place Theatre. He was imposing, his voice was rich and musical and a devilishly ironic look was the central feature of his distinctive face. He played small roles at the Shakespeare Festival in Stratford, Connecticut, and larger parts, such as Caliban, at the San Diego Shakespeare Festival, but *The Blacks* was his first big role in New York and he was selling jewelry in the East Village, he told me, when he came in to read for the part of Walter Lee Younger. He was very different from Ossie and Sidney, but just as believable. He was stepping into a larger role than he had ever played before and in top company. His future career was remarkable.[86]

Vernon Washington was terrific, as Bobo,[87] and Mel Haynes played the sole white character. He was effective and properly absurd in the role Howland and John Fiedler played so well before. But, unlike Broadway and the national tour that followed, Claudia was at the center of all things on and offstage and she and the cast decided not to like poor Mel. I could do little in his defense.

The cast was composed of career-driven individuals four of whom would be stars soon enough, but Gail was vulnerable because Claudia slapped her harder and harder every day, as opening night approached. And, just as Claudia, good Method actress that she was, did not, as was true of the character she played, like Mr. Lindner, the white man who would keep her family in check, and transferred her dislike to Mel, so, too, would she slap Gail Fisher, or

---

86   Starring in the classic 1970 film about two black detectives, Chester Himes,' *Cotton Goes To Harlem,* in which he played the role of Coffin Ed, the earlier *Pawnbroker,* starring Rod Steiger, directed by Sidney Lumet, *The Green Berets, The Comedians,* from a story by Graham Greene, starring Sir Alec Guinness, Elizabeth Taylor and Richard Burton, Raymond was the first actor to appear as Martin Luther King, Jr. – opposite Broderick Crawford's J. Edgar Hoover.

87   A World War II vet, he went to Hollywood and carved out a film career in *The Last Starfighter, Friday 13th Part V,* and *The Dark,* among others.

any girl who played Beneatha, with the same vigorous anger, Mama would, in reality, have employed.

I have not been able to locate Carlos Felice, who played nine year-old Travis Younger, but it appears he did not pursue an acting career. Otherwise, every other member of my cast is deceased.

****

From my point of view, rehearsals started to sour when it became apparent Claudia had no intention of doing anything but that which she had done before; that all the bullshit about learning from my knowledge and wisdom was a lie and she wanted the blocking, the moves of the other actors, to match the original; I was to be, simply, a traffic cop, the most abhorrent epithet in the profession. Whenever someone made a move she would say: "Is he (or she) gonna' do it like that?" or, when they said something it was, "Is she gonna' say it like that?"

But I shut up. It was debasement time and I was willing to cooperate because the cast was excellent and I was confident the production would be a success.

But toward the end of the rehearsal period, whether she knew of my urging Nemiroff and D'Lugoff to hire George Abbott, or whether she was referring to Glenna Syse's review of *Kicks & Co.*, in the *Chicago Sun-Times*, ("What this show needs is George Abbott" with those two words GEORGE ABBOTT in bold face), Claudia, during rehearsals and in front of the cast, began calling me, "Mr. Abbott." "What we gonna' do 'bout this flower pot, Mr. Abbott?" she'd say. The first time she said it, the cast burst out laughing. Then, and subsequently, I pretended as if I hadn't heard her. It was a new experience for me. Her game was divide and conquer. Unite the cast against management. There was no Sidney Poitier or Phil Rose to stand in the way.

She was a big lady with a big mouth and she knew how to use it; she was getting even at the world through yours truly. Now, *SHE* was in charge, in charge of another Sidney. It wasn't a matter of directorial incompetence. We weren't discussing motivations. The meanings of the play are clear. My knowledge of similar people and neighborhoods like those in *Raisin* and my indoctrination from boyhood, in addition to my defiant exploration of the South Side of

Chicago from teenage years onward, substantiated my competency. There was no excuse for McNeil's behavior. She had no offstage complaints. I catered to her.

And the situation between Claudia and Gail was worsening. Claudia was striking Gail with such force that Gail began crying through Claudia's eloquent speech that follows the slap. The first time it happened Claudia's eyes dropped to the floor and her body slumped like a tire deflated by an awl. After a long pause, she straightened up and came out of character slowly. Then, while Gail's eyes glittered with tears, Claudia's sought mine and the vicinity in which I was sitting, finally finding me at the rear of the rehearsal hall. In a voice from the depths of her oversized being, in ominous tones wavering between a mutter and a groan, she declared with an overabundance of solemn patience, as if speaking to a five year-old: "She can't cry there. I'm the only one can cry like that" and she was correct. It was her moment in the play, not Beneatha's. Gail would, bravely, from then on, control the natural tendency to cry, but it wasn't the end of the problem.

Rehearsals in New York ended and we were bound for our opening engagement. I went a day in advance and the cast was to travel the following day, with Claudia flying in independently.

13

THE SLAP

Proust profoundly proclaimed, "Remembrance of a particular form is but regret for a particular moment; and houses, roads, avenues are as fugitive, alas, as the years."[88] The road was ancient, the weather ideal and the sky pure Tiffany blue on that day in June, as I passed a huge acreage of fertile farm land, which I later learned had been the homestead of one Joseph Hayden, a 19th century farmer-speculator. Just around the corner from the western shore of Lake Wesserunsett, six miles outside Skowhegan, my destination was the Lakewood Inn, home to the oldest stock theatre in America.[89]

It was courageous of the management (and a tribute to their audience) to have booked the play. In North and South, there were violent physical confrontations and a constant call from leaders, such as Wyatt Tee Walker, James Farmer and Martin Luther King, for President Kennedy to tangle with Congress for action to combat Jim Crow. The young President had just recently made a speech calling for a new era in civil rights, and for legislation, which everyone on the Left predicted would never pass, but would be filibustered, as

---

88 *Remembrance Of Things Past*, by Marcel Proust. English edition published in seven volumes in 1922, in French: *A la Rechereche du temps perdu*, (*In Search Of Lost Time*). Alain de Botton, in his book, *How Proust Can Change Your Life*, Vintage International (New York) 1997, refers to the fact that Proust encouraged writers to quote from other writers and in following pages I quote from Proust profusely.

89 It is the oldest "resident" stock company, too (the Lakewood Theatre, founded in 1901). A long list of famous Broadway and film stars, beginning with the silent screen era, appeared at, what was touted to me as, and turned out to be, a gem of a theatre. *Life With Father* premiered there in 1938 before its long Broadway run. The theatre has been designated the "State Theatre of Maine." As stated previously, Victoria Crandall's Brunswick Summer Theatre at Bowdoin College, is now the "State Music Theatre of Maine" and there is no other connection between the two.

had always been the case. Meanwhile, Malcolm X. scoffed at the futility of achieving progress through peaceful non-violence. This was the atmosphere in which we performed and presented Hansberry's historic play.

Turning right, at the end of a short approach, I entered the vast campsite. A protective purlieu of trees appeared to the left, and then I saw the Lakewood Inn for the first time. Cabins peeked out from behind over one hundred stately birch trees and pines that towered above them. Finally, at the end of the road, there lay a heavenly vista, the placid, nearly torpid, lake that radiated spirituality. A sacred Indian campsite for centuries, it was overtaken by the white man only in the 1850's.

Then, it became Hayden's farm and, later, a meeting place for spiritualists and, finally, a swampy amusement park, before a Bowdoin graduate, Herbert L. Swett, assumed management in 1899, two years after a theatre had opened on the premises. And the Swett family was still in charge, though, when it came to the theatre, they no longer produced their own plays but had succumbed to the practice of booking "packaged" productions, which others, such as I, had mounted in New York.

A round building containing a restaurant stood before the lake so one could eat and view the tranquil waters simultaneously. Perched off to the right was the lovely theatre building, surrounded by larches of trees, with a Georgian-style façade and a portico fronted by white pilasters and lush foliage. It was (is) inviting. Inside was a wonderful proscenium theatre with plush, red velvet seating and a backstage worthy of a Broadway house.

That evening I was assigned to a comfortable cabin in the woods, not far from the lake and the theatre and, the next morning, Claudia, Velma and I met for breakfast at the "star" table, in the spacious dining room overlooking the beautiful lake. Claudia was beaming; she was in a terrific mood. The table sat six and Herman, the stuffed dog, was, once more, the fourth.

Claudia, making room for raucous asides from time to time, spoke with the dog and spanked him throughout breakfast for various infractions, barking commands, imprecations and low, surly insults to the phantom husband, while she demanded, throughout the meal and afterward, both "Cigarette" and "Light!" from Velma.

The waiters and waitresses, mostly kids working summer jobs, got a kick out of it, and the fact that Negroes were not only appearing at the famous theatre across the way, but eating in their dining room, a room resplendent with white tablecloths, shiny silverware and hardy Maine victuals, was a page in their respective memory books. Mainers, Yankees to the core, because of their proximity to nature and distance from the corrupting influences from nether states, are, generally, open-minded and kind, but, "What, the hell are they up to?" they must have said to themselves, "these matronly Negro ladies with the stuffed dog and the handsome white boy in a seersucker suit?"

The Lakewood Theatre was rewarded with a triumphant opening; the audience was deeply moved. The two-week run would be a great success. But trouble arrived the night after the opening, when Gail Fisher asked to see me following that night's performance. I wasn't surprised. "The slap" had grown in intensity until Claudia was slapping Gail much harder than she had ever slapped Diana.

The slap across the face, as utilized by modern playwrights, to create, further, or resolve dramatic conflict, may be as old as the Greeks, or perhaps was common stage deportment in Shakespearean comedies, tragedies and historical plays, but I believe, until someone more knowledgeable, with concrete evidence, shows otherwise, the slap across the face, though commonplace in today's plays and in films, is a theatrical device of mid-20th century usage and that, as far as the modern theatre is concerned, there is a point of origin and that origin has a through-line. My learned friends may say the slap IS an element in Shakespeare plays and cite *Romeo And Juliet* as an example. But if such business was intended by the author and his cohorts, or even interpolated later by a David Garrick or a Henry Irving, I say, the slapping was performed with a glove, something both sexes wore with regularity up until World War II. On stage duelists delivered challenges with gloves, not the bare palm of the hand. In every production of *King Lear* I've ever seen, in challenging his half-brother to a duel to the death in the denouement, Edgar, following both the fashion of the day and proper stage comportment, violently strikes Edmund employing the kind of large glove worn by horsemen and swordsmen of the period, in reality, a heavily padded mitt if the performance is to reach it's conclusion, for The Bastard has a lot more lines to say.

Eclipsed as a playwriting device by the revolver (see *Hedda Gabler* and *The Seagull*, among others), slapping a fellow human across the face is a barbarism reserved for moderns and, while it would take the combined mnemonic skills of John Mason Brown, George Jean Nathan, Brooks Atkinson and James Gibbons Huneker to ascertain the first instance of one actor slapping another as part of a theatrical offering, the practice was, probably, unknown to Capulets and Montagues throughout the ages.

"How the crowd does love slaps," says a character in the 1916 Leonid Andreyev play (which became the first film produced by MGM), but that pitiable, poetic paragon of self-effacement, the "HE," of *He Who Gets Slapped* gets slapped, in all, one hundred and fifty-five times, all but one hundred-fifty two of them occurring offstage; one of the on stage slaps is a mere "circus" slap and the evening's climax occurs through the more potent devices of poison and a packed pistol. A circus slap is not a real slap.

Oscar slaps Birdie in Lillian Hellman's *Little Foxes* (1939, directed by Herman Shumlin). The indignant Kate Keller, upholding her villainous husband, a manufacturer of faulty war weapons, slaps son, Chris, in Arthur Miller's *All My Sons* (1947), directed by Elia Kazan. Scarlett slaps both Ashley and Rhett, but that is a movie, it does not count; we are talking about plays.

Cleopatra may have beat-up on the messenger but I think not. Eventally the poor fellow would have gone to the director and complained and they would, mutually, in a fraternal manner, have substituted circus slaps, The Method be damned.

The slap is a key moment in the influential *Country Girl* (1950), written by Group Theatre member, Clifford Odets, Miller's forerunner. It is play about the theatre and is known to most every serious American actor. Lee Strasberg, who was, not only Kazan's close associate but also his mentor in the Group Theatre (which lasted the decade from 1931 to 1941), directed *Country Girl*. Kazan says in his autobiography, Strasberg was "the center," the force that held the Group Theatre together and that Lee was his teacher and guide. Strasberg was a masterful stage director, but known, for some time, to most people, primarily as the guru of the American spin-off of the Stanislavsky method, renamed The Method.[90]

Kazan, Odets and Strasberg met in the Group. Actors Studio was founded in that same year of 1947 in which *All My Sons* won the Tony for Best Author and Best Director, and also the New York Drama Critics Circle Award for Best Play of the Year, beating out *Iceman Cometh*. Kazan and two other members of the Group Theatre - producer, Cheryl Crawford (*Brigadoon*, etc.), and director, character actor, Robert "Bobby" Lewis (director of *Brigadoon* and *Teahouse Of The August Moon*, among others) were the Studio's three main founders. Bobby Lewis left the organization to teach his own version of Stanislavsky and Strasberg assumed the helm in 1951, soon after opening the *Country Girl*, and he remained in charge until his death on February 17,1982. I never met Lee and the only time I ever saw him, strangely, was the day before his decease, yet, Lee Strasberg affected my life and the lives of most actors of my time.[91]

Strasberg's direction of *Country Girl* was masterful. The play, which concerns an alcoholic ex-star who is a pathological liar and his enduring wife, who is attracted to the stage director of her husband's comeback vehicle, was rough stuff for 1950. With memorable settings by Mordecai Gorelik, it starred Paul Kelly, who went to prison for beating his girlfriend's boyfriend in a real life Hollywood love affair just a few years before and knew what it was to suffer, as the faded star. Steven Hill, the original D.A., in TV's *Law And Order*, played Bernie Dodd, the director of Elgin's vehicle, a character, supposedly, modeled after Kazan. Uta Hagen played the lady of the title. The play has often been revived, memorably with Jason Robards, Jr., and, not so memorably, with Morgan Freeman (in 2008). Bing Crosby nearly won an Oscar playing the role.[92] I

---

90   Strasberg, who was born in Austria-Hungary in 1901 and who, like Claudia McNeil, studied with Maria Ouspenskaya, but earlier, in 1925, and, also with Richard Boleslavsy in the mid-Twenties, returned to acting once more, in films, playing Hyman Roth, a thinly disguised Meyer Lansky, in Francis Ford Coppola's, *Godfather Part II* (1974).

91   Actors Studio, with Lee in charge, became home to The Method and operated in a variety of places before ending up in its present location, an old church on 43rd Street, between 9th and 10th Avenues in Manhattan. Al Pacino, Ellyn Burstyn and Alec Baldwin currently head Actors Studio. There is a Lee Strasberg Institute at another Manhattan location, another on the West Coast, and various teachers teach The Method throughout the world.

92   I have always been told that Elgin is based on actor Russell Collins, who played the leading role in the Group's production of the Kurt Weill musical, *Johnny Johnson*. I played a bit role, the

saw the national touring company at the old Erlanger Theatre, in 1952, with Hagen, Robert Young and Dane Clark.

Country Girl features, in fact, turns on the country girl of the title, Georgie Elgin, slapping Bernie Dodd resoundingly on the puss in an encounter in the Gorelik setting - a backstage basement dressing room, which prominently featured overhead heating pipes painted a putrid brown-ochre. It was like an explosion; it startled every member of the audience.

The production itself was electrifying; the acting visceral. You experienced, along with the actors, themselves, the emotions of the main characters. You were as surprised as were the pitiably magnificent, Robert Young,[93] the edgy, about to jump out of his skin, Dane Clark and the faithful and wrongly accused Uta Hagen, as the events in the play unfolded. Today, the slapping business is seen abundantly in films and playwrights employ it ordinarily.

As an apprentice at the Cleveland Playhouse, I appeared in a showcase presentation, an original play, in which Dom DeLuise, who was playing my father, slapped me rigorously throughout rehearsals and performances. The idea of Dom being my father was so risible I usually broke up each time he delivered the blow, which only made him madder and more vigorous in his slapping. I learned then that dealing with a stage slap, giving, or taking one, is a skill thespians should master early on, for, though the goal of acting is the revelation of life's truths in man's earthly existence, acting, it also may be said, is lying, dissembling, though some abominate the proposition and, understandably, claim the opposite.

But, just as, I would later learn, the prostitutes of Juarez, and other Mexican border towns, because of their Catholic upbringings and the Papal dictates under which they labor, abhor oral sex and, consequently, are educated in the technique of, first, insisting the lights of the bordello bedroom be extinguished and, then, by applying cold cream to the underpinnings of their chins, simulate the giving of a blow job, so, too, do actors learn the technique of cheating

---

stage manager, in a stellar Cleveland Playhouse production of the play in 1953, with its Artistic Director, K. Elmo Lowe, as Elgin, Eve Roberts, as his wife and Kirk Willis, as Bernie Dodd.

93   Those who know Robert Young (1907-1998) only from TV's *"Father Know Best"* and *"Marcus Welby, M.D."* would be surprised at this native Chicagoan's commanding talent on stage. He was, of course, a member of Alcoholic Anonymous, and had a long battle with the bottle just as did Elgin, the character he portrayed.

a slap by, without flinching, planting one's feet firmly and standing one's ground, as if unaware the blow is coming, and, only when flesh touches flesh, that is, only when the blow arrives and never before, it is allowable to "go with the blow," following its direction (upstage), deflecting the impact, but only doing so when flesh meets flesh, never before, never in anticipation. "Be brave; don't flinch; go with the blow."

When Diana and I had just met in Chicago, while she was appearing in the play with Claudia and we started going out together, and she was in the process of legally pursuing Claudia through Equity's auspices, I tried as I've said before, to convey some of the above to her, but she wouldn't listen. This, eventually, made me suspect her dispute with Claudia was predicated on some personal slight or arcane hatred. Throughout rehearsals of my little tour, I tried to impart to Gail the proper technique for receiving the slap; it was part of my repertoire. I was, evidently, as unsuccessful with her as I was with Diana.

And as my own mother called me a "dirty little kike" and didn't mean it, so, too do, all parents hate their children. In the theatre, verisimilitude is everything, and Claudia knew parents possess the capacity to hate their children, and she knew the *tessa tura* of her performance were the two separate moments in the play when she, individually, and for different reasons, chastises her son, Walter Lee, and her daughter, Beneatha. She raises her fists above her head to strike her son with full force, because of his opacity and foolishness in adopting Capitalist thinking, and there is the moment in question when she slaps Beneatha across the face. The former, the raising of her fist over Walter's head as executed by McNeil, is one of the greatest moments I have ever witnessed in the theatre and, remember, I have seen Chevalier enrapture the crowd with a gesture of his finger, bringing them to paroxysms of ecstasy and enchantment.

Gail and I (God she was beautiful!) took a sublunary stroll beneath a starry canopy, near the strand of the lagoon, at the edge of the woods. Simulacrum haunted the shadows, beams plied the placid lake and crickets chittered in the summer night, as this gorgeously desirable future star revealed her tortured tale of abuse at the hands of the fifth Mrs. McCoy.

One day, three years earlier, when I was working between summer stock engagements at the Palace of Dreams of Audible Dreams, I was standing alone, goofing off by myself, listening to a recording at the rear of the store. I was near the locked, side door, which was used only for stock deliveries, but never for the public, or even employees, only the bosses and the store manager were entrusted with a key. And that door suddenly opened and I looked up and directly into the eyes of Elizabeth Taylor. She was with Eddie Fisher and Ziggy had slipped them in the rear entrance. Fisher was wearing a black shirt with a black tie, something I had never seen before, it simply wasn't done, except in a George Raft movie, and, even then, it was a white tie on a black shirt; that was ugly enough. But what is most memorable is what Paul Newman called "the startling color of her eyes." I heard someone on television describe them as "lavender," but, they were not lavender they were violet blue, exquisite and unforgettable. They looked at you, into you, arrested and digested you all at once, like lightning. The orbs of Gail Fisher, though not violet blue, had a similar effect, but now, they were tearing profusely and there was little I could do about it. Go to Claudia and complain, adjure her to mitigate the blow? That was a bumptious notion. I don't believe Gail had any hope of my achieving that end; she only wanted a shoulder on which to cry. Gail was a strong woman and endured without further complaint "the slap" as administered by McNeil for more than a dozen consecutive weeks.

So, the show went on, as it always does, although Noel Coward asks, "Why?" Raymond St. Jacques, always on the lookout in real life, remained so as Walter Lee Younger; Gloria Foster, as Walter's forbearing wife, was stoic on and offstage and maintained a quiet sense of humor; Al Freeman, Jr., cool and cynical as Murchison, avoided controversy, while Ed Hall was an inspirational Assagai, the idealistic warrior, and a bit flaky, but fun.

After the third night in Skowhegan, I was off, as advance man, on my hegira, mostly by bus, to the next of the seven theatres we were to play, the Kennebunkport Playhouse located in the exclusive resort town of Kennebunkport, Maine, the "Summer Home of Presidents."

14

"The Summer Home of Presidents"

I arrived in the picturesque town of Kennebunkport to learn that, because of their skin color, no private home or public hostelry of the hamlet wanted to provide lodgings for my cast members with the exception of the lone white actor. At that time in the town's and the country's history, it was thought that giving shelter to African-Americans would set an unwelcome precedent or spread a disease of some sort. I was informed of this the moment I entered the theatre and met its producer and founder, Robert Currier, a sharp showman and brother of the successful popular singer, Jane Morgan, blonde, beautiful, winning on stage, blessed with a big, well-modulated, beautifully-projected mezzo-soprano voice which sold millions of London Records. Morgan, who played the theatre the week before our scheduled stand to sellout crowds, began her career at the Kennebunkport Playhouse, which, unlike the venerable Lakewood operation in Skowhegan, was a renovated barn seating just under 500 people. It struggled for years to become established with the locals and summer visitors, but through Currier's management and yearly sellout capacity appearances by Jane, the theatre had become (and still is) a successful operation.

Currier, whose responsibility it was to secure housing for my cast, was an artist at heart and a man of good taste. Other producers in other fancy Maine resorts, passed on booking Hansberry's play, but Currier thought differently about his audience's intelligence and potential receptivity and was, naively, surprised his town let him down by refusing to lodge my cast. So, he called up every newspaper in New York City and told them so. The story ended up on the editorial page of the *New York Herald Tribune*, not the lead editorial, just the third one down, but the editorial page, nevertheless. And it made a stir in Kennebunkport. Lodgings suddenly appeared, the whole cast were heroes, so was Currier, and the production played to full houses.

I was off, once more, to the next stop, the Hunterdon Hills Playhouse in Hampton, New Jersey. As I write this, there is a dinner theatre in that area today operating under the same name, but we were playing in a converted high school auditorium (with that name) and it was not to Claudia's liking. So, she stopped calling me "Mr. Abbott" and began calling me "Mr. Hitchcock." The other thing I remember about this stop on the tour was being backstage during the rehearsals conducted by Mike Nichols, for the show prior to ours, a new play bound for New York, by Jules Feiffer. I remember thinking, "If it's good enough for Mike Nichols it ought to be good enough for Claudia," but it wasn't.

Our next stop was Mountainhome, Pennsylvania and the long gone, burned down, historic Pocono Playhouse, where movie star, Zachary Scott (*Mildred Pierce*, *Mask Of Dimitrios*, etc.) starred the week prior to our arrival in *The Gazebo*, by Alec Coppell, a popular trifle of the then popular murder-mystery play genre. Scott was working on a transatlantic steamer when he met mogul Jack Warner who talked him into becoming a film star. He had fallen into a deep depression when the film industry and his career went south in the new age of television, and was just making a comeback with this summer stock appearance. He died of a brain tumor four years after I met him in the lovely dining room adjacent to the theatre.[94]

Canada was next, the Vineland Theatre in Vineland, Ontario, near Toronto and just a cross the border from Detroit, where, most of all, I remember the mammoth trees, the glorious sunsets and the audiences which adored the play. Next, was Detroit, the Northland Playhouse, in suburban Detroit, our penultimate engagement.

---

94 The affable Virginian was married to hotel heiress-actress Ruth Ford who conducted a literary salon at the Dakota until her death. Together they engineered an unsuccessful stage production of an adaptation of their friend, William Faulkner's *Requiem For A Nun*, in 1959.

"Critics," Laurence Olivier said to Michael Caine,[95] "are shit!" and a critic in a major Detroit paper liked the production, but said he disliked the "new" dialogue which had been added since the critic last saw the play. This resulted in Lorraine, who had been following the progress of the play, sending me "a cease and desist" telegram to which I responded by politely saying said critic was *fehrmisht*. Not a word had been changed. The telegram was a shock. It was poorly phrased and unnecessarily unkind, for the notion of my changing any of the dialogue was absurd. I (in conjunction with Herb Rogers) was the only person in the world presenting her play at that time, sending her weekly royalty checks based on receipts from nightly attendees (ranging from 500 to 1,200 customers per performance) to see her play. Perhaps, the tone of her letter was based on my relationships with her husband (and/or Diana).

Something else happened in Detroit. After I left *Kicks*, using part of the $2,500 given me by the producers, I optioned the phantasmagoric novel, *Malcolm*, the best-known work of the novelist, short story writer and playwright, James Purdy (1914-2009). He was represented by the diminutive Audrey Wood (1905-1985), the famous literary and theatrical agent, whose client list consisted of Tennessee Williams, Arthur Miller, Robert Anderson (*Tea And Sympathy*, among others), William Inge (*Bus Stop, Dark At The Top Of The Stairs, Picnic* and *Come Back, Little Sheba*) and newcomer Arthur Kopit (*Oh Dad, Poor Dad, Mama's Hung You In The Closet And I'm Feelin' So Sad*). Kopit, subsequently, wrote a play in which Linda Hunt[96] played the prominent role of Audrey Wood.

Audrey's father, William H. Wood, managed the Palace Theatre and she grew up in the Theatre District. A tiny woman with beady eyes behind fashionable frames, gray hair in a bun, she was infamous for picking up the phone or calling someone and speaking without any introduction whatever, no "Hello," but diving into the conversation with exactly what she had in mind, a technique designed to put one on the defensive. She could be kind and quite

---

95   Recorded in Caine's autobiography, *The Elephant To Hollywood*.

96   The four foot, three, 1980 Academy Award-winner for Best Supporting Actress, playing a Indonesian male dwarf in *The Year Of Living Dangerously*, Hunt is Henrietta Lange in TV's *NCIS*. Kopit's 1984 play was entitled *End Of The World*, ran for only thirty-three performances, was nicely staged and most enjoyable, and though not produced by him, was one of Harold Prince's few box office failures.

witty, but you would have to know her well in order to experience that aspect of her personality.

Aware of my money-raising activities for *Kicks* and my ambition to produce plays, she was gracious to me in our first meeting. Rising from the desk in her small office, she squinted in my face, stuck out her wee hand and said," Well, well, the new Elliot Nugent."To me, this was a great compliment. Since my boyhood I had identified with the Midwesterner who wore horn-rimmed glasses, spoke with a twang, as did I, and played the beleaguered professor, opposite Gene Tierney, in *Male Animal*, a hit he directed and co-wrote with cartoonist-author, James Thurber.

Originally, Elia Kazan optioned *Malcolm*, a serio-comical novel about a naïf who comes to New York and is devoured by dames and big city society, a familiar subject to me. But Gadge had allowed the option to expire. I asked for the rights to this quasi-homosexual nightmare populated by voracious women and Audrey said it was fine with her but up to Purdy. She gave me his number, I called him and we met at his apartment on Henry Street, in Brooklyn Heights, and then walked the nearby promenade built by Robert Moses known by fancier folk as the Esplanade, and viewed the great vista of Manhattan.

Purdy was balding, fortyish, and modest for a man who had received such high praise from the literary establishment.[97] We lunched at Sweet's, on Fulton Street, and he gave me the green light to hire my choice to do the adaptation, Academy Award-winning playwright-screenwriter, William Archibald.[98] If Kazan had decided not to continue with the property, I thought, "Why not get Bobby Lewis?" My experience with *Kicks* counseled me to "Go to the top; go for the best. You're nobody, attach yourself to proven talents and nurture what they have to offer." Sounds opportunistic, but pity the producer who lacks chutzpah. I obtained the director's number,

---

97 The Sitwells - Dame Edith Sitwell, brothers Sacheverell Sitwell and Osbert Sirwell, Harlem Renaissance activist-photographer Carl Van Vechten, John Cowper Powys (1872-1963) the American composer-critic, Virgil Thomson (1896-1989) and James T. Farrell (1904-1975), yes, the author of the *Studs Lonigan* trilogy, the Bible for growing up in Chicago in the 40' and 50's, all said Jim Purdy was a first rate talent. Dorothy Parker (1893-1967) writing in *Esquire*, said *Malcolm* was "the most prodigiously funny book to streak across these heavy-hanging times." Both Thompson and Van Vechten, highly influential figures, were very helpful to me. Purdy was a heavyweight and they knew it.

98 Best Adaptation – Henry James *Turn Of The Screw*, retitled *The Innocents,* in collaboration with Truman Capote. It starred Ingrid Bergman.

called, then, met him at his townhouse, on East 80th Street, purchased, in part, with the proceeds from *Brigadoon*. Known for his adept handling of fantasy, I thought him to be the ideal choice to stage Purdy's material.

Robert Lewis (1909-1997) actor, teacher, director, was one of the youngest members of the Group Theatre before he developed what Clifford Odets called "the need to sin," by going to Hollywood. Too "short and round," according to his own words, strictly a character actor, he played bit parts in films, the most memorable of which, perhaps, is his appearance in Fred Astaire's "Limehouse Blues" sequence in the MGM musical *Ziegfeld Follies* (1946) in which he plays a well-dressed john attracted to Lucille Bremer's poor Limehouse kid. Signed to MGM, Lewis co-directed the film with Vincente Minnelli, says some sources, probably meaning he staged many of the dialogue scenes, though it is true, in time, he developed skills as a director of musicals . Before the War he played gangsters, during the War, he played Japanese and German officers and a French collaborator, and in 1947, he appeared as Maurice Bottello, in Charles Chaplin's oft-banned *Monsieur Verdoux*.

When he formed Actors Studio with Kazan and they divided the teaching duties prior to Strasberg's coming to the fore, it was mutually agreed, because Gadge preferred the young ones, that Bobby's classes would be composed of advanced actors only, a partial list being: Marlon Brando, Montgomery Clift, Jerome Robbins, David Wayne, Mildred Dunnock, Herbert Berghof, John Forsythe, Kevin McCarthy, Karl Malden, Tom Ewell, Patricia Neal, E.G. Marshall and Beatrice Straight. Some class.

Dressed casually, Lewis answered the door himself. He was one of the first men to shave his head entirely – it was good for playing Nazis and other villains – and the features of his face, the shape of his nose, the small intense eyes behind oversized Swifty Lazar-type frames imparted a porcine aspect to his appearance. I did not make it to his living room, but, in a purple and red outer alcove of his stylish dwelling, the object of his blank-faced, quizzical stare, I, as it were, auditioned for him, but how could it be otherwise? I was in the presence of one of the greatest teachers of the art of acting; he was studying me, there was no time for false effusiveness.

He did not know what to make of me, but he agreed to direct and allowed me to "use his name" and now, a few months later, here I was in Detroit, about to lose my option on the property unless I came up with a thousand bucks, which I did not have. My contract with Audrey and William Archibald called for a renewal payment of $1,000 or I would lose Archibald and the option. Worse still, I would lose face with Audrey, whose power prevailed throughout the Broadway Theatre.

On a Friday evening, prior to the arrival of Claudia and the cast, I picked up a copy of the *Detroit Free Press* and turned to the sports section. It said tomorrow was the running of the Detroit Sweepstakes at the Detroit Racecourse. But there was no available *Daily Racing Form* on that Friday night unless I took a cab, way downtown, to the only 24-hour newsstand in Metropolitan Detroit, where the paper hit the stand around 2 A.M. The cab fare was nearly $40, a lot of scratch then. But, unless I were to be bad mouthed and blackballed by the most prestigious play agent of all time, it was essential I select the winner of the next day's big race, which, after ten minutes with the *Form*, was obvious to someone as experienced as I.

A couple of famous names in horse racing were involved in my choice, which won easily, at four to one: owner Peter Fuller and future Hall of Fame trainer, Eddie Neloy, unknown to Detroiters, but not to me. So I followed Neloy to the $100 window and bet the New York shipper, Half Breed[99], as did he, $200 on the nose, turning the two hundred into a thousand dollars, which I sent to Audrey on Monday morning. The next stop was the last on the tour – Chicago, where the great play had opened three years before.

✳✳✳✳✳✳✳✳✳✳✳✳

I am ashamed of what I am about to tell you but it is not only part of the story, it is indicative of my state of my mind and preparatory to what is to come and cannot, honestly, be ignored. Addi-

---

99   By Polynesian out of Pin Stripe by Hyperion, his philanthropist-businessman owner and civil rights advocate, in future, donated funds to Coretta King, in a crucial period, and won the disputed 1968 Kentucky Derby, with Dancer's Image, the only horse to be disqualified in that race, until Maximum Security's disqualification in 2019. Neloy would succeed the immortal "Sunny" Jim Fitzsimmons as trainer of the powerful stable of Ogden Phipps, and of the progeny of the equally immortal runner and stallion, Bold Ruler.

tionally, it fulfills an earlier commitment to which I have obligated myself – to tell the truth. It happened in the early morning of the sweltering day on which the play was to open at Herb Rogers' Tenthouse Theatre, in Highland Park.

I was driving down Clark Street, past "Bughouse Square," where, ten years earlier, I had seen the beloved comedian emerge from the Chrysler limousine, yell the "n" word repeatedly, and spit at the black orator on the soapbox, when I spotted a beautiful young streetwalker, of African descent, with prominent buttocks supported by languorous legs which were headed north, toward Division.

I drove behind the shapely whore in my mother's car (a 1962 Plymouth Fury, with a six-button, automatic transmission, a speedy car, shiny black, with red faux leatherette upholstery and white wall tires) observing the chippie's lovely legs which, exposed by a truncated skirt, ambled lazily on high heels. Her voluptuous rump, like a well-lubricated automaton, operated independently from the rest of her trollop self and, when I drew (forgive me) abreast, and regarded her considerable cleavage, the magnetic pull and desirability of this "working girl" increased accordingly. Along strolled the strumpet, past the tavern where Ira Sullivan used to play, seeing me now, and knowing I was her potential prey.

Her Cyprian eyes glanced at me, smiling the smile of a loose woman, and continuing her lascivious perambulation toward Division, she stooped slightly and said just loud enough, "Wanna' party?"

The show was all set technically, my responsibilities were discharged; I had been to Arlington Park to see Black Sheep[100] upset Ridan, in a six-horse field, and I had about $120 in my pocket when I smiled and answered, "Yeah; get in." She hopped in eagerly, ensconcing her lithesome, floozy frame beside me, and I spotted a bead of sweat on her upper lip eventuating from the sultry evening and the unseasonable red turtleneck sweater she wore, a sweater that simultaneously concealed and heralded the tantalizing mammilla which lay beneath.

Before some smart-ass social critic for the *Times* ordained the blue suit-red-til ensemble to be the "power" uniform, at a time

---

100 I don't invent these racist names - Half Breed, Black Sheep – they're real! This one was shipped in by Charlie Whittingham and ridden by Johnny Longden.

when bright, red ties were still considered swineish and the men who wore them *louche*, the sweater's color and the fact she wore it in summer was as much a warning as the red tie Faulkner's carny wears in *Sound And The Fury*, but I failed to heed the omen.

"Get over to La Salle," she directed, looking over her pretty shoulder to see if we were being tailed, and I complied with the quick coupe. "Hey, is that all you?" I asked the drab as I drove, gesturing at her boobs with a bob of my head. With an impulsive gesture the scarlet woman of easy virtue raised the sweater and displayed her ample breasts, pliant mounds on which brown nipples stood like succulent candies waiting to be devoured. This Delilah, this cocotte, ogled me evocatively and said, "All mine; you can touch them if you're friendly."

Knowing whores, I took "friendly" to mean "generous" and resolved to monitor, even more assiduously than usual, activities in the vicinity of my pants pocket (wherein resided my 120 clams) on the imminent occasion of this woman of the town going down on me. The slut's face was unmemorable, "Call her plain, you give her the best of it," says Erie of *Hughie*'s wife, but there was a vulnerability to her, unless I mistook her discomfort with the humidity for a nobler quality than the demi-courtesan, in truth, possessed, for even a whore can be off-kilter in the killing August heat of a summer in the Second City. Nevertheless, despite the humid stickiness of the early morning, which foretold another sizzling day, the young doxy's magnificent body was giving me an erection that interfered with steering, but I persevered and maneuvered the car onto La Salle Street.

Once there, the fallen woman directed me down a side street, then an alley and, finally, bade me turn left, where I found myself in a cul-de-sac, a dead end I did not like. But the *puta* lifted her sweater again and reached for the zipper on my pants and, suddenly, the car was surrounded by a six or seven black guys, my age and younger, armed with rocks and knives, most prominent among them, a guy with a gun to my head, the shape, model and caliber of which escaped my notice, but I felt cold steel where my *payot* ought to be.

I was suckered, disgusted and frightened, all at once, as the voice at the other end of the gun said, "Gimme all you fuckin' money!" I surrendered it gladly in receipt of my life, feeling fortunate I had the *gelt* on hand, though I was certainly sorry to lose it that way. Then, the gang ran off as quickly as it appeared and I confronted the young hustler, whose eyes were filled with fright.

"Hey, you set me up!"

"No, no, I swear, I didn't," the painted woman implored. She was sweating. This *nafkeh*, this *kurveh*, this call girl without a phone, if she was lying, was a good actress, but, while keeping her frightened eyes on mine, the Paphian queen felt for the door handle, pushed down, and scurried from the car, a sexy stew in high heels escaping in full flight through the glass and gravel strewn alley populated only by an audience of garbage cans, devoid of humanity in the miasmic morning, as the sun rose on another unbearable day.

Feeling like the schmuck that I was, the love juice/semen sticking to my hairy thighs beneath my summer pants, I headed back to the theatre in Highland Park on Edens Expressway[101] with hardly any traffic in the way and plenty of time to commiserate with myself upon my folly. It was an unpleasant journey, penniless, the sun beating down early in the incalescent morn, but I could just as easily have lost my life in the humiliating encounter that I had manufactured for myself.[102] I had plenty to think about aside from the Daughter of Shame and whether or not she worked in concert with the cutthroats who robbed me. I thought about my career and about *Malcolm*.

A few days before, I had met with Ken ("Hollow Me To Follywood") Nordine (1920-2019) for dinner at the Red Star Inn, on Clark Street, near the corner of Lincoln Park, where the Old Town contingent of Abbie Hoffman's Yippies were rudely confronted by Daley's stormtrooper cops. My intention was to induce Ken to invest "front money" in *Malcolm*.

Tall, sporting thick spectacles, with sucked-in cheeks and abundant black hair, Nordine, possessor of one of the most mellifluous and highly-compensated voices in the history of broadcasting, treated me to a dinner of wiener schnitzel a la Holstein, and then,

---

101 Named for William G. Edens, a banker, no less, and an early advocate for paved roads.

102 I think those who robbed me might have shot me. Just around the corner on La Salle Street, in years to come, a friend, producer Carl Stohn, Jr., was murdered while returning from "extra" work in a film, by a similar gang of youths.

we adjourned to the basement of his North Side home, where he had established a well-equipped recording studio.

Ken did not audition for voice-overs; he did not have an agent. Corporations, sponsors, came to him. He devised campaigns, wrote the copy and recorded it as only he could. His *Word Jazz* albums had been on the market for three or four years, and he had gained an international audience for his inventive linguistic excursions and, while he had earned a good deal of money, he remained egalitarian and accessible.

Ken said we were to be met by a friend of his who advised him on theatrical investments and when a fellow about my age arrived, Ken introduced him to me as "Billy" something and inferred that I should know him. I could have taken offense but after the breaded veal with country gravy, the Lyonnais potatoes and creamed spinach, the couple of scotches before and the Drambuie aperitif after, the charming conversation and the ride to Ken's in his small sports car, all of it free of charge, I was disinclined to be anything but agreeable.

"You know Billy, he does lots of stuff around town," meaning television, I guessed. We shook hands and the lack of enthusiasm he showed convinced me he was going to advise Ken to take a pass on *Malcolm*, which I understood "Billy" had read. He was a good-looking guy, fair-haired and he wore eyeglasses. Turns out he went to Senn and was, therefore, a natural enemy. Even the Jewish boys from Sullivan High hated the Jewish boys from Senn, and looked forward, each year, in vain, to beating Senn in the annual football game. My guess was Billy was Jewish and from the Northwest Side, which also made him an enemy and he, probably, felt the same. But I also sensed he was no fool.

We chatted for a while but Billy was not the patient type and once we mentioned *Malcolm* he produced a copy of the book, the one I had given to Ken, displaying it's orange cover and cartoonish picture of the title character, along with a shapely stripper, a decapitated female leg and a saxophone, all set against the background of a garish Manhattan. Then, Billy, with confident authority prophesied:

"I don't think it'll work, Ken; I'd pass on it."[103]

Billy was not alone in thinking *Malcolm* was unlikely to achieve commercial success, but, nevertheless, Ken, sweet, droll, wizard of words, gave me a check for $500. Billy knew it was *ts-dokeh*. So did I.

Much later I learned Billy's parents emigrated from the Ukraine after a pogrom, and that Billy saw and was influenced by the same films as I. He was directing at WGN when I met him and the next year, his documentary, *The People vs. Paul Crump*, won an award and he moved to Hollywood. His full name, of course, was William Friedkin (1935-   ) and he went on to direct two of the biggest box office hits of all time.[104] Billy's negativity gnawed at me considerably as I drove down Edens Expressway with the sun beating down on the Plymouth Fury. I turned on the radio.

"The Associated Press has announced actress Marilyn Monroe committed suicide last evening in her home in Brentwood, California. Her body was discovered by her maid and the L.A. coroner has ruled her death 'an apparent suicide.'" The report went on to say sleeping pills were discovered near her body.

I went to Herb's house and told him what had happened to me. He laughed uproariously – and gave me a hundred dollar bill. I felt shitty and drove around awhile, stopped for a Sunday newspaper, parked the car and sat on a bench near the tracks of the Northwestern commuter line.

I opened the paper; already there was coverage of Monroe's "suicide." I felt the tragedy and loss. Sitting in the noontime heat of that Sunday morning, on that bench by the railroad track, I pondered whether or not I was strong enough to stay the course, to stick to the difficult task of "making it" in the business Berlin decreed unlike any other. Marilyn had risen to the summit and, disdainful of success, not really wanting to be a "serious" actress, after all, I

---

103 Up until the time of which we speak, surrealistic, serio-comic fiction was practically nonexistent in American literature, exceptions being *Day of the Locust*, by Nathaniel West (1903-1940), *The Happy Island*, by Dawn Powell (1886-1965), and Purdy's *Malcolm*. There is more than a touch of the serio-comic in Twain, even in William Dean Howells *Rise of Silas Lapham* (1885) up to Saul Bellow's *Henderson the Rain King* (1952), but full blown, serio-comic novels from the pen of Americans were rare. Joseph Heller's *Catch 22* wouldn't arrive until October.

104 *The French Connection* (1971) and *The Exorcist* (1973). I'd be delinquent not saying Billy married the woman Orson Welles called "the greates actress in the world," Jeanne Moreau, and has been married to film maker (and former CEO of Paramount Pictures) turned philanthropist, Sherry Lansing, for over two decades.

guessed, ended up a suicide. To rise to the top in "the business," and, then, throw it all away didn't make sense; to build a career and demolish it, as she did, seemed ignorant. But who was I to talk? Especially at this time, with the show ready to open that night.

Later, no less a respected authority than director, Joe Mankiewicz[105] would opine, Marilyn "knew the jig was up," that she realized her fallibility and the ephemeral nature of her success. But that did not make sense if, as reported, she had just signed a long-term contract with Twentieth-Century Fox. I felt a loss with Marilyn Monroe's death, but I wasn't sure what was lost except a precious life. In my innocence I knew little about conspiracies and highly placed political Romeos who would fuck a snake.

****

The show opened that night to a standing ovation. When it closed its run, I said my good-byes to the cast and to Claudia, in her star dressing room. The ever-present Herman, the Dog, was perched on the makeup table. I was respectful; she was friendlier to me than she had been since I first met her in the basement where her predecessor had hung herself.

She was in a good mood and, for some reason, rhapsodizing about John Glenn's Friendship 7 spaceflight of February and our sticking it to the Russians. She was a very patriotic woman and her devotion to Catholicism shone through her words of belief in American superiority. But as collegial as she was in parting, she was not going to apologize for all the *tsores* she had given me. Everyone, at all the stops along the way, with the exception of those unwilling to offer accommodations at the second stand, had been kind to her, and, in return, she had been on her best behavior with the respective managements of the seven theatres at which we had appeared.

Claudia had never been more than civil toward me, never showed an interest in me as a person, moreover, was sardonically rude on numerous occasions. But she was a great actress and her consistently truthful performance was admirable. As wearying as the experience had been for me, travelling from location to location, usually in buses, sometimes for long hours, was unpleasant,

---

105 On the *Dick Cavett Show.*

but everything about the play and the production was aesthetically satisfying. And I was proud of the fact I had controlled my temper, humbled myself, and eaten her shit.

I never saw her, or Herman, or the stuffed dog, again.

****

Soon after were we back in Manhattan, *Variety* and *The New York Times* "News of the Rialto," published the astonishing (to me) news that both Claudia McNeil and Diana Sands had agreed to appear in a Broadway play entitled *Tiger Tiger Burning Bright*, by Peter S. Feibleman, based on his novel, *A Place Without Twilight*. It was to be the next production of the legendary director, Joshua Logan, who advised Bobby and Burt to produce *Kicks & Co.* with the white actors in blackface and the black actors in whiteface.

15

"Blackface in Whiteface, Whiteface in Black"

Joshua Logan directed a long list of successful productions including *South Pacific, Mister Roberts, Annie Get Your Gun, I Married An Angel, On Borrowed Time, Mornings At Seven, John Loves Mary*, and *Wish You Were Here*. He also produced the latter, turning a show with lousy reviews into a two-year smash hit. He had emerged from a mental institution to mount *Fanny*. That was the second time he had been admitted to a funny farm for bipolar disorder. Discharged from his initial visit, ten years earlier, he proceeded to direct a string of hits, which began with *By Jupiter!* and *Charley's Aunt*, starring José Ferrer, and artistic successes such as the Kurt Weill-Maxwell Anderson *Knickerbocker Holiday*, starring Walter Houston, and *Wisteria Trees*, which he wrote and directed, starring Helen Hayes - his version of Anton Chekov's *Cherry Orchard*, but set on a fading Southern plantation, similar to the home in which he lived as a child. In between stage successes Logan made the films *Sayonara, Picnic* and *Bus Stop*, enduring Marilyn Monroe's behavior in the latter.

He was now Joshua Logan Productions, which included a dutiful personal staff, another dedicated, directorial staff of gofers, a cook, his five times a week psychiatrist, and a chauffeur to drive him to and from his glamorous East Side Apartment to his Connecticut estate.

But at this juncture in his career, Logan was damaged goods. That same year he had had a monumental flop with Irving Berlin's *Mr. President*, starring Robert Ryan and Nanette Fabray, before that, *All American*, starring the redoubtable Ray Bolger,with music by Charles Strouse and Lee Adams and book by Mel Brooks, a production which, it was asserted, in *Variety*, the producer had over-capitalized, as was the case in a certain movie starring Zero Mostel and Gene Wilder. And Logan had had a flop play with *There Was A Little Girl*, starring Jane Fonda, and *Kind Sir*, which, though it starred Mary Martin and Charles Boyer, only lasted for 166 performances with so-so notices.

Now, though he earned an estimated $500,000 a year, mostly in royalties, he was a white haired, tired looking fifty-six year old with a big financial overhead and, what with two stays in the asylum and multiple, recent flops, he had become the butt of jokes at Sardi's and other Manhattan watering holes. Often, wags invented gags that centered on Logan's penchant for presenting shows with loads of bare-chested chorus boys.

As for Claudia and Diana, they knew, or their agents reminded them that, in the Theatre, if you court the bitch goddess Success, the ability to collaborate with others, to cooperate in order to do "what's best for one's career" must hold sway. Claudia and Diana, with a push from the ten per-centers, decided to bury the hatchet. Al Freeman Jr. was signed to play Claudia's son and Alvin Ailey, not known for his acting skills, much less his attraction to the female sex, was to appear as Diana's would-be lover and pursuer. The cast also included Roscoe Lee Browne, Ellen Holly, Robert (Bobby Dean) Hooks, and the only white member of the cast, Paul Barry. Cicely Tyson (for Diana) and Billy Dee Williams (for Ailey) were understudies.

Set in Louisiana, a synopsis of the affair read: "A woman (McNeil as Mama) builds a dream world around herself and her family in order to escape from her guilt over accidentally causing the death of one of her sons."

The venerable scenic designer, Oliver Smith, former co-director of Ballet Theatre (now American Ballet Theatre) was producing (as well as doing the sets) and sharing credit with him above the title was Roger L. Stevens. Smith has too many credits to list, just start with the ballet *Fancy Free*, the musical, *On The Town* and most everything else Leonard Bernstein wrote for Broadway. As for his partner, "ditto," too many credits, just say "No Roger Stevens, no Kennedy Center."

On the *Playbill*, Claudia's name was 100% the size of, and was placed above, the title. Diana and Al were featured in lighter script, 50% the size of Claudia's, but way down at the bottom of the page. Truly, Claudia had arrived. Not only was her's the only name gracing the prestigious marquee, cruel fate temporarily deemed her, once more (as when Sidney left and I sent her on the summer tour) the all important Giver of Life to a bunch of satellites who would soon, as refulgent stars, outshine her imminently fading Mother Planet, among them Cicely, Billy Dee, Bobby Dean, Roscoe, Diana, Al Freeman, and Alvin Ailey, who would have buildings and streets named in his honor. The show was in rehearsal and, surmising by then what the future held in store, Logan made sure his name was missing from the marquee and was unobtrusive on the printed page, in light typeface and only half the size of Freeman and Sands. This, considering it was a Joshua Logan Production, was uncharacteristic.

The play opened December 22, 1962 and closed less than a month later, on January 19, 1963, with 33 performances and 6 previews. Howard Taubman, in *The New York Times*, wrote a rave review, Walter Kerr's, in the *Herald Tribune*, was mixed, the rest showed respect, but none of them mattered because a newspaper strike was underway and, lacking the advertising outlet newspapers provided then, sensational reviews might not have kept the show alive. Still, Diana won the Theatre World Award and Claudia was nominated for a Tony but didn't win.

However, the play's failure was only part of the story. The trouble for Claudia, most of which stemmed from this production, was just beginning. Three months after *Tiger Tiger Burning Bright* closed, *Esquire* released their issue of April, 1963, featuring an extensive article by Gay Talese, exposing Claudia's combativeness with Logan during rehearsals

I could forgive the petty humiliations heaped on me by McNeil but I couldn't forget and I felt vindicated by the article. Entitled "The Soft Psyche of Joshua Logan," it concerned the rehearsal period of *Tiger Tiger Burning Bright* and portrayed an overly sensitive, vulnerable, Logan, sick and depressed and at the end of his rope because of the behavior of his star, a disrespectful Claudia McNeil.

Featuring a moodily-lit, full page, color picture of a white haired, scraggly mustachioed, brooding, looking-over-his-shoulder Logan, Talese's probing article showed a man full of self-doubt, his creative powers waning, in an unexpectedly challenging situation with Claudia, a Claudia in zealous pursuit of her career and her ascendancy to the place once occupied by Ethel Waters. For Claudia saw the diminution of Logan's creative power before her eyes and, in her continuing role as Mama, in rehearsing the play, exposed Logan's weaknesses to the cast and it troubled them greatly and made them fear for the glorified future/Bitch Goddess success they, like Claudia, so fervently desired. Claudia put Logan "on the spot" in the only available time and space, the rehearsal process, just as she had done with me. Logan was constantly rewriting in an offstage dressing room, with playwright Feibleman, and she couldn't stand it. Talese presented an angry McNeil:

"'Where the HELL is Logan,' she grumbled, on the third morning of rehearsing lines under the production stage manager, David Gray, Jr. Claudia was still furious at Logan for having left the theatre at mid-afternoon earlier in the week without having 'the courtesy, the respect' to let her know he'd not return that day; now with Logan working elsewhere on the script and ignoring the acting completely, Claudia was smoldering. With the other actors gathered around her offstage…she roared : 'Logan should be here! We ain't gettin' no direction.' 'And our reputations are at stake,' Diana Sands said. 'His is, too,' Claudia snapped. 'He doesn't realize it, but if he thinks he's going to blame this one on me if it's a flop, well, he ain't; I'll just get on the phone and call Sally Hammond at the *Post*, or that guy at the *Tribune* – what'shisname? one that married that actress? Mogenstern, that's it-and I'll tell 'em the whole story, about how we have to come here and listen to nine of his jokes, and all about LOU-iziana, and then he don't show up for three days!'

Then the others nodded and she went on, 'All this rewriting should be done at night! What the hell does he do at night? SHEET! People gonna look at me and think I shot my bolt in *Raisin In The Sun* and have nothing new to offer; well, that ain't fair…I got enough trouble, working with a lot of kids in this show, and carrying the responsibility for my whole race, being in the theatre thirty years, and this man Logan don't even show up! SHEET!'"

At this point, according to Talese, in walked Logan from the offstage room in which he had been working with Feibleman. They had a stack of papers of re-writes of Act I. Logan waved, walked offstage and up the aisle toward the rear of the orchestra with Mc-Neil watching his back intently. He sat in the rear of the house and, writes Talese:

"She waited; within ten minutes, she saw her chance. In the middle of one of her monologues, Claudia caught a glimpse of Logan talking to Feibleman….Flaring up, Claudia bellowed to Oliver Smith, the co-producer, sitting alone about nine rows back. 'MR. LOGAN IS TALKING! AND I CAN'T GO ON!'

'I am NOT talking,' Logan yelled from the back, his voice tense and angry.

'You WERE talking,' Claudia said. 'I could hear what you were saying!'

'I was NOT talking,' he insisted 'Somebody else was talking. It was NOT me.'

'YOU were talking!' she shouted, hunching her big shoulders and blazing her big eyes at him. 'And you spoiled the meter of my speech!'

'Look,' Logan said, stomping down the aisle toward where Oliver Smith sat, 'I don't want any more rages from YOU!'

'You're in a rage, not me.' she said.

'Well, I'm not going to stand for this!'

'You want me to leave?' she asked, challengingly.

'Look,' he said, more softly, 'everybody here is trying to get this play. I cannot s-t-a-n-d these outrages. What do you want me to do, close the show?'

Claudia now turned, hunched her shoulders again, and paced back and forth.

'Now,' Logan said, trying to get things moving again, noticing that the rest of the cast was standing in almost fixed, dumb-struck poses on the stage. 'Now, why don't you go back further –'

'I *can't* begin,' she said, casually. 'You spoiled my meter.'

'Oh-h-h, Oliver,' Logan groaned, his hand on his forehead, 'I can't stand these rages.'

'Well,' she shot in, 'that's *your* problem.'

'YOU'RE MY PROBLEM!' Logan screamed.

Now, everybody in the theatre was squirming.

Fortunately, Claudia did not answer him; she just shuffled around a bit, like a sumo wrestler waiting for the decision; in the prolonged silence, things calmed at bit, and Claudia did her monologue and David Gray yelled, 'Curtain,' and everybody sighed. There was a break."

Later after the break, resuming rehearsal on stage:"…back in the dark the lights of the stage beaming on the actors going through a scene in the garden of the Louisiana shack; Claudia McNeil's voice was now softer because she had had a touch of laryngitis a few days before. But at the end of the scene, she raised her voice to its full power, and Logan, in a pleasant tone, said, 'Don't strain your voice, Claudia.'

She did not respond, only whispered to another actor on stage.

'Don't raise your voice, Claudia' Logan repeated.

She again ignored him.

'C-L-A-U-D-I-A! Logan yelled, 'don't give me that actor's vengeance, Claudia.'

'Yes, Mr. Logan,' she said with a soft, sarcastic edge.

'I've had enough of this today, Claudia.'

'Yes, Mr. Logan.'

'And stop Yes-Mr. Logan-ing me.'

'Yes,' Mr. Logan.

'You're a shockingly rude woman!'

'Yes, Mr. Logan.'

'You're being a beast.'

'Yes, Mr. Logan.'

'Yes, Miss Beast.'

'Yes, Mr. Logan.'

'YES, MISS BEAST!'

Suddenly, Claudia McNeil stopped. It dawned on her that he was calling her a beast; now her face was gray and her eyes were cold, and her voice was almost solemn as she said, 'You … called… me…out…of…my name.' She stood there, rocklike, big and angry, waiting for him to do something.

'Oliver,' Logan said, turning toward the co-producer, who had lowered his wiry, long body into his chair as if he were in a foxhole. He did not want to be cornered into saying something that might offend Logan, his old friend, but neither did he want Claudia McNeil to come barreling down the aisle and possibly snap his thin frame in half. 'Oliver,' Logan went on, 'I just don't know what to do with her. She's like some queen up there, or something.….'

'YOU'RE THE QUEEN' she bolted back.

'All right, all right, I'm the queen,' Logan said, too weary to argue about it. 'What do we do now?'

'Get yourself another actress,' she said.

'All right, fine,' Logan said. 'Fine,' he repeated. 'We can close the show, and, we can….' Now he was walking up the aisle, and it seemed he might be leaving the theatre.

'Look,' Claudia quickly said. He stopped. 'Look,' she began again, realizing that if the show closed, she would be the reason for all the other actors' unemployment, 'I…I gotta man at home I can get mad at…and I been in the theatre thirty years…and nobody is ever going to point a finger at me and say that I walked off a show…and…'

She went on like this, and Logan knew he had her; he could have played with her for a while, letting her sweat it out, but he didn't. Instead he walked toward the stage, climbed it, and then, faster now he moved toward Claudia, arms outstretched, moved into her, his white mustache pressing against her cheek,- and then, dramatically, her big, black arms lashed around the back of his white shirt and pulled him close. They were almost tearful in their reunion, these two big, soft figures under the lights; they suddenly were spent, and the cast gathered around and whistled, hollered and clapped.

Then, cheerfully, Claudia pulled back and, grinning as she shook her fist, said, 'But when this show is over, I'm gonna hit you in the mouth so-o-o hard!'

'When this show is over,' he laughed back, 'you won't be able to catch me!'

'I'll catch you,' she promised.

'You'll need a long reach,' he said, 'because I'll be gone!'"

As far as Broadway was concerned, both were gone soon enough. Claudia would have other chances at Broadway fame, but something had changed. Then, on February 18, 1964, Washington, D.C.'s *Afro-American Gazette*, in a news article entitled "Claudia McNeil Seeks End To Marriage," stated "that the *Amsterdam News* (of Harlem) reported late last week that famed actress Claudia McNeil is seeking legal separation from her husband of little more than two years, Herman McCoy. The paper says that, according to Miss McNeil, McCoy attempted to strangle her with a silk stocking Sunday in the basement of their home….then reportedly locked her out of the house in the cold for an hour and a half clad only in a nightgown and her underwear. The incident reportedly took place at 1 P.M., Sunday at a time when many friends and neighbors of the couple were going to and from church. The actress says she was 'thoroughly humiliated.' She added that it was not the first time her husband had beaten her. Commenting on the breakup of her marriage, Claudia said, 'My greatest regret is that after putting all my investments to the extent of 15,000 into the house … which my husband owns, I was not given the dignity of being allowed to move out of the house. This is what a man would have done. There was nothing in my name,' she said. The couple met in October, 1961, shortly after the death of McCoy's wife, Madeline, who was one of Harlem's best known beauticians. Mrs. Madeline McCoy's body was found by her husband in the basement of the house at… She had been hanged. McCoy is 67. His marriage to McNeil was reported to have been his fifth. It was the second marriage for Ms. McNeil."

So, Herman, it appears, was the physically abusive partner in the marriage. She may have been beating on the stuffed dog, but the real Herman was beating on her. Tragedy seemed to follow her.

I did not read the article in the *Gazette*, nor did I hear anything about the breakup of the McCoy-McNeil marriage. But only a few months later, thumbing through *The New York Post*, walking downtown on Madison Avenue, near my hotel, I spotted, in a short, one column item ingloriously stuck adjacent to a vulgar, full-page ad for a supermarket chain, a report announcing the suicide by hanging, of Herman McCoy, in the post-nuptial, recently redesigned, basement of his Beaux Arts townhouse, the same Stanford White-designed basement in which I met the couple. Employing the overhanging pipes, as did the wife who preceded Claudia, the act had the flavor of a death pact. And it was tragic for Claudia. *The Post* article came as a horrific surprise to me. Mc Coy seemed gentle, unlikely to be argumentative. How poorly I had misjudged the situation!

The following year Claudia toured abroad, playing Sister Margaret in James Baldwin's *Amen Corner*, one of his early efforts from 1954. Claudia made only two other films, *There Was A Crooked Man* (1970) and *Black Girl* (1972) but she continued to make numerous television appearances and one of those, *Moon Of The Wolf*, was released in movie theatres. Her Broadway comeback, in 1967, placed her in Carl Reiner's *Something Different*, which he wrote and directed, with a cast including Bob Dishy, Gabriel Dell and Linda Lavin. It lasted nine performances.

In 1968, she won the coveted role of Fatatateeta, in the musical version of George Bernard Shaw's *Caesar And Cleoptra*, entitled *Her First Roman*, starring Leslie Uggams and Richard Kiley, with music by Erwin Drake. Flora Robson made a splash playing the role in blackface in the Vivien Leigh-Claude Rains Technicolor version, but this Broadway musical was a fiasco and closed after seventeen showings. Then, in 1969, Claudia appeared on Broadway in a straight play, John Gulden's, *Wrong Way Light Bulb*. It played seven times. Goodbye, Broadway.

She was absent for a number of years and, whether it was self-imposed or not, she did not surface until 1978, when she organized an act for a stint at Michael's Pub in Manhattan, featuring songs associated with Ethel Waters. She was nearly half the size she was before, weighing a mere 158 pounds. "I lost half a person," she publicly announced, via the press.

That year, Joshua Logan, after, a decade and a half absence, following *Tiger Tiger Burning Bright*, and, after flopping, rather monumentally, in Hollywood, with the musicals *Finian's Rainbow* and *Paint Your Wagon*, returned to Broadway to direct a play entitled *Horowitz & Mrs. Washington*, by Henry Denker, about the relationship between an aging Jewish man, played by Sam Levene, and an elderly African-American woman. One imagines Claudia was considered for the role. Perhaps, she auditioned for it, despite her previous "collaboration" with the director. He was, after all, a gracious Southerner, willing, at least, to appear to be a man of forgiveness, but Logan cast Esther Rolle (best known as Florida Evans, on the TV sitcom, *Maude*) instead. Claudia, however, appeared in a summer stock tour of the show.

Then, she returned to Chicago to play an emaciated Mama Younger in the play for which she had achieved a share of fame, but this time not at the Blackstone. It was at a place called the Forum Theatre, a 500-seater, appended to the Candlelight Dinner Theatre, in the far southwestern suburbs, a place called Summit, Illinois, a far cry from the Booth or the Barrymore.

She appeared in an off-Broadway revival of *To Be Young, Gifted And Black*, in 1981, and, also an Equity Library Theatre production of the musical *Rain*, but that was a non-paying affair and what is worse, the slimming down had caused severe health problems. She developed diabetes, a leg was amputated, and she retired to the place old actors go, across the Hudson.

Of her performance in Hansberry's play she said, "There was a time when I acted the role…Now I live it. "She died at the Actors' Fund Nursing Home in Englewood, New Jersey on Thanksgiving Day, 1993, at the age of 76. An online document, from the New York Public Library, Schomberg Center for Research In Black Culture, entitled "Claudia McNeil Scrapbooks," dated September, 1999, states she left behind three, or four boxes of items, including programs, scrapbooks, photographs, telegrams, letters, reviews, poems, advertisements, greeting cards, a wedding album and an "article on Joshua Logan, Director, *Tiger Tiger Burning Bright.*"

LOOKIN' FOR THE MAN & ETC.

16

JOSEPH E. LEVINE PRESENTS

I must have been losing my compass, but I did not realize it at the time. They say Gloria Vanderbilt said, "One phone call can change your life," but a million other people said it too; it's true.

At the height of the Cuban Missile Crisis, I returned from the summer tour of *Raisin* to the house on Washington Street, in the West Village, where I received a phone call about *Malcolm* from *The New York Times* gossip columnist-theatre writer, Sidney Skolsky (1905-1983). Calling at the behest of my publicist, Max Eisen, Skolsky subsequently placed an item in his popular "News of the Rialto" column that resulted in Joseph E. Levine (1905-1987), the most successful independent movie producer of the day, contacting me. Levine, who began as a partner in a dress business located in a basement store and ended up as the Embassy Picture Corporation, and about whom the Maysles Brothers made a full-length documentary entitled *Showman* (1963), is said to have been involved in 497 movies as producer, distributor or financier.[106]

It was Levine's theatrical representative, David Ivor Balding (1939-2014) who called. Balding's father, Ivor G., C.V. "Sonny" Whitney's stable manager and sometime trainer, was the man who told Johnny Rotz to go to the lead with Tompion.[107] I had read in

---

106 *The Graduate, The Producers, Carnal Knowledge, The Carpetbaggers, Godzilla, King Of The Monsters! Lion In Winter* and *The Night Porter*, are a very few he backed. With Ted Mann, he co-produced O'Neill's *Hughie* on Broadway, starring Jason Robards, Jr., in association with Gabe Katzka and Ely Landau and one Mr. Berne.

107 Whitney partially financed *A Star is Born, Nothing Sacred, Gone With The Wind* and many Broadway shows. Later he headed Pioneer Pictures and produced John Ford's *The Searchers*.

Variety of the Levine-Balding partnership and that Balding had started a theatre company of his own off-Broadway. David, who would go on to produce nearly two dozen Main Stem plays (including *Man In The Glass Booth*, with Robert Shaw, *Scuba Duba* and *Steambath*, etc.) and, then become a force in the circus world, helping produce the first Big Apple Circus, told me, "Mr. Levine would like to meet with you in order to discuss his co-producing *Malcolm* with you"

"Oh," I said slowly, stalling for time as I thought quickly, literally, on my feet, "I don't think that's such a good idea." "Whaaat?" Why not," said Balding, three years my junior and, now, slightly staggered. "Well, I don't think it's his cup of tea and I want my name alone above the title." In retrospect, that sounds idiotic, but that is what I said.

I am not a drunkard, but I vividly recall it was dinner time and I was imbibing a scotch and water as I picked up the phone. This incident is indicative of the ruinous extent of my egotism, lack of self-awareness and incipient insecurity.

"Well, let me tell you it IS Mr. Levine's cup of tea and you're foolish not to think so," or something to that effect, David Ivor Balding said, and soon hung up the phone.

It was a stupid move. If you're trying to be a big shot and a big shot wants to see you, never turn the big shot down. Forming a relationship with either of these men might have led to something of value. My reply to Balding was dictated by my not wanting to share credit, and because of the unfair reputation Levine developed thanks to those who thought a retailer of ladies' dresses was out of his milieu dabbling in art.

And things were not going well with the adaptation; William Archibald, having troubles of his own, had not delivered a script.[108] I neglected to take the obvious course, which was to try to at least organize the adaptation on my own. I wished I could have asked Kazan why he had dropped the option.

If he dropped it who was I to say he was wrong? He probably optioned dozens of properties, maybe for tax purposes, and then

---

108 I had spoken to other playwrights: Hugh Wheeler (1912-1987), who won three Tonys for the libretti for *Candide* (revival), *A Little Night Music,* and *Sweeney Todd* and Arnold Weinstein (1927-2005) author of *Red Eye Of Love.*

ditched them when he saw they wouldn't work. Who was I to mention my name in the same breath as Elia Kazan, much less question his opinions?[109] Rather than complain to Audrey, I decided to allow my option to expire.

It came as a shock to me, and to many others in the theatre, when Edward Albee, in a lead article in the "Arts and Leisure" of *The New York Times*, championing Jim Purdy, announced that his next play was to be an adaptation of *Malcom*.

I assume Albee did the best job possible.[110] By the time it opened, I was in Mexico. Nevertheless, mea culpa; I should have met with Joe Levine; I should not have relied altogether on an adaptor but should have had a go at it myself.

Mel Williamson helped me obtain entrance to the French state film school (IDHEC) in Paris (*Institut de hautes cinematographiques*), THE French film school.[111] A friend from high school, a film director with a degree from UCLA, told me I knew just about everything there is to know about directing a film, so (foolishly) I rejected the opportunity.

That summer I directed Larry Parks (1914-1975) and Betty Garrett (1919-2011) in *High Button Shoes*,[112] and Edgar Bergen (1903-1978) in Kauffman and Hart's, *You Can't Take It With You*, both at Herb Rogers Tenthouse Theatre in Highland Park, Illinois.

I sensed *High Button Shoes* would be difficult as soon as I picked up Larry and Betty from O'Hare. In a car, which the producer provided for the occasion and which the prop boy drove while I sat in the back seat with the stars, these two considerable talents, who had been rebuffed by La La Land and HUAC, were solemn through most of the ride. Recently, Parks had appeared prominently

---

109 I have collected and read published and unpublished plays my life through. Nearly two thousand of them, in a collection under my name, are housed at Chicago's Ray Lonergan Memorial Library of Actors' Equity. Another thousand volumes devoted to the history of theatre, biographies, and other aspects, are housed, again, under my name, at Roosevelt University.

110 Directed by Cain Park alumni, Alan Schneider, produced by Richard Barr and Clinton Wilder, it ran for 19 previews and 7 performances.

111 Today it is known as La Femis Ecole Nationale Superieure des Metiers de l'Image et du Son. To be considered for entrance required the sponsorship of a French citizen with clout and Mel's friend, Maurice Ghnassia (1921-2003), correspondent, novelist, poet, and French Resistance fighter, backed me, and I was accepted. The school, has graduated many of the world's great film directors, including Alan Resnais, Louis Malle and Costa Gavras.

112 Directed by George Abbott, it premiered on Broadway in 1947, with Phil Silvers and Nannette Fabray, songs by Jule Styne (m.) and Sammy Cahn (w.), and is best known for its Keystone Cops ballet, by Jerome Robbins.

in John Huston's *Freud*, with Montgomery Clift, but when I complimented him he became embarrassed and slightly annoyed. It's not a pretty ride from O'Hare to Highland Park and I couldn't help thinking what they were thinking, which was:

"How the hell did we ever get here?"

The year he portrayed Al Jolson in the *Jolson Story* (a role offered to, and refused by, James Cagney and Danny Thomas) when it was time for the Academy Awards, Larry was nominated for a Best Actor; his competitors were Gregory Peck, Laurence Olivier, James Stewart and the winner was Fredric March, for *Best Years Of Our Lives. Jolson Sings Again*, the *Swordsman* and an MGM contract, playing opposite Elizabeth Taylor, in *Love Is Better Than Ever*, followed. But that film was withheld from release because Parks and Garrett had been named as members of the Communist Party and Larry was called before HUAC.[113]

Film work dried up for both for a while. They replaced Judy Holiday and Sydney Chaplin in *Bells Are Ringing* and played the Palladium, in London, with a nightclub act. But the span of Betty's career went from Martha Graham to work in the Federal Theatre to playing opposite Frank Sinatra (*Take Me Out To The Ball Game* and *On The Town*) and Jack Lemmon (*My Sister Eileen*, the musical version) to her later appearances in *All In The Family* (Irene Lorenzo) and *Lavrne And Shirley* (Edna Babish).[114] After that first day, ride from the airport, Betty and Larry were exceedingly professional and cooperative and top-notch in the show, which received excellent notices from the very discerning Chicago critics.

It would have been okay with me if Edgar Bergen became my adoptive father, but he already had a son, and a beautiful wife and daughter, and didn't need me. I loved him when I picked him up at O'Hare just as I had when listening to him as a child, preferring Mortimer Snerd to Charlie McCarthy. He told me he and George Burns met every morning for lox and bagels at Jack Benny's house, just to tell each other jokes. He was wonderful on and off stage.

---

113 Prior to his Hollywood career, Parks had made his debut in in small parts with the Group Theatre, on Broadway, beginning with *Golden Boy*. He and Garrett met some years later through the auspices of that same institution.

114 In our production, Ray Rayner, a perennial favorite with decades of Chicago's youngsters, played the Phil Silvers role.

In the fall, Peggy Wood, who had been a famous Portia, was a member of the Algonquin Round Table, President of ANTA,[115] and is best known, perhaps, as the mother abbess in the film *Sound Of Music* (1963), being a native of Brooklyn, was dismayed, as were so many others, at the disuse of the beautiful main stage of the Brooklyn Academy of Music. So she threw her weight behind the formation of a theatre company for that facility. For the opening effort, I was hired to direct the Lerner & Loewe musical, *Paint Your Wagon*. Musical conductor, Paul Taubman (who also owned a fancy restaurant on 58th Street, overlooking Central Park) led a large orchestra, and, having directed the show twice already, I mounted a nice production with some actors who enjoyed enduring careers without becoming famous. It was well received but it was not a venturesome choice, the effort petered-out and Brooklyn would have to wait till Harvey Lichtenstein for a true rejuvenation of BAM.

But I met a pretty new paramour from that production and we were sitting on bench, that fall, around one-thirty in the afternoon, at the south entrance to Central Park, when a well-dressed, middle-aged man staggered up to our bench and, shaken, running his hand through his hair, over and over, sat down violently, saying, "I can't believe it, I can't believe it!" When my paramour asked him what was wrong, he said, "President Kennedy's been shot! I can't believe it!"

Like David Copperfield, I had seen enough by now to have lost the capacity for being much surprised by anything, but the world changed from then on, though we did not know it at the time.

With the death of the President I learned that my pretty paramour, a wispy Jewish sexpot from Brooklyn, and the star of the show, was an avid follower of Barry Goldwater. We were not in love and women of different shades and proclivities attended me at the Washington Street apartment, a three-story building, which, with its close proximity to the Hudson, must have been the home of sea captains when it was built in the 1850's. Now that Julian Barry had moved out, I was the sole occupant and, as winter approached, I had not paid the rent for three or four months. Everything was haywire.

---

115 American National Theatre and Academy.

My gambling and my credit with the bookies had gone sour. But worst of all, I was twenty-seven years old and wasn't famous!

The rent laws were different then, and one evening, at an unexpected hour, "the marshall" appeared with three or four associates to impound any "unnecessary items," such as works of art and other valuables not connected to my immediate and personal welfare. They took a baby grand piano and a second-hand drum kit, but the marshal, a well-dressed, middle-aged Jewish man, who resembled Milton Arbogast, in *Psycho*, was surprisingly affable. Smiling, as he touched the sleeve of my bathrobe, he said he had dealt with many artistic people who ran into bad times and not to worry about it "Just the other day, Mr. Edelstein, I had to do this very same thing to a famous, I should say, used to be famous actress, Julie Haydon, ever hear of her? Her husband was the famous critic, George Jean Nathan."[116]

The electricity went off the next day, but there were fireplaces in the living and bedrooms, but no firewood, so, while burning old *Daily Racing Forms*, in the few days allotted me before actual eviction, I received a call that launched an adventure - my Great Adventure.

Four years before, at Guy Little's Grand Theatre, in Sullivan, Illinois, I met a young man, Dick Lamb, who played, among other parts, the role of Julio, in *Paint Your Wagon*. When we returned to New York he'd call occasionally and we'd get together. Dick, who was a few years younger than I, liked jazz, played the piano and sang good songs. A handsome, well-mannered, six-footer with wavy, black hair and a baby face (a tenor, not a baritone), he was a graduate of Stanford and his father was among the richest lumbermen in Oregon.

We had discussed, many times, the fact that every major location in America, from Hyannis Port to Sacramento, Cain Park and

---

116 Author of *On Bacherlorhood* (and the model for George Sanders Academy Award-winning portrayal of Addison DeWitt), GJN married the considerably younger Haydon in 1955. Like his father a self-abnegating Jew, he converted to Catholicism on his deathbed, in his suite in the Royalton Hotel, in 1958. Five years had elapsed since then, as far as our narrative is concerned, and Haydon, who created the role of Laura, in *Glass Menagerie*, soon migrated to the College of St. Teresa, in Winona Minnesota, a Franciscan facility, where she became actress-in-residence, and did not return to the New York stage until 1980, where she made an appearance in the Laurette Taylor role, in a short, Theatre Row run, of *Glass Menagerie*. More about GJN and Julie in *Confessions Of An Unsuccessful Actor*, Book Two – "Rise & Fall in the Age of David Mamet."

the St. Louis Muni to the Texas Stare Fair and Herb Rogers' Tenthouse, whether in tents, geodesic domes or large amphitheatres, presented Broadway musicals and drew large audiences in the summertime, every major location, that is, except San Francisco. At this strange juncture in my life, Dick gave me a call.

"Sid, I know we've talked about this so much you're bored with it and you think I'm obsessed. But I've been thinking: what if I go out there with you, we go out there together...we'll drive. You know, my dad just bought me a Chrysler 400. Helluva car. Really, only eight made. We'll drive out there and I've got enough to take care of us both till we get there and start looking around, at least for a few months. I really think we ought to give it a try, but I want to do it with you."

I accepted.

It was the summer of "I Have A Dream," but they spit on Adlai Stevenson in Dallas, and with the suicides all spring and summer by Buddhist monks, the assassinations of Medgar Evers, in Mississippi, Diem, in Saigon, the four little girls in the Birmingham church and, then, Kennedy, plus the attendant mystery of the murder of Oswald by Ruby, it had been a really crummy year.

So, I accepted Dick's proposal, and, after some crunching of figures, meeting with attorney, David Marshall Holtzman, owner, with his sister, Fanny, of the successful Hyannis Port Summer Theatre, and getting advice from Herb Rogers, and formulating and printing a prospectus, I said "Goodbye" to the Washington Street apartment and we set off in Lamb's 1964 Chrysler Imperial 400 prototype, a black convertible, with white leather upholstery, one, as he said correctly, of only eight made.

To throw up everything, even when faced with eviction, to dispose of what little personal effects you might have and drive three thousand miles, to establish a fifteen hundred seat theatre in as broad a location as the San Francisco Bay Area is insane. But we did it...in a way, as you'll see (in a few brief pages) and let the reader decide whether or not my Great Adventure, which encompassed a couple of years, was worth the effort.

I still didn't know how to change a tire, but I was an experienced driver who survived two serious near-accidents while at the

wheel.[117] But driving the 400 was effortless entertainment. George
Furth (1932-2008), a caustic, funny man whose far-ranging talents included playing usually despicable, often slightly effeminate,
bit roles, in major films, as well as writing great libretti such as
Company and *Merrily We Roll Along* and plays as good as *Twigs,*
accompanied us as far as Chicago. Travelling the fabled "Mother
Road," "Route 66" (a song made popular by Nat "King" Cole) at
top speeds, stopping along the way at fabulous places like the Carls-
bad Caverns, navigating the curving roads of mighty mountains,
approaching Salt Lake City for the first time, as did the Mormons,
and racing through the salt lands of Nevada at 110 miles hour to the
miraculous City by the Bay was the first act of my Great Adventure.

All I knew about San Francisco came from the *Maltese Falcon*
and *Vertigo*, but Dick was a superb guide, from the Venetian Room,
at the Fairmont Hotel to Ernie's, from Lombard Street to Sausalito,
dinner at the Crystal Palace, the Museum of Fine Arts. It is the
most astonishing city in America, but when I understood the terrain
I realized the kind of theatre we proposed could only happen on
or near the Bayshore Freeway, somewhere between San Francisco
and San Jose, which meant somewhere near Palo Alto and Stanford
University.

After we arrived in San Francisco, each day, over a period
of many months (punctuated by a trip to Dick's home in Eugene,
to experience the glories of Northern California and Oregon) we
would arise early and Dick would drive up and down the Freeway
and I would make notes of empty lots and realtors, anything that
might lead us somewhere tangible. We found a local lawyer and that
led to a meeting with Marty Melcher, Doris Day's then husband,
and another gentleman who was a high official of a famous union

---

117 At Cain Park, in my '47 Ford sedan, travelling north, down the sharp decline on Lee Road,
heading toward a stop sign and the furious rush hour east-west traffic on Mayfield, I stepped on
the brakes and there were none and, then, took the only other path available, a violent right turn,
straight into a mailbox adjacent to an aged tree, saving myself and my three passengers. Then, in
the passenger seat of Mel's car, driving to his mother's funeral at 60 m.p.h. on the Turnpike, with
Lorraine asleep in the back seat at two-thirty in the morning, there appeared before me a 1928
canvas top sedan travelling at 20 m.p.h., without lights of any kind, like a specter of death in the
night. I yelled to the very near-sighted Mel, who screamed louder than I, and Mel braked the car in
time. His sight, as I say, was not good and had I not been there I feel it would have been fatal.

whose coffers had erected the lavish hotel-motel-restaurant in which we sat.

"Ain'chu kind of a lamb to be puutin' together a deal like this?" said the union big shot, while squinting a smile at Dick Lamb. It was upsetting and Melcher and the union boss passed on the deal. But shortly thereafter we made a breakthrough when I spotted the Burlingame Hyatt House hotel-motel, just off the Freeway, near the airport. There were only one or two other Hyatt Houses in the world at that time and one was not far from my old Rogers Perk neighborhood, on Touhy Avenue, just off Edens Expressway, in Chicago.[118]

I called and asked to speak with the owner, Donald N. Pritzker, who turned out to be the man behind the western expansion of the Hyatt Empire. An engaging, dynamic man, slightly past thirty, with a good sense of humor and the tough mind of a successful executive, he was likeable and, since we were both Chicagoans, it wasn't hard to make a connection. Not only had he heard of Herb Rogers and Herb's Tenthouse and Music Theatres, he had seen some of Herb's shows. That I had directed and produced with Herb impressed him and he liked the idea of a theatre on the empty lot he owned, across the street from his Burlingame Hyatt House.

We met with him in his office. He was very cordial and invited us to his home where we watched some friends of his play touch football, a ritual on weekends. Don's two sons and their sister were too young to participate, but some visiting family members and compatriots were earnestly embroiled in a vigorous back and forth battle, on a broad lawn adjacent to Don's home. The Pritzger family, much less the Pritzger Foundation and ancillary institutions with which they are associated, or which bear their name today, and the many philanthropies and *mitzvahs* they perform, had not yet attained the prominence they presently occupy in our society, but Don and his friends at play reminded me of the Kennedys at their best and I enjoyed seeing such a harmonious ensemble.

---

118 The first Hyatt House was an existing facility, at the L.A. airport, when purchased by Jay Pritzker (1922-1999). He delegated younger brother, Don, to manage the western interests of the newly reformed Hyatt Corp. Robert (1926-2011) was the third brother, all beings sons of A.N. and Fanny Pritzger.

At first, Don said he wanted me to raise the money to build the theatre and I said I believed I could accomplish that through a SEC offering, the California branch being easier to comply with than the New York office, where I had had experience pursuing a filing with *Malcolm*. Building costs were much different than today and we were talking about a tent-type structure or a geodesic dome, both of which were models then for theatres from Hyannis to Sacramento.

But one evening Dick and I were invited to Don's office, a large, two room affair in which only one lonely decorator lamp and the one on Don's desk were lit against the starless western sky. Outside, across the industrial road and the, then, vacant property, were the inlet waters of the great Bay and the strip of peninsula on which planes from the East would land. It was a dramatic setting and I sensed something memorable was about to take place.

No sooner had we seated ourselves than Don gestured to me to follow him into the adjacent room and to Dick to stay put in his chair. Don picked up a phone, said a word or two into the receiver, which he, then, handed me, with an amiable grin. It was Herb Rogers; Herb who had "given me" my Actors' Equity card when I played Frank in *Wonderful Town*, with Kay Ballard, and got a couple huge "house laughs" every night, Herb, for whom I directed, Bergen and Larry and Betty and co-produced Claudia in *Raisin*, all very successful. Herb, sounded guilty and apologetic; the gist of it was he was in and Dick Lamb and I were out.

It was impossible not to like Herb, and Don had been hospitable. Like the Pritzgers, but in a vastly different venue, Herb performed countless philanthropies in creating theatres and providing employment for actors, musicians and supporting personnel. That is what producers do.

Born in Seattle, a graduate of Washington University, where he studied under Professor Glenn Hughes (1894-1964), the father of theatre-in-the-round in America, Herb, prematurely bald, slight of stature, but good-looking, with dancing blue eyes, wanted to be an actor and was sufficiently charming to succeed in the endeavor, but his father, who owned a department store, gave him $10,000 and Herb started a tent theatre, in-the-round, in Highland Park, with a stellar group of actors, headed by Barnard Hughes and Helen Stenborg, husband and wife, and Marian Walters and director Mike

Ferral (also hitched) performing high-class dramas by Ibsen and Shaw, if you please. And Herb developed and maintained his intelligent, well-heeled audience, expanding his operation by erecting a tent nearby on the Lake County line, doing musicals with stars from New York and Hollywood, so that he had two theatres operating at the same time in the summer, all reviewed by the major newspapers. You could not blame Don for switching to Herb; it was a business decision.

Soon, I was back in New York, sleeping on a friend's floor, or staying in a horrid hotel just off Columbus Circle, on 58th Street, across from the Coliseum. I was broke and staying alive on borrowed money, from Dean Romanoff, among others, when, unexpectedly, a few months after I had last spoken to him on the phone with Don standing nearby and Dick Lamb waiting in the other room, I received a call from Herb, who tracked me down through the Palace of Audible Dreams.

Herb's natural demeanor was easy-going and intimate. This time, the intimacy was present but there was a note of urgency, too, and the words came as if rehearsed.

"If you come out here and help me raise the money, Don will put you up at the Hyatt House. He'll get you a new car from Hertz to drive around in and we'll give you some money for living expenses. But you'll have to come up with the air fare yourself."

I had estimated the cost of the theatre, be it tent or dome, and running expenses for the first show to be one million dollars, a lot of money then, yet I hadn't the dough to fly to S.F.

Only Macuilxochitl, Aztec god of gambling, knows how much *gelt* I have squandered playing ponies, but I savor the triumphs that solved pressing problems. This time it was a twenty-dollar, two-horse win parlay on two nags, with the unforgettable names of Sarsaparilla[119] and Scoresville[120] and the payout was twelve hundred dollars, you figure the pari-mutuels (the win price of horse #1 x the win price of horse #2, divided by two). The bookmaker, with whom I placed the wager, a denizen of the seedy hotel on 58th Street, a dour man from Middle Europe, paid me off with a look of one part

---

119 Scratch (GB) out of Star Melody(GB) by Stardust(GB).

120 Intent out of New Melody by Bimelech, the similarity in the names of the mares is coincidental but unusual.

wonder and ten parts hatred and I was on the plane within two days of Herb's call.

Back in S.F. sitting in the parking lot outside the Burlingame Hyatt House, in a 1963, white Chevrolet Impala convertible, with faux red leather seats, loaned to me by Don Pritizger, I listened to Cassius Clay (soon to be Muhammad Ali [1942-2016]) beat Sonny Liston. Only a month before, in NYC I was only ten, unobstructed feet away from the soon-to-be champ, as he strutted down Seventh Avenue, in front of the newly constructed Sheraton Hotel, trailed by half-dozen beautiful models. Boxing Hall of Fame promoter, Teddy Brenner, who would become the matchmaker at Madison Square Garden, frequented the record store regularly and was friendly with Gene Romanoff and his Brudder. Brenner, reserved, "cool" by nature, was unreserved in his enthusiasm for the newcomer from Kentucky and told us to get down on the comical braggart at 8 or 10 to 1. It was a sunny day, Clay was dressed in a suit and tie and yelling with arms outstretched, telling wide-eyed passers-by how great he was. And he was tall, powerful looking, young and funny, not like the bum he was going to fight, and as I sat there a few hundred feet from the Bay and the huge ocean beyond, I wished that I were back on Broadway and had had a bookmaker I could trust.

For a while, I worked with Herb in putting together a prospectus, but, after a few weeks going on months, he decided it would be better to have a SEC offering in California, Illinois and New York, and I knew that entailed a big effort. This stalled the forward motion of the project and I spent many afternoons ten minutes away from the Hyatt House, at the now defunct Bay Meadows Racetrack.[121]

Don, being a man of action, tired of the delay and decided to put up all the money without a public offering, and I, no longer needed, went the way of the lamb. But unlike Dick Lamb, I was given ten thousand dollars (minus the cost of a lot of lobster dinners and double vodka martinis from room service) and allowed to keep the sexy Impala.

---

121 At the time, they ran six quarter horse races a day. I knew nothing about those wonderful runners when I walked into the facility. They are a breed apart from thoroughbreds, and only run 440 yards to 3/4ths of a mile at the longest, and the races are over in a flash. I won $400 the first day, interpreting the past performances and learning something about the trainers. In time, I made lasting friends and even ran into Annette Funicello, in the paddock, one day.

There were two famous female show business residents in the city of Burlingame: Shirley Temple Black and Kathryn (née Grant) Crosby. The latter opened the theatre, starring in *Showboat*. Oh, how I would like to have met Bing Crosby, a mammoth figure, and I ain't no starfucker.

Shades of Eddie Lang, Harry Barris, Joe Venuti, and the real "Sunshine Boys,"[122] I am truly sorry I did not meet Der Bingle.[123]

Don Pritzger died tragically at the age of thirty-nine, in 1972, while playing tennis in Honolulu. His daughter, Penny Pritzger, was Secretary of Commerce, in the Obama Administration, his son, Anthony Pritzger, is managing partner of the Pritzger Group, and son, J.B. Pritzger, who bears a close resemblances his father, was elected Governor of the State of Illinois, in 2018. Maybe he will be President some day, maybe his sister. I would vote for either.

The building that housed the theatre was eventually converted into an office space and is an attractive structure in tune with the entire facility. Herb and I and Dick and I remained friends. I had had my Great Adventure, seen a large portion of the West, thoroughly investigated the beauties of San Francisco and the Peninsula, eaten in choice restaurants and enjoyed myself thoroughly thanks to the largesse of Dick, Don and Herb.

But none of it would have happened were it not for me.

I was tired of rehashing old musicals "I piss on it all from a considerable height," said the despicable anti-Semite Celine in the last line of his famous book and I felt the same way. The most memorable productions I saw during this period, the plays which influenced me the most, were Harold Pinter's *Caretaker*, with Donald Pleasance and David Merrick's production of Berthold Brecht's *Restistible Rise Of Arturo Ui*, starring Christopher Plummer. *Homecoming* was another great event, but that was a couple of years in the future. Now, I wanted a rest from the great Lyric Theatre.

Unhappy that the Burlingame project no longer included me, feeling old at twenty-eight and terrified of reaching thirty without fame and sorry I had eaten so many lobster dinners and drunk so

---

122 The Mooney Brothers, the great singer, pianist, accordionist, Hammond B-3 organist Joe Mooney and his equally gifted brother, Dan, who vanished in 1936.

123 And, for the unwashed and uninitiated, Crosby, with help from actor, Pat O'Brien, built Del Mar Racetrack.

many vodka martinis, I drove the Impala down to the Border, my destination El Paso/Juarez.

17

Dizzy Gillespie Meets José Ferrer

Lying on a lumpy mattress in a fourth-rate hotel in the oft' deadly, eternally corrupt Ciudad Juarez, cuddled in the embrace of a redheaded chippie named Ginger, whose skin and breasts were the color and succulence of honey-dew melon, I received a telegram from Julian Barry inviting me to come back to New York to produce *Lookin' For The Man*, a jazz musical about the relationship between the very popular Miles Davis and Charlie Parker, who had been dead for nine years.

A green-eyed beauty who looked more Hawaiian than Mexican, Ginger, the mother of a 13 month-old baby girl whom she attended assiduously whenever free from the grasp of hungry men, was introduced to me by her taxi-driver brother, Jorge, pronounced "hor-hay," with the emphasis on the "hor." In that border town named for the great Mexican emancipator, driving a taxi is a "cover" for free-wheeling rascals of every stripe, a "front" for peddling, or engaging in other nefarious undertakings and unmentionable sins of every variety known to humankind.

The first night I met him, Jorge thought to get me drunk, take me for all I was worth, and leave me in a ditch somewhere on the wrong side of the Rio Grande. Times were bad, the pickings small, and he had a family to feed, a family that included recently knocked-up sister, Ginger, a pretty *puta*. Jorge, when first we met, escorted me to a string of brothels where I interviewed the inmates and consumed a total of seventeen shots of Mexican brandy. One of the first things I learned to say in Spanish was:

"Dame un Don Pedro Domecq, por favor, con aqua por lado."
And to the prostitutes, I was taught to say:
"Quantos para tu, Chiquita?"
And throughout the bibulous evening Jorge was rendered helpless by the sight of a gold-plated Dunhill lighter with which I lit
my brown, Mexican cigarillos. It's the same lighter the replica of
which today sells for $700. Back then it was a sure pop for a twenty
or a thirty-dollar loan at a pawnbroker's. Each time I lit up with
the Dunhill, Jorge's eyes were drawn to my patented "Rollagas"
mini-torch as if Mesmer, himself, were spinning the flint wheel. He
smiled whenever I spun it. But he was a clever chap who smiled for
his clients whether he liked them or not.

And in a baronial bagnio on the outskirts of town, a sprawling
mansion of many rooms, the uniting factor of which was a foul-
mouthed madam of eighty who applied her face powder so massively she appeared to have emerged from the *Cabinet of Dr. Caligari,*
the ever-smiling Jorge, sure enough, pocketed *my muy expensivo*
Dunhill lighter.

Pointedly, in Jorge's direction, I announced it was missing, and,
after first insisting it was stolen by one of the girls, he shamefacedly
confessed, brought forth the pilfered item, and, making a desperate
about-face, invited me to his poor abode for dinner. Jorge liked me;
like you like a souvenir, or a benefactor. He introduced me to his
family as a celebrity from Times Square, showed me his babies in
their cribs, and fawned over me for his aged mother and his somewhat mystified wife.

Jorge became my Man in Juarez, my guide and confidant in
sinful undertakings, small dealings, for my personal use and those
of my friends in the marijuana trade, the prices being laughable by
U.S. standards and the quality acceptable. Jorge need merely drive
me out to the fields beyond town, and we would pick it from the hill
on which it grew, and drive back across the border. It was beautiful
as long as the border guard passed you through, without question,
if not, the penalty was a mandatory twenty years, by federal edict.
An ounce of pot cost $15 in Manhattan then, and was often sold
in a can of Prince Albert pipe tobacco in order to assure its proper
weight. In Juarez it sold for $80 to $100 a kilo, a kilo being approximately two point two pounds.

Ginger and I (still partially influenced by the seventeen bran-dies) were in love for all of sixteen minutes, but I also had some-thing going with the cashier in the restaurant at the legal horse parlor/bookie near the Border. Ramona was slender, brunette and devoutly Catholic. She had beautiful, brown eyes and we ogled each other all day long, as I handicapped and wagered on the daily racing cards, from racetracks operating East to West and Agua Caliente, too, below the Border. On her lunch-break we would drive around going nowhere and kiss like school kids in a stolen car. But when she became serious and invited me to her home for dinner to meet her parents, I smelled the bonds of marriage, sold the white Impala (which now had expensive wire wheels), for *bubkas* to an avaricious and deceitful used car dealer, in El Paso, whose name, believe it or not, was Tex, and made plans to depart for NYC.

But something ugly happened before I left for Gotham. It was around 9 P.M. I had dined at the Alcazar in Juarez and was plan-ning to take the streetcar, at the Border, to Downtown El Paso, where friends would, come to meet me. On this routine crossing of the famous pedestrian walkway between Juarez and El Paso, in the month that saw Lyndon B. Johnson masterfully force the Civil Rights Act through Congress, I was detained, when I reached the American side, by a detective of the El Paso Police Department, and asked to step aside and into a detention office. The detective who led the way was a heavy-set fifty year-old of Mexican descent. His pockmarked face, approximating the color of his brown suit, bore a resemblance to Benito Juarez but he (we'll call him Sanchez) lacked the peasant president's humility. This was his beat and he was on federal property, which meant no-holds barred. An Anglo-looking partner joined him, they asked me to take off my clothes, searched my pockets, took my wallet and, told me to bend over and spread my cheeks so they could look up my asshole.

Fifty years later I am still wondering what they expected to find there. I protested but cooperated because I had nothing to hide. Sanchez or his partner had probably seen me traverse the Border, at this main point for foot traffic, on a previous occasion. I looked out of place. I was dressed in a tropical weight, light blue plaid, tailor-made suit, which, if you found a suitable tailor to cut the pat-tern, and found comparable fabric, would cost about $4,000 dollars today. Too heavy for the sun baked days, it was light enough for the cooler early-summer desert evenings. Two button and conservative, to the eye of a crooked dick who worked for a Benjamin a week and all he could shake down, it looked too expensive. Then, Sanchez began a new phase of the interrogation while fondling a card from my wallet.

"Say, Edelstein?" he asked in a mocking tone,"what's a Jewboy from New York like you doin' with a buncha niggers in the NAACP? You ain't no secret nigger, are you?"

He was holding my NAACP card. "You don't have to be a Negro to belong to the NAACP," I responded mildly.

He continued questioning me in an insinuating manner, repeating "Edelstein" insultingly, as he looked through my wallet, until he produced a scrap on which I had drawn a street diagram indicating a drugstore where I purchased cartons of brown Mexican cigarettes at a bargain rate. I planned to take some home. It was perfectly legal.

I explained the map but Sanchez insisted the pharmacist was supplying me with illegal controlled substances, and, on the basis of the scrap-of-paper-map and the fact I was a Jewish member of the National Association for the Advancement of Colored People, he tossed me in the legendary El Paso County Jail.[124]

I used my one phone call to contact a high school sweetheart of my sister's, who was now the head of New York's ACLU branch. Released in the morning, I was escorted by the El Paso representative of the American Civil Liberties Union to the office of the Sherriff of El Paso County, who happened to be running for Mayor in the next election. He shook my hand warmly and apologized for my arrest. Then he rang a buzzer on his desk. Sanchez and his partner entered and solemnly shook my hand and apologized. But every

---

124 In my 28 year-old life, I had been incarcerated overnight on two previous occasions. The reader already knows of the night in the Tombs, but the most recent had been in Chicago, in 1960, where I was arrested in a bookie joint located in a TV repair store, on Clark near Devon, an establishment operated by the Lenny Patrick branch of the Outfit. When the raid went down I had one marijuana cigarette in my raincoat pocket and they sent me to the State Street Jail. Early the next morning of a sleepless night, an Outfit lawyer, for a $500 legal fee, bailed me out. I was broke, but I convinced the poor bookie, who was terrified by the whole affair, to call in a one hundred dollar wager on a winning 5-1 shot in the last race at Santa Anita Racetrack, ridden to victory by Bill Shoemaker. The horse paid $12, the bookie paid me and I gave it all to the Outfit's lawyer. It was the most expensive joint I never smoked and it showed, once more, the absurdity of the Marijuana Laws. The case was thrown out.

time I saw Sanchez through the coming years, he would harass me with that insulting smile and ask," Hey, Edelstein, what crime are you up to this time?' or "Say Edelstein,[125] how's everything with Martin Luther King and the NAACP?"

With the proceeds from the sale of the Impala and the finder's fee from the deal with Pritzker running low, I returned to Manhattan in August of 1964, the first year in which the miniskirt made an appearance, the first year in a decade in which I did not perform or direct in summer stock. In Times Square, by chance, I bumped into a con-man friend whom I befriended at the Palace of Audible Dreams. He had wangled entry to the Beatles concert at the Steel Pier, in Atlantic City. As the reader knows by now, I had no interest in seeing Mopheads, but I was delighted to stay at the four-star Marlborough-Blenheim Hotel and visit the Atlantic City Racecourse, where the con-man and I met Perle Mesta who did not invite us to her party that night.

We visited the Democratic Convention where security was amateurishly lax and walked the convention hall floor without official passes of any kind. When I hear the words "Gulf of Tonkin Resolution" (which had been passed three weeks previously with little debate) or the name "Fanny Lou Hamer," a mental picture forms in my mind of the view from the lobby of the giant hall overlooking the Boardwalk and the mighty Atlantic itself.

****

Lookin' For The Man is about a young trumpet player (Sonny Lewis, a thinly disguised Miles Davis) who comes to New York to meet "The Man" (Ray Baker, a thinly-disguised Charlie Parker) and, hopefully, to play with him. Sonny achieves both goals, but like Ray he becomes addicted to heroin. I talked Dizzy Gillespie (through his agent, Joe Glaser) into playing the role of "Fats," a big band leader and friend of Sonny and Ray, in other words, a thinly disguised version of Dizzy, himself.

The music by Warren B. Meyers (1929-2010) is authentic and original. Bop-oriented, there isn't a bad song in the score. The

---

125 Again, despite what Mencken said, "Edelstein" is a distinguished name in this country, as it was in the Pale and elsewhere.

lyrics by Julian Barry are hip and consequential, and the book, for which they shared equal credit, creates an authentic world of jazz . "It might have been a great Broadway musical" is a familiar refrain throughout the history of Broadway musicals, but in this case "might have been" is true. I refer you to the recording. But I'm getting ahead of my story.

Before I left with Dick Lamb for California, Julian and his childhood best friend, Warren, played the score and read the script for me. They did not ask me to produce the show then, but when they contacted me in Mexico, they said if I became involved, José Ferrer might agree to direct. Julian had been stage manager for Joe on *Andersonville Trial* and was currently serving in the same capacity for Ferrer's starring appearance, as the Prince, in Noel Coward's musicalized version of Terence Rattigan's, *Prince And The Showgirl*, now called *The Girl Who Came To Supper.* He was playing opposite Florence Henderson and Coward had directed. Playing at the Broadway Theatre, down the street from the Palace of Audible Dreams, the film with Marilyn Monroe and Laurence Olivier was well known, but Coward's version was going to be short-lived.

In recent years Ferrer, as director, had failed to save the musical version of *Juno And The Paycock*, and his own production of *Oh, Captain!*, starring Tony Randall, a musical comedy adaptation of *Captain's Paradise*, which had been a successful film, starring Alec Guinness. But I was indelibly impressed by Joe's staging of *Andersonville*, that 1959 Saul Levitt drama about the Confederate Civil War camp with its all-male cast: George C. Scott, Herbert Berghof, Albert Dekker, Ian Keith and Robert Burr.

The score, the book, and the idea of Ferrer directing motivated my return to Gotham. Following the jaunt to Atlantic City I checked into a fine hotel across from the Waldorf.

I awoke in the middle of the night with a horrible pain in my belly, a pain of such ferocious intensity I was unable to rise from my bed. I knew something awful was happening and my life was in danger. Crawling on my side, struggling to reach the phone, which connected to the desk downstairs, I knocked the receiver off the stand, mumbled a few words and passed out. An ambulance and the "house" doctor, who lived nearby, were dispatched, and I awakened just as I was about to enter the operating room of the old French Hospital, on 30th Street, where my appendix was summarily removed. Had I not been in a hotel, and connected to a switchboard, I would not have lived, said the doctor, who performed the procedure and saved my life.

It took a couple of weeks to recover. By then *Girl Who Came To Supper* had folded and it was time to meet José Vicente de Otero y Cintron Ferrer (1912-1992) the scion of a wealthy attorney, and his then wife, the singer, Rosemary Clooney (1928-2002) at the Warwick Hotel. (He had previously been married to actresses Uta Hagen and then, Phyllis Hill.)

José Ferrer had long been one of the people whom I most admired in the theatre. Introduced to him originally as the dopey Dauphin wowed by Ingrid Bergman's *Joan Of Arc*, my young chums and I were fourteen years old when his performance in *Cyrano de Bergerac* earned him an Academy Award for Best Actor. Viewing it many times in its initial run, fascinated with, and imitative of, his swordplay, we were not too young to sense that the beautiful words he spoke in praise of his white plume represented an ideal beyond parochial Rogers Park, something to which we should aspire. He was moved when I told him this and we became friends forever.

It is impossible to summarize his gargantuan career with only a few words, but, thankfully, we are dealing, now, with only the first portion of his career. Following *Cyrano*, his performance as painter, Henri de Toulouse-Lautrec, in the John Huston masterpiece, *Moulin Rouge*, added to Joe's luster and almost won him another Academy Award. I was too young and in the wrong place to have seen him in *Charley's Aunt* or *Silver Whistle* (by Robert E. McEnroe) or the series of revivals he presented with producer Jean Dalrymple, at the New York City Center, much less the Theatre Guild's famous presentation of Margaret Webster's production of *Othello*, with Hagen, as Desdemona, and Joe playing Iago to Robeson's jealous Moor, though I, like many aspiring actors, listened devotedly to the award-winning recording of the show on Columbia Records.

In this earlier period, Ferrer's returns to Broadway from Hollywood eventuated in potent hits. He directed *The Fourposter*, produced and directed *Stalg 17*, and produced, directed and starred in *The Shrike*, to which may be added, *My Three Angels*, which he only directed, but which ran for 344 performances, starring Walter Slezak, and then was sold to Hollywood, for big bucks, as a vehicle for Humphrey Bogart.

And, while his appearances as a blackmailing hypnotist, in Otto Preminger's *Whirlpool*, and as the hypocritical minister tempted by Rita Hayworth's *Sadie Thompson*, as Captain Alfred Dreyfus, in *I Accuse!* (which he also directed) and in his role as a Russian émigré, opposite Kim Hunter, in *Anything Can Happen*, were financially profitable, and artistically satisfying, his portrayal of a Latin dictator hoping to be saved by surgeon, Cary Grant, in *Crisis*, his assaying of the life of Sigmund Romberg, in *Deep In My Heart*, his debut as a Hollywood film director, *Shrike*, starring opposite the miscast June Allyson, the comedy *The High Cost Of Loving*, opposite Gena Rowlands, (which he also directed) and *The Great Man*, which he co-wrote, starred in and directed, were less rewarding at the box office. Joe was not your average, good-looking Hollywood star and it was not easy to find him leading roles. "I didn't come across the same way in film. I wasn't made for the screen," he told me.

His role as Barney Greenwald, playing opposite Bogart, who appeared as psychotic Commander Queeg, in *The Caine Mutiny*, a box office success, was salubrious for his career, but the film failed to capture the play's riveting appeal. Of Bogart, he said, "I had little to do with Bogie," which I found strange, not so much because he called him by his nickname, but because he said they had little in common. They both grew up on Manhattan's Upper West Side, Bogart having been the son of a Riverside Drive, society physician, and Joe spending much of his youth living in the Ansonia Hotel. Both were members of the same club, The Players, in Gramercy Park, and had many mutual friends, but they were not chums. Maybe Bogie resented Joe's lack of defiance when summoned by HUAC. "It was a very bad time for everybody," were Joe's only words to me on the subject.

He first appeared as a professional actor in 1934, in a "show-boat" theatre, on Long Island. The following summer a fellow Princeton alumni, in the class a year before him, Joshua Logan, operator of the new Suffern Country Playhouse, hired him, as stage manager. "Stage managing is the best way to learn about the theatre," he claimed, but I thought attending the Cleveland Playhouse and watching directors mount productions was better.

Actresses Ruth Gordon and Helen Hayes, who worked at Suffern during that summer, became early facilitators of Joe's future success by introducing him to the prodigious producer, director and champion womanizer, the almost universally hated, Jed Harris (1900-1979).[126] A theatrical genius, Harris mentored Ferrer.

Four of his five initial Broadway appearances as an actor were in flops, but among them was the long-running hit, *Brother Rat*, produced and directed by George Abbott. Ferrer played small supporting roles in *High Tor*, starring Burgess Meredith, and *Mamba's Daughters*, starring Ethel Waters.

"I have no agent," Joe told me soon after we met. "I've never had an agent. Eddie Reiskind, my lawyer, handles everything." So, Joe always had something on the fire, juggling two or three projects at a time.

Recognizing him as a great man, I realize he was not without his foibles and faults. Balding prematurely, despite his athleticism he was not an imposing figure and he had a funny walk and an interesting, but not conventionally handsome, face. Still, women adored him and found him the very personification of Love. Some because they had seen him play *Cyrano*, some not. He was in love with the female form, a mutual interest that contributed to our friendship, another being our love for Bix Beiderbecke. Joe didn't know a lot about Charlie Parker, but he sure knew about Bix.

He could be arrogant, but he was never that way with me. Still, I once saw him send a plate of food back to the kitchen of a highly touted restaurant, on Chicago's Halstead Street, throwing the entire staff (and most of the customers) into a discombobulated turmoil. He grew up in luxury, attended a Swiss boarding school, and spoke eight languages fluently: French, Spanish, German, Swiss, Portuguese, English, most memorably, Italian, for which he exhibited great facility when we ate at Patsy's Restaurant, on 56th Street,

---

126 Harris, of whom the equally prodigious George S. Kauffman said, "When I die, I want to be cremated and have my ashes thrown in Jed Harris's face," produced *Front Page, Broadway, The Royal Family,* directed *The Crucible*, and *The Heiress*, and produced and directed *Our Town*, to name a very few.

and I know not what else. Versatile, he replaced Danny Kaye, in Cole Porter's 1943, *Let's Face It*, learning and performing, on short notice, one of Porter's most syllabically difficult songs, "Let's Not Talk About Love," bringing the house down with his rendition. He had one of the most exquisite speaking voices in the world, and starting out as *Philo Vance, Detective*, on the radio, made a fortune with his voice alone.

Facile, usually the smartest one in the room, graduating from Princeton with a B.A. in Architecture, he was a gifted caricaturist. He had his own band "The Pied Pipers," all through college, even toured Europe, and a fellow member of the Triangle Club, Jimmy Stewart (who was in Logan's class), recorded "Sweet Georgia Brown" with Joe's band. He had the guts to produce and direct the 1945 stage adaptation of the Billie Holiday-inspired novel *Strange Fruit*, by Lillian Smith, a play which dealt with miscegenation, Jim Crow and lynching, and which raised wild controversies in Philly, Boston and on Broadway. He could be as snooty as a Vassar girl, or as egalitarian as a waiter at Lindy's. After all, his grandfather, Gabriel Ferrer Hernandez, led the Puerto-Rican fight for independence from Spain. The father of five beautiful children from his current marriage to his lovely, movie star wife, so far as I was concerned, he had a right to be arrogant.

Now, since playing the sadistic colonel in David Lean's *Lawrence Of Arabia*, Ferrer was much sought-after, and could afford to be at liberty and select his projects carefully. A past "Blindfold Test" in *Downbeat* showed his love of jazz. He still played the piano (rather well, his favorite being Erroll Garner) and the clarinet (not as well, though he took some lessons from Benny Goodman) and would, in future, have his own cabaret act (with Warren Meyers, on piano and conducting). The only person to ever win Tony Awards as actor, director and producer, jazz was important to him and he truly wanted a cutting edge, hit Broadway musical.

When Julian, Warren and I met with him at the Warwick, Rosie was sitting up against a headboard, pouting in the bedroom, obviously upset that we had interfered with her plans for the day, and Joe was making up for it by being welcoming in his energetic way.

Nothing much was accomplished but his enthusiasm was vibrant and our rapport instantaneous.[127]

A couple of weeks later, to cement the relationship, I flew out to the Ferrer-Clooney home in Beverly Hills, on Roxbury Drive, an abode once occupied by George Gershwin. I exited the cab to find an unpretentious residence which required no Sherlock Holmes to detect that children, love and affection dwelt within. I entered the living room where Gershwin wrote "Foggy Day" for Fred Astaire, looked through the doors that led outside to the pool where Billie Holiday tried to recuperate in an extended, unpublicized stay, spied across the yard to where Ira Gershwin still lived, and looked for the tennis court where they played with Harold Arlen and other celebs. Joe took me upstairs and introduced me to sons Gabriel and Miguel (1955-2017) and their friends from school. There was a drum set and guitars and they were rehearsing. Rafael, the youngest son, was a toddler, then, and I did not meet daughter Maria until years later.[128]

I went back to New York and "hired" Wally Fried as general manager and began putting together a prospectus for SEC approval. Julian's parents and Warren's brother put up some "seed" money, but insisted I hire Elias Goldin, as g.m. He was a great person and, like Wally, respected in his field. Eli's next show would be *Funny Girl*, with new singer, Barbra Streisand. Wally, who was in the initial weeks of *Man Of La Mancha* (playing in the Village, in a geodesic dome on the former location of the Open Door) was pissed and never forgave me.

****

---

127 This is true in Julian's case, too. Joe's final appearance was with Mandy Patinkin in the musical version of Ionesco's, *Rhinoceros*, presented by Sir Peter Hall, at the Chichester Festival of 1991. Unsuccessful with critics, Barry and Hall wrote the libretto.

128 I have never met daughter, Monsita, or the daughter from his marriage to Uta Hagen, the first Mrs. Ferrer, whose affair with Paul Robeson caused Uta and Joe to divorce. Uta was supposedly the model for Eve, in *All About Eve* (1950) directed by Joseph L. Mankiewicz, from his own script, which was a transmogrification of author-actress, Mary Orr's (un-credited, in the film), 1946 short story, *"Wisdom of Eve,"* which she, with husband, Reginald Denham, adapted into a play, of the same name. It was never produced until 1979, when it appeared off-Broadway. However, *All About Eve* was made into a musical called *Applause*, with music by Charles Strouse, lyrics by Lee Adams, book by Betty Comden and Adolph Green, starring Lauren Bacall, in the role of Margo Channing, which was created by Bette Davis in the film. The real life Margo was the German-British actress, Elisabeth Bergner (1887-1986).

I spent an entire day with Dizzy (John Birks) Gillespie (1917-1993), picking him up in the morning and taking him back home at night. He had many errands and I drove him all over Manhattan. He was known and loved wherever we went. Just as, at the Palace of Audible Dreams, I observed but did not engage in conversation with certain celebrities, but divined their essence (or thought I did) by watching them perform mundane activities, so, too, I learned a great deal about Diz by not talking as much as is my usual wont. We had mutual friends and he knew where I stood politically. Had he talked politics or religion with me he would have confirmed what I already knew. I grew up in the vicinity of the Baha'i Faith House of Worship, in Wilmette, and was aware he had converted to that humanitarian religion.

Lights glaring, cameras rolling he exclaimed with astonishment (to Ferrer and I) "They can't do that! We can do that, but they can't…they can't improvise. They're great and they play beautiful but they can't play it unless it's written down." He was speaking of classical musicians and I have seen him say this in documentaries other than mine. Celebrities who give frequent interviews often give the same answer to different interviewers; their answers become routine.

Asked how he got the name Dizzy, he replied slyly, with a broad grin, "Because I'm so smart." Born in Cheraw, South Carolina, his first instrument was the Jew's harp (mouth organ), he gravitated to piano at age six and before his father died, when Diz was only ten, he taught the boy to play the trombone. For a long time Dizzy thought there was only one key – Bb. He wanted, after he first heard Roy Eldridge, to become the best trumpet player who ever lived. The filmed interview went well and was particularly informative when Diz, playing the piano, showed us that his well-known composition "Con Alma" was based on Jerome Kern's "All the Things You Are," which many consider the greatest popular song ever written.

In my apartment I had (still have) a wonderful framed picture, of the 1933 Duke Ellington Band. Diz was a teenager in '33 but he named every band member in the photo. Soon he would be playing with the bands of Frank Fairfax, Edgar Hayes, Teddy Hill, Les Hite, Cab Calloway, and the two bands which (largely, through arrangements and solos which featured flatted fifths and modern harmonies), promoted and popularized bebop: Earl "Fatha" Hines and Billy Eckstine. In 1940, he had married Lorraine Willis, an enduring partnership. While so many of his contempories compromised their careers by abusing alcohol and drugs, Lorraine helped create a world bereft of these ever present temptations. She contributed stability.

And I have another rare photo of Ellington. It comes from the 1944 *Esquire* jazz poll issue. Taken by the celebrated Anton Bruehl, it shows Duke at the piano with two soldiers and one sailor standing behind him, their eyes fixed on the keyboard. The caption reads: "Servicemen invited to the all night party at Café Society Downtown, rushed to the piano when Duke Ellington arrived. The urbane Duke, often reluctant to jam, kept going for a half-hour on 'Lady Be Good.'" But there is something strange about this late wartime photo and its caption. There is another person in the picture, a trumpet player with his horn to his chops, standing right next to Duke, completely un-credited in the caption, as if he weren't there, but clearly playing along with Duke. It is a 27 year-old Gillespie. One year later, with his black, horn-rimmed glasses, beret and goatee, he would be internationally famous. As a kid, I was late keeping up with Birks for I heard him for the first time playing "Anthropology," the RCA Victor version of that tune, with Charlie Parker, Denzil Best on drums, Marjorie Hyams, on vibes, and Bill D'Arango on guitar, the sound coming from my sister's maroon Emerson radio, designed by Raymond Loewy.

Ushering at the Civic Opera House I had seen and I was well acquainted with, (though I had not yet met), the Dizzy of the early 50's, who clowned through duets with hipster Joe Carroll. Known as an entertainer as well as the most accomplished trumpeter and a major force in jazz, Dizzy was, underneath it all, a serious man, not just because he became fatherless at ten, not because he carried his mouthpiece in his pocket everywhere he went and blew through it at odd moments, particularly when walking up stairs, because it imposed another burden and he wanted to be the greatest ever, serious, not just because of his two campaigns for the Presidency. He was always political. Look at his proposed cabinet members: Duke Ellington for Secretary of State, Malcolm X. for Attorney General.

That's serious. The beautiful, 1933, sepia picture of Duke's Band, in its mahogany frame with a gold stripe and a beige matte, still, nearly covers the wall above my bed and, each time I look at it, it pains me I did not give it to this great man when I had the chance.

I first met Dizzy in the basement of his home in Corona, Queens,[129] at twelve midnight. He was half asleep, but he was playing with his spectacular train set, which covered the entire floor of his large basement. I had taken a cab and was greeted by wife Lorraine. We talked about the bossa nova, which had just reached these shores, largely through Stan Getz and Diz. He said, "We was the first," meaning himself, not Stan, whom he admired greatly and with whom he recoded a near perfect album, with Oscar Peterson, on piano. "I was there first; they was listening to us. Then I got me Lalo," (Schifrin) and with Leo Wright, playing alto and flute, they recorded the famous "Dizzy at Juan-les-Pins" album.[130]

When I left his house at 4 A.M., he called a local "gypsy" cab for me and we travelled through his backyard and emerged on 107th Street. "That's where Louis Armstrong lives," he said, pointing to a modest dwelling, which has now become a museum/monument to its former occupant. "That's Pops' place." Armstrong was not an early fan of bebop and was initially critical of Dizzy, but Dizzy and his music were hard to resist and, sharing the same agent, Joe Glaser, Diz and Pops and their wives became friends and neighbors.

---

129 Dizzy and Lorraine would later move to Englewood, New Jersey
130 One of the greatest jazz bossa nova records and one of the earliest.

18
MILES DAVIS IN MUFTI

I never met Miles Davis. I wasn't sure I wanted to. All the women I loved were in love with him; I knew all his recordings by heart. Except for the early postwar years when he was a sideman in the trumpet section of Dizzy's big band at Birdland, he no longer visited the Palace of Audible Dreams. He was royalty now, but I had seen and been around him on occasions. He was off-putting and could be mean. I was standing next to him at the bar in Birdland, his drummer, "Philly" Joe Jones, was standing on his other side. We were watching Buddy Rich, on the bandstand, taking an elongated solo. In his raspy bari-tenor (the result of a botched boyhood tonsillectomy), in a manner requiring no answer, and very loudly, so that everyone at the bar would hear, Miles said to his star percussionist: "Why can't you play like that, Motherfucker?"

New York concert promoter friends[131] booked the Civic Opera House and came to Chicago with a hip bill for 1960; Miles-Muligan-Monk. It sold out. I watched from backstage and when Miles approached Donnie for his payment after the show was over, Donnie was counting out cash money from an enormous bankroll. Then he handed a large wad to Miles with a smile, and Miles, a well-practiced pugilist, countered with a right hook which sent Donnie to the floor; Donnie's knees just crumpled and he fell to the stage floor. Not even looking at him, Miles, always cool, turned away, and counted the money while walking toward the band members,

---

131 Don Friedman and Ken Joffe, who also presented the famous Billie Holiday *"Lady Sings the Blues"* and the Lenny Bruce concerts at Carnegie Hall, both recorded.

who stood nearby. The reason he floored Donnie involved the order in which the acts appeared, Miles not wanting to be last on the bill, which is illogical, since the best is typically saved for last. So, he punched out Donnie to get even. It was frightening and uncivilized.

Which is not to say that there was ever anything typical about Miles, or that he hadn't justifiable reasons to use his fists. In the summer of the previous year, while standing outside Birdland conversing with a female friend, he was accosted by a NYPD patrolman and told to "Move on!" When Miles protested the police officer, soon joined by another, hit Miles savagely upside the head, drawing considerable blood and arresting him for being a sassy nigger.

Born in Alton, Illinois, on May 16, 1926, Miles grew up in East St. Louis, the son of a well-to-do dentist. The area (near Ferguson) produced talented players, among them trumpeter Freddie Webster, a contemporary of Miles. Davis met Bird in St. Louis and both were members of Eckstine's band, prior to Miles trek to New York (supposedly paid for by his father) to go to Julliard School of Music.[132] But he left that institution to join Parker's quintet from 1945 to 1948. It was then that he became addicted, like Bird, to heroin.

In *Lookin' For The Man*, after the overture, and a voice-over of D.J., "Classical Sam," who sounds much like "Symphony Sid" Torin, we are set plumb in the middle of 52nd Street, surrounded by nightclubs and accosted by barker-doorman, Marcus, a takeoff on Gilbert J. Pincus, longtime Jimmy Ryan's club shill. [SEE APPENDIX #3]

Marcus is hawking the wares of musical giant, Ray Baker, (the Parker character) who is appearing at the joint at which the little doorman labors. Enter Sonny Lewis (the Davis character) who quizzes Marcus on the Man's whereabouts, before Marcus, tells him to move on. Sonny sings "The Autobiography of Sonny Lewis." A song of countless measures, requiring eighteen pages of music manuscript, it is full of haunting bop-like twists and surprises, and accurately portrays the young man who comes to the Apple with

---

132 Lonnie Levister, a classmate and life-long friend of Miles since Juilliard, and who spent much time at Miles' New York brownstone, though the years, long ago convinced me that Miles' rough exterior is self-manufactured, a device to ward off squares and conceal his true gentleness.

stars in his eyes. It is the main motif ot the score and, once heard, hard to forget.

In A, the relative minor of C, beginning on the accidental G#, the title song commences with a hypnotic vamp conducted by piano, bass and drums, the latter employing a "Philly" Joe Jones chop. Many measures later it will burst into a jubilant bridge-like "second chapter" in the key of F, encompassing many skips along the way. It is a remarkable melody and all the words are appropriate.

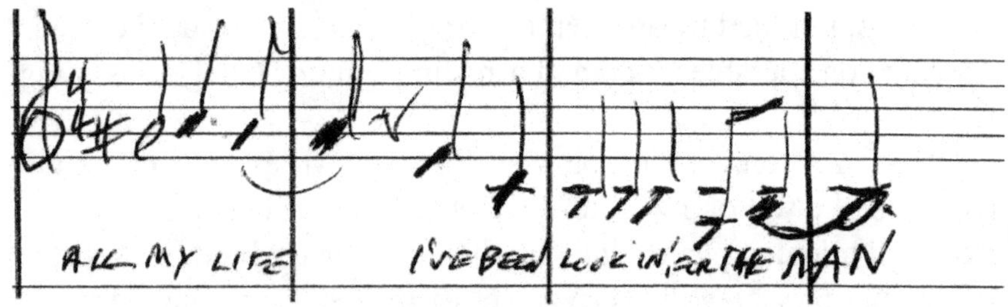

And for those who can't read notes but have a keyboard: between the above and the following, you should be able to piece it together.

"All (G#) my (A) life(G#) I've (E) been (C#)
look (D#) in' (D#) for (D#) the (C#) man (D#)."

The song completed, we are transported inside to the kitchen of the club in which the Man is appearing. The Man enters and plays a scene with a non-English speaking chef, then, gets high, i.e., has a fix, and delivers a stunning aria entitled "The Man Wails," a soliloquy directed to the Almighty.

Then the kitchen set moves off, the inside of the club appears and the Man's group swings through a number before The Man, always elusive, splits. Sonny, still seeking an intro to The Man, meets a beautiful African-American woman named Dee-Dee. Till this point, the show has been hypnotically taut and the audience has heard two impressive songs. We will be back on track when Ray and Sonny soon meet and play together and bond. This eventuates in a production number "The Word Is Out," announcing the arrival of a great new talent in Sonny. It is authoritative in its depiction of the New York world of jazz.

Till its close, the show chronicles Sonny's newly acquired addition to smack (despite the warnings of his mentor) and Ray's continued use. While Sonny resurrects himself in Act Two, Ray is forced to join a big band led by the character played by Dizzy, and go on the road. Ray disintegrates, and ends up dead in a cornfield in the sticks. There are other remarkable numbers, including "Big Band Bus," which should be a jazz classic. There is no weak song in the entire score, lest it be the ballad. And the book, credited to both Julian and Warren, is often electrifying.

I decided to produce a condensed version of the show, including all of the songs, just as Bobby, and Oscar had done with *Kicks*. I assembled the cast of José Ferrer, to narrate and play the minor roles, Pat Suzuki, of *Flower Drum Song* fame, as the female lead; and the three characters whom I had projected for a Broadway presentation: Carl Lee, son of the great Canada Lee, as Bird; Al Freeman, Jr., as Miles and Dizzy, who read a few lines and sang a duet from the show with José, which is a highlight of the recording, the show's comic relief.

I circulated a mere 50 copies of the LP, with a cover by Mel Williamson. The two record set is a collectors' item which sells for $30 to $100, or more, a copy, The last one I bought cost one hundred and sixty-six dollars, tax included (SEE ILLUSTRATIONS). The seller told me it was well worth the price, "a unique collectors' item" if you can find it. I have received e-mails from people whom I do not know remarking on its merits. A friend said he saw a copy in Noel Coward's garbage. Julian Barry told me composer-saxophonist Benny Golson, whom he never met previously, approached him in London singing one of the show's best numbers, the afore-mentioned, "Big Band Bus."

We invited a small audience to the recording session, on a Sunday, at Bell Sound, and among them was Warren's landlord, who contacted me Monday morning and said, "I want to buy you. I want to buy you for five years for twenty-five thousand dollars for twenty-five percent of everything you make." At this point I hadn't the money to pay for the recording session, which cost a little over four thousand dollars. "Come on over," the landlord said. "Are you doing anything right now? Come on over."

He was a man of action and I complied, cabbing it over to an enormous skyscraper he owned and commanded from his penthouse residence. He owned many other such buildings. He greeted me at the penthouse elevator and showed me around the apartment. On the walls hung the works of Picasso, Matisse, Gauguin, Renoir, Cezanne, Braque. The view from his terrace was spectacular, and yet the man was boorish and I sensed that I could never relate to or ever get along with him. I suppose I didn't like the idea of being purchased for a price.

But like Sir Robert in Oscar Wilde's *An Ideal Husband*, "I sold myself for money," and accepted a bad deal. I had hoped Joe Glaser might kick in some *shekels*. But he turned me off terribly, as I was leaving his office after a convivial meeting, when he grabbed my elbow and, eyes wide open, said to me with great enthusiasm: "Say, I gotta' a nigger broad would be great for you in the Billie Holiday story: Dorothy Dandridge!!!" That remark with the 'n' word was the end to my relationship with Joe. Oh, why did I have such a weak stomach? Why was I so intolerant?

I went to Chris Mankiewicz and Joyce Selznick at Columbia Pictures, on Fifth Avenue, and received the kind of sympathetic reception you would expect from people with such names.[133] "Well, well, the new Irving Thalberg," Joyce greeted me, as I entered her small office. She and Audrey Wood evidently practiced the same flattery in dealing with young producers. She and Chris were kind, but they declined. So did Quincy Jones, working at Mercury Records, under owner Irving Green (1916-2006).

I had anticipated negativity pertaining to the authorship by whites of so-called black subject matter. This was unfair because the authors had been haunting "The Street" since being schoolboy interlopers from the Bronx. When he was young, Warren's piano teacher took him backstage to meet Erroll Garner, on 52nd Street and Warren became his occasional student.

But I began to recognize a greater flaw and discussed it with the authors. I did not see how a serious and stark work of lyric theatre

---

133 Joyce was not related to David O. but had quite a reputation re: actors and writers, having discovered Tony Curtis, among others. Chris, son of Joseph L., is warm and knowledgeable and he and Joyce comprised the talent and story department at Columbia Pictures, NYC, 5th Avenue branch then.

dealing with this kind of material could sustain a vapid and unnecessary love affair, and felt the ballad they wrote was weak, some of the comedy banal, and a detraction from the overall seriousness of the play. Warren disagreed and refused to make corrections. They, but mostly Warren, felt defying music comedy conventions like boy-girl love affairs and comedy relief, was a recipe for failure. Those conventions, said Warren, were necessary for commercial success.

Warren Meyers was one of the most talented people I have ever met, an ingratiating and hip pianist, an authoritative musical conductor, a competent actor, an adept professional voice-over man, and author of the book "Who's That?"[134] But he insisted there be a love interest as most every Broadway musical had had till then. When Lehman Engel started the famous Composers Workshop at BMI,[135] it included Warren, Jerry Herman and Mary Rodgers. By that time Warren had been accompanist and conductor for Diahann Carroll, Pat Suzuki and Connie Francis. Years later, according to Warren, Jerry Herman encountered Warren on Fire Island and told him everyone in Engel's class thought Warren "the most likely to succeed." But, brilliant as he was, he was opinionated, too, and he refused to change the book. I was so perplexed that I made a poor decision in another direction.

I had taken Ferrer to hear Gerry Mulligan's Band at Birdland with a view toward asking the great valve trombonist, Bobby Brookmeyer, who was Gerry's top arranger, to do the charts for our show. Everything was agreed to (it was just a matter of verbal commitments, with no contracts involved at the time), but now I got it in my mind to contact Duke Ellington, that having him involved would give legitimacy to our enterprise.

Everyone knew of Ellington's desire to have a hit in the theatre. I was one of the few people who had seen his *My People, My People* in its limited run at McCormick Place, in Chicago, in 1960, in a space quite different from the huge auditorium in which *Kicks* appeared. His unsuccessful *Beggar's Holiday* (an updated *The Beggar's Opera*, with Alfred Drake) and the later *Pousse Café* (a musi-

---

134 *The Late, Late Viewers Guide To The Old, Old Movie Players, Who's That!*.
135 Broadcast Music, Inc.

calized *Blue Angel,* with Theo Bikel) both failed. Preminger employed Duke's talents in *Anatomy Of A Murder,* but Duke, sincerely wanted to participate on Broadway and said so when queried.[136] Joe and Rosemary knew Duke well because she made an album singing to a pre-recorded soundtrack of the band, and she and Duke were both under contract to Columbia Records. I asked Joe to call Duke and let me speak with him.

And in a phone booth in the lobby of the Warwick, I heard the mellifluous tones I had heard so many times on record, radio, television broadcasts and in person, that elegant voice of refinement with a dash of slightly slangy syllabication.

"Well, look here, Sidney, why don't you write down this number, Joe knows where I'm at and …uh…you'll call me again and we'll get together," Duke said with a smile in his voice. And when I called him a couple of days later he said, "Look here, why don't you come down to Basin Street East, on Wednesday night and we'll talk; you know Basin Street East?"

"Oh, yeah, it's right down the street from my hotel."

I was still holding court at the fine hotel across from the Waldorf. Now I had a two-room suite paid for by my bookmaker to whom I was deeply indebted. A tall, thin, white-haired man of forty, who wore conservative gray suits and rimless spectacles and carried thousands of dollars in his pants pockets, he looked more like an intellectual than anything else, and, years later, when I bumped into him at Belmont, he told me that after being framed and convicted and, then, finally released from Sing Sing, he became a ghostwriter for celebrity tell-all autobiographies.

His name was Eddie and I allowed him to use my digs one hour a day. He employed a bagman, a man of Chinese descent, named Harry, a very discreet and similarly suited, middle-aged family man who was also deeply indebted to Eddie because of his addiction to gambling on baseball games. Eddie was a high stakes guy and bets averaged five hundred dollars a pop, though, in the hour spent in my suite, he had numerous satellites calling in small-time numbers action, too. He was a good man; very good to me.

---

136 *Dick Cavett Show.*

Alas, I feel it incumbent upon me to once more address the correlation that exists (albeit the strain has grown weak in passing years) between the theatre and horseracing. For a long time theatrical news and thoroughbred racing shared the pages of the same metropolitan journal – *The Morning Telegraph*, the eastern edition of the *Daily Racing Form*. Outside of theatre and film, where else does adventure lie?

From producers Max Gordon, Herman Levin and Martin Gabel to movie moguls Louis B. Mayer[137] and Cubby Broccoli[138], from Andrew Lloyd Webber[139] to Burt Bacharach,[140] Steven Spielberg[141] to Raoul Walsh, the racetrack has been, for many show folks, a home away from home. Fred Astaire, a close friend of Joan Payson Whitney, owner of the New York Mets, Greentree Stables, and the *New York Herald-Tribune* and a serious student of horse breeding, married jockey, Robyn Smith. War of Will, winner of the 2019 Preakness, is owned by South African-born Gary Barber, former head of MGM and producer of *Seabiscuit*, along with a passel of box office hits. The number of actors involved in the sport is endless, from Robert Mitchum[142] to Betty Grable, Bo Derek[143] to Cary Grant.[144] In my case, had I not worked at the Palace of Audible Dreams I might not have become a horseplayer.[145]

"Though shalt not invest thine own money in thine own show," is a fiat producers have frequently violated. It is verboten to wager with the money of investors, but taking advantage of a betting op-

---

137 Owner of the great sprinter and sire, Busher. Mayer's interest in the sport is one of the reasons he was fired by the MGM Board back East.

138 Owner of 1993 Breeders Cup Juvenile winner, Brocco, Broccoli owned the James Bond franchise with Harry Saltzman. His daughter runs it now.

139 Owner of 2013 Breeders Cup Turf winner, Fugue.

140 Owner-breeder of Afternoon Deelites, winner of the Hollywood Futurity.

141 Part owner of Derby contender Atswhatimtalkingabout.

142 Prominent breeder of quarter horses, he won numerous such races and spent much time on his Maryland horse farm.

143 Member of California Horse Racing Board.

144 Longtime board member, then, President of Hollywood Park, he claimed never to have wagered more than $2 per race.

145 The racetrack is also a place to meet potential investors. And somewhere, somehow, there may be someone out there who does not know, so I am going to tell them, that in most every State in which pari-mutuel betting is conducted, the government's share of the handle is mandated for spending on schools and roads alone. It is an industry that employs thousands of people nationally, yea, internationally, most of whom love the equine breed. Moreover, thoroughbreds were bred to run. It is what they like to do.

portunity (I speak only of betting on horses, not men) is theoretically, the privilege of the General Partner, just as would be betting on the Stock Market.

A young man recommended by Julian was working for me as an assistant. I could not allow Eddie to see that I was betting with someone other than he, so I arranged to send the assistant (we'll call him Louie) to the track on my behalf. Andre Malraux said, "Gambling is suicide without death," but who knows if Malraux, who wrote one of the greatest novels in the history of mankind,[146] ever went to Longchamps?

I studied the next day's (early) daily double at Belmont all night long, as if hypnotized. I swallowed a bunch of No Doz and smoked a couple joints. I studied and studied. I had to get it right! I concentrated on the first three races and made a plan. I wrote a letter to Louie as to what to bet and slipped it through the door so Eddie or Harry wouldn't notice. With the instructions was the cash required to make the wagers.

My key bet was in the second race at 4-1. In the first race I preferred the horse Eddie Arcaro was riding in a race for 2 year-olds down the still viable Widener chute, but made a "wheel," betting all of the twelve horses in the first race with my pick in the second. That cost $120 and an extra $100 double using Arcaro's mount made it $220. If I won the double, Louie was to bet a maximum of two thousand, of the potential winnings from the daily double, on a 10-1 shot I had selected in the third race, but not to win, to place, that is to say, to run second.

Now, here is the part non-horseplayers might not understand and I'll make it fast. Even a novice knows "scratched," means a previously entered horse is removed from running as scheduled and has become a non-starter. Each horse has a betting number and that number usually corresponds to the horse's post position in the starting gate. An "entry" means two or more horses racing for the same owner, i.e. #1 and #1A, in which case the betting number and the post position number may become different. In the old days, when a horse in an "entry" was "scratched" all the numbers changed. That

---

146 *Man's Fate*

is what happened in this case. There was a scratch in an entry in the second race and my horse's number changed.[147]

I did not take this possibility into account when I slipped the envelope of instructions and cash through the door to Louie, who knew nothing about horse race betting, so he came back with $220 worth of wrong tickets instead of what should have been over ten thousand dollars, for all my selections ran as I had predicted, including Arcaro's horse in the first race, the double paying $150+ dollars. This was a terrible blow at a crucial time. In a fancy bar on Lexington Avenue, I tore up the worthless tickets and threw them in the air. It was not Louie's fault it was mine for not giving him the names of the horses instead of just their numbers. (See Appendix F#16 for further details and authentication.)

The state of my sex life was not much better. The incision resulting from the removal of my appendix had taken time to heal and, in the interim, the nature of my venal activities had been limited. Yet I managed to be accommodated by numerous women, though I harbored a preference for bleached-blonde prostitutes and saw them, sometimes, two at a time. Some were so lonely they wanted to stay the night; some even reached the point of visiting, if you can believe it, without financial compensation. One showed up with her suitcases and wanted to stay on a permanent basis.

I believe I was destined not to find contentment with a decent women, for something deep inside me, ultimately connected to the fact I was brought up by two proper women, contributed to my decision to avoid marriage to a "normal" woman as was the case in my first marriage. Was it a curse, or a disease?

And I was running out of the money I had received from the vulgar realtor and Warren remained adamant about not changing the script. Finally, I was to meet with Duke Ellington the following night and did not know what to say to him.

Basin Street East was located on the southeast corner of Forty-Fifth Street and Lexington Avenue, directly across from the Grand Central Station post office, a space inhabited since by Horn and Hardart, MacDonald's and other purveyors of fast food. I sat at a

---

147 After many years the system was revised and the likelihood of making this mistake has lessened. Nevertheless, there are many ways of making such mistakes in the process of wagering. Of course, cell phones were non-existent and outside telephone calls were not allowed at racetracks.

table off to the side, as close as possible to where, I was told, Duke's dressing room was situated. I was not a dummy; I had directed dozens of shows, I knew what I was doing (I told myself).

I knew most of Duke's repertoire; I had been listening to and collecting his recordings since Bar Mitzvah days and knew rare numbers from "T.T. on Toast" (Tough Titty on Toast) to bootleg copies of V-Discs which they sold from under the counter at the Palace of Audible Dreams.[148] But I did not listen fully to what was played that night; I was too nervous about going backstage to meet Duke as planned.

I barely heard the band or what Duke said during that set, but once he left the stand, and just as I was about to pull back the curtain and walk down the hallway to his dressing room, still nervously thinking just what to say and how this great man would fit into my tarnished plan, there suddenly began a hullabaloo, a hub-bub filled with eruptions of unified laughter, all coming from that dressing room so near my table. The noisy chatter, punctuated by belly laughs and guffaws, never ceased during the five minutes I procrastinated in my seat, not daring to intrude on a frenetic Ray Nance or whoever was engaging in this boisterous merriment. Someone was putting on a show and making my entrance difficult. It was bound to cock-up my act, my pitch, my speil, of which I was uncertain to begin with.

I rose from the table, walked to the curtain, and peered down the darkened hallway to the dressing room, all alight and bulging with people, some regurgitated into the corridor, some standing on either side of the doorway, some with drink in hand, all awaiting a chance to inch further in to see and be seen by Duke.

I couldn't go. No longer the man of action, who escorted Joe downstairs to Birdland and summoned Gerry Mulligan to sit with us at the star table, as the band wailed in the background, my attentive friend, Oscar Goodstein, asking "Is everything all right?" I could not go past all those people and fabricate a bunch of bullshit. I have been bragging, reader, I could perform for an audience of

---

148 As they also did with the famous Dean Martin-Jerry Lewis "Cocksucker" record, a blooper recording where, from their early days, when they flubbed while recording a radio commercial and said "cocksucker" in aggravation, then repeated it 20 or 30 times while everyone broke-up in the recording studio. Someone got ahold of the blown take and sold the blooper recording nationwide. Such were those innocent times.

any size but I could not face that assemblage. I could not embarrass myself and lie before my hero, so I, who considered himself a prince of chutzpah, left in defeat, humiliated and angry with myself. It was apocalyptic.

I felt similarly when I was pushed on the radiator by the Tiny Tots and once, when I was eight, dumped in my pants in the back seat of one of my mother's boyfriend's car. At the age of twelve, in front of the school assembly for the National Spelling Bee contest, I was victimized by a sadistic pedant, know-it-all teacher, who, under the influence of the first page of *Strunk's Elements Of Style*, trapped me with "its," the possessive, while it was "i-t- apostrophe – s," "it's," the contraction meaning "it is," that he was really requesting. He succeeded in making a fool of me before the assembly, but my freezing up with Duke at Basin Street East surpassed all my previous humiliations for, I adored him with all my being.

I, who believed in my ability to speak with almost anyone with whom I desired to speak, to get any S.O.B. at all, on the phone, I, who had a publicist and a general manager and subscribed to Earl Blackwell's Celebrity Bulletin and had a little, red leather address book whose cover bore the gold imprint "EAST, WEST, ABROAD" and contained the addresses and telephone numbers of countless celebrities from Fred Astaire and Judy Garland to Orson Welles and Danny Kaye, I, who could "cold call" and pitch anyone alive and was operating under the illusion I had invented the technique of putting the person on the other end of the on the defensive with "Hello, do you know who I am?" until I had a theatre I could rent to other producers, and Phil Rose, who you would think I had met before but I hadn't, called one day saying "This is Phil Rose; do you know who I am?", yes I, jerk that I am, suffered a catastrophic defeat in not going backstage to meet Ellington and, practically speaking, was a broken man, humiliated, embarrassed, amazed at my lack of gumption.

Then, without discussion or notice of any kind, the multi-millionaire realtor-investor who had purchased me for twenty-five thousand dollars for five years, the morning after the recording session, and loved me five months earlier, now wanted to ruin my career and forthwith sued me. I was served with papers by the firm of Nizer, Benjamin and Krim, charging me, as did an unjust Parliament the noble Marlborough, with petty peculations and poor practices of accounting. Louis Nizer (1902-1994) whose clients ranged from Salvador Dali to Johnny Carson was, at that time, the most famous lawyer in America because of his status as a best-selling author.[149] My realtor-investor was accustomed to telling contractors and workmen what to do and probably thought the process identical with a Broadway show. Producers know investor lawsuits are not uncommon when plays close prematurely without profit. I did not think he would win his suit and hired an attorney.

Julian had a new comedy I thought funny and workable and, when Ferrer read it and agreed, we managed to get Julian, who was free at the time, to fly to Miami and spend some time working on the play with Joe. But, with the multimillionaire suing me, my choking-up with Duke, my loss of the $10, 000 after Louie bought the wrong tickets, and my indebtedness to Eddie, the bookmaker, it all became too much and I was evicted from the hotel.

I went back to El Paso-Juarez. But the magic, or novelty of the place, was gone. My lawyer in New York called to tell me I had won the lawsuit and that if I sent him $500 more he would initiate a suit against the landlord/investor that I was certain to win, for my reputation, according to the law, based on the disproved accusation of defalcation on my part, had, theoretically, been damaged. But I did not have a spare $500 to send to my counsel in New York.

Then, on an excursion to L.A., driving a rented car on an extremely slippery US 1, with fog so dense you could see but two feet in front of the hood and barely that, my car suddenly careened off the highway, I know not how to this day, but it seemed to accelerate, and travelled some one hundred feet before crashing into a tree. I was unable to drive the car any further and hitched a ride to the airport.

Somehow the Fates decided to prolong my destiny once more and after spending some time with my family in Chicago, I returned to New York City, just after New Year's of 1967 to make the biggest mistake of all.

---

149 *My Life In Court* (1960) and nine others.

19

PSYCHO-BITCH

In the last days of winter, just before spring of the year of the "Summer of Love," she came to the door with no clothes on. When she parted it a crack I saw a cascade of blonde curls and wicked blue eyes that said she knew all there ever was to know or do. She was twenty but her eyes said forty and she was smiling almost manically. Desire often drives us to what is most opposite in ourselves and forces us to love what will make us suffer most, like a beautiful poisonous flower which attracts, then destroys us. So said Proust; or something like that.

Then she opened the door and I stepped in as she turned and led the way through a barren living room to an alcove just large enough for a queen size bed. She had done so hundreds of times. It was a well-rehearsed move designed to show her nakedness, her long legs and her appetizing derriere, which she wiggled with lascivious precision. She was just what I was looking for.

"Take off your clothes," she invited with a casual wave of her beautiful arm. "What do you do for a living?"

"Look for girls like you," I replied. She slapped her hands together and bent forward with laughter.

"You're funny!"

"You think I'm kidding?"

She laughed a little more, them looked to gauge my seriousness.

"What do you mean, 'Like me?'"

She was a little puzzled after that and watched me closely from then on, her cordiality, however, never waning, in fact, increasing steadily in the few minutes involved.

"I'd spend more time with you but I gotta judge coming," and she laughed naughtily.

"Oh, yeah?"

"He likes the vibrator," and she held up such a one and laughed slyly some more. I wondered what she and the judge did with the vibrator but I did not pursue it.

When our activities were concluded she pointed to the bathroom and asked me, "Would you like to take a shower? It's okay," she gave a knowing look, that implied she thought she knew more than I. In my experience it was a ploy to fleece my pockets while I was in the shower stall, so I declined. She did not know I was a spy…yet.

She said her name was "Yvonne" (which I doubted) and I left her laughing as she, in all her nakedness, closed the door and let me go. But, even as I turned away to take the elevator, I knew what my next move would be.

****

When I returned to New York, I found the cheapest apartment available in what they were now calling the "East Village" but which was really an extension of the Lower East Side.

I had lived all over New York City though never in a tenement. But the flat I moved into, for a thirty-six dollar a month rental fee, was on one of the most happening blocks in Manhattan. Any knowledgeable historian, hipster, or junkie of the time will be familiar with its location.

In the middle of the downtown side of the block, the side on which I lived, is a former Irish bar, in which poets are reading their rambling writings and budding guitarist-singer-poets are auditioning for other kids as young and as poor as they. In three or four years the scruffy joint will organize under new leadership, begin performing plays on their small stage, and take the name Nuyorican Poets Café.

An unknown singer-guitarist, not yet "discovered" by Albert Grossman who "discovered" Bob Dylan, lives directly across from me, in a storefront basement. He plays all day long and the amplification produced by the underground acoustics make his powerful singing and playing available to anyone in the vicinity. His name is Richie Havens and he is adjacent to my butcher, a Polish-American who refuses to leave the neighborhood, though the buildings are crumbling from age.

Though rundown, the block still has a drugstore on the corner, with an old fashioned phone booth. And at the far end of the street there is an all night automobile repair shop cum parking lot refulgent with overhead klieg lights atop tall stanchions. A young Jewish man named Carl, who is in his late twenties, wears glasses and looks intelligent, operates the facility, which has four bays and is always bulging with taxis, autos and trucks. There is a cheap (and extremely greasy) fried chicken, take-out joint, run by a wise-cracking black man, operating near the middle of the block, wedged in between grim, six-story, shabby tenement buildings.

But the most important feature of the block, especially at night, is a small bar across the street from Carl's parking lot. Originally patronized by painters and jazz musicians, it features the often cacophonic, but interesting, "astro-infinity" music of the "Arkestra" of the great Sun Ra (1914-1993), an oddly-harmonized sound unlike any other. The joint is called Slug's Saloon[150] and now you know you're on a ratty old block on the Lower East Side that is becoming famous, you're on East Third Street, between Avenues B and C, in what is now euphemistically called "Alphabet City," a term originated in the opprobrious climate of a budding drug culture.

In my "railroad" apartment there is a bathtub in the kitchen and a toilet in the water closet. There are mice and rats and roaches, and someone broke in and stole a television set and a typewriter the first month of my occupancy. But other families live there, too, up and down the block, and I am friendly with everyone, or try to be, and befriend a teenaged neighbor who turns out to be a gang leader by the name of Alonso. Only a teenager in high school, I am nice to him, invite his mother and grandmother inside my flat, which I have cleaned and decorated with framed pictures, bedspreads, and furniture. I have a seventy-seven key Wurlitzer piano and intend to

---

150 Later, Ornette Coleman, Albert Ayler and Sonny Rollins will appear there.

buy a dog or cat to combat the bugs and rodents, which invade all spaces of the rattrap building.

Dick Lamb obtains a cushy job for me writing liner notes for all MGM and certain Verve Records albums. I haven't the liberty to say anything bad but in most cases it isn't necessary, and when they are just puff pieces it is simple to sign with the pseudonym, Tom Rolfe, one of my favorite horses. It is a cinch to write good things about Oscar Peterson, Jimmy Smith, Cal Tjader, Cy Coleman,[151] Kenny Burrell, Erroll Garner, guitarist, Johnny Smith, Brazilian performer-composers, Walter Wanderley and Marcos Valle and to meet producers like Angela Lansbury, Martha Glaser and Merv Griffin, who are pushing artists they represented. It is rumored I might be groomed to become head honcho at MGM Records. I have the clothes for it.

In April of 1967, I bet two thousand to win on Dr. Fager to beat Damascus in the Gotham Stakes, the beginning of a great rivalry, the main feature of which is Dr. Fager's attempt to savage his rival when they draw abreast in the stretch, that is, by reaching out and biting Damascus (which is not considered a foul). Dr. Fager wins by a half-length.

The next day I buy a 1948 Lincoln Continental convertible, the most photographed car in history,[152] the last internationally accredited classic car. At first I have the twelve cylinder car professionally restored, painting it a discreet but improper Rolls-Royce burgundy. And I finally start to learn about cars, buying and restoring them for the next few years. I park the showy car in Carl's lot, where the police and everyone else notice it, so say the young gang leaders, including Alonso, who have my back, and with whom I smoke weed and bond.

---

151 Rejecting a piece by Douglas Watt of the *New York Daily News*, Cy Coleman could not find someone who would write an acceptable liner note for his *"Ages of Rock"* album so I wrote an excellent piece myself. For sometime, whenever I could find a pianist, for I had not, yet, taught myself to play, I had been singing Cy's songs and following his career. He and his "secretary" at the time, the singer, Claire Hogan, liked me and invited me to a party but I never followed-up on this important contact.

152 *Lady From Shanghai, Eddy Duchin Story*, the list is endless; the body was basically the same during the years of pre-war and post-war production, only the grille was changed. Cary Grant drives one with Ingrid Bergman at the start of *Notorious*. Lizabeth Scott crashes one at the end of *Dead Reckoning*, with Humphrey Bogart. It is the car Sonny Corleone is driving when assassinated on the NJ Turnpike in *Godfather*.

That summer I had an idea and put it into effect almost immediately. I called Diana Sands and asked her to meet me for dinner with Joe Ferrer to discuss my producing a revival of George Bernard Shaw's *Saint Joan*, with Joe directing. I had contacted the Shaw Estate and was given the green light.

This is the first time I had spoken to Diana since our affair and I had seen her only once, and it was in front of the Winter Garden. She was unfriendly, but her new husband, Lucien Happersberger (1932-2010) was over-flowing with cordiality. I did not know at the time that this was a marriage of convenience, arranged by James Baldwin in order to obtain U.S. citizenship for Lucien, his life partner.

I took Joe and Diana to dinner at Cavanaugh's, on Twenty-Third Street, off of Eighth Avenue, in a 1928 chauffeur-driven Cadillac Town Car, the kind with the driver exposed to the elements. Throughout dinner, Diana barely smiled. Maybe she was uncomfortable being in a place with such a name as that. The near-ancient eatery, only a couple of blocks from her linoleum apartment, hardly catered to African-Americans, but it was time they changed that policy was my attitude. Grim through the meal, at the end of the evening, she agreed to play Joan, under Joe's direction and my aegis, a seemingly sincere affirmation.

Two months later, I was shocked to learn that the Lincoln Center Repertory Company, now run by Jules Irving and Herbert Blau, was presenting George Bernard Shaw's *Saint Joan*, with Diana Sands. No one called to let me know they had secured a deal with the Shaw Estate. Diana should have called, I would have understood, but, I would have said: "Watch out! I know how I would present it and I fear I know how they might and there is a difference, and I want to help you." But we never ever spoke again.

Since 1957, and with the publication of *Lady Sings The Blues* the prior year, there had been efforts to bring a story about Billie Holiday to the screen. David Susskind was number one in the effort, for he was the only one who had developed a script. Joe Glaser, as the narrative has shown, because he represented Dorothy Dandridge, stood for another faction, but she committed suicide in 1965 and Diana, who had been in the running since *Raisin*, was now, in some people's minds, the prime candidate. She did not need a flop, but that is what she got. The reviews were so bad the run was cut short. Mel and Lorraine Williamson and I saw it a few nights after it opened in January and found the acting mannered, the direction tedious and Diana unconvincing. The critics agreed and it closed in February.

As far as Diana and I were concerned, I imagine she felt, at some point, that she had wreaked her revenge on me, but it backfired.

In the meantime, as far as the world, the country, and the city, were concerned, things, the reader must now be told, were changing. Middle class families fled to the suburbs as blacks and Puerto Ricans arrived from the South. Teachers, transit and sanitation workers went on strike, while the fight for civil rights continued and MLK denounced the Vietnam War in his speech at Riverside Church. And despite Mayor Lindsay's efforts to ease them, racial tensions increased in Fun City.

Sexual mores were changing even more rapidly. I regarded myself a sophisticate, had read *1,000 Nights Of Sodom & Gommorah*, and, because Kazan said "a director is someone who knows something about everything," I knew about bestiality, even learned, from actors I had met in summer stock and with whom I had had intimate conversations, about the Black Mass, met a leading man who whored as a male prostitute in Paris and had a go with Marlene Dietrich who wore diamonds and nothing else when they made rumpy-pumpy.

But, because things were changing with such rapidity I realized, once more, that I was naïve. Hefner's Crusade against Calvinism and recent court decisions had eventuated in a climate where "porn houses," showing licentious films and porn shops, where magazines and, even, sex toys, proliferated, and the Kama Sutra, it seemed, had replaced the Holy Bible.

But my own far ranging experience had not yet prepared me for, nor had I yet encountered, had no yearning for, or even knowledge of, improbably horny shop girls who yearned to be tethered and slapped in the face before penetration; girls screwing each other in the front seat and yelling "Hello!" to passers-by while being driven up Park Avenue; fist-fucking exhibits on Eighth Avenue, "Five bucks to see the show;" inflatable, fuckable dolls dressed in French maid costumes and stiletto heels; *Screw Magazine* and oversized dildos in shop windows all over town.

Nor could I imagine that in only a couple more years, young Scandinavian-American teenaged girls of 42nd Street's Minnesota Mining Strip would be working out of fetid barrack-like facilities worse than the holes in fourth-class steerage suffered by their fathers' grandfathers in times gone by; that celebrated novelists would write about oversexed socialites taking two-way joyrides on the sitting room settee with a couple of linebackers from the Pickle Bowl, or create an anti-hero cursed with the urge to masturbate to excess, or sell two million copies about a transsexual intent on world dominance? Who could imagine that there would eventually be fucking on television, much less in the movies?

All through childhood and into high school (which ended the year Christine Jorgensen became the first [widely known] transsexual), there was another audacious *shaigetz* such as I, a Scandinavian-looking boy, who was my friend. He had been adopted by an elderly Jewish couple. This boy immersed himself in trouble throughout his youth, attending the same whore houses as I, flirting with the same schoolgirls, playing on the same ball teams, a decent outfielder and home run hitter, a very masculine boy. We felt it our right, then, to steal what we could not afford to buy: books, records, pictures from lobbies, a bass drum from Lyon & Healy. Then he ended up a Communist Party functionary writing opinion pieces and drawing cartoons for the Chicago branch of the *Daily Worker*, while laboring in a lab to support his young wife and newborn son. Three years into his marriage, after I had seen him in the early Sixties, he went missing and his cousin and I had not heard rom him for five or six years. In 1967, that cousin, visiting me in New York, showed me a picture of a girl standing under a tree and asked me, "Do you know who this is?"

I knew it was his missing cousin by the look of his/her fingernails, which clutched the trunk of the tree; they were unique. He had undergone the sex change operation and was head of a coven in a Midwestern state. (My friend ended up in California with a new mate and reunited with his son and his son's family.)

At this point in the century, trans-sexuality via medical procedure was still rare. Beautiful women with succulent breasts and abnormally large penises were soon to be ubiquitous and at the heart of a powerful political movement. Near-naked women making erotic love and being whipped by strippers, to the delectation of a boisterous audience, on the *Jerry Springer Show*, was in the future, but the Sexual Revolution was well underway in 1968. Oh, Brave New World, indeed, which brings me back to Yvonne at the beginning of this chapter.

When we left her, I told the reader I knew my next move, but it was not an original device, it was flowers. I sent her a bouquet of red roses the morning after our encounter.

Now, I have said, perhaps too often, that I sang in school assemblies and what were called variety shows[153] and the girls swooned and the boys booed, and, through the years I sang with pianists and musical directors with whom I labored putting on productions. But in 1966 I met Joe Derise (1926-2002), one the great jazz singers, and we became friends, and on April 7, 1968, Joe produced and I recorded an album with an all-star band.[154] It was three days after the assassination of Martin Luther King and riots were raging.

The night of the day on which Yvonne received the red roses, she called me and came over to the tenement building in a cab. I met her downstairs where she was holding a rose between her teeth, like Rita Hayworth, in *Carmen*. The personification of Cole Porter's streetwalker who chides the childish ways of poets and bids one climb the stairs, she had a good sense of humor but she was the lewdest girl I had ever met.

"No liquor shall pass these lips of mine," she was fond of saying, and was a fanatical teetotaler in reaction to her father's perpetual drunkenness, but her language and mode of expression was that of a salacious sailor and, I was soon to find out that, relatively speaking, she had more stories to tell about herself and her customers than Bergen, Burns and Benny had jokes at the lox and bagel breakfasts at Benny's house.

And, while she was not averse to making herself the victim in occasional tales, self-effacement deserted her entirely when it came to asking her direct questions. Then, her general comportment be-

---

153 "Blue Moon," "I Could Write a Book," all Rodgers and Hart.

154 Zoot Sims, tenor sax, Clark Terry, trumpet, Jimmy Raney, guitar, Richard Davis, bass, Stash McGlaughlin, piano, Mel Lewis, drums.

came that of Proust's Albertine, that is, to reflexively lie whenever questioned. At the same time, she could see a beggar on the street and feel true compassion, get all teary at the sight of some homeless wino begging for a dime.

When we gained entrance to my apartment that second night encounter we started sticking our tongues down each other's throats and I put my hand inside the elastic waistband of her pantyhose and attempted to finagle my finger up her asshole. But she began biting me, and placing hickies on my neck, so that other women, with whom she knew I was involved, would see them.

"Cut that out!" I said.

"I haven't kissed a guy like this since I was in high school, " she whispered. She wore no makeup. Her lips were very pink and sans lipstick, but she wore false eyelashes. Despite the pleasures of her pliant tongue, her breath had a sour taste and I figured I was chocking on what Nabakov called "the fumes of sin."

We were naked now. I gave her twenty dollars and walked away to the nearby kitchen as she said regretfully, "I gotta feeling this is the last time I'm gonna see any money from you." I was in the other room now, but I heard her clearly and drily replied, "You can say that again."

We were both correct. That night she told me she had a five year-old daughter, a little black girl, and that she had $36,000 saved for herself and the baby. She said the child, Cleo, was boarded at the Dale House, a new private home for children of unwed mothers, which was located uptown, in Harlem.

"Have you got a pimp?"

"Hell no!"

"Then who's the baby's father and where is he?"

She couldn't stand the pressure and started laughing.

"He USED to be my pimp!" she said, biting her fingernail closer to the nub.

I told her not to do that.

"I can't stop!"

"You're nervous."

Then, I played her the test pressing of my record session and she said she didn't like it and used it as an excuse to say the only man she had ever been in love with was Sam Cooke, with whom she had sex each night, in his dressing room, before he performed at the Latin Quarter. She was so sincere I almost believed her.

"You must have been very young at the time."

"Fifteen. I hung out at the Peppermint Lounge, started working at the Barrett Hotel, turned thirty tricks a night without using my pussy, I was so cute. You like my body?" she asked standing up now and modeling herself. She had slight scars, stretch marks, near her belly button, but otherwise she had the kind of body the voluptuousness of which makes men commit acts of supreme foolishness. Women wouldn't call her beautiful; they'd say, "She's cute." Her breasts were not large.

"Nipples are everything," she told me, and hers were exquisite, brown, inflated, *muy sabroso*. He feet were small; size seven. Just as the trainer of thoroughbred horses estimates an aspiring jockey's potential by the size of his or her foot, so, too, do I admire the dainty foot of sexy women, and value highly she that has one.

And if she had the feeling that the future of our relationship no longer involved my giving her money, I also had the mounting feeling that I was going to do something foolish because of her. It was an even trade…sort of. I drove her home to Forty-Fifth and Eighth, in the 1948 Lincoln, with the top down. We had had a good time, though she faked the orgasm I attempted to provoke.

She called me the next evening and sounded spaced-out.

"Come over," she managed to say. "I need you to come over."

When I arrived she opened the door, stark naked, of course, but she was not smiling and there were enormous black bruises on the soft, ivory skin of her hip and on part of her buttocks and thigh.

"He himme me with a chair…twice." She slurred her words as she said them. She seemed to be high on something.

"Who's he. Who are you talking about?"

"Ronny."

"Your pimp."

"He's NOT my pimp. My EX-pimp."

"You're fucked-up on something, that's for sure."

"He got me some smack, I just sniffed it. Ronny's my baby's father."

She was speaking softly; one barely heard her.

"He used to be my pimp. I hate him. Will you get me some Marlboros?"

"Sure." I went down to the deli and bought a carton and brought it back. She was more coherent, but still crying.

"You haven't told me why he did this to you."

"Fuck's the difference?" Then, "Why do you *think* he did it?" She answered her question, "He did it because of you. Whaddaya' think?" I told her she was better off coming home with me and she agreed.

On the way, and that evening and the next, she told me the usual story: raped by her drunkard father, she escaped from the bosom of her family, displaced refugees from a disputed part of Poland, the very scum of Europe, the residue of generations of drunkards Emile Zola references in the introduction to *La Bête Humaine,* she arrived at the Port Authority, where Ronny picked her up and turned her out. Sound familiar? It was one week into our relationship when she announced:

"I've never gone with a white man, you know? I mean, sure I've gone with plenty," she laughed, "No, no, I mean I've never been in LOVE with a white man…except, maybe, Gregory Peck."

"What made me the lucky guy?"

"That picture on the wall for starters."

I had a very large, professionally framed poster of Malcolm X. hanging on the wall in the kitchen.

"You mean that large picture of Malcolm?"

"That and my aunt."

"Your aunt?"

"She's a tarot card reader; she said I'm going to meet a white man and fall in love and I told her she's crazy."

And yet, when the big, black bruises healed she went back to work. "I'm a working girl, whaddaya' expect me to do? I need the money. I gotta pay for the kid."

But she left Ronny and moved out of the apartment he had established for her and into a hotel on 57th Street. I picked her up in the Lincoln most every night after her "work" and we went to Chinatown for food. I thought I was "playing" her; she thought she was "playing" me. She said rotten things about her perversities and Gomorrahaan practices with fellow girlfriend-hookers and paying female tricks, who ranged from wealthy lesbians to strippers and sick, socialite "submissives," rotten things designed to enrage me and, once, succeeding so successfully that I obliged her by putting a hot plate of spaghetti on her lap upside down, and leaving her in an Italian restaurant in Chinatown, at 4 A.M. in the morning, to get home by her own devices (which were plentiful, believe me; a cab would stop for her if the world were crumbling all around; most men would just look at her and get a hard-on). She was wearing a white linen outfit (as was I) and I reveled at the sight of the enormous puddle of marinara sauce, which, now, flooded her miniskirt and dripped down her lovely thighs and pretty knees.

But she phoned me the next day.

Hey, I was ready to dump her fast, preferably after I got the $36,000 she had saved, that's what I told myself. But she wanted me to go with her to see her child and I took them to dinner at the Seafarer, where Bobby and I had met Burgess Meredith for the first time. The child, Cleo, was beautiful but extremely introverted, and she kept staring at me as if she had never seen a white man before.

I had purchased two Fox Terriers, brothers, Jesse and Frank, who caused the rodents and bugs to vanish, but, now, Yvonne, in order, it was clear, to prove my sincere interest in her and her daughter, asked me to buy a dog for Cleo, specifically a black Cocker Spaniel puppy. Fox Terriers are feisty and unfriendly compared to Cocker Spaniels and this one fell in love with me the moment I offered my hand for him to sniff, in the pet store on 14th Street, near Third Avenue.

He became MY dog no matter what anyone, including myself, could do about it. "It is not the effect of chance if men who are intelligent give themselves to insensitive and inferior women. The instinct to sacrifice everything else in the attempt to keep such a woman with them, is the instinct to suffer."[155]

Still she continued to "work," said she hated it, hated white men who touched her, but continued because, she said "Like Tippy Hedren said in *Marnie*: Money answereth all things," and she considered herself to be an industrious ho (that's how they pronounced it:

---

155 *Remembrance Of Things Past*, Marcel Proust

"ho"), "not some ho who lays around all day taking morphine, like the 'Laziest Gal In Town.'"

People who are in love have little time for other people and she had me on the phone constantly, wasting my time, showing up and not showing up, complaining she was missing out on fifteen hundred dollars on account of me, fifteen hundred dollars to tie up some poor little rich girl, put a dog collar around her neck and lead her around the room on a leash. Like the girls in the bordello whom Proust's Albertine visited, Yvonne would know just what to do.

And, like Albertine, she had "as many personalities as an unopened deck of cards,"[156] only, unlike Albertine, she knew it. Though she could be nice, and often funny, she had the short sighted cunning of the schizoid and knew the meaning of the word "libertine," for a trick had told her that she was one and she agreed. But basically she was a tramp and I could not break the growing addiction she had incited within me.

"Why aren't you rougher with me?"

"You mean why don't I smack your ass when I fuck you?"

"Yeah."

"Well, I want to be tender. I love you," I lied.

The proverbial "bad girl, " she thought herself the sine qua non of the little South Jersey town in which she grew up after she and her parents reached their destination on the trip from Stuttgart, in steerage, when she was five years old, the point, she opined, when she started being bad. She resembled Dietrich, but, if you can believe it, had better legs, and though I was far from being an old professor, she often made me feel, and frequently behave, like Emil Jannings in the *Blue Angel*; surely I felt the same passions and was subjected to the same humiliations as the scenery-chewing school-master.[157]

Her father and mother had prayed for a son and were mad at Jesus (whom Yvonne rejected entirely) for giving them a daughter, which, in turn, accounted for their daughter's penis complex, a condition to which she freely admitted and practiced with enthusiasm on any john who would pay for it.

---

156 Ibid.

157 Dietrich herself, in documentary *Marlene*, directed by Maximillian Schell, in 1984.

Additionally, in this regard, she had a taste for black girls of varying hues whom she would hog-tie with electrical cord, and penetrate, while admiring the contrast of ebony and ivory, raven and platinum blonde, in the reflection which projected itself from a strategically-placed mirror. Sometimes she would have them wear a blonde wig. She taunted me in saying she had a girlfriend with whom she went on dates when johns requested two girls.

"Me and my girlfriend Anita got introduced by Ronny and her pimp, Jerry; he's cute. I let him fuck me and then I fuck her, she's cute, gotta' big luscious bum, that girl."

In truth, I should have beat on Yvonne's succulent ass with a rolled-up newspaper, as other courtesans and straight girls had requested I do, and called her "Slut," over and over again, something it would be impossible for her to allow a john to do to her, no matter how much money she was offered; nor would she submit to it from a pimp, for she was a Leo, the opposite of submissive. If I had hit her, then hit her harder, she would have loved me longer.

She would do things to hurt me, such as, after being away and having no contact with her for a few days, she would call long distance from Baltimore and tell me in a muffled voice that she was working in a bordello there and was at the moment in the process of fucking some guy up the googaloo.

"I'll be back soon. I'm thinking only of you, you know," she said softly, while someone grunted in the background and she breathed heavy sighs. This was done, to repulse me, in order to attract me once more. Once, after being away again for a week, she said a wealthy lesbian, who lived on West End, was "keeping her busy."

At one point I tried to break away by calling the madam to whom I owed the pleasure of Yvonne's company and requesting that a new acquaintance be dispatched. I thought that was the way to rid myself of Yvonne, to see if she was replaceable, at least, sexually.

"Hey, honey, I'm surprised to hear from," said Amber Lytel, the madam. "Where you been?" she said teasingly, and, a bit knowingly. She was an overweight blonde in her forties and her favorite singer was Joe Williams. "Sure, I got someone to see you, someone you'll like, but she's a little older than Yvonne, dear," Amber ventured with a tinge of sarcasm.

When Sandra (for that was the name she gave me) arrived I was not disappointed, for I was confronted with a very sharp-looking blonde, with a nice figure, ample cleavage, wide hips, which suggested an ample rump, and a pretty and sympathetic face. She was in her early thirties. She ogled the apartment with wonder and the dogs came and sniffed her and we exchanged pleasantries, as she started to disrobe, when all of a sudden she said: "Oh, my God!" in a hushed voice, with her hand over her mouth.

"What?"

"The dogs! You're the guy with the dogs, the guy Yvonne's in love with!"

I knew immediately she was Anita and "Sandra" was the name she used as a "working girl." I realized she was the girl Yvonne had mentioned so often, the girl with whom she "partied" along with Anita's pimp, the girl she had fucked atop the bar in a Mafia-owned strip club in New Jersey, that time when and they were stiffed by the gangsters who watched them perform, and were forced to hitch a ride home, penniless. It left an indelible erotic impression in my memory. I could see, at once, how Yvonne could wrap Anita around her little finger, or artificial penis, or vibrator, or whatever was available, for Anita, though hardened by The Life, was a true submissive and could not resist a dedicated pimp.

"Listen, honey," she said with great sincerity, "I promise not to tell her. I wouldn't tell her in a million years, I promise. Here, fuck me, it's my best feature."

In my shock and guilty embarrassment, I believed her, as she turned and stuck her ass in a position for me to engage. This was Yvonne's preferred position, though she, unlike Anita and other girls, totally prostrated herself with her arms outstretched and her head to the side, probably imagining she was having sex with Gregory Peck or Sam Cooke.

Anita was good, but nowhere as good as Yvonne in this position and I was distracted, as you can imagine, after being "found out." Afterwards we spoke for sometime and I drove her all the way home, which is something she didn't expect.

"Yvonne is in love with you, you know," said Anita. She kept her word; Amber, the madam, never told, either. It was a much more critical event in my life than I divined at the time. If they had told Yvonne, no matter what Yvonne felt for me, she was too proud to accept the fact that I had been Anita's trick and she would never have seen me again, and my life would have taken an entirely different course.

Two days later Yvonne called and taunted me by saying she had just partied wildly, for two days, with a fly pimp and his redheaded whore. "The redhead was really something. Wanna' know what we did?" I told her to cut it out or move in with me. She moved in and stopped "working" altogether. It was a big deal for her. I quit my job writing liner notes for MGM.

20

BIRTHDAY AT THE ROSE ROOM

I was hoping for Yvonne's redemption, but I did not realize, yet, that I was dealing with a genuine sociopath. For her twenty-first birthday I put on my tailor-made tuxedo, of pre-war English worsted, which my mother had saved for me for years, and took Yvonne to the Rose Room, of the Algonquin Hotel, for dinner. She made her own dress. Before she told them to go to Hell, the nuns had taught her to sew and to be an adept hair stylist; she wasn't stupid, just dyslexic (and seriously mentally deranged).

I knew the Rose Room well. A well-lit dining room situated at the western side of the lobby, opposite the Oak Room, home of the fabled Round Table graced by wits who livened the Twenties and Thirties coast-to-coast from this outpost, the two establishments share one kitchen but there the similarity ends, the Rose Room being vaster, quietly elegant, tastefully formal.

Because of the way we were dressed they gave us the best and most conspicuous table. I long ago learned how to make an entrance, how to carry myself when following the maître d. to the designated table. She went between us, shaking her ass in her sexy manner, she knew no other way. Her dress, a patterned, tight-fitting affair of fuchsia, and my tailor-made formal attire (satin lapels disgust me, only grosgrain will do) became the focal point of the room. No one else was similarly attired.

Once seated, I looked across the room. Sitting alone, with his back against the wall, and directly in our line of vision, so that he could not avoid looking at us (or visa- versa) was someone whom I had never met but knew rather well. I had studied his life for years, acted in, auditioned for, and directed his plays since my youth, and, as the reader may remember, silently observed him observing everyone and everything around him whenever he came into the Palace of Audible Dreams, completely unnoticed by others; never waited on him, never introduced myself; not a starfucker. Arthur Miller had recently premiered *The Price*, at the Morosco, his most commercially successful play since *Death Of A Salesman*, but the guy scoping us, Tennessee Williams, was just as famous.

"I'll bet you your mother has sucked as many dicks as I have," Yvonne said, out of the clear blue, as she perused the menu. I don't know why she said it, but that's what she said, if I'm to report things faithfully. It wasn't supposed to be funny and I hoped the man from an eccentric Midwestern family, with the name of a Southern State, this man whose friend, Gore Vidal, dubbed the "Glorious Bird," this man, whose plays changed the theatre lacked the power to read lips, as he stared at us throughout the entire meal, trying to figure out the story we embodied, and then, timed his exit so as not to coincide with ours.

I never believed in the credo "Treat a lady like a whore," but I devoutly reconciled myself to the notion that I should "Treat a whore like a lady." So after dinner, I took Yvonne to see Bobby Short at the Carlyle Hotel. The place was packed and we were surrounded by millionaires, the "cream of society," an element so unlike the tramp whose birthday we were celebrating. By the time we returned to East Third Street and she took off her false eyelashes and set her hair in curlers, my stomach was turning and I was telling myself disaster was waiting in the wings.

The last people to empathize with such a situation would be third parties. When I took Yvonne to meet Mel and Lorraine she embarrassed me by flirting with Mel. When she spoke with my sister on the phone she said, "Oh, he's at the racetrack. He takes such good care of us. I just love the guy. He's a genius!"

When I spoke with my sister later she said sarcastically:

"Boy, you got a real winner there."

Just as sarcastically, when my mother met her she said, with eyes wide open, as if she were about to faint, "She's so wholesome!"

Moreover, as Proust so cogently observes, third parties not similarly engaged always view horribly failed marriages as if the man thus bitten has some kind of choice in the matter and they fail to observe that the object of the man's affection is really "an exquisite mirage" which envelops the woman whom we love. And, I would add, completely blinds us.[158] She was a whore but she was all mine for a while, as Touchstone says of Audrey, "An ill-favored thing, sir, but mine own."[159]

We took LSD and ran down Fifth Avenue in the heat of a summer night like wanton juveniles. We watched the murders at Kent State, Robert Kennedy's assassination, Nixon's election, the continued outrages in Vietnam, the protests, the momentary growing strength of the Left, the teachers' strike, the garbage strike, Mark Rudd and the student protests, the raids at Stonewall, the riots. Cleo, the five year-old child, moved in. We put up a sheet to separate the room in half, as in *It Happened One Night*, while we searched for a better place to live.

One evening in early December, as Yvonne and Cleo (and the three dogs) were watching television, I went downstairs to the chicken shack, near the middle of the block, for take-out food. After I made the purchase and exited the fry-joint carrying the bags of hot food, I was immediately accosted, surrounded and maneuvered into the small outer hallway of a contiguous tenement building by eight young black men. We were, for a minute, crowded like the Marx Brothers, in that tiny space in front of the mailboxes, but it was long enough for the spokesman-leader of the group, a handsome young man dressed in suit and tie, with a pencil-thin mustache, and wearing a topcoat, to say, "Gimme your watch."

He spotted the expensive alarm wristwatch my mother had just sent me as a pre-Christmas present. I didn't argue as it was eight to one, and half of them stood guarding the doorway and the sidewalk in front of the building. The one who seemed to be the leader, the one who had made the demand, I now noticed, was carrying a walking stick of some kind, a cane, or was it a truncheon? Whatever it was it symbolized his power.

---

158 *Remembrance of Thing's Past.* (On the other hand) "the coupling of contrary elements is the law of life."

159 *As You Like It*, Act V, scene IV, by Wm. Shakespeare

The door leading into the building was ajar, too; there was no security in a building so derelict. Even the rat-hole of a building in which we lived, a few tenements to the west, was better than this. I surrendered the one hundred and twenty-five dollar alarm watch reluctantly, but, then, the trouble really started. A push was suddenly on and we were moving down the main floor hallway and the leader was shouting, "Get him up to the roof!"

I started copping a plea immediately and commenced fast-talking over my shoulder, as loudly as I could, as they shoved me down the hallway and up the flights of stairs. At one point I felt someone clipping my heels from behind as I made my struggling ascent, talking over my shoulder all the time. My ankle, then, was jabbed by a stick; it was the leader with his lever of authority poking at my ankles. I wanted to say, "Don't you understand? I have a little black girl I am going to adopt who is back there waiting for me with her mother? Why kill me?" I wanted to further say, "Hey, my sister has taught in the ghetto for twenty years; my sister and brother-in-law were at the Lincoln Memorial when MLK spoke; my mother is with Legal Assistance. When she visits the black community in Evanston everyone yells: 'Hey, Fay Edelstein is here now; our troubles are over. She'll get us a lawyer!'"

I wanted to tell them I had seen Paul Robeson four times and Du Bois, that I knew many famous black actors and musicians and had been around and loved black people all my life, that I almost married Diana Sands. But they would not have known any of these names, so it was pointless to mention them.

"Hey, you know who she is, don't you?" I would say just as they were about to shove me to my death, I fantasized, to myself. I was exhausted once we ascended to the top, where they pushed me roughly through a doorway that led to the roof itself. "Hey, listen, I gotta family, I got people waiting for me, don't do this!"

My heart was beating fast; I was in a panic. They manhandled me to the edge of the roof; just one push I'm dead. I looked down at Third Street and I was terrified. I was ready for someone to make a move and I braced myself to respond. But then, whether it was telepathy or auto-suggestion that I employed on the mustachioed, good-looking leader, I focused on him and something clicked in my favor. He said, "Fuck 'em, let's go."

I didn't hear any complaints from the others; I don't know why, but, like their leader, they did not look like ragamuffins. "Stay here till we're gone," the leader told me and they made a hurried departure.[160]

****

The day Yvonne finally said she loved me – I mean, directly, for she had told Anita, Amber, my sister and some other girls but never me — declared she wanted us (including her daughter), to start looking for a new abode. It was in early December. At that time, she made a whorish confession of all her perverted and sinful transgressions, such as sewing up, with the aid of a fellow whore, a drunken john's asshole with needle and thread, or spoon-feeding johns their feces, often disclosing the particular sums she received in recompense for her services. She and Baron de Charlus would have been bosom buddies for when she alluded to the cat o' nine tails an irrepressible gleam came to her eye. "There is in woman something of the unconscious function of drugs which are cunning without knowing it, like morphine"[161] is the only explanation that makes sense. (Did I forget to tell you there was no $36, 000?) After her confessions that evening, she rewarded me by saying, "I want you to fuck me in the bum, now."

She put on her black patent leather stilettos, positioned herself before the bureau of drawers with her ripe, prideful, protuberant ass and bade me puncture her pretty posterior; that was to be my recompense, the meed usually offered only in submission to one's pimp. It was an ineffaceable pose of erotic grandeur and it is not within my scope to describe how enticing a sight I beheld. She moaned, "Oh, fuck me, Daddy."

But my pecker went stale. I was disenchanted by her graphic stories of vile acts that would mortify Albertine and even the more experienced Odette. Nevertheless, I was sucked in now, or pixilated, and felt responsibility of a strange sort, and, in December, with a hired van and a couple of young moving men, we occupied a 120 year-old farmhouse of stone and wood, in beautiful Bucks County,

---

160 That was death encounter number eight. Number nine is included in Book Two and concerns my appearance as a CIA munitions expert in the cult film *Spook Who Sat By The Door*.

161 *Remembrance Of Things Past*, by Marcel Proust.

just above New Hope, where the Delaware River takes a turn. It included an adjacent 15 acres, and we moved with our furniture, the Wurlitzer piano and the three dogs. Yvonne, who loved the old house, wanted, immediately, to hang pictures of nudes all over the walls, the kind which glow in the dark, the kind they feature in cathouses.

She also wanted to fuck one of the moving men the night we took possession of the place. Was she serious? She didn't want to wear a wedding ring and gave a strange name when we filled out the marriage papers before a Justice of the Peace. As erratic as a straight-eight operating on seven cylinders, like Albertine, one could never be certain if she was telling the truth.

Cleo, who was absent for the initial trek to Bucks County, moved in with us in time for Santa; we had a fat friend play the part, and we enrolled her in an integrated pre-school program. Still, she was strange and introverted, though she now had three dogs with which to romp around the spacious and safe grounds that included a few acres of forest, which once had been an Indian burial ground. The Tohican Hill Creek served as a boundary to the property. German settlers inhabited the plot of land at least as early as 1848, for, in a discarded stack of firewood, I discovered a thick cut of lumber to which a local German paper of that date had been attached by the elements and left to dry.

No matter how idyllic an experience it was for Yvonne and me, Cleo had difficulty adapting to her surroundings and often cried all night. And once, when I entered her room in the daytime, I saw her masturbating. I found it troubling and spoke with her mother, who was in denial and did nothing about it.

With all the rustic charm of it, Yvonne and I, nevertheless, had a horrible fight the first two weeks and she took Cleo and left me behind with the three dogs. I could have let her go, I could have gotten an annulment, but, instead, in a bout of sheer madness, I brought them back.

At this point, after we reconciled amorously, the Maid of Orleans Personality #25 manifested itself and I returned one night from New York, to find her shorn like Jean Seberg, in *Joan Of Arc*. It looked good. And from then on, when I came back late, she met me at the door, naked, wearing white leather stilettos and silver-sequined pasties, looking like the blonde Rita Hayworth, in *Lady From Shanghai.*

"Say, don't I know you from somewhere, fella?" she would greet me; that was the routine. It made us hot. But that personality could be gone just as easily the next day and she'd be grousing about something stupid. She said she wanted to start a collection of models of classic cars, the kind you put together yourself with parts made of balsa wood and metal held together by mucilage, models which require a great deal of patience, skill and time.

It was the summer of the Moonwalk, we played a lot of badminton, friends came to visit and we made new friends in the countryside, though Yvonne was good only with men. She could only relate to women sexually or work with them side by side only if they played second banana to her in a bagnio. We drove to Saratoga, to Maryland and to Delaware Park. My hair had grown long. We had many cars. Wherever I went, little girls were standing by the roadside holding their fingers up in the peace sign.

Cleo came out of her shell a jot and her father came to visit and turned out to be an okay guy who was concerned about his daughter. You could see he thought Yvonne was crazy and I, too, for being with her, and for wanting to assume the responsibility of parenting Cleo. But he would not resign legal fatherhood and obviated my being the child's adoptive dad.

Even though he had thrown a chair at Yvonne a couple of times a few months back, it had become apparent to me that he was the saner of the two parents. But it was, with the exception of certain forthcoming incidents, a time of "happiness which neither the present or the future can restore to us" one which we may taste only once in a lifetime "for even for a little prostitute (there are) motives more determining than the pleasure of making money."[162]

She wasn't just a "little prostitute," then, as far as I was concerned, she was a perfect five-foot six, or seven, and was swell to cuddle up to at night in the curve formed by her perfect back, rump and shapely legs. In truth, she had shed, for the time being, and one hoped for all time, her libertine ways for a life in the country.

---

162 Ibid.

In mid-summer we drove to Doylestown to see her doctor, a routine examination, she said, when she went in. I waited in the car, in the parking lot, with the dogs, and she went in holding Cleo's hand. When they came out she said she was pregnant. Pledged to continue to take every precaution NOT to become pregnant, she had betrayed me.

"You don't want it, do you?" she said, as she seated herself in the car.

"I DO want it, but you never told me. How come?" I said calmly, holding on to the steering wheel.

"I wanted to give you a present."

Such a present was enough to ruin a career in the theatre in most but not all cases. Alan Alda and Dom DeLuise were two exceptions I knew of, but they had responsible women as helpmates. Carol Arthur, Dom's wife, an adept comedienne whom I helped cast in *Kicks*, temporarily retired from theatre in order to bear him sons.

When I directed *Guys & Dolls*, for Guy Little, in 1959, and our Sky Masterson suddenly became unavailable, I searched the *Players' Guide* for a replacement and saw a picture of Alan Alda. I was unaware that Robert Alda's son was an actor, or that he even had a son. But I called Alan directly.

"Oh, I can sing the part; I was backstage listening to it enough times," he said. From the beginning, I was impressed by the fact he had spent the previous season at the Cleveland Playhouse and we discussed, with amusement and pride, that unique institution. Alan was very good in the role. We went to the racetrack together that fall and he out-handicapped me. We came back on the subway and I went to his apartment on 115th and Broadway, on the second floor, above commercial, street-level stores, where I met his wife, Arlene, who was playing clarinet, then, with the New York Philharmonic. I believe they had only one little girl at that time, but two children and his wife were sitting on the floor playing. I could see it was a happy home.[163] Knowing Dom's wife, Carol, and, having met Alan's wife, I knew their supportiveness was instrumental in their

---

163 To my recollection Alan is a modest person. I wonder what he would say of the remarks of social critic, William A. Galston, of the Brookings Institute, who said, on C-Span (9/17/13): "An important fact about American culture is we've gone from Gary Cooper to Alan Alda, that is, from the strong silent type to one who wears his feelings on his sleeve."

husbands' successes, and I hardly expected Yvonne to reach their standards.

I am all for a woman's right to choose but couldn't sanction the abortion of a child I had conceived, even though I was finding my wife to be unbalanced, or maybe psychotic. Soon after the initial visit, the doctor declared that it was to be a boy.

****

In our dining room there was a nearly ceiling-high cabinet of Colonial design, a fancy shelved affair, lighted from within by fluorescence and encased behind hinged glass doors, in which we had assembled a stunning collection of classic car models, all of them purchased by me and painstakingly assembled by Yvonne. I never assisted in any way; this was her new hobby, that is, Personality #26's new hobby. Up until this point I have not uttered the phrase "I don't remember," but you'll hear it in this chapter.

I don't remember what it was that upset one of her personalities, or whether or not it was something I said that made her do it, but, just as Charles Foster Kane erupts in the dollhouse-attic scene in the great film, Yvonne, too, became so violently upset that she completely lost control of herself and destroyed the entire collection. She began ripping the delicate constructions she had so lovingly measured, and glued together, and painted, and waited for hours while they dried, and, then, smashed them tall to pieces, every last one.

Packard, Hispano-Suiza, Rolls-Royce, a model of our own 1948 Lincoln Continental, Mercer, Bugatti, Lagonda, Bentley, Cadillac, Duesenberg, Delage, Delahaye, Isotta-Fraschini, Mercedes, Cord, Alfa-Romeo (we were in Bucks County, the Capitol of Classic Cars) all were represented and all came cascading to the parquet floor, or were thrown at the walls of the dining room of French blue, while the dogs scattered and Cleo, who first watched her mother with wonder, then solemnity, then stark fear, finally turned abruptly and ran from the room to hide. The floor was littered with pieces of rubber, tin, alloys, and plastics, which had been bumpers and tires and fenders, painted all colors, but now were completely smashed to crummy smithereens, relicts of a childish pipe dream of Resurrection and love ever after. The still illuminated cabinet now stood forlorn, ugly, barren.

Ten minutes later, not crying but rather like a person recovering from a spell, still in shock, she began sweeping up what was now junk and wasted dreams, never fully apologizing, merely muttering a weak, "I'm sorry."

"It is a terrible thing to be tied to another person like a bomb"[164] which can explode at any time. I replaced the cars with a beautiful set of costly dinner plates and life went on.

---

164 *Remembrance Of Things Past*

21

GOIN' TO CHICAGO

We went into semi-isolation in Bucks County for good reasons: for Yvonne to isolate herself from the The Life, for Cleo to get away from the city and have a taste of the country with a loving family - Yvonne and I and the dogs. But another reason was to "woodshed" my way back into the acting profession.

I was aware that I had diverted my attentions from trying to be an actor because my mother and sister thought directing move refined, a peg above being a mere ham. But friends, to whom I thought myself equal in talent and experience, had become big stars, Dom and Alan Alda, in particular. I felt I could, at least, earn a living. So I broke the back of every one of the plays of the man called Shakespeare.

> *"Down, down I come like glit'ring Phaeton....Let's talk of grave's, of worms, and epitaphs, make dust our paper, and with rainy eyes write sorrow on the bosom of the earth....Virtue, a fig!....Tomorrow and tomorrow and tomorrow creeps on its petty pace.....You lie, in faith, for you are called plain Kate , And bonny Kate, and sometimes Kate the curst.....I do much wonder that one man, seeing how much another man is a fool when he dedicates his behaviors to love, will, after he hath laughed at such shallow follies in others, become the argument of his own scorn by falling in love... "*

All these speeches and plays and characters – both Richards, Iago, Petruchio and Benedick, Macbeth and Hamlet, of course, - I knew since high school, cut acetates to send for scholarships to college acting schools, knew most of Olivier's and Gielgud's and Brando's, even John Carraidine's well-articulated but slightly florid, line-readings. But now began a methodical program of making less familiar plays like *Measure for Measure* and *The Winter's Tale* part of my being, immersing myself in them, discovering the appropriate role in each for myself, and to know everything there was to know about the man called Shakespeare, from traditionalists Dover Wilson and Northwestern's Professor Schoenbaum to non-believers, mainly the Ogburns, father, mother and son.

I did not think I would devote the rest of my life to being a classical actor, though I had most of the attributes, certainly the voice, the timbre, the breathing, intellect and energy, both mental and physical, to succeed in some repertory company somewhere. I had seen how it worked at the Playhouse. It was an honorable life. But I did not do this particular kind of woodshedding for that purpose, but because it is the most demanding material, emotionally and in terms of technical requirements. Through this regime, I believed I would eventually receive work in every area, including voice-over commercials. And I was right!

I followed the play script with the Caedmon recording of every play then, memorized and rehearsed the best speeches of those characters. I was a jazz person; long ago learned acting is spontaneous and organic, was never afraid of copying, of not being original. I also taped and listened to my recordings, repeatedly.

And during Yvonne's pregnancy, Joe Derise, who told me he became a junkie because of his inadequacies as a pianist, came and stayed with us and kicked heroin. Joe became the number two guitarist and boy-singer with the famous band of Claude Thornhill.[165]

Then, going on his own, Joe taught himself to play the piano in order to accompany himself and play in nightclubs and on records. When your life is dependent on something as fragile as accompanying yourself appropriately while singing properly and, then, taking a piano solo for sixteen bars, you are walking a tightrope. It looks and sounds easy, but it is one of the most difficult feats in the show

---

165 Gil Evans, arranged, and Gerry Mulligan, Lee Konitz, Red Rodney, Bob Brookmeyer, Billy Bauer and other superb soloists played for Thornhill.

biz. And the pressure and the availability of dope with friends like Chet Baker and Charlie Parker put the monkey on Joe's back.

Helping Joe go "cold turkey" was the best thing Yvonne ever did. When he left, he was, because we were the same size, wearing my expensive tailor-made suits and had a new point of view that kept him productive for many years to come.[166] While he was with us he played for me every day, while I sang, which helped, and became a part of my regimen for returning to acting. Yvonne appeared to enjoy it.[167]

My son was born on Duke Ellington's birthday. Nearly eight pounds, his mother declined to breast-feed him and deeply resented the presence of my mother who had come to be of assistance. She irritated my mother in a dozen ways the most humorous of which was her insistence that my chaste, respectable mother read the *Kama Sutra* I had purchased for Yvonne.

No doubt my mother was too possessive of her new (only) grandson; a more decent girl would have understood, but not Yvonne. After a few days they fought with each other up and down the long gravel driveway to our home, hitting each other upside the head with each one's purse. I did not want to, but had to take my wife's side and my mother went back to Chicago.

A few days later Yvonne, whether in a fit of post-partum depression, or simply because a new personality invested her person, she once more became the victim of her energumen self, and destroyed the set of new plates I had purchased, and she had appreciatively placed, in the dining room cabinet, where the antique car models had been housed. Every plate in the cabinet, including, platters, charger plates, salad plates, finger bowls, cream and sugar bowls, all were broken, every one, by my twenty-two year-old wife who hurled them right and left against the walls and to the ground.

---

166 When it came to singers of his material, Jimmy Van Heusen put Joe on a par with Crosby and Sinatra. I told Joe he should make the definitive collection of that composers work and took him to Bourne Music, Van Heusen's publisher and, subsequently, Joe made the four volume set of Jimmy's songs, wherein lies the substantiation for the bold comment which begins this footnote.

167 Though her taste tended to "Shimmy-Shimmy-Coco-Pop," and Al Green, our opinions conjoined on Ray Charles and Fats Waller, whose works were in current re-issue. I went to ASCAP at this time and proposed to its very congenial President, Herman Hupfeld, that he assist me in an effort to obtain the rights to put together a revue about Waller, someone to whom I had been listening devoutly since grammar school. A few years before, in 1931, Hupfeld had written a little ditty called "As Time Goes By." Needless to say, I was beaten to the punch by Richard Maltby, Jr. and his *Ain't Misbehavin'*.

Dangerous shards of sharp glass littered the dining room's parquet floor this time. Pieces big and small spilled out into the hallway and the kitchen. You could never be certain you had successfully swept up everything and it was especially unsafe for kids and dogs.

But ten minutes later, there she was, again, broom in hand, attempting to contain and dispose of the mess, while she quiescently apologized for the flagitious behavior. Her daughter and the dogs stood by immobile and scared once more.

And she was not an enthusiastic mother. Cleo showed more interest in her new half-brother than her mother did. Then Yvonne began talking of going back to "work," at first, jokingly. "I'll set it up as a classic car chauffeuring service but the drivers will all be 'working' girls, all hos." And, as it became harder and harder to pay the rent and bills, she became insistent. "Yer getting' old, yer losin' yer looks. Ya coulda have plenya' women and I'd be yer wife-in-law, and we'd have plenya' cash."

****

It was two o'clock in the morning and I was in Manhattan heading back to Bucks County, supercharged on Dexedrine and weed, a combination that made me savagely horny. Driving the Continental down Madison Avenue (still a two-way street then) on the northeast corner of Twenty-Ninth, I saw a beautiful, young blonde on the phone in an illuminated booth on the corner. There was a street lamp overhead. My instinct told me she was tricking, probably in the nearby hotel, in the middle of the block, the only thing open in the vicinity at this hour, except the 24-hour parking garage just east of the timeworn hostel.

Stately office buildings built before the Stock Market Crash of '29 stood on both corners and one contained a bank. Some lunch counter restaurants and an office supply company shared either side of the block. But all of these were closed. The light from the hotel signage and the streetlamp were the only source of light on either side of the block, except when the one in the phone booth was activated by a the blonde with long legs and a tantalizing body. It was a haunted scene of gloomy disrepute Edward Hopper might have painted.

I parked the car and waited till she exited the phone booth. My suspicion was confirmed and I had no problem picking her up. I parked the car and followed her slender gams past the registry desk and into a strategically placed first floor room of the funky caravansary. The room was redolent with the smell of sex. There was a water closet, a small washbasin and towel rack on the wall and a nearby unreliable looking straight chair. But the unkempt room's dominant feature was a double bed with rumpled sheets.

Loquacious she wasn't. There was no badinage between us. Hers would have been the usual:

"So, what do you do for a living?"

Mine would have been:

"What's a nice girl like you doing in a place like this?" and it would have been entirely appropriate, except the phrase "beautiful girl" might have been applied. We undressed. She lay her sylphid body on the bed and spread her legs. She was fair-skinned and her ivory bosom featured sweet pink nipples. There was a refinement about her that she was unable to conceal, not exactly wholesomeness under the circumstances, but a sort of sophistication.

I stood over her, removing my jacket, then my shirt, and shoes and pants, all the while observing her closely. We didn't speak. She watched me watching her. She was voluptuous. But unlike Yvonne she did not flaunt it. If Yvonne was cute, this girl was beautiful. Both were blondes, but Yvonne's blondness was courtesy of Nice n' Easy, this girl's was natural, shoulder length. Though I see the features of her face only dimly now, intelligence was its main ingredient. Tall as Yvonne and as shapely, but, whereas Yvonne was outgoing and funny in one part of her bi-polarity, this girl was serious and reserved and I suspected it reflected her general temperament.

Her eyes were limpid, empathetic; Yvonne's told a story as sinful as Ganaiden's snake. Both were the same age and would give you boners but this one did not appear to be a tramp. Like Yvonne she wore no makeup or lipstick, probably paradigmatic for prostitutes of the period, hardly "painted ladies" at all. In such situations prostitutes assume the initiative and perform fellatio but she just lay there watching me closely She was a big turn-on.

I was not so much interested in coitus as I was in performing cunnilingus. Whether subconsciously or not, I believe now that I wanted her to fall in love with me. I decided she was not going to make love to me; it would be the other way around. I got on the bed on my knees and put my head between her legs and, with the benefit of acumen acquired through the terrific tutorials of the talented Twomey Twins, with my lips and tongue, surrounded by the soft, buff-colored hair of her muff, I made love to her.

This amorous degustation led to a search for her clitoris, which I discovered with alacrity owing to its stiffness. I couldn't do that with Yvonne and wasn't even sure she had one, though she always wanted to be serviced. My subtle attack on this beautiful whore produced restrained but passionate moans that were contagious and urged me to persevere until my efforts effected orgasmic relief. Afterwards, lying there for moments, she placed her slender fingers on either side of my head as she lay breathing softly in a mood far removed from the depressing surroundings. I raised my head slightly, looked up at her and smiled.

She smiled back and I rose to my knees, taking hold of her compliant legs just above the ankles. I twisted them slightly, gently urging her to face the bed, which prompted her to turn over and place her body in a position of suppliant prostration. I was very stiff now and entered her by way of her already lathered lips and loved her thusly for some minutes thanks to the Krauts who invented uppers for the troops to kill more Jews.

There is not much a woman can do when you make love to her in that manner, she doesn't have to shake her can or do a thing, and, as I have said, no one was ever as good as Yvonne in that particular pose, but this girl was better than good, *emes*. And, unlike Yvonne, my not beating on her behind and calling her "Slut," seemed not to be an impediment to her pleasure. On the contrary, I believed she appreciated the tenderness of my riff for I WAS making love to her, though it seems a dream to me, now. When it was over I dressed myself, while she sat up in the bed, silent, mysterious, *sans causerie* or b.s.

Then, she looked for a piece of paper and a pencil and began writing. Still naked, she rose from the bed and came close to me. I drew her to me; I embraced her; I kissed her as if I loved her and, when she backed away, she gave me the piece of paper with her phone number. Clearly, she was living in a hotel for it was one of those numbers with zeros on the end and an extension number as addenda. She looked deeply into my eyes and said, "This was different for me. Call me."

No plaintiveness, very sincere, she might have been an actress who wasn't getting anywhere. I thoroughly believed her. The oldest acting school in America was right around the corner. Maybe that is why I remember so well those parting words and no others. She could have been a student down on her luck. Maybe her mother or father was dying and needed money for an operation back in Kansas, or from whence she came, for she wasn't a New Yorker and was without accent. I asked nothing; instead of conversation there was magic. Or was she playing me? I don't think so, though it might have been the other way around. I couldn't wait to see her again.

I left her, then, without promises or further comment. It had taken a half hour at the most, but here I am still pondering the event in my eighties. And if you and I have a Good Angel and a Bad, my Bad Angel was rejoicing for I was going to have a stable of beautiful *odalisques* or call them what you will.

In a flash, getting back into the Lincoln to drive back to Bucks County under the sway of my Bad Angel, I wondered what would happen if I called her in the early evening at her hotel, took her to dinner, took her back to the hotel and fucked her again, then brought her back home to Yvonne to form a beautiful *ménage a trois*? I would realize the most extravagant sexual fantasies of which Proust only dreamed of bringing to fruition with a compliant Albertine and her girlfriend, the even more malleable, Andree.

Then, the Good Angel might have asked: "Was I the vessel of a Jungian imperative that dictated I recreate the sins of my father?" But that cannot be, for I did not yet know my father had been a bigamist, a womanizer.

Nevertheless the Good Angel forcefully asserted, as I turned on the ignition, that I was in a ridiculous situation. I knew nothing of the lovely whore's no doubt recondite past. Obviously not another Yvonne, she must, like Yvonne, be sick, my Good Angel whispered in my ear, "An apodictic threat to your future as an actor or participant of any kind in the theatre."

My Bad Angel intervened and said: "This girl has no pimp, don't worry, the situation can be managed. You can have your cake and eat it, too!" My Bad Angel had a point.

I thought to myself, as I continued west, in the direction of the old Tenderloin, "What am I, a reformer, a latter day Comstock? In the first place, a woman has a right to sell her body and do-gooders be damned. Secondly, I've already got one depraved soul to reform. How many can I handle and at the same time manage two small children, three dogs and my career?"

"But what if you two are kindred spirits, what if you shared the same interests and were both outlaws and spies, for that's what you are. Maybe you were destined for each other?" the Evil One queried with profound emphasis.

That really scared me. And in these back and forth tergiversations that enflamed my frazzled mind as I traversed Chelsea on the way to the Holland Tunnel and eventually Bucks County, where awaited a haven of non-blissful connubiality, the Good Angel triumphed, for, as if it were a death warrant or tainted with poison or raging with an ungovernable flame, I threw the scrap of paper out the windscreen window of the fancy car by the time I reached Fourteenth Street and Seventh Avenue. I did not want to be Mickey Jelke after all.

Was it an act of the same cowardly reticence I evinced in the episode with my mother in the Palmer House restaurant involving the girl with the goo-goo eyes? It was pusillanimous perhaps, but I couldn't be sure the lovely whore, who was under some kind of pressure and showed it in her phone call on the corner, was stained beyond recall, that her attraction to me was a matter of pathogenesis and that two whores together were too much to handle psychologically if I wanted my career back, especially if they were both beautiful, or one beautiful and the other exceedingly cute.

This much is certain: if I had called the lovely and mysterious whore I would not have completed my plans to return to the theatre. I would have adumbrated my career. In other words, reader, I was trying to do the right thing.

I could never have imagined the awful events which were about to transpire but had I done so I would have waited till the lovely whore was through work that morning and insisted she tell me everything there was to tell and only the Fates know what might have been in store. What halcyon days I might have spent with her, what halcyon days conjoined in contented propinquity we might be spending now in fond recollection of our "magical" meeting? "The only real Paradises are the Paradises that are lost."[168] And right now, I would, if I could, trade everything I have been if I could be with her now.

Yvonne deserved a fat kick in her beautiful behind for her querulous and greedy hortatory that I endow her with a position as wife-in-law, and her speculation regarding my inability to do so was a spurious argument at best, as the above event memorializes. The fact is I was in my absolute prime and could have brought home attractive girls and women from New York or from among the fly females I saw along the roadside thumbing rides, now and then, day or night, between the Apple and Bucks County. I could have become her procurer. I could have engineered intricate orgies. I had the perfect car; I had the perfect setup; I had the perfect mate.

But I also had two children to take care of now and I considered myself to be an artist not a pimp. In short, when it comes to adventures with women I was a coward, for a stable of women, especially co-managed by Yvonne, while it might enhance my sex life, would not improve my career but only get me into more trouble.

Though I had never heard of the term before, Yvonne now began accusing me of "duty fucking" her. "Does that mean I'm not fucking you enough, or that I'm not fucking you to your satisfaction?"

"Both!"

Shortly thereafter, she was particularly sullen one rainy day, so I asked, "What's wrong?"

She looked at me as if I had killed the dogs, and then bounded from the room, only to return with my green fishing tackle box, which served for many years as my makeup kit for stage work. It had been sitting on a shelf in the closet for over a year. "What's this?" she demanded, holding the container of green plastic away from herself as if it were the box for which Mike Hammer searches

---

168 *Remembrance Of Things Past.*

all through *Kiss Me Deadly*, the box that holds the nuclear bomb that kills Creation in the last few seconds of the film.

"It's a makeup kit, what do you think it is?"

I had been very good at making-up even before I went to the Playhouse because I was playing character roles all the while attending high school. The box was filled with rolls of fake hair for moustaches and beards, clown white, nose putty, two different shades of Max Factor pancake makeup, eyeliner, rouges, powder brushes, spongy applicators, spirit gum and spirit gum remover, Stern's Derma Wax (light flesh color) and even an ancient powder puff. It is still in my possession though greasepaint and pancake makeup are seldom used today and "makeup artists" abound. The kit had sentimental value and represented my time as a young actor.

Now, staring at me maliciously with her sky blue eyes, Yvonne said, as rottenly as she could spit out the word:

"Faggot!"

"Hey, don't get me mad. What are you, crazy? That's my old makeup kit."

"Faggot!"

"What are you, some kind of moron? Use your head, dum-dum, I've told you before," I said, trying to control myself.

She had warned me never to hit her and I never did. I never hit any woman, I never took advantage of one or ever forced myself upon a female; I let them come to me. And at this point, reader, I give you not only my exigent reply, I interpolate for your benefit, other information transmitted to Yvonne a long time prior to the event that I now attempt to depict.

"I had one homosexual experience in my entire life and I've told you about it; I was fifteen years old, I was in a play, this older guy, a black guy with a barbershop, a bit player, starts flattering me one day, says he knows a lot of girls, lures me to his place, feeds me gin, which I never drank before, and, while I'm fucking a white hooker, who, by the way, looks like you do now, the guy comes up and starts putting his tongue in my ear and so on. THAT'S IT! He molested me; he could have gone to jail; I didn't do anything about it. It really wasn't that big a deal, but, yeah, you KNOW that's the only time, what are you crazy? Why are you doing this?"

She responded by repeating the epithet once more.

"Faggot."

"Say it again and I'll kill you."

This, evil, vindictive girl, for whom I stuck out my neck, this unhinged virago with whom I found a few months of love, screamed, now, defiantly, at the top of her lungs, "FAGGOT!"

It would be a hallmark in the history of fatuity for me to ask the reader: "Have you ever seen Gil Turner, a top-ranked welterweight who faced Kid Gavilan?" because you're, probably, all too young. But I saw him box in the old Garden and I could never forget his famous "Bolo punch." It was an exaggerated right uppercut that emanated from somewhere below his kneecap and was sheer devastation to his opponent when it landed on target, which was the opponent's chin.

And in one swift movement that propelled me across the bedroom floor to where she stood naked, framed by the doorway, completely conscious of what I was doing and with the image of Gil Turner firmly in my mind, I wound up my fist from below my kneecap and applied it to the point of her chin as forcibly as I could. She left the floor six inches, in a momentary disabling of her body, with arms pinned to her side, and, then came down hitting the floor with a soft thud and crumpling into a heap. It was exhilarating. I never hit a woman before; never hit one since. I am not a sadist. But oftimes, especially when I am blue or, worse, disconsolate, I think back to that awful night and take solace from the perfect trajectory of that blow, the almost comical rise and silly, rag doll fall of the one I once so foolishly loved, and my being fills with heady satisfaction and an abundance of joy.

Two days later, she brought up the subject of going back to "work" in order to bring in some money. "Look, I know some guys, just wanna talk with me and they give me three hundred dollars." We had not spoken much during the two days following the accusation of faggotry, but I said, "Yes, " and on the third day and, with Cleo and the dogs in the car, I brought her to the bus and she left for New York. I confess, reader, I was at that point happy to get rid of her and to test her loyalty. It would have been the first unselfish thing she ever did for me.

She called a couple of times from New York, during those two days away, and sounded very weird. She said she had met an old madam friend and things were fine. But she didn't sound fine, she sounded as if she was high on cocaine. She arrived at the nearby bus stop on the morning of the third day and it was clear she had not slept at all and was operating under the influence of a mixture of uppers and downers. She barely slept that evening and was uncommunicative. She arose early and, with Cleo, went shopping.

Now, in the words of Mr. Dickens' alter ego, "A dread falls on me here.…It is no worse because I write of it. It would be no better, if I stopped my unwilling hand. It is done. Nothing can undo it; nothing can make it otherwise than it was."

When Yvonne and Cleo returned up the long gravel path and entered the house, Yvonne walked straight up to me where I was standing by the dining room table adjacent to the now-empty cabinet which had once exhibited the models she had laboriously constructed, and the plates she had maliciously broken, and said, "Cleo says you've been having sex with her."

I exploded spontaneously, grabbed the child.

"What? What have I been doing? Tell me, I want to hear, I want you… I want SOMEONE to tell me what I've done," I shouted, as Olivier did, falling from the platform to his death in *Titus Andronicus*, I mean I was REALLY pissed after all I'd done for these two!!!

But I heard the sound of a car speeding down the gravel driveway and two armed detectives jumped out of it, guns drawn, and ran into the house, one rushing behind me and pulling my wrists behind my back, in order to handcuff me. This was the most awful moment in my life, bar none, before or after. Hitchcock got it right in *Wrong Man*; the experience, the sight of your hands in handcuffs stays with you forever.

The trip to the prison near Doylestown was no fun either.

"Ya know we take child rape pretty seriously here in Pennsylvania," said one offensive detective. Nor was the fingerprinting pleasant.

My brother-in-law saw to it that I was released that afternoon. The bail was set low. There must have been a reason. I realized that the madam (whom I never met but about whom I had heard from Yvonne) was the one responsible for this act of injustice. The madam coked her up and filled her head with made-up, suppositional lies about me, and, then, Yvonne, who was nuts to begin with, talked Cleo into something, too, whatever that was, meaning the specific charges (which, as you will see) never came to light.

But on the way back from the prison in a taxicab, I thought of something which had happened and on which, I believed, I had, at the time, placed too little significance, even imagining that I had imagined it to happen at all, if you get my drift.

I was thinking of a time when Yvonne had driven the Lincoln to the shopping center in Doylestown and I was stretched out on a lawn chair at the rear of the house with the dogs and Cleo nearby. I almost dozed off, but then I heard Cleo approaching slowly and I looked up at her. She had the strangest look on her face. By now, she was only six years old but it was clear she was attempting to look older, as if she were imitating a movie star in a love scene, or her mother. I had always respected her shyness, but, at the same time, showed her appropriate affection. I was seldom alone with her and never remember seeing her naked. Her mother was always there for that.

But now she was approaching me, arms outstretched, like Greta Garbo, in *Queen Christina*, reaching out for John Gilbert. It was very odd. I let her embrace me, as if it were a hug, though it seemed to be more than that to her, and I gave her a kiss on the cheek and forgot about it. Kids do the strangest things I thought, at the time. Now I was beginning to wonder if she weren't plain batty like her mother.

Yvonne didn't plan on my returning so soon from the penitentiary and when I entered the house she was tearing up pictures in the family photo album we had started, all the pictures in which she and Cleo appeared. I restrained myself and she departed, with Cleo, in the morning, under the influence of I know not what, for how could she ever have thought such horrid things about me, Bolo punch or not? She left me with my nine month-old son and the three dogs.

I imagine she dropped Cleo off with Ronny, or perhaps re-enrolled her in Dale House, but she would have had to do it right quick for she was arrested the next morning in New York City for prostitution and, what's more serious, for assault and battery of an NYPD Vice Squad detective. There was a lot of coke involved. She called my brother-in-law to bail her out.

"I've never heard such language before even from a barge captain," he remarked, refusing her request. When she appeared before the judge she was sentenced to six months in the Women's House of Detention and would serve approximately three.

In Pennsylvania, the judge, in a short sentence consisting of five or six words, dismissed the child abuse charges against me, whatever they might have been, and no evidence of any kind was ever presented by anyone because nothing ever happened. The two detectives who arrested me were there and I bad-mouthed them on the way out and had to be restrained by my attorney.

Nevertheless, still obsessed, I visited her in jail twice and set up an apartment for us after she was released. We planned to pick up my son in Chicago, where my mother had taken him. You say I was crazy to be loyal to her; that some part of me was still in love with her? But in reality I was most concerned with my son's future and blowing her off entirely, especially if she showed some remorse, seemed precipitous.

But she never showed anything approaching remorse. That's how it is with her type of madness. In fact, when she came out of prison (with hickys all over her body) instead of showing she was sorry, she taunted me and bragged about her conquests in prison. She never accounted, much less apologized, for the child abuse charges, never told me what Cleo alleged or said because she knew it was all invented in order to destroy me. She would not admit it.

When she was released she flirted with every man with whom we came in contact, on two occasions whispering in my ear, with the target of her affections within earshot," I want to suck this guy's dick." Once she jumped in a new male visitor's lap and looked at me defiantly as she started necking with him.

I had put all our furniture in storage to be sent for when we were ready. I found good homes in the country for the Fox Terriers and Puddin', the black Cocker Spaniel, was to leave with Yvonne and myself in the '48 Continental, my only asset and presently on the market for sale. But on the day we were to leave for Chicago, I came back from Belmont Park to find her gone. Puddin' was all that was left. "Good riddance to her," I thought.

"And indeed when we are no longer in love with women whom we meet after many years, is there not the abyss of death between them and ourselves, just as if they were no longer of this world, since the fact that we are no longer in love makes the people or the person that we were then as good as dead?"[169]

I saw her three years later. She came to Chicago. It is the only time she has seen my son since his birth. The previous year she had been at the Democratic Convention in Miami and had fucked seventy-five per cent of the superdelegates and Teddy Kennedy twice, (so she told me) and the Hall of Fame jockey, Willie Hartack, who, she tauntingly averred, gave her one helluva good ride. She admitted she had been seeing psychiatrists and learned she had twenty-seven different personalities and could not accept the responsibility of parenthood. She, also, admitted that her mother was mad. "They say there's something wrong with her mind," she said with a laugh.

She was in essence, however, admitting by her presence that she wanted to be accepted back as wife and parent. That is, that is what one of her personalities wanted that particular day, so I sent her back to Jersey at the end of the week. She had taken our son to the Lincoln Park Zoo while I was rehearsing for the Chicago premiere of Lanford Wilson's new play, *Hot L Baltimore*, and our son told her: "I hate you!"

I was cured. I had learned that "being in love is like being in an evil spell, such as those in fairy stories, against which we can do nothing until the spell is broken."[170] I saw her once more, a decade after our marriage. Her tits were sagging; she looked awful and said she was heavily into intercourse with canines.

"They're so beautiful, especially the Doberman pinschers," she disclosed with the same maniacal look of sexual enthusiasm on her face that I encountered the first night we met, the night when the judge who dug the vibrator was next in line.

With her final visit I realized her core personality was that of a straight-out nympho-maniacal prostitute with insatiable desires and a capacity, and a willingness, to bring men to ruin in order to revenge the sin of her father (who had been killed the previous summer crossing a road while drunk to the gills, an event which did not prompt his daughter's shedding of a single tear).

---

169 Ibid.
170 Ibid.

Decades later, I learned she was married to someone else – not Ronny - when she married me, some felon convicted of weapons possession and burglary. Who knows, they may be together still. True love never dies. As for Cleo, who knows?

And incidentally, I forgot to mention that I met her, indirectly, through the Palace of Audible Dreams.

****

The day Yvonne walked out on me was July third, 1971. The next day, with Puddin' panting heavily as he lay on the floorboard of the Continental, his mouth wide open and his tongue hanging out, I drove to Chicago, keeping the top down in the horrible heat of the holiday of our national birth.

Well, that's the story, though I'm aware it doesn't make me look good. But, at least, it's the truth and that's a virtue in itself, as far as this bullshit world you and I live in is concerned.

I was now thirty-five. Seventeen years, nearly two decades, a score of years, had passed since Gandy came to Gotham with high hopes. No matter how deep the hole I had dug for myself, I now had a son, a healthy baby boy, and, as I drove the eleven hundred miles with my canine companion on that scalding-hot day, I wondered could the nation's rebirth, also be a new beginning for me? Chicago theatre was burgeoning; I had some history there, some credits and I was hopeful I could get work. Today was, after all, a celebration of independence and I was free of the psycho-bitch. I began with a cliché when I said my back was to the wall, and, now, I end with another because they're both true - the best was yet to come.

THE END

Appendix

Note: Unlike the main body of the book, the names, places and events listed in the following appendices are *NOT* listed in the Index.

#1. – PRELUDE – Jimmy and "the Shuberts" at the Pinnacle. Here is my list candidates for Erie Smith, the leading role in Eugene O'Neill's Hughie. (Though I had the rights and the budget in hand, I had no star and composed the following in a state of desperation, from client lists and memory, while in town overnight to see agents and actors.) Ed Asner, Karl Malden, Martin Balsam, Robert Preston, Lee Strasberg, Howard Da Silva, Broderick Crawford, Shelly Berman, Sam Levene, Jason Robards, George Kennedy, Jack Weston, James Coco, Clifton James, Morris Carnovsky, Sanford Meisner, Peter Boyle, Dana Andrews, Eddie Albert, Neville Brand, Tony Franciosa, Darren McGavin, Leonard Nimoy, Vince Edwards, Ben Gazzara, Howard Duff, Richard Crenna, Jack Gilford, Richard Widmark, Soupy Sales, Dick Shawn, Ray Walston, David Wayne, Dennis Weaver, Martin Landau, Mike Kellin, Burt Lancaster, Tony Lo Bianco, Ed Mc Mahon, Cliff Robertson, James Whitmore, Victor Buono, Arthur Kennedy, Ray Milland, Robert Duvall, Ed Flanders, Gary Merrill, Laurence Luckinbill, Simon Oakland, Pernell Roberts, Jack Warden, Robert Vaughn, Stacy Keach, Robert Culp, Frank Gorshin, Warren Oates, Ralph Meeker, Theodore Bikel, Joe Campanella, Carroll O'Connor, Tony Randall, Tom Ewell, William Shatner, Richard Basehart, Nehemiah Persoff, Jack Palance, Robert Alda, Alan Arkin, Burgess Meredith, Ernest Borgnine, Tom Bosley, Richard Castellano, Arthur Hill, Pat Hingle, Kevin McCarthy, Patrick O'Neal, George Peppard, Anthony Perkins, Tony Roberts, Albert Salmi, Roy Scheider, William Windom, Jack Albertson, Eddie Bracken, Abe Vigoda, Burt Young, Gene Hackman, Rip Torn, John Cassavettes, John Saxon, Cliff Gorman, Harry Guardino, Bradford Dillman, James Daly, Jack Cassidy, Barry Nelson, Hal Holbrook, Ricardo Montalban, George Grizzard, Richard Kiley, Steven Hill, and Robert Lansing. A good friend of mine worked with Burt Lancaster. It turned out I only approached two actors Jason and, then, Ben Gazzara.

#2. – PRELUDE -Jimmy and "the Shuberts" at the Pinnacle. These following articles militated for non-profit theatres, namely for the Illinois Repertory Theatre of Evanston at, initially, the American Hospitals Association Building, in Downtown Evanston (with a theatre designed by the noted architect, Harry Weise), then, at the nearby Levy Center, and, later, for use of the theatre at Navy Pier, as the Illinois Repertory Company, with sponsorship from Helen Hayes and John Cassavettes, among others (years before the Chicago Shakespeare Company): *Chicago Tribune* "Tower Ticker" by Aaron Gold, October 22, 1973; *Chicago Tribune* "How Evanston Got its Arts Together" September 17, 1975; *Chicago Guide* "Silver Dreads Among the Gold," by James Maronek; *Chicagoan* "Mr. Eden Plans His Paradise for the Drama," by Richard Christiansen, January, 1974; "Energy

Crunch Or Not at Chicago Theaters The Show Goes On," by Peter Jacobi, *Chicago Daily News* April 1974; *Chicago Tribune* "Tower Ticker" by Aaron Gold, August 24, 1976, and in the architecture section of the *Chicago Tribune* Arts & Fun – November 14, 1976 in a lengthy article with pictures by architecture critic, Paul Gapp, entitled "Theatrical Dream Shapes Up Out At Navy Pier;" "Some Big Plans And Few Small Items," by Glenna Syse, *Chicago Sun-Times*, Thursday, July 8, 1976. A prospectus was drawn for both the Evanston and Navy Pier projects and I was to meet with Mayor Daley's Park Commissioner, re: Navy Pier, the day before His Honor, the Mayor, died.

#3. – BANDITS AND BOPPERS ON BROADWAY, CHAPTER ONE, Palace of Audible Dreams, RE: Geography of Times Square Area in 1954. Built by B.B. Moss in 1924 and named the Colony, the Broadway Theatre, at 53rd, opened as a vaudeville-movie house, but led a schizophrenic life, shifting from live to film presentations. In 1930, Moss changed the theatre's name to the Broadway and presented stage productions, but not for long, reverting in the mid 1930's to films. In 1938, it was sold to the Shuberts, Lee and Jake, who, in 1942, premiered *This Is The Army,* with Irving Berlin singing and playing himself. The showstopper was his "God Bless America," first written in 1917, revived in 1938 and today our second national anthem. It was a convenient arrangement for the composer; his office was a mere block away, next door to the Winter Garden Theatre. The jazz club Iridium is in that space at present and sits above a high class, highly-priced delicatessen. After a decade of stage productions, the Colony, now called the Broadway, once more, became a movie house, this time showing *Cinerama*. In 1954, it became a legit house. When the play was over, hundreds would exit and walk toward (past or into) the Palace of Audible Dreams, sometimes, to buy a copy of the show which they had just seen. *Most Happy Fella* and *Gypsy* played there, and *Fiddler On The Roof* ended its long run there. Birdland was across from the Broadway and, in 1954, next door to the Band Box.

Skipping a block, going downtown, Joe Kipness's Hawaii Kai Restaurant was just a door downtown from the Winter Garden and adjacent to Tony Canzoneri's, where the five-foot, four-inch fighter could usually be found standing at the east end of the bar. The drugstore on the corner included a Le Blang's ticket office. There were newspaper stands on both corners of 50th and Broadway and one vendor took Aiden's (and many other people's) bets. A hot dog emporium was on the southeast corner until Chock Full o' Nuts took over in the mid-60's. Adjacent to it was a second floor walk-up dime-a-dance establishment. A small store that, eventually, housed a tiny retail record outlet, was next door to that. Then came another small fast food place. The next southerly tenant was the huge Rivoli Theatre, a premiere movie house, which occupied the rest of the block, except for a popular Howard Johnson's on the corner of 49th.

Up 50th, going toward Eighth Avenue, near midway in the block, on the south side of the street was a famous bar called Beefsteak Charlie's, an establishment which had nothing to do with the franchise restaurants operating under that name, some years later. It, like many establishments midtown (Toots Shor, Dinty Moore's, Tony Canzonneri's) had a sawdust floor. Its customers were mainly black musicians. It was a regular hangout for Coleman Hawkins, Max Roach, Sonny Greer and others.

Across the street from the Rivoli and Howard Johnson's was the Brill Building. On its corner was the Turf Club, an egalitarian eating-place for the sporting crowd. There, Aiden and Dean watched Iron Liege beat his stablemate, Tim Tam, Bold Ruler, Round Table and Gallant Man, when Bill Shoemaker, riding the latter colt, misjudged the finish line, stood up in the saddle and blew the Kentucky Derby. It had previously been called the Paradise Club and the Hurricane Club before that. Today it is a CVS. Heading back north, was the Art Deco entrance to the building, which housed the new Tin Pan Alley that had long ago departed 28th Street. Next to it was Jack Dempsey's, with the Champ, almost always, sitting in the window. Kitty-corner from Howard Johnson's and the Rivoli was McGuniess Clam Bar, which was on the southwest corner of 48th and Broadway. A newsreel theatre was next door going downtown. Above McGuiness was the Tango Palace, with its compelling signage reinforcing its promise of beautiful ladies waiting within. Cobb's Restaurant was across from McGuiness, going uptown. The Brass Rail (not to be confused with Chicago's Brass Rail, at Dearborn and Randolph, a jazz club) was at 48th and Seventh Avenue and up the street was the Latin Quarter, run by Barbara Walters' father, Lou. The big sign on the 47th Street side of Times Square, was advertising Planter's Peanuts then.

Across from Duffy Square, the western block of Broadway, between 47th and 46th Streets, was dominated by Horn and Hardart, sometimes known as, "Horny Hard-on." Just as there were multiple Horn & Hardarts, so, too, was there was more than one Hector's Cafeteria, one on Seventh Avenue in Times Square proper and another on the southwest corner of 50th and Broadway. Both were referred to as "Hector the Garbage Collector," and served fine fare. The Globe movie theatre was next door to H-H and other prominent movie theatres in Times Square proper were Loew's, the Strand, the Embassy, and, of course, the Paramount Theatre which ceased booking stage shows in 1952, though briefly revived by Alan Freed presentations. The Astor Theatre and another first-run movie house, below the Johnnie Walker sign, were on the following downtown block, and, then came the great Astor Hotel itself, with its high-ceilinged bar on the southwest corner. In 1954, the old Childs Restaurant was still on Seventh Avenue between 44th and 43rd and Toffenetti's was where NASGDAQ is at present, 43rd and Seventh. The Camel's sign was still blowing smoke-rings. Next door to Toffenetti's was a movie theatre. Above it was McGirr's pool hall.

Back toward 52nd, the Capitol Theatre, showing films, was on the corner of 51st and Lindy's was directly opposite. A few doors west was the Mark Hellinger Theatre, where *My Fair Lady* had its run. Nola's Recording Studio was above the Penny Arcade on the southwest corner of 52nd and Broadway, where very important sessions were held.

As mentioned, there was a newsstand in front of the Palace of Audible Dreams; it did NOT take bets, but race results, which were not, then, transmitted until one half hour after a race became official, made news stands a haunt for horseplayers and bookmakers who thrived in this neighborhood made famous by Damon Runyon. Newspapers had two or three editions daily and the racing results were posted at the top of each new, updated edition. The Night Patrol, a twenty-four hour barbershop, operated up another block from the Stage Deli, which places it between 54th and 55th on Seventh Avenue. Back to 52nd, going toward Eighth Avenue, and across from the Penny Arcade and Gallagher's Restaurant, was a small, inexpensive restaurant, The Capri, which specialized in exquisite Northern Italian cooking and whose frequent patrons included Ezio Pinza, the producer, Walter Fried, and Aiden, when he could afford it.

Next, came the space where the final incarnation of Roseland, the Mecca of Ballroom Dancing, was being built. It did not open until 1956 and its forerunner at 51st Street and Broadway, second floor, was about to be torn down. The 1956 location would last until 2014, when it, too was demolished. Next door was Confucius, a Chinese restaurant which, around the time of which we speak, featured the Lennie Tristano Quintet, and, then, the ANTA Theatre, now called the August Wilson, which was (is) across the street from the Alvin Theatre, named after producers Alex Aarons and Vinton Freedley, and which has been renamed the Neil Simon, a Nederlander Organization theatre.

Jilly's, the bar owned by Frank Sinatra's sidekick, where the singer parked his limousine, from time to time, and where Frank could be found sometimes sitting at the bar, was west of the Alvin and a parking lot was on the southwest corner. 888 Eighth Avenue had not been built yet, nor had the Sheraton Hotel on Seventh Avenue between 52nd and 53rd Streets. The Band Box, next to Birdland, going uptown, featured Art Tatum as late as February, 1953, but was soon superseded by its neighbor, which opened on December 15, 1949 with Max Kaminsky (trumpet), Tristano, (piano) and Charlie Parker and Lester Young. The space had previously been called The Clique and was operated by the owner of the Downbeat Club, before it was taken over and renamed by Morris Levy after Charlie Parker.

The Ham n' Egger, on the northeast corner, was housed in an office building which still stands. A rib joint was adjacent. It operated under the sway of "Spare Rib Red," a light-skinned African-American, with a freckled-faced, a former band boy who was tight with neighbor "Pee Wee" Marquette, and who, having no conscience whatever, sold salt for cocaine. The opposite northwest corner of 52nd and Broadway, right next to the Palace of Audible Dreams, was the location of a diner called Rudley's. As said before, it consisted of a counter with a dozen stools and a few stand up spots facing downtown. The record clerks could grab a fast bite there and famous jazz musicians favored it, similarly.

It must be reiterated that, the "old" 52nd Street, famous from the late 30's through the wartime years, was shuttered. The clubs which featured Art Tatum, Coleman Hawkins, Bird and Diz, the comedian B.S. Pully (the climax of whose act hinged on the revelation of his penis, hitherto, secreted in a cigar box, and produced as the punch line), the Three Deuces, the Onyx, Samoa, Downbeat, Jimmy Ryan's, the Spotlight, the Famous Door (all rip-off joints) and Tony's (which never featured bop, and where Spivy held forth, at the piano) – all located between Fifth and Sixth, in four-story brownstones, originally built for upper middle-class families, turned speakeasies during Prohibition and, now, during the daytime, housing all kinds of commercial enterprises, from photographers to private detectives, were gone, by 1949-50. Kelly's Stables had relocated and only Jimmy Ryan's, moving to 54th Street, and the Hickory House, remained in that vicinity.

Gilbert J. Pincus (1907-1980), the doorman at Jimmy Ryan's at both locations, was known as the "Mayor of 52nd Street." "A short, stocky man," according to John S. Wilson's obituary of him, "Pincus was known to the musicians of 52ndd Street as 'Yizill' because he would tell crowds blocking the entrances to his clubs 'Yiz'ill have to move on.'" Wearing an "oversized overcoat with a newspaper protruding from a pocket, a battered doorman's cap and a long cigar jutting from his grizzled face…(he) served patrons of other clubs and restaurants on the block as well as Ryan's, waddling energetically on sore feet to get them cabs, open doors or find spaces." Managing all this with aplomb, generally directing traffic on the block lined with nightclubs (even when he moved, temporarily, to the Peppermint Lounge, in its heyday) he was struck by a truck, and survived only three weeks, dying at the age of 73.

The action, now, in 1954, was Broadway and 52nd, Birdland, the Palladium and the Palace of Audible Dreams. The Royal Roost had been located at 1580 Broadway (47th and Broadway) but was gone by 1954.The entire block bounded by Broadway, Seventh Avenue, 51st and 52nd Streets, was demolished a few short years after Aiden's 1954 residency. The City Squire Hotel (now called The Sheraton Manhattan) became the main occupant of the block, with retail stores located on the Broadway side. It dislocated Roseland to the location on 52nd Street and did away with Charley's Tavern at 788 Seventh Avenue, near 51st Street, which was on the rear side.

Charlie's was another famous hangout for musicians. Finally, at the northernmost boundary of the turf of which we speak is the theatre referred to in recent days as the David Letterman Theatre and, before that, the Ed Sullivan. Arthur Hammerstein, eight years after the death of, and in honor of, his father, impresario, Oscar Hammerstein I, built it. It was a memorial to the man most responsible for the development of Times Square as the center of the New York theatre district and, quite naturally, was called the Hammerstein. Because of the Depression the ownership of the theatre changed hands and was renamed the Manhattan. Then it was purchased by impresario Billy Rose in 1934 and named the Billy Rose, then renamed the Billy Rose Music Hall. Purchased by CBS in 1936, it took until 1967 to rename it the Ed Sullivan. As an addendum, for it would be a glaring inadequacy to the learned if missing, Moondog (1916-1999) still stood on the corner of Sixth Avenue and 55th Street in his hooded monk's robe, with staff in hand, often at 5 or 6 A.M. For those too young to know, Moondog (Louis Thomas Hardin) merely stood there. He did not move, he did not play or compose at that time and location.

And, for some years during this period, there was a black woman who dressed in party costumes and funny hats and paraded down Broadway with a cat in a wagon who wore the same clothes as she.

#4. – BANDITS AND BOPPERS ON BROADWAY, CHAPTER TWO. "Hotbed of Human Power." RE: Further opera productions, recitals, plays, jazz club appearances, and concerts seen, through elementary and high schools up to June of 1953, when he entered the Cleveland Playhouse. Aiden saw the entire repertoire of Gilbert & Sullivan in the D'Oyly Carte's tour of the U.S., sitting in the top balcony of the Great Northern Theatre. Martyn Green and Sydney Granville, among others, were featured. At the age of fifteen, with his own money, on a Saturday evening, in the heat of July of 1951 he took the train to Ravinia to hear the still young, sensationally popular pianist, William Kapell (1922-1953) play the 1935 Piano Concerto of Armenian/Russian composer, Aram Khachaturian (1903-1978), with Eugene Ormandy (1999-1995) conducting the Chicago Symphony Orchestra. Claudia Cassidy had championed Kapell since the outset of his career and particularly liked his dynamic rendering of this very considerable work, a mixture of Lisztian Romanticism and Borodinian Orientalism, all united by a lyrical motif that runs through the opus. It was exciting to see and hear Kapell pound away at the flashy concerto, the great, by now familiar, Ormandy exhort the huge orchestra, all in white tuxes, as they lustily performed this dramatic work Aiden had listened to repeatedly, in a superb recording by Oscar Levant, with Dimitri Mitropoulis, conducting the New York Philharmonic. He perambulated the band shell he knew since his wee childhood, walked around the parameter, studied the people on the blankets who listened, for the most part, with wonder. No one knew it would be the brilliant pianist's final Ravinia appearance. The young man from Brooklyn died in a plane crash, on tour in Australia, two years later. Aiden also saw Pierre Monteux, Sir Thomas Beecham, Ernest Ansermet and Rafael Kubelik conduct. He saw Segovia, Gregor Piatagorsky, Zino Francescatti, Ruggerio Ricci, Mishca Elman, He saw the majority of recitals Sol Hurok presented at Orchestra Hall. In addition to some of the above soloists, he bought tickets to the impresario's piano series, which included Solomon (Gutner), Dame Myra Hess, Aldo Ciccolini, Byron Janis, Gary Graffman, Benno Moiseiwitch, the ancient Cortot (Alfred), Rudolph Ganz, Josef Hoffman and Robert Casadesus.

Among the ballet Aiden saw were the entire '51-'52 tour of the Ballet Russes de Monte Carlo, '51-'53 showings of Ballet Theatre (ABT) Saddler's Wells and New York City Ballet, under Balanchine. He way was an usher for *Rite Of Spring, Pillar Of Fire, Gaite Parissienne, Fancy Free, Rodeo, Fall River Legend, Appalachian Spring*, standards like *Giselle, Les Sylphides, Coppelia, Swan Lake, Sleeping Beauty, Nutcracer Suite, Petrushka, Firebird, La Valse, Serenade, Symphony In C., The Scotch Symphony, Promenade, Façade* and *Billy The Kid*. He saw Margot Fonteyn,

Moira Shearer, Alexandra Danilova, Alicia Markova, Nora Kaye, Igor Youskevitch, Frederic Franklin, Leonid Massine, Oleg Tupine, Nina Novak, Leon Danielian, John Kriza, Toumanova, along with sets, and, sometimes, costumes, by Leon Bakst, Pablo Picasso, Henri Matisse, Cecil Beaton and Oliver Smith. The Bolshoi had not, yet, arrived in the USA, but, courtesy of Sadler's Wells, Aiden saw choreography "after" that of the ballet masters, Petipa, and Fokine, and viewed the works of De Mille, Martha Graham, Anthony Tudor, Frederick Ashton, George Balanchine and Jerome Robbins, among others. He saw Massine dance de Falla's *Three Cornered Hat.* He saw baritones from Leonard Warren, of the Met, to Lawrence Winters, of the NYC Opera Co.; tenors from Ferruccio Tagliavini to Jussi Bjorling; sopranos from Lotte Lehmann (in a "farewell" recital on the campus of Northwestern University) to Kirsten Flagstad, as Brunhilde, in *Der Ring das Nibelungen*; bassos from George London to Italo Tajo, both superior actors capable of arousing great emotion. Aiden saw many of the major operas, such as, *Faust, Carmen, La Traviata, La Boheme, Tosca, Madame Butterfly, Pagliacci, Aida, Il Trovatore, Rigoletto, Hansel And Gretel*, and lesser-known ones such as Prokofiev's *For The Love Of Three Oranges* and the original touring productions of Menotti's *The Counsel* and *The Medium* and *Ahmal And The Night Visitors*. Aiden saw the Budapest String Quartet, the Pro Arte Quartet, and systematically listened to the main body of chamber music.

After *Winged Victory*, Aiden saw a tired, third road show company, of J.J. Shubert's production of *Blossom Time* (at the Civic Opera House, i.e., the "House That Insull Built") featuring a long-suffering Franz Schubert expiring from T.B. to the music of Sigmund Romberg, though, factually, he died of syphilis. This is a partial list of what Aiden saw theatrically from 1951 through the summer of 1953, before entering the Cleveland Playhouse as a full-time, living away from home, apprentice: the legit theatre presentations of the national touring companies of *South Pacific* and *Call Me Madam* (with Paul Lukas), both at the Shubert and both starring Janet Blair; Jule Styne's stellar production of Rodgers & Hart's *Pal Joey*, starring Harold Lang; and, as mentioned, the failed production of the musical adaptation of Barrie's *Peter Pan*, with music by Leonard Bernstein, starring Jean Arthur and Boris Karloff. He saw *Point Of No Return*, with Henry Fonda, Helen Hayes, in *Mrs. McThing, Tea & Sympathy*, with Deborah Kerr, John Kerr and Leif Erickson, *Don Juan In Hell*, with Agnes Moorhead, Sir Cedric Hardwicke, Charles Boyer and Charles Laughton, and Tyrone Power in *John Brown's Body* (these last two at the Civic Opera House) and the production which Holden Caulfield satirizes in J. D. Salinger's *Catcher In The Rye*: The Lunts (Alfred Lunt & Lynn Fontanne) in *I Know My Love* (adapted by S.N. Behrman from the French play "Aupres de Ma Blonde," by Marcel Archard) at the Erlanger. The play, which gave Holden the opportunity to tell how much he hated the Lunts, only made Aiden love them more.

In seeing these plays as a fifteen and sixteen year old, Aiden was not simply entertaining himself; he did not consider himself to be a fan. He knew he was a future professional and the expense involved, the homework assignments from high school, work at the record store, and appearances in, or rehearsals for plays did not deter him from his duty to see and learn from the great artists of his youth. And this is an appropriate place to mention the vast importance and awareness, on Aiden's part, of the Decca recording of *Death Of A Salesman*, in its entirety, with the original cast minus its leading man, Lee J. Cobb, replaced, instead, by Thomas Mitchell; Tennessee Williams' recording of *Glass Mengerie* (Aiden first played Tom at 15, with a Chicago Park District production); and the very first long-playing 331/3 RPM record ever issued, the original cast recording of *South Pacific*.

As far as jazz is concerned, after the Duke's appearance at the Chicago Theatre in 1945, Aiden saw Ellington numerous times at both locations of the Blue Note. He saw the Art Tatum Trio twice, with Slam Stewart, on bass and Tiny Grimes, on guitar. (Slim Gaillard, who removed most of his clothes as the finale of his act, was on the other half of the bill.) Though he purchased the monumental 13-disc LP collection of one hundred twenty standards played by Tatum, produced by Granz, and knew at least one hundred eighteen of them by heart, could sing them to you with most of the lyrics intact, as well as tell you who wrote them, despite his awful precocity Aiden did not yet know, was unaware, that on his first trip to New York in 1939, as a nineteen year-old, Charlie Parker washed dishes in the kitchen of the Chicken Shack, in Harlem, in order to listen to Tatum, who played there regularly. Some dopes found Tatum "flowery" and some said, ridiculously, that Bird played too many notes, but that was not the only similarity. Aiden came to believe they heard identical harmonies. Aiden saw Buddy De Franco, with Sonny Clark, on piano, and Sonny Igoe, on the drums, in a warehouse operated by the Outfit. He attended many clubs, but standouts were the revived Benny Goodman Sextet, with Jimmy Rowles, on piano, Terry Gibbs, on vibes, at the Blue Note; the saxophonist, Flip Phillips, extremely popular at the time, at the Hi-Note on Clark Street, whenever he appeared there; and Miff Mole and Art Hodes at the Reinhardt's Jazz, Ltd. Chicago jazz entrepreneur, Joe Segal was just beginning his series of presentations and Aiden made sure to attend those, as Joe was a regular at the record store in the Loop. He saw Charlie Ventura, also, with Sonny Igoe (who really got around), then, the Count Basie Septet, featuring Wardell Gray, tenor, and De Franco, at the Brass Rail. And he saw every JATP event as well as the famous D.J. Al Benson's concert where "Big Sid" Catlett died backstage, at intermission. At his height, Stan Kenton invaded the Civic Opera House, with Maynard Ferguson, etc., and Aiden made it his business to attend. Arranger-bandleader-trombonist Bill Russo's concerts, during the period, were obligatory for Chicago jazz enthusiasts, and Aiden saw two of these performances. At 14 and 15, the lone teenager present, Aiden attended jam sessions with ancient African-American players, in a room holding three or four dozen of his elders, on one of the upper floors of a commercial building on Wabash, past Van Buren atop Manny's Record Shop. And Aiden saw the superb violinist, Eddie South, "The Dark Angel of Jazz," twice, once in a club, once at the Al Benson concert. He even saw Charlie Ventura play the bass sax, the one that's so big you can't pick it up.

5. – BOPPERS & BANDITS ON BROADWAY, CHAPTER FOUR "Lester Leaps Out" re: CAIN PARK / CLEVELAND PLAYHOUSE, 1953-54 Season.

Cain Park is celebrating its 81st season in 2019. It is still very much alive each summer, and into the fall, with a wide variety of acts playing to large audiences. In the recent past, it curtailed production of musicals because of their cost and booked touring productions every summer. The 2019 season featured a production of the Broadway musical *Ragtime*; also Just For Laughs, presented in conjunction with The Musical Theatre Project, and For Good: The New Generation of Musical Volume 4. Also appearing in the 2019 season were Dionne Warwick, Chris Botti, Dudu Fisher, Octo Jazz, Olympic Brass, Verb Ballets, Black Squirrel Wings, The Singing Angels, Athena String Quartet, Groundworks Dancetheater, Lyle Lovett and his Big Band, Ani Difranco, Judy Collins and others.

As for the Playhouse, formed in 1915, by a group of civic leaders, Raymond O'Neil, a devotee and disciple of Edward Gordon Craig, was named as its initial director. It was the country's first regional theatre. In 1921, O'Neil stepped down and was replaced by Frederic McConnell and his associates, K. Elmo Lowe, a versatile actor and McConnell's eventual successor as Artistic Director, and Max Eisenstadt, the business brains of the operation. By 1953 the very prosperous Cleveland Playhouse consisted of three professional stages in two different buildings located a few blocks from each other. The new one on Euclid Avenue, a former church, was the largest of these, but the Playhouse Building on 77th, off Euclid, built in 1927, had two excellent theatres: its main stage, the Drury, and a studio theatre. (They currently perform in the Allen Theatre in the Playhouse Square Center.)

The '53-'54 company was composed of players from whom one could learn a great deal: William Swetland, William Patterson, (who would shine at William Ball's ACT, in San Francisco), Rolf Englehart, who had been the numero uno actor in Cleveland for years before I arrived, and Eve Roberts, who was brilliant in *Country Girl* that season, and who would have a long stay at the Seattle Repertory Company. Also prominent that season were Max Ellis, Robert Allman, Kirk & Sue Willis, Clayton Corzatte, Jeannette Atkinson, and fellow apprentices Ann Sudek and Nancy Nutter, who later married the actor-director Howard Da Silva. Dom DeLuise, June Squibb and Jack Lee (who acted in, and was the musical director of *Bloomer Girl* and *A Tree Grows In Brooklyn*), were with me at the Playhouse, and we three went to Cain Park together the following summer. Under the name of Sidney "Edelstein," I appeared in a dozen shows at the Playhouse, always playing bits, but I played the lead and directed a studio production of Irwin Shaw's *Assassin*.

Everyone agreed that Dom, who was doing his frustrated magician's act even then, was much too "undisciplined" to ever succeed in the Big Time. June, though she was a replacement for the original Mazeppa in *Gypsy* and continued working and studying her craft, waited until her mid-70's to become a star, again proving that what Berlin said about show business is *emes*.

Among shows presented in the 1953-54 season were *Male Animal*, in which I made my professional debut, in the role of Nutsy Miller, who McConnell had opening the show, leading a supposed parade, high-stepping and twirling a baton, at which I was lousy. That season they presented *Twefth Night, Bell, Book And Candle, Stalag 17, Family Portrait, The Lady's Not For Burning, The Innocents, State Of The Union, Tree Growes In Brooklyn* and *Come Back, Little Sheba*. Harriett Brazier, McConnell's wife, was one of the greatest character actresses I've ever seen. Many who saw her performance in *Come Back, Little Sheba* that season, shared that opinion. K. Lowe's major film appearance is in the 1949 *Kid From Cleveland*, starring George Brent and Rusty Tamblyn. Alan Alda, Eleanor Parker, Ray Walston, Jack Weston, Thomas Gomez, Carl Benton Reid, Paul Newman, Joel Grey and Margaret Hamilton are listed as having begun their careers at the Playhouse, but a couple of these, I suspect, were members of the Curtain Pullers, the Playhouse's children's' theatre adjunct.

#6. – 'KICKS & CO," CHAPTER FIVE, "Good Intentions" Re: History of the African-American theatre and film prior to 1960. When I began this book in June of 2012, and came to *Raisin* and *Kicks*, it was clearly necessary I tell the prior history of African-American theatre in the United States because no comprehensive book on the subject had been written. But the long chapter I wrote (copyright 2014) is no longer necessary because of Stewart F. Lane's monumental book entitled *Black Broadway*, published in 2016, by Square One Publishers (Garden City, N.Y.).

Nevertheless, if only because I saw three seminal presentations in its history (*Anna Lucasta, Carmen Jones* and Robert Breen's famous 1952 production of *Porgy & Bess* [multiple times]), and in my early youth entered into an everlasting bond with people of color, and because I must, perforce, throw away all my other writing on the subject and refer you to Lane's beautifully-illustrated book instead, allow me, at least, to summarize, in an appropriately left-wing manner, events prior to *Raisin's* premiere. What I wrote and copyrighted in 2014 is reduced, herein, to a few paragraphs. History is history and free to all, but I do not want to be accused of plagiarism, and again refer you to Lane's excellent *Black Broadway*.

The history of the African-American Theatre begins with the African Grove Theatre in New York, in 1823, performing the works of Shakespeare, among others, catering to both white and black audiences. It lasted but a few years and its leading actor, Ira Aldridge, found greater fame in Europe. Minstrel shows conceived and performed by African-Americans morphed into a new genre in the mid-ninetieth century: minstrel shows controlled by and featuring white performers in blackface, occasionally assisted by black performers in demeaning supporting roles. Aside from a few works by 19th century ofay playwrights, such as Dion Boucicault's *OCTOROON*, in the Jim Crow era, from post-Reconstruction until the time of which we speak, 1959, employment for African-Americans on the legitimate stage – in plays about African-Americans - was rare.

But there was black vaudeville and there were musical revues and certain long-running Broadway productions where singers, dancers and comedians found work in largely so-called "all-Negro" or "all-Black" revues, chief among them Noble Sissle & Eubie Blake's *Shuffle Along,* (backed by Arnold Rothstein) *Blackbirds Of 1928 and 1930* (with Ethel Waters), and the 1929 production of *Hot Chocolates*, with music by Fats Waller (1904-1943); *Shuffle Along Again.* Waters (1896-1977) on Broadway, in Irving Berlin revues, and Bert Williams (1875-1922), in Ziegfeld's *Follies*, would achieve great success. To truly understand the significance of Williams and his profound cultural influence, see Professor Louis Henry Louis Gates, Jr.'s 2019, PBS documentary *Reconstruction*. For a bio of the great Ethel Waters SEE APPENDIX 14.

And there was work in black-owned films, which I can only touch on. D. W. Griffith's *Birth Of A Nation* (1915) presented bronzed-up white men as animalistic African-Americas, an image all too acceptable to the bigoted. Early films desecrated the African-American experience, enforcing crapulous stereotypes in films such as *Nigger In The Woodpile, Rastus, Sambo* and the *Wooing And Wedding Of A Coon*. African-Americans responded with the pioneering films of Oscar Micheaux (18884-1951), the Chicago-based, Ebony Film Company and the Lincoln Motion Picture Company, formed by Missouri-born actor, Noble Johnson, and, later, in films by Clarence Muse (1889-1979) and other black-owned companies, organized in the 1920's. These firms employed dozens of African-American actors and actresses. Micheaux's 1925 film, *Body & Soul*, starred Paul Robeson.

But on the Broadway stage, before *A Raisin In The Sun*, there were only the few plays that follow below. In the main, African-Americans did not attend first-run houses in big cities because they were discouraged by theatre managements from doing so. This was all too true on Broadway, too.

However, black amateurs, in communities throughout the country, engaged in staging one-act plays from the turn of the century until the mid-1930's. Called "lynching" plays, *Crisis Magazine* the organ of the newly-formed NAACP, edited by W.E.B. Du Bois, printed and licensed many of these dramatic pieces. Contests were conducted to see who could write the best one, and the short, didactic plays were performed in churches, meeting places, universities, and small theatres. Tickets were bought; royalties paid. In the winter 2016 *Journal Of The Stage Directors And Choreographers*, Northwestern University Professor Harry Young, Chairman and Head of the Drama Department, and President-elect of the Association for Theatre in Higher Education (ATHE) speaks of this in his essay entitled "Sustaining Black Theatre," in which he chronicles "how the stage offered an opportunity to raise awareness and bring attention to experiences of racial violence and abuse...Throughout the 1920's and 1930's, communities of artists gathered to revise the depiction of black life with an aim to create art that reflected the complexity as well as the beauty of African American culture." Prominent among those theatre groups, Professor Young lists Georgia Douglas Johnson's famed S Street Salon, at the heart of the Baltimore-Washington corridor, Beale Street, in Memphis, and "the Stroll" in Chicago to name a few. The Lafayette Players, in Harlem, was a

professional stock company composed solely of African-Americans. It was
the first of its kind and vintagenews.com claims the old Lafayette Theatre,
at 132nd and 7th, "became the first major theater which did not segregate
African-American audiences in New York."

Karamu House theatre, on Cleveland's East Side, the home of interracial
casting in the United States, where anyone can play any part in any
play, was founded nearly one hundred years ago and is still operating
successfully today. When I attended the Cleveland Playhouse, the energetic
German, Benno D. Frank, one of Max Reinhardt's many assistants, headed
the Karamu Theatre. Benno was also one of my teachers at the Cleveland
Playhouse, where he directed a swell production of *Bloomer Girl*, which ran
for seventeen weeks.

The first African-American to author a Broadway play was Anderson
Garland (1888-1939). A San Francisco bellboy and a life-long exponent of
constructive thinking, no one wanted to finance his 1925, *Appearances*,
about a bellboy falsely accused of raping a white woman, so he raised
the money himself with aid, it is said, from Al Jolson (according to
Blackpass.org Anthony Duane Hill, Ohio State University). In 1920, The
Provincetown Players presented Eugene O'Neill's *Emperor Jones*, off-
Broadway, first starring Charles Gilpin (1878-1930), then Paul Robeson
(1898-1976), who later starred in a highly censored, but now-restored and
magnificent film version of the play in 1935. The role of Joe in *Showboat*
(1927), written by Oscar Hammerstein 2nd from Edna Ferber's novel, with
music by Jerome Kern, was intended for Robeson, but he did not appear in
the part until the London production, in subsequent New York revival and
in the 1936 film, singing, of course, "Old Man River." The All-American
fullback, lawyer and political activist (on behalf of his people and workers
everywhere) played *Othello* in London, in 1930, opposite Dame Peggy
Ashcroft. The London critic and Shakespeare scholar, John Dover Wilson,
called Robeson's Othello, "the greatest of the Twentieth Century," but the
actor had to wait thirteen years before playing the role in New York, in
a Theatre Guild production, directed by Margaret Webster (1905-1972),
with José Ferrer (1912-1992), as Iago and Ferrer's wife, Uta Hagen (1919-
2004), as Desdemona. (Robeson, it is said, quickly bedded the lady). After
touring with *Othello*, Robeson was drawn deeper into the political sphere he
always inhabited. He was a teller of truth, a spokesman for the oppressed,
and, because he became so outspoken in his support of world peace and
detente with the evil Stalin, he was deemed unemployable, his passport
was revoked, and he was forced to confine his performance activities to
concertizing. However "duped" he may have been, he was, nevertheless, not
afraid to wok behind the scenes in the "Doctors Plot," of 1953, on behalf of
the accused and in opposition to Stalin's murderous regime.

I saw Paul Robeson four times in my youth, twice at the Chicago Stadium,
along with a crowd of thousands. Once I sat close-up and saw him face-
front. Another time I was on the wrong side and saw only his powerful
back. When I was in high school I purchased tickets and saw him at
Orchestra Hall, in concert with his wonderful accompanist, pianist,

Lawrence Brown. But the most memorable occasion was when my sister took me to see him at a longshoreman's hall, on the Southwest Side of Chicago, where he spoke to a small group of unionists. Afterwards he came down from the platform, came up to me, said "Hello," and patted my cheek. Dr. Gerald Home, Moores Professor of History and African-American Studies, at the University of Houston, and the author of biographies of W.E.B. Du Bois and Robeson, among others, stated, "The younger reader must be told Paul Robeson was the predecessor of Martin Luther King and Malcolm X." Stalin attempted to deceive him. But, like Martin Luther King, Robeson was willing to tolerate Soviet Communism rather than pursue war. King, accompanied by Harry Belafonte, echoed Robeson when interviewed on the *Merv Griffin Show*. But Robeson was not so blind to Stalin's atrocities as critics or appeasers claim. No matter what one believes about Robeson, the American government bears responsibility for hounding him, attempting to dishonor him, and ruining his health and career.

The Stock Market Crash of 1929 had a stultifying effect on Black Broadway, but the play with music by elfin, born-in-a-trunk Marc Connolley, the Pulitzer Prize winning, *Green Pastures*, a folk version of the Old Testament, with its all-Black cast of 80, plus the Hall Johnson Choir, provided much employment for African-American actors and singers in its 640 performance run on Broadway, followed by a Hollywood film, national touring companies and subsequent revivals. The leading role of De Lawd, was played by William Marshall (1924-2003), a friend and supporter of Robeson. Du Bose Heyward's pre-Gershwin, "straight" play, *Porgy* (1930), was essentially as apolitical as the all-Black musicals of the period. This was followed by the Gershwin Brothers collaboration on *Porgy & Bess*, along with Heyward, which introduced Todd Duncan (1903-1998) as Porgy and featured the great John W. Bubbles, as Sportin' Life, a role written for Cab Calloway (1907-1994) and finally assayed by him in the fabled 1952 revival. That was a sensational production and people who were fortunate enough to have seen Bobby Breen's staging find it hard to imagine it having been surpassed in subsequent revivals. I saw it four or five times as an usher. The 1952 cast included William Warfield, Leotyne Price, Cab Calloway, and in a small role, Maya Angelou. It toured the States, then, Europe (accompanied by Truman Capote) and, finally, Latin America, all under State Department auspices. (SEE Truman Capote's *The Muses Are Heard* [Penguin-Random House] 1956.)

"Serious" black actors found temporary homes when the Federal Theatre Project of the Works Progress Administration (WPA) organized in the 1930's, an effort strongly endorsed by Eleanor Roosevelt. A Negro Theatre Unit was created and divided into two groups, one contemporary the other classical. In New York, twenty year-old radio star, Orson Welles, was hired by producer John Houseman to direct the all-Black *Macbeth*, with former prizefighter, Canada Lee (1907-1952) originally as Banquo, then, in the title role, and a cast of mostly non-professionals. The Communist Party believed the effort to be a plot and picketed when rehearsals began, claiming the production was designed to make the participants appear foolish reciting iambic-pentameter. This, transferred-to-18th century-Haiti, *Voodoo*

Macbeth (1936) was a sensation when it opened in Harlem, at the La Fayette Theatre. And when it moved to Broadway, streets around the theatre were blocked-off and the riot police stood by on the ready. The protest musical *Cradle Will Rock*, by Marc Blitzstein, and the more satirical, but very political *Pins* and *Needles* (political, if only because it was the Labor Stage unit of the International Ladies Garment Workers' Union which commissioned the show, through its, and the FTP's, funds), with songs by Harold Rome, had only one African-American performer, Olive Pearlman, between them. But, after its premiere, *Pins And Needles* added the dance troupe of Katherine Dunham (who gave classes at the Labor Stage), and it included Archie Savage, who had been in Orson Welles' Mercury Theatre production of *Dr. Faustus*. Whether Claudia McNeil had, as yet, joined Dunham's troupe is a question for which I have no answer. But the third edition of the *New Pins And Neeles*, in 1939, made a conscious effort to feature black performers by incorporating Dorothy Harrison and Dorothy Tucker. Harold Rome's second revue, *Sing Out The News*, directed by Charles Friedman, opened on Broadway and featured, as its major production number, a Harlem block party celebrating the incumbent President with the song "FDR Jones," sung by Rex Ingram, accompanied by a young Hazel Scott, (who would later marry Adam Clayton Powell, Jr.), at the piano.

ILGWU's Labor Stage, spurred by the success of *Cradle* and of their first revue, commissioned Langston Hughes and the composer, James P. Johnson (an influential jazz pianist, too, and mentor to Fats Waller) to write a show entitled *The Organizer*. It was a hit at ILGWU's 1939 convention, but could get no further, and was rejected as being "too controversial" for radio. Less controversial were the *Hot Mikado* and the *Swing Mikado* which both, eventually, ended up on Broadway.

Langston Hughes, who was part of the Negro Cultural Committee, which presented *The Bourbons Got The Blues*, then formed his own theatre, the Harlem Suitcase Theatre and produced *You Want To Be Free?* a series of skits, poems, and songs, a musical revue; *The Bourbons Got The Blues*; and *Imitations Of Life*, in which Rex Ingram played Frederick Douglass and Frank Wilson, who appeared with Robeson in *Emperor Jones*, played Denmark Vesey, planner of an 1822 South Carolina slave rebellion. Langston Hughes's 1935 drama, *Mulatto*, ran for 373 performances.

The success of NCC's efforts in the East prompted Hollywood's Left, in the spring of 1939, to form the Hollywood Theatre Alliance, whose members included Lillian Hellman, Dashiell Hammett, Langston Hughes, who had moved out West, and Ira Gershwin. Their first production was *Meet The People*, which toured nationally, and, for their second production they wanted a "Negro Revue," and what they got was Duke Ellington's *1940 Jump Joy*.

Langston Hughes had close affiliations to the production, which was about the "new times 'a comin,' but *Jump For Joy* never made it out of California, despite introducing Dorothy Dandridge, and featuring the great singer, Ivy Anderson, a young, Roy E. Glenn, Herb Jeffries (who starred in many westerns as Herbert Jeffrey) and a grab bag of great songs – 41 musical numbers, in all, and all written by Duke, with aid from, according to the original program, William Strayhorn and the often mysterious, ofay, Hal Borne, who collaborated with Fred Astaire, among many others. The score included not only the great title song, but also the classic "I Got It Bad And That Ain't Good." The important lyrics for the all-Black extravaganza, important because they said a new day was dawning, were by Paul Francis Webster, with additional lyrics by the likes of Mickey Rooney and, said, Langston Hughes. The all-Black cast (as you might guess, just because Duke was involved), included, a bevy of beautiful women in the chorus. Marie Bryant, the future Mrs. Nat "King" Cole, was a featured singer, along with the Rockets, Wonderful Smith, a trailblazing standup comic, altogether forgotten today, and the dance team of, get this, Pot, Pan and Skillet. The prestigious, Nick Castle staged the numbers, but the Hollywood radical, Henry Blankfort, stage manager of *We The People*, received credit at the bottom of the page, in large letters "Entire Production Supervised by." Castle and Blankfort were both ofays. The show was funded partially by John Garfield and movie producer, Joe Pasternak, each anteing up $15,000. All this plus Duke's greatest band ever – Ben Webster, Johnny Hodges, Lawrence Brown, Sonny Greer, Freddie Guy, Ray Nance, Rex Stewart, Otto Hardwicke, Joe Nanton, Juan Tizol, Wallace Jones, Barney Bigard and young, immortal, soon-to-die, Jimmy Blanton on bass – Duke's great 1940 band, still, the revue never left La La Land.

The Provincetown Players, which had become the Experimental Theatre, presented Eugene O'Neill's *All God's Chillun,*' in 1924 with Paul Robeson and Paul Green's *In Abraham's Bosom*, in 1926 with Charles Gilpin. These plays, Hughes's long-running *Mullato*, on Broadway, and the 1945 main stem success, *Deep Are The Roots*, by Arnaud d'Usseau and James Gow, directed by Elia Kazan, starring Barbara Bel Geddes, all concerned miscegenation. Dorothy and Du Bose Heyward's 1939 *Mamba's Daughters*, starring Ethel Waters, and Richard Wright's (1940) *Native Son*, co-authored as a play with Paul Green , starring Canada Lee, appeared on Broadway. Both *Native Son* and Langston Hughes' entire body of work have close connections with Hansberry's play. Wright was a Communist until he broke with the Party over the Hitler-Stalin Pact. Hughes flirted with Marxism.

In 1940, Frederick O'Neal (1905-1992) and the writer, Andrew Hill, founded the American Negro Theatre in Harlem, giving career starts to Ossie Davis, Ruby Dee, Harry Belafonte and Sidney Poitier, among many others. The theatre produced 19 plays before closing in 1949, but its biggest hit, *Anna Lucasta*, was its downfall. Premiered in Harlem, it was moved to Broadway by ofay producer, John Wildberg, all in 1944.

Written by Chicagoan Phillip Yordan (1914-2003), originally, it concerned a Polish family similar to his own, but he was unable to obtain a production and rewrote it. Shocking in language and content, the play is about a prostitute who returns to her family and the ex-G.I. with whom she dallies, and it was still touring when I saw it in 1945, at the Civic Theatre in Chicago, while running concurrently in its third year in New York. Because of its Broadway (and touring and film sale) success, the ANT seemed less community-based and O'Neal and the others moved onward and upward. Onstage *Anna Lucasta* gave employment to its star Hilda Simms, and, among many others, Frank Silvera, Rosetta LeNoire, Alice Childress, Ossie Davis and Earle Hyman. It was made as a film in 1959, with O'Neal, as well as Rex Ingram (1895-1969), Le Noire, Childress and James Edwards (1918-1970), but the stars of the picture were Eartha Kitt (1927-2008) and Sammy Davis, Jr.(1925-1990) and the film is little remembered and seldom shown today. Frederick O'Neal later succeeded Ralph Bellamy as President of Actors' Equity from 1964 to 1973.

Produced by Billy Rose (1889-1966) at the Broadway Theatre in 1943, direction by Charles Friedman, staging by Hassard Short, orchestrations by Robert Russell Bennett, and with Muriel Smith and, then, Inez Matthews, in the title role, Oscar Hammerstein 2nd's theatrical ingenuity and love of African-American culture inspired him to transport Prosper Mérimé's shocker of 1848, *Carmen*, with music by Georges Bizet, from Spain to a cigarette factory in the Deep South, with an Army base nearby. Don José became G.I. Joe and the toreador, Escamillo, became a champion prizefighter. The show was a great source of employment for African-American theatre artists in New York and on tour. Everyone in the original cast was appearing on Broadway for the first time.

The Vernon Duke-John La Touche *Cabin In The Sky* was a hit on stage and screen. The 1949 Kurt Weill-Maxwell Anderson musical, *Lost In The Stars* was an artistic success. *My Darlin' Aida*, an "all-Black" version of the Verdi opera, with Charles Friedman and Hassard Short, attempting, but not succeeding, in repeating their success with *Carmen*, premiered in 1952, as did a revival of the Sissle-Blake *Shuffle Along*. Two shows which featured black headliners, *Mr. Wonderful*, with Sammy Davis, Jr., and *Shinbone Alley*, with Eartha Kitt, appeared in '56 and '57 respectively. There were occasional Hollywood films through the 1950's with African-American actors such as *The Jackie Robinson Story*(1950), *The Joe Lous Story* (1953), as well as Otto Preminger's film version of *Carmen Jones* (1954).

Five Harold Arlen musicals, which had integrated or all-Black casts were: *Bloomer Girl* (1944), starring Celeste Holm, which featured the freedom song "Eagle and Me;" *St. Louis Woman* (1946), featuring Avon Long as the jockey, "Little Augie," flopped stateside, then later toured Europe, led by young, Quincy Jones; *House Of Flowers*, featuring Diahaan Carroll, with Geoffrey Holder, luscious sets by Oliver Messel, dances by Herbert Ross, direction by Peter Brook, and book and lyrics by Truman Capote and Johnny Mercer, and which closed after a few months at the Alvin in 1954-55 season. The last two shows starred Pearl Bailey, who made her Broadway debut singing "A Woman's Prerogative" in the Theatre Guild's 1950 presentation of the musical adaptation of Bernard Shaw's *Arms & The Man*, called *Arms And The Girl*, starring Nanette Fabray, with music by Morton Gould. The fourth Arlen show with roles for African-Americans was *Jamaica* (1957), starring Lena Horne and the last, *Saratoga* (1959), was a musicalized, *Saratoga Trunk*, with Carol Lawrence and Howard Keel.

It featured Carol Brice, Harold Pierson and Virginia Capers (1925-2004), who would win a Tony for her performance as Mama Lena Younger in the musical *Raisin,* in 1974.

And, in 1957, a nascent off-Broadway saw a musical production called *Simply Heavenly*, based on writings of Langston Hughes, and featured a relatively new face, a singing actress named Claudia McNeil. Before Hansberry's play closed on Broadway, Jean Genet's *The Blacks*, with James Earl Jones, Godfrey Cambridge, Raymond St. Jacques, Maya Angelou, and Roscoe Lee Browne, Louis Gossett, Jr., the powerful, Moses Gunn (1929-1993) and Cicely Tyson, all appearing in a "whiteface" production, directed by Gene Frankel, opened at the St. Marks Place Theatre.

This is a summation of the pre-*Raisin* days of the African-American actor. Eliminating the musical shows ("all-Black," or not) and activity generated by the New Deal and the American Negro Theatre, there was a great paucity of work for the serious actor, especially on the Great White Way where African-Americans were underemployed, underappreciated and, as paying customers, unwelcome.

(**Addendum** re: African-American film actors, dancers, etc. prior to 1959.)

Tap dancers abounded: Bill "Bojangles" Robinson (1878-1949), Ford Lee, "Buck" Washington (1903-1955) and John W. Bubbles (1902-1986) of Buck and Bubbles fame and other dance teams such as the Step Brothers; the Nicholas Brothers (Fayard and Harold); Stump and Stumpy (James "Stump" Cross and either Eddie Hartman or Harold J. Cromer (1921-2013); Chuck and Chuckles (the fabulous Chuck Green and "Chuckles" Walker). Other soloists were Honi Coles, Cholly Atkins, "Cookie" Cook, Ernie Brown, Pete Nugent, Jimmy Slyde, "The King of Slides," "Baby" Lawrence, Henry Le Taing (a versatile dancer and choreographer, more than tap dancer), Bunny Briggs and "Sandman" Sims. Frankie Manning (1914-2009) personified the best in swing dancing. "Baby" Laurence (Jackson) traded 4's and 8's with Bird on 52nd Street, and danced with Tatum, too.

Among actors who appeared in black-made films in the 1920's, let us celebrate: Ernest "Sunshine Sammy" Morrison, Samuel "Sambo" Jacks, Eva Jessye (also famed as a choral conductor), Jack Johnson (The Champ), Anita Bush, Bill Pickett, Mamie Smith, Laura Mae McKinney, Mildred Washington, Trixie Smith, Matthew "Stymie" Beard, bandleader Clarence Williams, an entertainer since 12 and author of standards such as "Baby, Won't You Please Come Home?" the classic "West End Blue," as played by Louis Armstrong, considered one of the 10 great jazz recordings of all time, and "I Ain't Gonna Give Nobody None o' This Jelly Roll, Kelly," "Madame Sul-Te-Wah" Conley and Allen "Farina" Hoskins.

More followed in the 30's: Ralph Cooper, who eventually, became the M.C. at Harlem's Apollo Theatre for years, and Henry Armstrong, featherweight, lightweight, welterweight and middleweight champ, both starred in films in the 1930's and 1940's. Other players of the period were Sheldon Brooks, Lillian Randolph, Woody Strode (of John Huston's *Moby Dick* (1956), Ethel McDaniel, Johnny Lee, Willie Best, Oscar Polk, Eddie Green and Billie

"Buckwheat" Thomas, Dooley Wilson (who played and sang "As Time Goes By" to Bogart and, in real life, couldn't play the piano), Les Hite (who also had a band – one of Dizzy Gillespie's first gigs), Emmett "Burke" Wallace, and Dusty "Open the Door Richard" Fletcher.

From the late Twenties, Spencer Williams, Jr. (1883-1969) was involved in directing, producing and acting in films with all-Black casts. He directed the 1943 *Blood Of Jesus*; later he was TV's Andy of *Amos 'N Andy*. Clarence Muse (1889-1979), like Orson Welles, played in other folk's movies in order to finance his own and accepted roles which ranged from his un-credited appearance as a runaway slave, Henry Prince, in Henry King's film *Chad Hanna* (1940) starring Henry Fonda, to his featured appearance in Frank Capra's *Riding High* (1950), as groom to Bing Crosby's horse trainer, in which they sing the Jimmy Van Heusen-Johnny Burke "Anywhere Road" (in the strange key of A natural). Stepin Fetchit, whose real name was Lincoln Theodore Monroe Andrew Perry (1902-1985), Mantan Moreland (1902-1973) and Eddie "Rochester" Anderson (1905-1977) were comedian-actors who achieved great status (none so high as Perry, who, by contract, commanded a luxurious dressing facility) but there were no serious roles available for them as there would be for comics Milton Berle, Red Buttons and Jackie Gleason.

Florence Mills (1896-1927), "The Queen of Happiness," more a singer-comedian than an actress, was, nevertheless, known for her winsome stage presence. She famously introduced "I'm a Little Blackbird Looking For a Bluebird." Duke Ellington memorialized her in the composition, "Black Beauty." Florence E. Williams (1905-1995) appeared in Edward G. Ulmer's *Her Sister's Secrte*, as Matilda, and continued working in film into the 1970's. Harry Bolden appeared as T.T. Williams in the stage film versions of *Member Of The Wedding* and was on Broadway in 1933 in *Run, Liitle Children*. As previously mentioned, though the role of Joe, in *Showboat*, was created for him, Paul Robeson did not open in the original 1927 Broadway production, but a year later in London. Instead, the role was created, in New York, by Jules Bledsoe (1897-1943), a famous baritone, who had long associations with the composers, William Grant Still, "Dean of African-American Composers," and Hall Johnson, of Hall Johnson Choir fame.

Hattie McDaniel (1895-1952) became the first African-American to win an Academy Award when, in 1939, she won an Oscar as Best Supporting Actress, in *Gone With The Wind*. Her brother, Sam McDaniel, who began in minstrel shows, went to Hollywood during the talkies craze with his brother, Otis McDaniel, mostly playing butlers.

Ruth Attaway (1910-2006) had a long and distinguished career in theatre and film. She originated the role of Rheba in Kauffman & Hart's *You Can't Take It With You* and, decades later, appeared with Peter Sellers in the 1979 film, *Being There*. The role of Rheba was played in the Frank Capra film of the play by Lillian Yarbo. Rbeba's boyfriend, Donald, was created by Oscar Polk in the play and Eddie "Rochester" Anderson, in the movie.

Two ladies who gained prominence in the films of Oscar Micheaux were Ethel Moses and Dorothy Van Engle. Moses began as a dancer, then, in films, was considered the "Black Jean Harlow," until her retirement in the early 40's. She appeared in Micheaux's *Temptation* (1935), *Underworld* (1937), *God's Stepchildren* (1938) and his *Birthright* (1939) and married Benny Payne, a pianist with Cab Calloway's Orchestra. Van Engle starred in three of Michaeux's most popular pictures: *Harlem After Midnight* (1934), *Murder In Harlem* (1938) and *Swing* (1938).

The beautifully photographed *Hallelujah!* (1929), directed by masterful King Vidor, featured Daniel L. Haynes, Harry Gray and William Fountaine, in addition to Nina Mae McKinney (1912-1967), Victoria Spivey and Fannie Belle Dee Knight. The film meant to display, with dignity, the life of poor African-Americans in the South and succeeded to an extent, but, by today's standards, it also succeeded in making them, occasionally, look foolish. It featured the sensational sixteen year-old McKinney singing an Irving Berlin song in a Northern, big city dance hall. She is one of the delights of this heralded film. Known as the "Black Garbo," she was a gravel-voiced scat singer and appeared in British films in the 30's.

Lorenzo Tucker (1907-1986) was prominent within the African-American film community throughout the 30' and 40's and was known as the "Black Valentino." Blue Washington (1898-1970) is best known for *Haunted Gold* (1938), starring John Wayne. But, to repeat, the 1940's and '50's were bad years for Hollywood's black actors. The great Clarence Muse played a railroad porter in 1943's, *Sherlock Holmes In Washington*. After the War, Evelyn Ellis was brilliant in Orson Welles' *Lady From Shangha* (1947). There was, of course, *Harlem Globetrotters* (1951) and *Jackie Robinson Story* (1950). Billy Walker played Jack Palance's butler in Robert Aldrich's faithful rendition of Clifford Odets' play, *Big Knife* (1955). Woody Strode and the dancer-actress, Carmen De Lavallade, appear in Delmar Daves' 1954 film, *Demetrius And The Gladiators*, starring Victor Mature, while William Marshall was a prominent cast member, in the role of Glycon. Tennis star, Althea Gibson, in a fling at acting, played a role in John Ford's magnificent 1959 film, *Horse Soldiers*, starring John Wayne.

Hilda Simms, the original *Anna Lucasta*, made a single-scene, Technicolor appearance in 1954's *Black Widow*, starring Ginger Rogers, Van Heflin and Gene Tierney. Libby Taylor played Suzanne, a maid, in the 1938 film, *The Toy Wife*, starring Luise Rainer and Melvyn Douglas. Hattie Noel auditioned in vain for the role of Mammy, in *Gone With The Wind*, then played a maid in *Lady For A Night* (1942) starring Joan Blondell and John Wayne. Ruby Dandridge, mother of Dorothy, appeared as a maid, in John Cromwell's 1947 film noir, *Dead Reckoning*, starring Humphrey Bogart.

Pearl Bailey and Lena Horne found secure places as box-office draws on Broadway, but only in musical comedy. Many consider Lena Horne, always in the vanguard of those celebrities active in the struggle for civil and human rights, to be the premiere singer, but her career as a serious actress on the screen, which was unthinkable under the studio system, never took flight after her top-billed performance in the film *Stormy Weather* (the song was introduced by Waters in a Cotton Club revue), a movie in which Bill "Bojangles" Robinson made his final film appearance. There were no serious roles on Broadway for Lena Horne, nor was there interracial casting, so she starred in the musical *Jamaica* and continued her career in clubs and in television until she returned to Broadway in her 1980 one-woman show, along the way winning numerous awards for her political and humanitarian activities.

Actress-singer, Elisabeth Welch (1904-2003), born in Englewood, New Jersey, grew up on Manhattan's 63rd Street as a neighbor of jazz great, Benny Carter (1908-2003) but, after appearing on Broadway in *Liza* (1920), and three all-Black revues, *Runnin' Wild* (1923), wherein she sang and introduced "The Charleston," *Chocolate Dandies* (1924) and *Blackbirds* of 1928, she escaped to England where she made a sensation singing "Solomon," in the West End production of Cole Porter's *Nymph Errant* (1933). Welch played Paul Robeson's wife in the English film *Song Of Freedom* (1936) played opposite him in *Big Fella* (1937) and pursued a long and successful career living in London, singing in clubs there and in Paris. Internet postings erroneously have her introducing "Love for Sale" (she was a replacement in Porter's 1930 *New Yorkers*, upon returning, temporarily to the USA), but she was the first to record the jazz evergreen "When Lights Are Low," in Europe with the song's author, the multi-talented Maestro Carter. Elisabeth Welch returned to Manhattan in her last years, and was recorded by Hugh Forden, for DRG Records, accompanied by pianist-composer Murray Grand.

Dorothy Dandridge, born into a theatrical family, one-third of the Dandridge Sisters 1934, (the third member being friend, jazz singer, Etta Jones) debuted, in 1940, in Duke's *Jump For Joy*, then appeared in the 1941 film, *Sundown*, starring Gene Tierney, the 1953, *Bright Road*, with Harry Belafonte, and got a break as the lead in Preminger's 1954 film, *Carmen Jones*, but ended up a suicide (in 1965).

Maya Angelou (1928-2014), who subsequently played the guitar and sang in Village clubs and later became Poet Laureate, Alice Childress (19162-1994) playwright and author of note, and Rosetta Le Noire (1911-2002), who created the AMAS on Theatre Row, dedicated to interracial casting, appeared in *Anna Lucasta*.

Louise Beaver (1902-1962), whose most famous role came in 1934's *Imitation Of Life*, as Delilah Johnson, appeared in dozens of films from the 1920's on, but usually as a maid. In 1960, Juanita Moore (1922-2014) was cast as Dominique, a maid, in *Affair In Trinidad* (1952), with Glenn Ford and Rita Hayworth, a follow-up to *Gilda*. She was nominated for an Academy Award as Best Supporting Actress for Ross Hunter's 1959 re-make of *Imitation Of Life*, which starred Lana Turner. In 1959, she appeared, as a maid, Hilda, in *Girl Can't Help It*, starring Jayne Mansfield and Edmond O'Brien, and is the only person present who responds when the new music called "Rock and Roll" is introduced to the principals of the film.

Another Juanita, Juanita Hall (1901-1968), the original Bloody Mary in Rodgers and Hammerstein's *South Pacific*, was a featured player, a singer, in musical comedy, not legit. The career of Ada Moore, who first came to serious attention in *House Of Flowers*, despite the promise she showed, on her album for Charles Mingus, on his Debut Records, did not flower.

Both Theresa Harris in *Velvet Touch* (1949) with Rosalind Russell and in other films, and Lillian Yarbo of *You Can't Take It With You* fame (1938), *Destry Rides Again* (1939) and the 1949, *Night Unto Night* (starring the odd couple of Ronald Reagan and Viveca Lindfors, exemplars in opposing political camps), specialized for years in playing, mainly, maids.

Eartha Kitt (1927-2008) after being discovered by Orson Welles, found temporary success on Broadway both as a singer and actress in *New Faces Of 1952*, *Mrs. Patterson* (1954) *Shinbone Alley* (1957) and the short-lived, *Jolly's Progress* (1959). But she, likewise, faced great obstacles, because of her outspokenness.

Mention should be made of stage and film actress, director, playwright and first female taxi driver in New York City history, Gertrude Jeannette, who died at the age of 103. She had been a member of the American Negro Theatre. Also Aubrey Lyles, sometimes known as A.L. Lyles, was someone who did everything: performed in vaudeville, wrote plays, lyrics, and appeared for decades with partner Flournoy E. Miller, in the comedy duo Miller and Lyles.

Esteem for Ruby Dee (1922—2014) would increase with the size of her roles, but she and husband Ossie Davis had been around since 1941 at the Negro Repertory Company and in films since 1950, including *The Jackie Robinson Story*, in which Dee played Robinson's wife, in *No Way Out*, with Richard Widmark, Stephen McNally, Linda Darnell and Sidney Poitier, directed by Joseph L. Mankiewicz. Great parts failed to come along until later years, but Ruby Dee raised a family, wrote extensively and was a vibrant activist.

Ernestine McClendon, who appeared in the long-running *Mulatto*, became a talent agent, initially, and developed a standup comedy routine in her later years. *Little Foxes*, both the play and the film, provided roles for Jesse Grayson, as Addie, John Marriott, as Cal and Henry "Hot Shot" Thomas, as Harold.

Also appearing in the 1950 film *No Way Out* were Dots Johnson (1886-1986), who was in the *Joe Louis Story*, too; Mildred Joanne Smith, who appeared as Cora Brooks; Amanda Randolph (younger sister of actress Lillian Randolph), who appeared as Gladys, and who began in Black Vaudeville, and was also seen in *Heller In Pink Tights* (1960) among other films. Ossie Davis and Frederick O'Neal both played small roles in this 20th Century Fox film.

Maude Simmons enjoyed a long career beginning the 1920's. She appears as Mrs. Morgan, in *Portrait Of Jennie*, and as Sidney Poitier's mother in *No Way Out*.

Lorenzo Tucker (1907-1986) was prominent within the African-American film community. Blue Washington (1898-1970) is best known for *Haunted Gold* (1938) starring John Wayne. James Edwards (1918-1970) appeared in *The Men* (1950) with Marlon Brando and, as the kind attendant, cruelly murdered by Tim Carey in the parking lot of Santa Anita, in Stanley Kubrick's *The Killing* (1956). Warner Brothers contract player, Juano Hernandez (1896-1970), of African descent, but born in Puerto Rico, toiled in vaudeville before prominently appearing in *Intruder In The Dust* (1949), directed by Jean Renoir, *Young Man With A Horn* (1950), Jacques Tourneur's *Stars In My Crown* (1950) and in numerous other major films. In later life on television, he was a featured player, in the ABC-TV series, *Adventures In Paradise* and other primetime shows.

Orlando Martens (1899-1985) was a featured player in a couple of dozen feature films, of which, perhaps, his most famous is as the African, in *Hasty Heart* (1945), with Patricia Neal, Richard Todd and the fortieth President of the United States. Vince Townsend played Toby, in *Alligator People* (1959) and assayed other small roles in films of the 1950's. Percy Rodriguez (1918-2007) had considerable success in Hollywood, in film and television before he appeared on Broadway, as Henry Simpson, in 1960, in Lillian Hellman's *Toys In The Attic*, with Maureen Stapleton, Irene Worth and Jason Robards, Jr., and Rodriguez would play a key role in James Baldwin's play, *Blues For Mr. Charlie* and, as Dr. Copeland in the underrated film version of Carson McCullars, *The Heart Is A Lonely Hunter*, with a cast that included Alan Arkin, Cicely Tyson and Stacey Keach. When I saw the Hellman play on the road, Clayton Corbin was playing the role Rodriguez created and Corbin progressed to Broadway with the play *Mister Johnson*. One of the first prominent black stars, Robert Earl Jones (1919-2006), father of James Earl, starred in *Lying Lips* in 1939, but worked for years thereafter in films such as *The Sting* (1973) and *Cotton Club* (1984).

Butterfly McQueen (1911-1995) was a popular and familiar character actress in Hollywood films, always a dippy servant. Fredi Washington (1904-1994), best known for her appearance in the film *Imitation Of Life* (1934), sang with Duke Ellington and appeared, with Robeson in the film of *Emperor Jones*, directed by the jazz-loving Hollywood maverick, Dudley Murphy.

Joseph Papp, among others, pioneered interracial casing, at the Shakespeare Festival in Central Park and, certainly, I have missed other productions and individuals prior to the production of *A Raisin In The Sun* who contributed toward enlarging opportunities for African-American actors. Symbolically, in lieu of all the African-American actors I might have neglected, I mention the usually unheralded Leigh Whipper (1876-1975), one of the founders of the Negro Actors Guild of America. The next time you see the original black and white film *Of Mice And Men*, observe more closely his subtle performance in the key role of Crooks. He made his film debut in the 1920 silent *Symbol Of The Unconquered*.

A curious appendage to the above is the case of John Larkin, a distinguished ofay actor who, after his Hollywood career, became radio's

Perry Mason, on a longtime basis. In the 1931 MGM film, *Sporting Blood*, starring Clark Gable, one of the best films about horseracing, because it shows authentic pictures of Churchill Downs on Derby Day, John Larkin plays an important role, is the last one to speak on camera, and has numerous close-ups throughout. As Uncle Ben, he played the role of the African-American groom of the thoroughbred, Tommy-Boy, which is at the center of the plot. Only John Larkin is playing the entire role in blackface! Of course, Griffith's riotous ex-slaves were in blackface, but that was 1912; this is a major sound film from MGM! But, when I think about it, they were still doing minstrel shows in some Chicago schools in the late 1940's, early 50's. So, there are many other examples, I'm sure, similar to what happened in *Sporting Blood*, i.e., with African-Americans being cheated out of jobs by whites.

The careers of so many African-American actresses blossomed after 1960 –particularly the afore-mentioned Diahann Carroll who starred in Richard Rodgers (words and music for the first time) *No Strings* (1962); Barbara McNair who followed in the role; Leslie Uggams who rose to stardom in some people's favorite musical, *Hallujah, Baby!* (1967), being among them. But, again, I make no attempt whatever to compile the long list of actors who have followed after *A Raisin In The Sun* (1959).

#7. – "KICKS & CO." CHAPTER ONE, "Good Intentions" Re: Author's parody song for character playing John F. Kennedy for pre- presidential candidate selection/endorsement for Independent Voter of Illinois banquet in ballroom of Hilton Hotel in spring of 1960. Sung to tune of Rodgers & Hart's "Everything I've Got Belongs To You," from the show *By Jupiter!*

I've a background that is steeped in Eastern wealth
And I'm full of boyish charm and vibrant health
I've courage to spare and energy, too.
And everything I've got belongs to you.
I've hobnobbed since I was ten with royalty
Even Henry Cabot Lodge confides in me.
I've youth on my side, just turned forty-two
And everything I've got belongs to you.
All the polls throughout the land
Say that I'm in big demand.
Lord knows I've campaigned enough
Who gives a damn for James Hoffa?
There's no doubt that ladies swoon at my good looks
Who the hell else authors slick best-selling books?
I've a beautiful wife, a baby to boot
And everything I've got belongs to
Everything I've got belongs,
Everything I've got belongs to you."

#8. – "KICKS & CO." CHAPTER EIGHT "Love At the Palmer House:" re: Limited Partnerships, replete with capitalization befitting such legal documentation as follows. Broadway shows, then and now, when more than a certain number of potential investors are solicited, are governed by Limited Partnerships and must be filed with the Security Exchange Commission. The SEC must also approve the prospectus, used by a Producer to attract funds.

In a Limited Partnership the General Partner is the Producer and bears all financial responsibilities and risks. The Limited Partners are only responsible for their original investment which, if lost, can be used only as a tax write-off. If the General Partner runs out of the funds from the original capitalization because of lack of demand at the box office, and decides to keep the show afloat and must raise additional funds, he or she is empowered to go to new Investors, the consequence of which would be a diminution of the original Investor's share in future profits, if any. Investors are also limited insofar as only the General Partner is vested with the power to make any and all decisions.

The General Partner, who did not at that period in the theatre receive any salary until two to four weeks before the opening of the show, conveys to the Partnership the rights acquired from the authors. The General Partner owns 50% of the Partnership and collects 50% of the profits after the original investment is repaid to the Limited Partners, the Investors. The units in *Kicks* sold for $8,000 each (though each share could be split between two people, each assuming a $4000 loss) and a person who invested that amount owned 1% of the Limited Partnership and earned 1% of 50% of the net profits of the show once the initial investment was recouped.

Again, the $400,000 raised for *Kicks*, according to the Broadway League's Economic Impact study of June 7, 2012, as reported by Ken Davenport in "Producer's Perspective," equates to $9,660,000. Today, Producers (the General Partner) receive a fee up front for services. And today, it usually takes, at least, a cadre of people to produce a show.

#9 KICKS & Co. - CHAPTER NINE Continued synopsis Acts 2 & 3.

As the play continues, Kicks and the Students, among them, are discovered in the school's gymnasium, which is decorated for a party. There's a reprise of "While I'm Still Young," which features Kicks waltzing with June. Kicks, who, magically transforms June's prom queen crown of paper into one of rhinestone, samples the punch and pours it into a potted plant, which "suddenly pops into bloom." Then Kicks turns ginger ale into whisky, which undergraduate, Eggy, mistakenly serves to Dr. Crieger, the University's stereotypical head professor, who spits it out in outrage. Realizing his mistake, Eggy, in shades of *Hellzapopin'*, samples the punch and blows a mouthful into Dr. Crieger's face. Crieger loses his glasses, Eggy steps on them, Kicks intervenes, makes Eggy make Crieger lose his pants, and exits with Eggy in chase. Pages and pages of dialogue involving Kicks tempting June ensue.

Enter Hazel accompanied by Silky. Ernest approaches June sings "Beautiful Girl," with choral accompaniment, and dances with June. It is one of Oscar's best efforts in the show.

"Rhythm and poise
Musical voice
Sepia soul
Lovable role
Beautiful Girl."

Ernest and June continue their dance into the next scene, a "Terrace," adjacent to the gymnasium. The next 16 pages of dialogue are about nothing whatsoever except Ernest's love for June and visa-versa – she saw him in Hazel's arms, is he in love with her or with Hazel? (Ed note: Clichéd musical comedy stuff that died out in the 1920's.)

Finally, Hazel enters with Silky, who drags a "reluctant" Ernest offstage in order that Hazel may play a scene, as nearly interminable as the previous, in which June avers that Ernest is NOT in love with Hazel, but with June.

In order to prove it, Hazel sings "Love is Like A Newborn Child." Then, much more dialogue ensues between the two until Kicks suddenly appears. So, too, do the Students, and the scene ends with Kicks and Silky singing "Virtue Is Its Own Reward," a Brechtean "It Ain't Necessarily So." It is addressed to the Students who, in a style reminiscent of Vienna operettas and Marx Brothers movies of the 1930's, join in singing with the antagonists:

STUDENTS

"The crooks are eating high up on the hog

SILKY

They're drinking all the fancy grog
And really putting on the dog.

STUDENTS

But virtue is its own reward!"

The next scene is in Ernest's room. Kicks enters, introduces his Hadean self and starts in pulling Ernest's coat to write garbage songs, not the high tone stuff to which Ernest aspires. Finally, Kicks sings "Most Folks Are Dopes."

"Getting no place
Running in a rat race...,"

But Ernest is perseverant, that is, until Kicks magically produces a letter that he found lying downstairs near the mailbox. It is a letter of rejection of Ernest's compositions by the "National Composers Foundation" and the Act mercifully comes to a close with cacophonous music, and Ernest sick of being poor, and ready to compose crap in order to achieve commercial success. Shades of Thomas Mann's *Doctor Faustus* .

This act is the approximate length of an entire evening in the contemporary Broadway theatre.

After intermission, the show resumes with a ballet sequence against the backdrop of a "Chicago Panorama." One critic decried the show's "pelvic choreography," but the dancing was one of the show's best aspects. According to Oscar, Donnie and Walter's creations inspired "the Twist."

The final act included a Ballet Sequence and, since it was a musical comedy, everything was resolved in musical comedy fashion - a happy ending for all but the evil ones.

And there was an epilogue. As the curtain dropped and the audience applause begins, Kicks reappears atop the curtain and slips to the apron of the stage. He whistles, holds up his arms, stops the applause, and the audience from departing.

KICKS (To Audience)

"Hold it! What are you getting yourselves in an
 uproar for? You know better than that….The
traditional happy ending. Very reassuring. If a
trifle maudlin. But you're practical people…So I lost
a couple. Well, you can't have 'em all. But—

(Quietly)

*I'll be back. I'll be around. I'm always around. And
the next time it just might be for—"*

and he makes a gesture toward the audience and smiling sweetly he steps back though the

C U R T A I N"

#10. – "KICKS & CO." CHAPTER SIX, Re: - NOTES on **Casting Kicks & Co.** I was delighted to have Carol Arthur in the chorus. She was ideal for a bit part, the *Waitress*, to be cast from among the chorus members. The critics took very special notice of her "bit" and three years later, when Noel Coward allowed Hugh Martin and Timothy Gray to make his 1941 comedy classic, *Blithe Spirit*, into a Broadway musical, *High Spirits*, starring Beatrice Lillie, Tammy Grimes and Edward Woodward, Sir Noel, who directed the production, cast Carol in the choice role of Edith, the maid. When I saw Carol Burnett, the first week of *Once Upon A Matress* (1960), or when, at the first public preview of *Fantastiks* that same year, sitting in an audience of less than fifty people, I saw Jerry Orbach enter on the small stage and sing "Try To Remember, or when, seventeen years later, I saw an actress in the Weill-Brecht *Happy End*, named Meryl Streep, who I knew I would be seeing for a long time to come, well, that's the way I felt about Carol, but she dumped a full-time career and married and devoted herself to another actor-comedian whose star was in the ascension and whom she loved. While she has appeared in some of Mel Brooks' films and even been involved in film and television production, her main productions have been the three sons eventuating from the former Ms. Arata's happy marriage to Dom DeLuise, who passed away in 2009.

I knew Buck Henry, to be a witty man and accomplished comedian-actor and that the would shine, in the role of Willy Wenchin. He was, by the late 50's, a guest on late night shows, but a year away from his initial appearance on *Saturday Night Live*. Buck read for the role, but turned it down and the it went to William Dwyer. Buck's script for *The Graduate* heads his long list of writing credits for major films.

Ensemble cast members: Betty Anders, Carol Arthur, Drrell J. Askey, Miriam Burton, Leu Camacho, Gino Conforti, Barbara Creed, Chuck Daniel, Jack Eddelman, Mercedes Ellington, Louana Gardnr, Jack Goldin, Lavinia Hamilton, Herman Howell, Bernard Johnson, Tommy Johnson, Ross Lashbrook, Carmen Morales, Nancy Rae Noel, Thelma Oliver, Caryl Paige, Rod Perry, Harold Pierson, Gilbert Price, Pearl Reynolds, Mabel Robinson, Jaime Rogers, Paul Reid Roman, Gus Solomons, Jr., Mark Taylor, Kent Thomas, Ella Thompson, Barbara Wallach, Zabethe Wilde, Dudley Williams, Joseph Williams. Dance Captain: Kathleen Stanford.

#11. – KICKS & Co., CHAPTER TEN, "Tell Me About The Rabbits, George"

Re: Martin Ritt's "Casting" Story: Deep in thought, perambulating the Main Stem in the season of '38-'39, twenty-four years old and facing a crucial career decision because he's been cast in two different plays and must choose between them, Marty encounters his actor-dancer-singer pal, from Pittsburgh, who's played a bit in Cole Porter's *Leave It To Me* (he appeared with three other chorus boys and Mary Martin when she sang "My Heart Belongs To Daddy") and has been slated to appear in one of the two productions Marty was, just then, choosing between. The play in which they both might appear together was unconventional, to say the least, though its playwright had had an outing already on Broadway, a financial failure, directed by Robert Lewis, and produced by the Group Theatre, which nevertheless received acclaim in some quarters.

Because Kazan was directing, Marty chose the role in Irwin Shaw's *Gentle People*, produced by the Group (Bloomgarden, G.M., Wally Fried, C.M.) It opened in January of '39 and lasted but 141 performances. The play was later adapted into the film *Out Of The Fog* (1941), starring John Garfield. Kazan or Marty had no part in the film production, which was directed by Anatole Litvak.

In the fall of the '39-'40 season, the "unconventional" play opened, with his Pittsburgh pal, Gene Kelly. Directed, produced and staged by Eddie Dowling, with a cast including Julie Haydon, Celeste Holm, and the, till then, unknown William Bendix, in the role Marty might have played, the play was William Saroyan's *Time of Your Life* and it won both the Pulitzer

Prize and the N.Y. Critics Circle Award, the first ever to win both. John le Carre (David John Moore Cornwell) in his piece, "Richard Burton Needs Me." has written brilliantly on the subject of who was Martin Ritt. (See Bibliography).

#12. – "KICKS & CO." CHAPTER TEN "Tell Me About The Rabbits, George," RE: Harold Prince. Imagine the American musical theatre without the contribution of Harold Prince, as director/ producer: *A Funny Thing Happened On The Way To The Forum, She Loves Me, Fiddler On The Roof, Cabaret, Follies, Company, A Little Night Music, Candide* (revival), *Side By Side By Sondheim, Pacific Overtures, On The Twentieth Century, Sweeney Todd, Evita, Merrily, We Roll Along, Kiss Of The Spiderwoman, The Phantom Of The Opera*, and that is a partial list (leaving out straight plays and flops), of a man who "studied" under George Abbott. Mr. Abbott first hired Prince as ASM for the revue *Touch And Go*, then, *Call Me Madam* and, when Prince went off to the Korean War, Mr. Abbott promised to re-hire him when he returned. And he followed through, making Prince ASM for, *Wonderful Town* (as reported by Forest Hirsch in "Harold Prince and the American Theatre").

#13. – "KICKS & CO." CHAPTER ELEVEN, "Down the Drain and Then Some." Complete Reviews Of Kicks & Co. from *Chicago Sun-Times*, Glenna Syse; *Chicago Tribune*, Claudia Cassidy; *Chicago American*, Roger Dettmer and Sydney J. Harris in the *Chicago Daily News*. Also *Lerner Newspapers* blurb by Ann Gerber, and *Chicago Defender* reviews and follow-up commentaries by Bob Hunter and Al Monroe.

Chicago SUN-TIMES October 12, 1961:
"Kicks & Co. Needs Play Doctor with Moxie
By Glenna Syse

What 'Kicks & Co.' needs is a play doctor – one part witch and part wizard. A call should be posted for someone with a loud voice, a whip, a carrot on a stick and a sense of humor. Someone who can wield a long pair of shears with the nonchalance of a Saville Row tailor, someone with magnificent moxie and a live cigar, a Broadway graduate who has known the despair of a flop and the exhalation of a hit; a grizzled, conscienceless veteran who has re-written a many a first act in a smoky room hotel room at 2:30 in the morning after room service has closed down.

GEORGE ABBOTT WOULD DO NICELY. But if he's busy, I suggest the producers of this brand-new musical start going through the rest of the alphabet. Some people will say it's not worth the struggle. But they could be wrong. This Oscar Brown, Jr. musical, which opened Wednesday night at McCormick Place, has many attractive people onstage. And behind that entire message, delivered with the finesse of a sledgehammer, there is talent.

It will take time, but a stall is better than a stalemate. And it will take money, but Chicago composer, author Oscar Brown, Jr., who elicited $400,000 from an audition on the Dave Garroway show is that rare species, previously unknown to show business, who ended up with more money than he needed. Another polite suggestion – one cook to stir the broth. And another, perhaps not quite so polite - satire should be light fingered not strong armed.

AND IF YOU DON'T agree with that, you will have to admit there is something just really wrong with a show in which a waitress's cough excites the only spontaneous laugh of the evening. It needs pointing out that Chicago is not used to the try- (The rest of the article has been lost over time.)

****

Claudia Cassidy, famous as she was, needs no further introduction here than the mentions she has, so far, received in my tome. She appears as a character in Book II of Banished. Suffice to say, here, she was a brilliant and knowledgeable about all matters artistic and could, if you listened, tell you how to fix your play better than just about, anyone else.

****

Chicago TRIBUNE October 12, 1961
ON THE AISLE
Of All "Kicks'" Ailments This One
Is Lethal: It's Deadly Dull
By Claudia Cassidy

More as confirmation than as information this morning, "Kicks & Co." is a poor excuse for a show. It is not difficult to understand why when Oscar Brown, Jr. auditioned some of his better songs he became a Pied Piper with a string of eager angels in tow but the difference between a song and a musical comedy is a vastness that challenges the highest skills of the professional stage. A pleasant song or two, some attractive and amusing people, some energetic dancing – these are not enough to offset the tedium of an amateurish show dwarfed by the big theatre and blasted into a forest of microphones.

Taking on two things not previously compatible even in bitter jest "Kicks" starts out satirize segregation and Playboy magazine thinly disguised as "Orgy" which is contemplating Playboy's satire is in built and as far as I know unapproachable. And ugly as the manifestations of segregation can be, it proves nothing theatre-wise to label those who practice it as stupid, filthy and lecherous in rabble-rouser called "Turn The Other Cheek."

Egging all this on is Mr. Kicks of the title role, a Devil's advocate played by the painfully miscast Burgess Meredith as a kind of sulfuric leprechaun. Descending upon Freedman university for Negroes he tries to get the sit-ins to stand up and fight, lures a campus queen to Orgy fame, and urges a discouraged young composer to cash in the easy way. None of this makes much sense, but that is the way the book goes.

****

High in the cast of this or any show that could use him is Lonnie Sattin as the lad who wants to write music. He makes a good appearance, he has the easiest way imaginable about him, and his voice is warm baritone with a lilt to it that makes "Opportunity, Please Knock" the high point of the evening. Both Vi Velasco, as the selfish campus beauty and Nichelle Nichols as the waitress not as tough as she looks defeat their material much of the time, and that takes doing. When Ms. Nichols is less nervous, she does a good job with the plaintive "Love is like a newborn child."

But all of them are up against the hazards of a clumsy book and awkward staging. About the nearest thing to professionalism in the production is the outer curtain design by Jack Blackman in the color rectangle style of Mondrian. Marked by a red false proscenium, it gets the evening off to a good start – while it lasts.

****

At intermission John Crown, grandson of the late Arie Crown, accepted the dedication of the theatre from James B. McCahey of the Metropolitan Fair and Exposition authority.

Chicago AMERICAN
October 12, 1961
ROGER DETTMER
'KICKS & CO.'
A SHAMBLES

"'KICKS & CO.' the victim of a first public performance Wednesday, is amateur night not in, but about Dixie. Some of Oscar Brown, Jr.'s two beat music, and a few of his lyric ideas could be the basis for an original cast recording if only there were a show. What the audience in the Arie Crown Theatre at McCormick Place saw from a great distance, and heard, through aggressive amplifiers, was a hideously costly junior college workshop.

The book, charged to Mr. Brown "in collaboration with Robert Barron Nemiroff" [the latter a co-producer whose wife, Playwright Lorraine Hansberry, is reputed to have been director], is simply and irremediably a shambles.

Instead of a new era in musical theatre, taking "Faust" as its cue, "Kicks and Co." turned out to be an integration harangue - when it was comprehensible at all – in the worst imaginable taste. As a book it lacks little basics like sequence, motivation, originality, humor, connection, and dignity.

All this doesn't seem to be Mr. Brown's sole responsibility by any means, but there he is, holding the bag.

THIS SOCIAL TRAVESTY is a catch-all for jigsaw scenery, pelvic choreography, a preposterous stage performance, and the tardiest "8 p.m.

sharp" curtain possible in the history of Chicago theatre. House lights went down at 8:27 p.m., intermission lasted a half hour and the audience was sent home at 10:55.

This is not to deny talented, even gifted people in the cast who must wear their environment like albatrosses

hung about their necks. Especially there is Lonnie Sattin as the hero, Ernest Black (oh yes, the show is symbolic], a big young man with a man's big baritone and that quality you call presence. There's Nichelle Nichols as Hazel Shapre, a hippy waitress gone bad who suddenly turns good at the final curtain.

And there's Burgess Meredith, poor blighter, as Mr. Kicks, the pivotal villain from Down Below, who arrives in a mobile picture frame, who resembles a Chinese Og from the Shanghai company of "Finian's Rainbow" and who must hate these surroundings with a true artist's and actor's passion.

THE HUMOR, of its kind, concerns a Chicago mans magazine called "Orgy" which conducts an Orgy Girl of the Month contest: "You'd be propane." "Propane?" "Yeah, a natural gas!" Not to draw on the Orgy business though the book does so with insistent monotony, it's owner is called Will Wenchin. And a chorister got a laugh calling one race or another "Ofay." When "Kicks and Co.," got serious Mr. Sattin was obligated to enunciate "I want say, 'look at us world - e're black and beautiful'" and to be knocked down by two white boys in a balletic lunch counter sit-in.

It struck me that the NAACP ought to picket the place until, of its own plain awfulness, "Kicks and Co." tells all those backers that their $400,00 somehow went wrong. One of those ways is the militant advocacy of integration by racial caricatures that libel the Negro perhaps even more than minstrel shows, "Ol' Black Joe," the motion picture of "Porgy and Bess," and Steppin Fetchit."

****

The Chicago critics, writing in the tradition of Ashton Stevens, were not only tough but learned, and Sydney J. Harris (19917-1996), who wrote both for the *Daily News* and the *Sun-Times*, was a weekly nationally-syndicated columnist on matters political, practical and philosophical, in addition to being the first-string drama and music critic for both sheets. He was knowledgeable in all the arts and politically liberal in the best sense. His review in the *Daily-News* was respectful of Oscar (because of Harris' liking the "Sin & Soul" album) and the kindest of all four major newspapers. Harris, who had written a "puff piece" for the show days before, now said in his review:

"It would be a pleasant civic and dramatic duty to report this morning that the first legitimate venture in the new Arie Crown Theatre at McCormick Place was a rousing success. But despite the tantalizing promise of better things to come from young Chicago composer, lyricist and librettist, Oscar Brown, Jr., it is my melancholy task to record that *Kicks & Co.*, which made its delayed opening Wednesday evening, has pathetically little to recommend it.

Apart from the few rhythmic tunes, a couple of sprightly ensemble dances and one or two pert or poignant scenes this strange mélange of a musical is much like Leacock's horseman who mounted his steed and rode off in all directions at once.

"KICKS & CO." is at the same time a tedious tract on racial integration, a wild lampooning of girlie magazines, a dully conventional love story and a vapidly modern adaptation of the Faust legend and each of these themes keeps getting in the other's way. This is not t say that a madly improbable story cannot come to life on the stage. "Finian's Rainbow" remains unforgettable after fifteen years and that dealt with leprechauns, pots of gold, racial injustice in the South and such combinations.

And incidentally "Finian's" satirized segregation in the South with a grace and wit that made it twice as devastating as Wednesday night's clumsy jabs at the subject.

What is basically wrong with "KICKS & CO." be a lack of unified taste: it operates on a several levels at once; it lacks continuity and flow and becomes a series of static scenes.

Nor is the cast especially professional. Burgess Meredith, of course, is a highly trained actor, but his Devil is precious and coyly mannered; at any moment to I expected him to fly out of the of the scenery, like Peter Pan.

Lonnie Sattin , as the serious composer who redeems himself from Satan just in time, posses a robust and commanding voice and plays his role with dignity, but he has not yet acquired sufficient prescience as a performer.

Nichelle Nichols is seamlessly appealing as the good bad girl and displays more potential for the legitimate stage than most of this company. Her body is a work of art, and she uses it with tact – except for that dreadful imitation Agnes de Mille ballet sequence in the second act.

Others in the cast range from adequate to embarrassing.

The choreography by Donald McKayle and Walter Nicks is animated and makes up with vigor what it lacks in style; while Jack Blackman's settings reflect the show's general unevenness, veering from the imaginative to the quite banal.

Oscar Brown, Jr. is a gifted composer, but his lyrics are often strained or obvious while his powers as a librettist seem wholly undeveloped.

This honest hard working crew who have labored so
long and lovingly on "Kicks & Co." simply cannot
measure up to the mark particularly when tackling
so formidable a dramatic tradition as the
Faust legend.

****

Here is a positive critique attached to listings of current and coming attractions, written by Ann Gerber of the *Rogers Park News*, a local paper published by Lerner Newspapers on October 18, 1961, which is printed in its entirety:

"KICKS & CO., although kicked and bruised by some critics after opening night last Wednesday, was thoroughly enjoyed and praised by most of the audience. Fresh, daring, and zingy and bittersweet as good dark chocolate, it combines an integration theme with love and the Devil and some of the finest singing and dancing you'll ever see. We liked Burgess Meredith as "Mr. Kicks" and felt this seasoned actor provided an excellent contrast and foil for the less sophisticated members of the cast Lonnie Sattin, Vi Velasco and Nichelle Nichols. Although Oscar Brown's music was much appreciated by the audience, although one critic slighted his score by stating they weren't "show tunes." What special degrees make a "show tune," we wonder. Both morning daily paper critics showed they never read Playboy Magazine, paralleled Orgy Magazine in Kicks. Both refer to the heroine as "cover girl" for the publication which anyone curious enough to look even once, knows it is the inside "girl of the month" photos the Devil Was touting."

****

"'KICKS' TOO MODERN FOR MOST"

Chicago Defender, Bob Hunter, dated October 16th,:

"Now that most of the reviews for Kicks & Co. are in – and all of them bad, it appears that the Faust opus is in for the fight of its life – even in Chicago. (Ed. Note: The show had already closed.) Although the show played to a packed house, which seemed to have gotten a kick from the yarn, most critics, or (rather) experts, turned thumbs down…

Possibly, it's because the theme of Oscar Brown, Jr.'s attack on segregation is all too true. The play is of the day, the hour and the minute. As one writer wrote, 'it's all black and white.'

In viewing Kicks, it must be remembered that the theme "IS" as controversial, as Mr. Kicks states. Interracial sex is certainly not something to be taken lightly. Yet, looking at it from another angle, it has always been with us – and like it or not, always will be. One has only to look around and it is readily seen that miscegenation has been occurring for centuries...

Kicks & Co. …does not condemn all white people. It merely takes a much needed whack at the race issues of 1960-61-62.

As for the acting, only Burgess Meredith, who tries like the Devil to be a Devil, and fails, is an established stage performer. The others are more closely associated with night clubs than with the legitimate theatre.

For Ms. Nichelle Nichols, this is her big chance. She has a right to be excited and nervous, who wouldn't be?...she turns in a superb job.

Al Freeman, Jr. as Silky Satin, in convincing in his stereotyped role of a sharp dressing, jive talking, self-styled philosopher. He is completely against the non violent pledge of the sit-ins, placing all his faith in the almighty dollar.

These two are the bright spots in the cast..."

After a complete and accurate synopsis, Hunter ends:

"Chicago is a town that is used to getting the plays following long performances on Broadway, but in this case, the Windy City is getting a chance to say if a play will make it to the Great White Way, or not.

Times have changed but the theatre and most of the old guard haven't. They have failed to keep abreast of the hydrogen age. Kicks & Co. is much too forward for stagnant minds."

The popular entertainment columnist, Al Monroe in his "So They Say," said:

"The 'experts' were a little rough in their reviews, in fact, they were downright nasty and short sighted, in this corner, Oscar Brown, Jr. came home with a winner."

Not my punctuation or syntax, the popular Monroe continues:

"Although the theme is a conglomeration of sex, sin and satin, it is none the less real. Miscegenation is going on. Maybe behind closed doors but still going on.

And know something, there has never been a spotted child born yet At least I haven't seen one. When all grown ups realize that time moves on, and with it evening then possibly they will become more enlightened.

It will be interesting to see how it (Kicks) fares on Broadway, the capitol of critics. It would be a crushing bore to some folks I know if it hit reallllly big."

The Defender, October 17, Monroe, "So They Say" Complete text:

"They say two sides to every story - at least there used to be. So let's look once more at the life and times of Kicks & Co., which should be entitled The End of Oscar Brown By The Knives of Four Critics.

It is considered well known that O.B., Jr. the originator of this romping satire on sex and sin, was dissatisfied with the final draft of the script. His Mr. Kicks was a college music instructor, not a Faust farce such as portrayed by Burgess Meredith.

There are those who are versatile enough to take on any type role, and then there are those who can not. Meredith is a cannot this time....

Basically, Kicks & Co. is a good play. However, the fact must be faced, that despite the up-to-the-minute theme, most settled theatre go'ers are not ready for this type of show. Kicks is much too progressive for them Four critics, (oops, pardon me) I mean experts, murdered the song and dance extravaganza. They also made a great number of the show's angels sick.

Every American is entitled to a free mind. No individual or individuals should have the power to either directly or indirectly, choose for others, and this what has happened in the American theatre today.

Their motives might be professional, but their emotions aren't. After all, they're human too. Kicks & Co. stresses miscegenation, and brother, that hurts right down to the white. Nuff said."

KICKS & Co. GET CHANCE TO 'LIVE IT UP' IN NEW YORK"

More complete text:

"The assassination attempt on the life of Kicks & Co. by Chicago's four 'expert' critics, was a damaging blow to integration and the play but, not quite fatal. Oscar Brown, Jr.'s romping, up-to-the-minute extravaganza depicting the life of today's Negro, is now in New York.

According to Mrs. Maxine Brown, wife of the composer, a full-scale dress rehearsal was held there Thursday. As for the title role, Burges Meredith is still out front."

After mentioning Merrick, Belafonte and Susskind, the article continued:

"Despite the lynching the new born baby received from the hands of the critics, Oscar Brown, Jr. is 'still optimistic about the future,' said Mrs. Brown. 'He knows that if this play doesn't make it, then there will be others that will.'

In New York, the company will revert to the original script, the one that was seen on the night of the Urban League benefit…However, it will not run three hours as it did here.

'Oscar and I are not angry at the critics for causing the flop of Kicks here,' said Mrs. Brown, 'but we are displeased at their failure to face the fact that time have changed; the Negro is here to stay. For the first time they have seen the true spirit and determination of today's young Negroes and they are afraid of them. They saw *Porgy & Bess* and *Raisin In The Sun*, but both are concerned with bygone times.

Kicks & Co., although meant for entertainment, has a message to tell and relates it in no uncertain terms. There is no attempt at conservatism. The point on miscegenation is rammed home with all the force of a jackhammer. Kicks is much too modern for the decrepit."

Al Munroe,11/23/61 *Chicago Defender,* More complete text.

"If by chance I'm beginning to bore you with these bits on KICKS & Co. then kick me. Other hand, if you aren't, then read me loud and clear. Until convinced otherwise, I will always believe that its debut in our town was deliberately butchered because some people are not ready to open their eyes and see what the new world is like. The course of history is changing, and so is the theatre.

The tragedy of the Negro is the fact that he was forced to come to a country, which he did not want to do, and then once here ordered to do the biddings of 'the master.'"…

In reality the Negro was an undesirable import, but a valuable piece of working flesh. The Negro women were good enough (and still are) to feed the blue-eyed child (sic) but not worthy of sitting at the family dinner table.

They were also a welcome outlet for illicit sex, but not quite "polite" enough to sleep in the big house. And even today, in 1961,the situation still persists, only no one cares to look.

A second class citizenship is slavery itself. Therefore, the emancipation proclamation of 1863 freed the Negroes in theory but not in practice. If it had, there would be equal rights.

Oscar Brown, Jr.'s, the originator of Kicks & Co., is the first Negro play with guts and imagination to conceive a musical bearing such a message, so powerful, that not even Western Union can not deliver it."

The grammar and syntax are not my own. Mr. Monroe continues and, then, concludes:

"Kicks & Co. is just another way of informing America that a social revolution is underway demanding the fulfillment of that statement which reads: 'All men are created equal.'

The young Negroes of today are not going to sit back and be content with laboring in steel mills and seeking entertainment in roach infested booze barns. They know that something must be done, and their (sic) doing something about it. Their (sic)weapons – passiveness and sit-ins."

#14. – "RAISIN ON THE ROAD" CHAPTER TWELVE, "Debasement," Re: Ethel Waters. Born in 1896 in Chester, Pennsylvania, as a result of the teenage rape of her mother, under-appreciated today, but at the pinnacle of fame from the mid-1920's until her retirement in the late 1950's, first as a jazz singer, then as a Broadway headliner in Irving Berlin's *Music Box Revues* and his *As Thousands Cheer* (1933) and later in Carson McCuller's 1951 drama, *Member Of The Wedding*, Waters was, it is said, the first woman to sing W.C. Handy's "St. Louis Blues," (though this most recorded blues song of all time was first waxed by Ted Lewis in 1924 and Bessie Smith in 1925). She introduced Hoagy Carmichael's "Am I Blue?" "Happiness Is Just A Thing Called Joe," written for her by Harold Arlen and E.Y. "Yip" Harburg, and the Arlen- Ted Koehler, "Stormy Weather" (originally written for Cab Calloway), among other standards. Other great African-American singers, such as Ivy Anderson, Lena Horne, Maxine Sullivan, Billie Holiday, Ella Fitzgerald, (and before them, blues singers Ada Cox, Bessie and Mamie Smith and Mama Yancey), achieved celebrity during Waters' heyday but their fame pales in comparison to that achieved by Ethel Waters, whose name was the first of any African-American woman to appear on the marquee of a Broadway theatre.

There never were any black woman stars until Ethel Waters and, then, Josephine Baker, who, like Ira Aldrige, decades before, travelled to Paris in order to achieve stardom.

Ethel Waters began in clubs in Chicago, in 1925, and appeared on the same bill with Bessie Smith. The famous raconteurs and historians of early jazz, guitarist and club owner, Eddie ("I may get drunk as hell but I never vomit on my best friends") Condon, clarinetist, Milt "Mezz" Mezzrow and tenor saxophonist, Bud Freeman, all wrote memoirs emphasizing the depth of emotion present in Bessie Smith's renditions. Her musicality and powerful lungs were formidable, too.

The much younger Ethel Waters must have learned from Smith when they appeared on the same bill. Waters' appearance a couple of years later at the Plantation Club in Harlem, her starring in an all-Negro revue on Broadway, her being featured in Cotton Club revues, and the enormous popularity of her records led to her becoming a theatrical headliner in *As Thousands Cheer*, then Irving Berlin revue in which she introduced "Heat Wave," "Harlem On My Mind" and "Suppertime."

The pose Waters strikes in Edward Steichen's anguished 1933 portrait is said to be proof of the manner in which she performed the last two songs. Like Bessie Smith, who confined herself, mostly, to the blues, Waters, lived every song she sang. When the white singer, Lee Wiley (1908-1975) sings "Suppertime," the premise seems absurdly strained: her husband is not coming home because he has been lynched, she must tell the children about it and, instead, she's singing about it.

But Waters, according to contemporary accounts, delivered it less as a lament than an indictment and it was performed against a cyclorama that depicted a lynching place, heavy stuff for a Broadway revue. She interpreted the song "Suppertime" in a state of accusatory fury, devoid of self-pity.

She was an actress, not just a singer, but there were no parts for her to play until Du Bose (and Dorothy) Heyward wrote *Mamba's Daughter's*, with her in mind, and she starred in the 1936 production. (In a supporting role, José Ferrer made one of his first appearances.)

The stage, and film versions of a *Cabin In The Sky*, both directed by Vincente Minnelli, followed. It featured unforgettable songs by Vernon Duke and John La Touche: the great, lovely title song, plus "Taking A Chance On Love," and "Honey In The Honeycomb," all assayed by Waters. Playing Petunia in *Cabin In The Sky* afforded her a strong dramatic role in which she reached a wider audience.

Later, the stage and film versions of *Memebr Of The Wedding*, with Julie Harris, directed by Harold Clurman, won Waters praise and further fame and she topped it all with her best-selling autobiography, *His Eye Is On The Sparrow*, the 1949 film, *Pinky*, directed by Elia Kazan, and a second autobiography, *To Me It's Wonderful*, but her performing career was at its nadir by the late 1950's.

Waters and McNeil met at a time when Claudia was working mainly as a singer. Waters influenced McNeil to concentrate on acting. Both had had rough childhoods; both were devout Catholics. In this new, blooming era and with Ethel Waters no longer on the scene, Claudia aimed for nothing less than royalty on the American stage and was poised, with no visible competition, to inherit the matriarchal mantle of her mentor, the great actress-singer, Ethel Waters.

**#15. – RAISIN ON THE ROAD CHAPTER THIRTEEN, 'The Slap."
Re: Mama vs. Walter Lee**. In writing *Raisin*, Hansberry made Mama the central character, whether she wanted to or not. Phil Rose said he may not have been able to raise the money for the show without Sidney's commitment. Sidney Poitier, without causing unnecessary trouble, worked through rehearsal and performance to elevate Walter Lee Younger and, in the Third Act of the play, bring the focus to himself as the apex and future of the play, addressing individuals in his family, most pointedly his son, and rejects the ofay Lindner's offer. Once Sidney left the cast, Claudia was able to change the focus. Also, she was able to rally the cast (most of them) around her character. In the 2014 Broadway revival starring Denzil Washington, the proper balance – that which Sidney Poitier had defined - was restored and there was no question as to who was the play's central figure. Phil Rose had long advocated for such a revival – one starring Washington - and the star had more than a decade to develop a full understanding of the play's dynamics.

**#16. – "LOOKIN' FOR THE MAN" CHAPTER EIGHTEEN: Miles
in Mufti. Wrong tickets for #10,000 payoff**. Though not gifted with hyperthymesia, I have a damn good memory, so, I am perturbed I cannot successfully research the names of the horses listed in this sad event. I have no reason to research the matter further, for I know what happened. But if you do, look for any horse ridden by Arcaro which won on the no longer extant Widener course, a straight chute which ran diagonally across the Belmont infield and was exclusively for two year-olds. "Bananas" could not have won that many races (there weren't that many run on the Widener) on that course at that meeting. Then, look for a horse, which, absolutely, paid $10.00 even in the second, (the double paying around, as I've said $140) with, in the third race, a horse that paid $6 to $10 to place. In conclusion, on the general subject of my betting on horses, I have never won more than ten thousand dollars on a single day, but since the introduction of "exotic" betting (the Pick 6, Pick 5, trifecta, superfectas, etc. and million plus pots, offered by racetracks today) I have won that amount on at least three occasions: Alysheba's Derby and Preakness, and a horse owned by J.W. Shield's, trained by Dominic Galluscio, which paid $154, on the first day of spring of 1992. At Gulfstream, two years ago, I won a $4,500 Pick Six on a $3.60 ticket.

BIBLIOGRAPHY

Afro-American Gazete, Washington D.C. 2/18/64 "Claudia McNeil Seeks End To Her Marriage"

Albany, Joe "Portrait of An Artist" CD on Wounded Bird Records (2008) 1982 "Conversation with Joe Albany"

Andreyev, Leonid "He Who Gets Slapped" Samuel French New York (1921)

Armstrong, Louis "Satchmo" Signet Book, New America Library New York (1955)

Asbury, Herbert "Sucker's Progress: History of Gambling in America" Thunder's Mouth Press 161 William Street, New York (1938)

Barry, Julian "My Night With Orson" Create Space Independent Platform Publishing (2011)

Barry, Julian & Warren Meyers *Lookin' For The Man* Manuscript (1964)

Berg, Charles Ramirez *"latino images Stereotypes, Subversion, Resistance"* University of Texas Press Austin (2002)

de Botton, Alain "How Proust Can Change Your Life" (1997) Vintage International New York (1997)

Brightwell, Eric Internet postings "Black Cinema Parts 1 & 2" Amoeblog.

Brown, Oscar Jr. KICKS & Co. Manuscript (1960

Caine, Michael "The Elephant to Hollywood" Holden & Staughton London (2011)

Cheney, Anne "Lorraine Hansberry" Twayne Publishers Boston (1984)

Chicago American, Dettmer, Roger "KICKS A Shambles," 10/11/61

Chicago Daily News Lindner, Lionel "Persistence Pays Off For Oscar Brown, Jr." 10/7/61; Harris, Sydney J. "Reviews Musical KICKS & CO." 10/11/61.

Chicago Defener- Hunter, Bob "Kicks Too Modern For Most 10/16/61; Monroe, Al "So They Say" 10/16/61; "So They Say 10/17/61; "So They Say," 10/18/61; Hunter, Bob "Kicks Gets A Chance To Live It Up In New York," 10/21/61; Monroe, Al "So They Say," 10/23/61.

Chicago Sun-Times- Syse, Glenna "Kicks & Co. Needs Play Doctor With Moxie," 10/11/61; Kupcinet, Irv "Kup's Column" 10/12/61; 10/18/61;

Chicago Tribune- Cassidy, Claudia On The Aisle "Of all KICKS Ailments This On Is Worse; It's Deadly Dull," 10/11/61; Weitzel, Tony 10/14/61; Weitzel 10/16//61; Lyon, Herb "Tower Ticker," 10/16/61

Coward, Noel "Letters of Noel Coward" Edited by Barry Day Knopf-Doubleday New York (2012)

Crouch, Stanley "Kansas City Lightning: The Rise and Times of Charlie Parker" (2011)

Dannen, Frederic "Hit Men" Vintage New York (1991)

Down Beat Magazine- Tynan, John A. 9/2/62 Review Oscar Brown, Jr. and Miles Davis

Gelly, Dave "Lester Young" Spellmount, Ltd.(UK) Hippocrene Books 161 Madison Ave. New York (1984)

Giddins, Gary "Celebrating Bird: The Triumph of Charlie Parker" Beech Tree Books/William Morrow New York (1987)

Gitler, Ira "Bud Powell: Bud Plays Bird" Roulette Records CDP 724383713721 liner notes(1996)

Gold, Robert S. "Jazz Talk" Bobbs-Merrill New York (1975)

Grauer, Jr., Bill and Keepnews, Orrin "A Pictorial History of Jazz" Crown Publishers, Inc. New York (1955)

Green, Benny "The Tatum Solo Masterpieces" Liner notes

Pablo Records 13 LP set 2625 703, Pablo Records Re-issue of 1953 Sessions. Produced by Norman Granz(1975)

Henderson, Mary C. "The City and the Theatre" James T. White and Company Clifton, New Jersey (1973)

Hentoff, Nat "Jazz Is" Avon Books New York (1976)

Hentoff, Nat and Shapiro, Nat "Hear Me Talkin' To Ya'" Dover New York (1955)

Hentoff, Nat "The Jazz Life" Da Capo Paperbacks New York (1978)

Hirsh, Forest "Harold Prince and the American Theatre" Applause Books (2005)

Hopkins, Arthur "The Directing Theory and Practice of Arthur Hopkins" University of Iowa, (1961) edited by Delmar J. Hansen (Des Moines) previous brief editions called "On Directing"

Israel, Lee "Kilgallen" Dell Publishing Co. New York (19879)

Kahn, Albert E. "Matusow Affair: Memoir of a National Scandal" Moyer Bell Limited Mt. Kisco, NY (1987)

Keepnews, Orrin and Grauer, Jr. Bill, "A Pictorial History of Jazz" Crown Publishing, Inc. New York (1955)

Kogos, Fred "A Dictionary of Yiddish Slang & Idioms" Kogoss Publishing. Castle Books Seacaucus, New Jersey (1968)

Korall, Burt Liner note to "Tony Scott, Sung Hero: Featuring Bill Evans, Scott La Faro and Paul Motion. Sunnyside Records

Lane, Stewart F. Black Broadway An Illustrated History of African-American Struggles and Triumphs On the Theatrical Stage/African-Americans On

The Great White Way - Square One Publishers (Garden City, New York (2015)

le Carre, John (David Cornwell) The Pigeon Tunnel: Stories from My Life "Richard Burton Needs Me" Thorndike Press 2016

Leonard, William Editor "Chicago Stagebill Yearbook – 1947" Chicago Stagebill Publishing

Lerner Newspapers, *Rogers Park News* – Gerber, Ann 10/18/61 Review of *Kicks*.

Malraux, Anre Man's Fate, trans. by Haakon Chevalier Harrison New York (1933)

McNeil, Claudia "Scrapbooks" New York Public Library, Schomburg Center for Research In Black Culture, 515 Malcolm X Boulevard, New York New York, Processed by Paula Williams September, 1999; Processed by Dina Lachatanere, April, 1995 Provenance: Gift of the Actors' Fund of America.

McKusack, Patricia C. and Frederick L. "Young, Gifted And Determined" Holiday House, New York (2000)

Mencken, H. L. "Happy Days" Alfred A. Knopf, New York (1940)

Mencken, H.L. "The American Language" Fourth Edition Knopf New York (1977)

Meyers, Warren B. & Julian Barry Lookin' For The Man Manuscript (1964)

Mitchell, Koritha "Living With Lynching: African-American Lynching Plays, Performance and Citizenship University of Illinois, Champaign, Illinois (2011)

Nabakov, Vladimir "Glory" translated from Russian by Dimitri Nabakov McGraw-Hill New York (1971)

Norris, Frank "McTeague" Doubleday-McClure New York (1899)

Nisenson, Eric "'Round Midnight, A Biography of Miles Davis" Da Capo Press New York (1996)

Nordine, Ken Musicmelon Volume One CD liner notes (author unknown)

O' Neill, Eugene *Hughie* Yale University Press New Haven (1970)

Poitier, Sidney "The Measure of A Man" Harper San Francisco (2000)

Proust, Marcel "Remembrance of Things Past" (Better known in France and the Continent as "In Search of Lost Time") Translated by C.K. Scott Moncrieff Random House, New York (1924)

Reisner, Robert George "Bird: The Legend of Charlie Parker"(New York) Citadel Press (1963)

Riedel, Michael *Razzle Dazzle* Simon & Shuster New York (2015)

Roctober Magazine #15, 1996 interview of Oscar Brown, Jr. by James Porter and Rick Wojick

Rose, Phillip "You Can't Do That on Broadway: " *A Raisin In The Sun* and Other Theatrical Impossibilities (Limelight Editions, New York (2001)

Rovere, Richard "Senator Joe McCarthy" University of California Press (1965)

Russell, Ross "Bird Lives!: The Hard Life and Hard Times of Charlie "Yardbird" Parker Charterhouse New York (1973)

Scheader, Catherine Lorraine Hansberry: Playwright and Voice of Justice Enslow Publishers, Inc. Springfield, N.J. (1998)

Shapiro, Nat "Hear Me Talkin' To Ya" with Nat Hentoff Dover New York (1955)

Sinnot, Susan "Lorraine Hansberry: Award Winning Playwright and Civil Rights Activist" Conaki Press, Berkeley (1999)

Stagg, Jerry "The Brothers Shubert" Random House, New York (1969)

Stravinsky, Igor "The Poetics of Music: In the Form of Six Lessons" Harvard University Press, (1959)

Talese, Gay "The Soft Psyche of Joshua Logan" Esquire Magazine April, 1963, Conde Nast Publications New York

Tanner, Lee "Dizzy: In His 75th Year" Pomegranate San Francisco (1992)

Taylor, J.R. "Lester Young: Pres/The Complete Savoy Recordings" liner notes

Tripp, Barbara "The Importance of Lorraine Hansberry, "Lucent Books, P.O. Box 28901, San Diego, California 92198 (1998)

Wilson, John S. The New York Times 1980 obituary of Gilbert J. Pincus

Young, Prof. Harvey "Sustaining Black Theatre" Journal of Stage Directors and Choreographers Winter 2016, Edited by Anne Fliotsos and Ann M. Shanahan

Zinsser, William "Easy To Remember: The Great American Songwriters and Their Songs. David R. Godine, Publishers New York (1987)

Acknowledgements

Thanks to Judy Davis and her husband, the novelist, Marc Davis, for being the first to read and comment on this book. Marc was encouraging and helpful in many ways and I might not have written it at all if it were not for his urging.

I am grateful to the Newberry Library of Chicago, Illinois and to Ms. Lisa Schoblasky in particular. I want to express my gratitude to Ms. Denise Garrett and Ms. Ingrid Abbott of the Library of Congress, U.S. Copyright Office, and to its distinguished Head Librarian, Dr. Carla D. Hayden. Thanks to J.J. Johnston, my friend of many years, for reading my first few pages and steering me in the right direction. Only Amy Albani and I know how much she helped me. Ditto that witty and versatile actor, Dennis Wit. Alan and Juanita Light have been faithful friends for decades. Thanks, too, to Dave Schnitter, world class saxophonist and ex-Blakeyite, and to my friend, Tom Brooke.

It was not until August of 2019, long after I had written and copyrighted and sent to the formatter, my manuscript, that I first learned that Nica's niece had written a book about her aunt and that it was made into a documentary. I have never read or seen this material and would not have consulted it during the course of writing my memoir. The reason for this is at the end of this paragraph. I confess that I have, long ago, seen Clint Eastwood's fine *Straight, No Chaser*. I am less enthusiastic about his *Bird*. As they were published through the years, I read all the books about Charlie Parker up to and including Stanley Crouch's fairly recent one, but have not, in writing this tome, consulted, nor do I own, any of them, except Gary Giddens' *Celebrating Bird*. I am not aware of biographies of Dizzy, have not read any, but in documentaries have seen and heard him repeat things he said to me. This is not unusual. I have my own copyrighted documentary of Diz being interviewed by Joe Ferrer in my living room, saying things he has said to others and things he never said before. I understand there is an excellent biography of Thelonious Monk but I have never read it. Books about Lester Young abound. I have only read Dave Gelly's biography and comment about it in the text. There is, as I promised earlier, a point in all this: my writing about the aforementioned is based entirely on my personal experiences and interactions with them.

About H.L. Mencken: I quote from him often, and employ some of the lovely and archaic words he used, like "sylphid" for instance, or "vomitous," words that are unrecognizable by Microsoft, and may strike the reader as a sign of ignorance on my part. I am well aware that, though he began as a Liberal/Libertarian, he became an arch Conservative, during FDR's presidency (largely because of Roosevelt's mocking him at the Gridiron Club Dinner) and has long been a doyen of right wing, Conservative politics, i.e., people I don't represent. But, at Sullivan High School, in Rogers Park, where we studied not only *Ulysses* but *Finnegan's Wake*, too, HLM was the darling of the English teachers because he was as devoted to our (American) language as Dr. Johnson was to his.

Had I their gifts, I would write many words in praise of the artistry of Gay Talese, his keen eye, wonderful words, and kindness in allowing me to reprint the Joshua Logan/*Esquire* article.

Aware that I was the lone survivor of the production staff of *Kicks*, though not yet fully aware I was the only one who could tell the truth about matters known only to Bobby, Burt and Lorraine, I was contacted by Charles J. Shields, Hansberry's forthcoming biographer, early in July 2019. My book was complete and in the process of being formatted. Soon after, hipped now that I was the real deal and knew all that went down, Mr. Shields kindly sent me numerous documents from his research of the Hansberry-Nemiroff papers at Yale, some of which I already had in my possession. The others were not of importance to me, the exception, as cited in the text, being Nemiroff's telegram to Harold Prince, which I have used because it directly involves me. I thank Mr. Shields for that.

Of course Bobby would never keep anything incriminating or damaging in the Yale collection, so there is little there to inform Shields, or others, of the true facts of the show. For instance, the document of most importance, and which seems to be missing, is the final prospectus with Mrs. Roosevelt's encomium and those of others, which were added after the first two of such prospectuses. Aside from the manner in which the budget was expended, that prospectus, designed partly by me, was, I am assuming, the most, or one of the most, important document(s) presented by attorneys representing the investor lawsuit initiated by General Lefkowitz after *Kicks* closed; if not in legal arguments before the court, still, in all likelihood, submitted to the court as being in violation of basic SEC regulations. To repeat, it was comprised of a page for each (admittedly, well-intentioned) quote from Mrs. R., Rosa Parks, Sammy Davis, Jr., Dave Garroway and Harry Belafonte, added to those already obtained from Dorothy Kilgallen, Steve Allen, Lorraine Hansberry and Martin Luther King. My brother-in-law had a copy and a limited partnership agreement because he was an investor, but he passed away years ago.

Though I circulated the document as much if not more than the producers, I was not named in the "Lefkowitz" suit. General Lefkowitz was acting as one of a group of angels, but, in truth, also as a government official, and he wanted the laws already on the books to be enforced and new ones enacted so that no producer would ever try the stunt again. Question is: "Did he know he was going to do this when he bought a unit in the show?" He did not invest because of the Garroway broadcast because I was looking at his partnership agreement on the very day of the Garroway show; I saw the "cease and desist" telegram on that same afternoon, meaning Lefkowitz's signed agreement had been consummated before the "illegal" broadcast.

In autumn, Mr. Shields twice expressed an interest in knowing when my book was to be published and we had a nice correspondence into November, he trying to be of assistance by sending me further materials (which I did not employ in my story), and I by opening my big mouth too much regarding my relationship with Diana Sands and hers with Lorraine and other relevant arcane matters. But in a pre-arranged phone call on November 19, the central subject of which was the respective publishing dates of his and my book, he suddenly hung up the phone on me, forgive the syntax. I have no idea why, but it necessitated my serving him with a legal missive that evening around dinner time, specifically demanding he make no mention of information I imparted to him relative to my relationship with Diana, Bobby or Lorraine, their relationships to each other, information regarding the authorship of any works involving Hansberry, as author, and Nemiroff, as executor and adaptor and editor. Shields responded saying, "Nothing by you – said or written – will be used."

I expect that will be the case and 1.) You will not hear the truth about *Kicks*, if at all and 2.) If he does write about it, his main sources will be Phil Rose's book (which is extremely limited) and his archival research at Yale, about which I have already expressed an opinion. I suspect he will base his reporting using the only available mentions extant, meaning Phil Rose's autobiography, which yields only that *Kicks* was auditioned for him in Oscar's Chicago living room; that he said it needed work, which offended Bobby and caused strained relations vis-à-vis he, Bobby and Lorraine; that he recommended Vinnette as director; that Lorraine called for Phil's advice when Bobby fired Vinnette and begged Lorraine to assume the director's position; that he (Rose) attended the run-through at the Imperial; and, finally, that he told Bobby to buzz off , terminating their relationship in a meeting also attended by Burt, about whom he evinced no gripe, at least in his tome. That's all Rose knew, or wrote, about *Kicks*. I do not expect Mr. Shields to mention my name at all. I am sorry to have, thus, lost contact with Mr. Shields for he seemed to be a very nice guy till he unexpectedly hung up, and I have no concrete idea as to why he did so.

I am aware this book will cause controversy, but one area particularly offensive to many may be my reference to *To Be Young, Gifted and Black* as a presentation not a play. For lunk-heads who need a diagram: playwrights, as well as most theatre professionals, know the difference even though both genres have in common dramaturgical similarities. It started when some storyteller told a tale over and over until Homer, or whoever, wrote it down and called it the *Odyssey.* That's not a play. Aeschylus and Euripides wrote plays. Charles Dickens could be credited as a modern progenitor of the one-man show, then, came Mark Twain, and Ruth Draper, Larry's mom, a famed monologist – and I'm sure I'm missing similar examples. None of these are plays, they're presentations. You may have a better word than mine to describe these evenings in the theatre, these events, but I'll stick with "presentation." Revues – which barely exist anymore, and I've seen some of the best of them – are not plays nor are they presentations, they're revues. Producer Paul Gregory fits into the discussion, for his *Don Juan in Hell,* directed by Charles Laughton, starring Charles Boyer, Sir Cedric Hardwick, Agnes Moorehead and Laughton himself, was a great success of the Fifties with a nationwide tour beginning a new trend – staged readings, this one black tie. Brilliantly talkative and consummately performed, it could be called a play only because it is a selected, rarely performed portion of George Bernard Shaw's *Back to Methuselah.* Myself, I saw it; I call it a "presentation," ditto Tyrone Power performing/reciting Stephen Vincent Benet's *John Brown's Body,* with rear projections and a dynamic soundtrack, if I remember correctly. That was definitely a "presentation." But the Paul Gregory-Charles Laughton production of the *Caine Mutiny Court-Martial* (AS MENTIONED IN THE APPENDIX), THAT was a play, even though it was 16 men sitting around a table with Henry Fonda, questioning Captain Queeg (Lloyd Nolan) and John Hodiak, or whomever, on the witness stand.

A presentation may have vignettes or scenes, may even have the all-important dramatic ingredient of conflict that is so indigenous to a play. In one- character shows, one actor may play many roles, even simultaneously, so to speak, but such theatrical events are just that, theatrical events, not plays. Shows from *Thurber Carnival* to *Brecht on Brecht* from *Spoon River Anthology* to *To Be Young, Gifted and Black* evoke a writer's essence by the arrangement of their words, and like plays, have beginnings, middles and endings and, if they hold together and work as evenings in the theatre, it is only understandable they be advertised as plays, but they are presentations.

Though by no means as glorious and memorable as *To Be Young, Gifted and Black*, I, too, composed such a theatrical event myself, in the late Seventies, in Chicago, at Goodman Theatre's Stage 2, on their subscription series, what its producer[171] called "a paste-up job." He also gave it its title: *George Jean Nathan in Revue.* It was very successful, received very good reviews. Claudia Cassidy came to rehearsals, can you believe it?

But, like Bobby's adaptation of Lorraine's words, and just as he adapted the letters of German soldiers into an evening, I used other actors playing: H.L. Mencken, Sinclair Lewis, Eleonora Duse, etc. A play came later. More about that, in the second volume of this memoir, from 1971 to today. That book will lack footnotes and an appendix, no index, no bibliography, the framework and all necessary elements having been introduced herein.

— Sidney Eden
March, 2020, NYC
As the Pandemic reached Manhattan.

---

171 Gregory Mosher (19949-   ), longtime director at Lincoln Center and Goodman theatres, original director of *American Buffalo* and *Glengarry Glen Ross* (both by David Mamet), among others.

Rights & Permissions
"The Soft Psyche of Joshua Logan" by Gay Talese (Conde Nast Publications). "You Can't Do That On Broadway" by Phillip Rose, by permission of Hal Leonard Corporation. 'Hazel's Hip's" and "Mr. Kicks" and other songs from *Kicks & Co.* by Oscar Brown, Jr.- Kicks Music Co. (BMI).

Photo Credit: Cleveland Playhouse production of musicals, *A Tree Grows in Brooklyn*, by Hastings-Wilinger & Associates, Cleveland, Ohio.

Lookin' For The Man recording session photographs, of December 13, 1964, at Bell Sound, NYC, Frank Dandridge and Aaron Heller.

Many thanks to actor, Doug Barron, and his Plaza Desktop Publishing for his artistic formatting.

ABOUT THE AUTHOR

SIDNEY EDEN, actor, producer, director, playwright, TV critic, teacher, a native Chicagoan, has directed at that city's Goodman Theatre, the Brooklyn Academy of Music, the State Theatre of Maine, the State Music Theatre of Maine, the Cleveland Playhouse, where he made his professional acting debut, and at numerous other theatres in the U.S. and Canada. He founded the First Chicago Center, the first first-run theatre in the Loop in over forty years and his second show, Eugene O'Neill's till-then neglected *Hughie*, starring Ben Gazzara (Tony-nominated), went all the way to Hollywood and Broadway. He followed with Mark Medoff's Obie-winning *When You Comin' Back, Red Ryder?* with the playwright starring. Making his film debut in the cult classic, *Spook Who Sat By the Door*, Eden created the role of Leonard Poetry in Julian (*Lenny*) Barry's controversial "*Sitcom*," at the David Mamet-W.H. Macy famed St. Nicholas Theatre Company, acted in regional, winter and summer stock, in support, or opposite a long list of stars of stage and screen, and on and off-Broadway in *Are You Now Or Have You Ever Been*, starring Liza Minnelli. He has appeared on most of the soaps and in countless commercials on and off camera. His play *George Jean Nathan in Revue* was a hit at the Goodman, his *Mencken, Nathan and God* premiered at the Lincoln Center Workshop, *Atlantic City Lost*, played off-off-Broadway. He served as resident critic/interviewer on NBC-Tempo's nationally syndicated, pioneering *Broadway Magazine*, and as a teacher initiated his Acting for Non-Actors course, a title appropriated worldwide. Eden sings and plays most every song in the great American Songbook and has recorded with jazz greats Zoot Sims, Clark Terry, Mel Lewis, and the legendary Joe Albany.

SidEden.com   sideden7@gmail.com

****